08/24
STRAND PRICE
$ 5.00

SOFTWARE PROTECTION

SOFTWARE PROTECTION

Practical and Legal Steps to Protect and Market Computer Programs

G. Gervaise Davis III, Esq.
President and Senior Principal
Schroeder, Davis & Orliss Inc.
Monterey, California

VNR VAN NOSTRAND REINHOLD COMPANY
New York

This publication is designed to provide accurate and authoritative information in regard to the subject matter covered. It is sold with the understanding that the publisher is not engaged in rendering legal, accounting or other professional service. If legal advice or other expert assistance is required, the services of a competent professional person should be sought.—*From a Declaration of Principles jointly adopted by a Committee of the American Bar Association and a Committee of Publishers and Associations.*

Copyright © 1985 G. Gervaise Davis III

Library of Congress Catalog Card Number: 84-25718
ISBN: 0-442-21903-2

All rights reserved. No part of this work covered by the copyright hereon may be reproduced or used in any form or by any means—graphic, electronic, or mechanical, including photocopying, recording, taping, or information storage and retrieval systems—without permission of the copyright owner.

Manufactured in the United States of America

Published by Van Nostrand Reinhold Company Inc.
115 Fifth Avenue
New York, N.Y. 10003

Van Nostrand Reinhold Company Limited
Molly Millars Lane
Wokingham, Berkshire RG11 2PY, England

Van Nostrand Reinhold
480 Latrobe Street
Melbourne, Victoria 3000, Australia

Macmillan of Canada
Division of Canada Publishing Corporation
164 Commander Boulevard
Agincourt, Ontario M1S 3C7, Canada

15 14 13 12 11 10 9 8 7 6 5 4 3 2

Library of Congress Cataloging in Publication Data

Davis, G. Gervaise, 1932-
  Software protection.

  Includes index.
  1. Copyright—Computer programs—United States.
2. Computer programs—Patents. 3. Computer contracts—
United States. I. Title.
KF3024.C6D38 1984   346.7304'82   84-25718
ISBN 0-442-21903-2   347.306482

Preface

SOFTWARE PIRACY

The unparalleled growth of the microcomputer industry in the past six years has been accompanied by an even more explosive demand for "user friendly" computer software for the personal computers produced by the industry. This has led to serious concerns on the part of software authors, publishers, and the computer industry about what is called "software piracy"—illegal copying and distribution of valuable computer programs. The true extent of this practice is unknown, but it is large enough to cause serious economic harm to a software industry that expects to generate $10,000,000,000 in annual revenues by 1990.

TECHNOLOGICAL CHANGE

In a society based, among other things, on laws and property rights, the computer industry and the general public may assume that the American legal system provides a protective legal web around the ownership rights of software authors. Unfortunately, the technological changes wrought by the computer industry have outpaced the ability of the legal system to adapt to these new forms of intangible property. Lawyers and laymen alike are often confused and unable to ascertain with certainty how best to protect commercially valuable computer software from illegal use and copying. Lawyers are having to learn a whole new vocabulary in order to advise their software clients. Such problems are not unique to the United States, but exist on a worldwide level.

THE AUDIENCE FOR THIS BOOK

To date there has been no comprehensive source of information on the subject of software protection. The purpose of this book is to provide guidance in this area. The book is intended to give both practical and legal assistance to those persons in the industry concerned with software protection—whether they are software developers, software publishers, industry executives, or lawyers working in the software industry. The book should also be of value to members of the general public or to business-men concerned about their business responsibilities when they are using computer software under license from the computer industry.

Furthermore, this book is intended to be used as a reference or guide for someone looking for information on just a portion of the subjects covered, or as a starting point for research into the field. However, there can, as yet, be no definitive work on the subject of software protection because the law remains so undeveloped in many aspects. Rather, the effort here has been to see that the material takes into consideration the most relevant of the existing law and points up practical problems. For this reason the coverage of licensing is limited to Chapter 11, although it provides an adequate starting point for further research into the subject.

MICROCOMPUTER ORIENTATION

Because the great majority of this book's readers will probably come from the expanding microcomputer part of the industry, the orientation here is towards those involved in software for microcomputers rather than mainframes or minicomputers. The legal principles, however, are the same at all levels of the industry; only some of the practices differ. This material should be of use to anyone who is trying to understand the in-terrelationship of intellectual property law and the technology of com-puters and computer software.

ORGANIZATION

The materials are logically organized and grouped so that you can quickly see from the Table of Contents where you will find a particular subject. The book is extensively indexed, since one of the most common frustra-tions in using books like this is the inability to find material that "must be there somewhere." The book also contains near the back a Bibliog-raphy and a list of legal citations so that lawyers and others can find the source of the materials for further research.

You may find it helpful at the outset to review the subjects of interest to you in the Table of Contents. Then read, or at least skim, all the related chapters, but only after you have carefully read Chapter 1, which ex-plains the relationship of the various parts of the book. If you want more background still, you should carefully read the first three chapters, which are intended as precursors to the rest of the book. A Glossary of Computer Terms is included at the end of the book.

NOT A FORMS BOOK

While this is not a legal forms book, it does contain a number of forms actually in use in the industry, which forms are intended as much for illustration as for actual use. Those readers not experienced in the field should recognize that there are serious dangers in using forms that are either not completely understood or slightly out of date.

STEPS YOU CAN TAKE

On the other hand, I have identified many important steps to protect software that can be taken by those in the software industry, without the day-to-day services of a lawyer. I am not one who believes that lawyers are the sole source of knowledge and competence in the world. The book tries to strike a balance between economic ruin from lack of legal advice and economic ruin from excessive legal fees.

CUT-OFF DATE

The materials in this book are current to December 1, 1984, the last point at which I could make any significant changes to the manuscript. No matter what the cut-off date, Murphy's Law of Legal Authors and Publishers says that the most important case on the subject will always be decided three days after the press run is finished.

My editor and I discussed the possibility of publishing this material in microcomputer diskette form, but the world is not quite ready for that since we have still to solve the piracy problem with diskette-based book materials.

FEEDBACK TO THE AUTHOR

As a means of feedback to the author, I would encourage you to correspond with me about suggestions for improvement of this book, about apparent errors, or about possible subject matter for related books and materials.

G. Gervaise Davis III
Post Office Box 3080
Monterey, California 93942

Acknowledgments and Other Thoughts

The decision to write a book is rather like the decision to have children. Sometimes the decision is made for you, sometimes you have some choice. But the similarity does not stop there for, like children, books have their own character, can bring you a combination of joy and despair, and seem to be with you always even when you would like them to go away for a while.

For the past three years this child has been gestating, and now it is time for it to be born. It was conceived at the suggestion of several people and would have died prematurely were it not for the encouragement of my wife Kathleen, my four biological children (Virginia, Cindi, Susan, and Shauna), my law partners (George and Ted), and a series of persistent editors who seemed never to give up. Only time will tell what kind of person this child (like other children) turns out to be, and its father will have anxious moments for many years watching it make its way in the world. Please be kind to it if you have occasion to work with it, for it and the subject matter are still very young and inexperienced.

As with all books, this is a product of many hours spent at the computer terminal, in law libraries reading and researching, years of struggling to solve complex but fascinating problems presented by clients of my law firm, and a lot of thinking about what others might like to know about the subject of software protection. Upon reflection, it seems like most of my time was spent trying to figure out how to present the material so that it was understandable by a diverse audience, ranging from computer programmers to experienced lawyers and judges. Only you can tell if I was successful.

I must acknowledge here the particular contributions of two friends, starting with Robert T. Daunt, Esq., one of my partners in my law firm, who researched and wrote an initial draft of the chapter on warranties. He also assisted me in obtaining materials that allowed me to put this book together. The other friend is F. David LaRiviere, Esq., a patent and trademark attorney with Hewlett-Packard who reviewed and corrected my errors in parts of the book where his professional judgments and knowledge were vastly superior to mine. My 1983 summer law clerk, Anne Gundelfinger, did an in-depth research job on the problems of the First Sale Doctrine. As usual, however, the final responsibility for errors due to omission and commission is mine alone.

Others who made direct contributions, in the form of reviewing and suggesting material, were Robert English, Esq., of ITT (Government Contracts), David Gerber, Esq., of Los Angeles (Video Games), John Michaelson, Esq., of Monterey (Tax), David R. Terrill, Esq., of Chicago (numerous chapters), Paul Vapnek, Esq., of San Francisco (Patents), Camilo Wilson of Monterey (Technology), Kristen Shannon (general editorial comments), and a number of fine people people at the Library of Congress Copyright Office.

Encouragement in many ways came from other professionals who work in this field of the law, such as Paul Carmichael, Esq., of IBM, Jackie Daunt, Esq., and Gordon Davidson, Esq., of Palo Alto, Duncan Davidson, Esq., formerly of Los Angeles and now of Denver, Ron Harwith, Esq., of Reynolds & Reynolds, Henry Jones III, Esq., General Counsel of Ashton-Tate, Ron Laurie, Esq., of San Francisco, Ron Palenski of ADAPSO, Ron Reiling, Esq., of DEC, and Rainer Stachels, Esq., of Frankfurt, Germany.

All of these fine people acted in their individual capacity, of course, and not on behalf of their respective employers. It is, however, encouraging to know so many highly competent professionals from this exciting industry, who cared enough about this subject and about those who work in the industry to assist me.

The illustrations were prepared by my young artist friend, Lynn C. Harrison of Monterey.

G. Gervaise Davis III

Contents

SOFTWARE PROTECTION

1

Introduction—A Magnetic Image in Time

The Moving Finger writes;
    and, having writ,
Moves on: nor all your Piety
    nor Wit
Shall lure it back to cancel
    half a Line,
Nor all your Tears wash out
    a Word of it.

The Rubiyat of
Omar Khayyam, Verse LXXI

When I was a child, my father loved to read to me from the Rubiyat of Omar Khayyam, and this verse always captured my imagination—a big finger in the sky writing human history on a slate, history that no one could change. Unlike most history the rapidly changing law pertaining to software protection is like a magnetic image in time, which keeps being rewritten and changed with each spin of the computer disk drive. Capturing the present state of this law in a book is akin to photographing a moving target at one point in time.

PROTECTING THE ECONOMIC VALUE OF SOFTWARE

With the explosive growth of the microcomputer and the emergence of the "personal computer," software has become the driving force of the dynamic computer industry. Moreover, software is a form of property. Protecting the economic value of software has become of paramount

1

importance to the industry and to the lawyers who work in it. But, as the value of commercial software increases, it is apparent from the ensuing litigation that present legal theories are less than adequate to protect this valuable magnetic property. It has become clear that the law of software protection is in a state of rapid development that will take many years to stabilize.

The fundamental problem is the inability of an established legal system, based on protection of *tangible* property, to cope with a form of property that can appear and disappear with the speed of light. Software is a unique form of sometimes invisible property, which often seems little more than the embodiment of an idea in magnetic or silicon form. Because you cannot touch it, it is as though you cannot own it. We will return to this troubling legal concept many times as we explore the law together.

THE ORIENTATION OF THIS BOOK

Since business and professional men and women connected with this industry need some guide through the legal thicket, my twin purposes in writing this book were those of explaining why such a frustrating legal situation exists and suggesting effective ways of protecting software under present law and industry marketing practices. When you complete this book, you should have all the information and background needed on the subject.

The primary orientation of this book is prescriptive and not descriptive, so it presents only enough of the actual laws and cases to allow you, the reader, to appreciate the significance of the various legal principles. Throughout, once the necessary legal context has been made clear, I have sought to present practical solutions and suggestions. For this reason, the book is of value to *all* persons connected with the computer industry, be they businesspeople, programmers, or lawyers.

INTRODUCTORY CHAPTERS OF THE BOOK

In writing a book intended to be of value to more than one audience, as here where the audience consists of both computer professionals and interested lawyers, there are several compromises one is tempted to make. First, I might have decided to oversimplify the legal aspects to carry along the computer professionals, or I could have watered-down the computer terminology to avoid scaring away the lawyers.

I hope that I did neither, for both groups have much to gain by working together toward a better understanding of what the other is doing. What I did do is provide each profession with an introductory chapter (Chapters 2 and 3) intended to bring each group up to speed in the other's territory. The rest of the book assumes the basic knowledge derived from these chapters.

Chapter 2 on computer technology is intended for lawyers, businesspeople, and others who do not have a technical computer background. It provides some grounding in computer science, at least in those areas relevant to the legal principles discussed later.

Conversely, Chapter 3 is a quick survey of American law, essential for non-lawyers or those without a legal background, as that law relates to the protection of "intellectual property rights." These are essentially the subject matter of copyrights, trademarks, trade secrets, patents, and other forms of industrial or commercial property of an intangible nature. Chapter 3 develops the relationship between each of these subjects and with the law in general.

THE WEB OF SOFTWARE PROTECTION

Whenever I speak on the general subject of software protection, I show an overhead or slide of the diagram in Figure 1.1, because it seems to help in understanding the relationship between the various legal theories underlying software protection. Reliance by a software business on each of these theories is akin to the attachment points of a spiderweb, one or more of which might fail without creating a disaster for the spider. When you don't know for sure what will work, you use everything available, just like the spider.

This interrelationship is such that I have intentionally tied together the materials in Chapters 4 through 10—the chapters on trade secrets, copyright law, patents, and trademarks. A software business will encounter problems of trade secrecy from the first day of business. As the business progresses, the various aspects of copyright law, the primary method of protection of most microcomputer software, will assume more and more importance. Since patents and trademarks are usually of less importance, they are treated last.

These seven chapters provide a complete background to the legal and practical principles of each subject, and should be reviewed carefully. Each contains numerous suggestions and forms, addresses for making filings and obtaining further information, and warnings about traps or problems for the unwary. However, these materials are not intended to substitute for *competent* legal advice, which should go hand in hand with the steps outlined.

TEN OTHER RELATED SUBJECTS

Failure of a software company, and its attorneys, to consider the implications of each of the subjects covered in Chapters 11 through 20 could result in economic disaster or serious problems with government agencies and the law. The introduction of each chapter describes in some detail the purpose and scope of coverage of the material. I would recom-

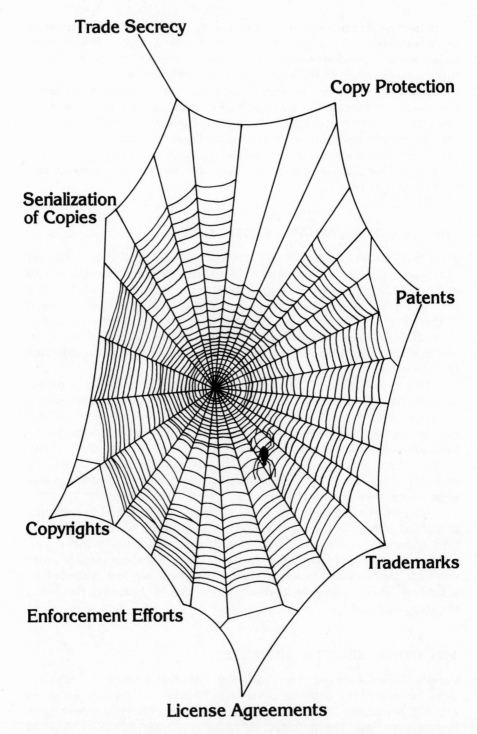

Figure 1.1. The "WEB" of Software Protection.

mend delving into each of these chapters, even if you only skim them at the outset.

There are, however, two or three chapters that I should comment upon in more detail. Chapter 11 on the subject of software licensing is a vital and complex subject. Its principles are deeply involved in any day-to-day computer law practice, but are much misunderstood by lawyers and laymen alike. Read Chapter 11 in detail if you have anything to do with contract negotiations for the licensing or use of software. The coverage here is limited to the principles behind licensing and to the use of end user licenses. At present, I know of little or no other material in print on this subject.

Once the basic principles of software protection are understood, Chapter 12 on warranties and limiting liability becomes another key portion of this book. It does you little good to protect the ownership of software and then lose a million-dollar judgment for defective software products. Some might argue that this subject is not an integral part of software protection, a position with which I disagree. It is a subject that will not go away by ignoring it, for it necessarily involves the reader in some of the most picky, detailed statutes ever passed by Congress.

The content of Chapter 18 is primarily of interest to lawyers, since it is on the subject of bringing suit for copyright infringement. However, many of my software clients have also found portions of this material helpful. So rather than list laws and cases in detail here, I have provided a good summary of the subject for any reader and also created a means for lawyers to obtain more detail on a current basis.

CONCLUSION

I invite you now to join me in the search for truth. Indeed, "The Moving Finger writes" the truth, but it also moves on. Time may work against us, but it does provide our incentive to move on to the future. Surely the future is the computer industry—and the future is here.

2

What is This Thing Called "Software"?

"I'm glad they've begun asking riddles—I believe I
can guess that," added Alice.
"Do you mean that you think you can find out the
answer to it?" said the March Hare.
"Exactly so," said Alice.
"Then you should say what you mean," the March
Hare went on.
"I do," Alice hastily replied; "at least—at least I
mean what I say—that's the same thing, you know."
"Not the same thing a bit!" said the Hatter. "Why,
you might just as well say that 'I see what I eat' is
the same thing as 'I eat what I see'!"

Lewis Carroll, *Alice's Adventures in Wonderland*,
Chap. VII.

To do more than guess at the riddles of the law in the field of software
protection, you will, like Alice, have to be sure you *say what you mean*
when describing computer technology. Yet computerese is no more
intelligible to the lawyer than legalese is to a computer programmer. Both
metalanguages are intended as a shorthand form of communication to
the initiated, but both serve as a barrier to understanding to the
uninitiated from another profession.

Recent software-copyright and patent-protection cases have been
concerned with the technical aspects of computers and computer software. Lawyers and other non-technical persons must understand what

software is, in the technical sense, or risk missing the factual basis of the legal issues.

This chapter and the glossary are designed to bring the nontechnical person to a reasonable level of technical knowledge through a brief exposure to the more common computer concepts. You should not expect to understand the technology in depth, but to end up with a good grasp of the relationship of the principles discussed to the problems of software protection.

COMPARING HARDWARE AND SOFTWARE

A computer is a system consisting of hardware and software. So let's begin with defining these two most basic computer terms. In computer parlance, the term *hardware* refers to the physically embodied parts of the computer—the metal box, the circuit boards, and the integrated circuitry soldered or plugged into the boards. *Hardware* also includes the various component parts of the computer system, like printers, disk drives, and terminals used to communicate with the other sealed boxes. In short, the hardware is that part of the computer you can see and touch.

The *software,* or the computer program, is the second necessary part of the system. A computer program is a set of written instructions to the computer, initially prepared by a human operator. These instructions are used by the computer to perform the desired work. The actual software used in the computer is recorded magnetically on a diskette (floppy disk), which is then read into the computer from the disk drive, or the software may be embedded electronically in the cartridge of a video game.

The instruction books and manuals, which accompany the diskettes and provide information to the user, are also considered part of the software. These materials are sometimes called *documentation.*

Software is unusual in that you cannot normally see it, but you know it is there because it makes the hardware do useful things, like calculate numbers in a payroll or print out words in a word-processor or personal computer. With most microcomputers, the only way you can "see" the software is by looking at the small magnetic diskette or program cartridge, which you insert into the computer when you want the computer to do something. Even then, you only see the physical object that carries the software, and not the software itself. It is this conceptual problem of "invisibility" that has bedeviled legal systems worldwide.

The one exception to "invisibility" is the original computer program written by the author. This is called *source code* and it can be seen and read when listed or printed out by the computer.

Before we learn more about software and software terminology, let's now quickly go over the physical parts of a computer system in more detail, so that the hardware terms don't confuse us later when we discuss how software is created and used by the computer.

A COMPUTER SYSTEM
AND ITS COMPONENTS

Most of us have seen and examined personal computers, so we no longer think they are magic, but there is still a mystique about them that intimidates people. A computer is little more than an electronic device that can perform the four mathematical operations of addition, subtraction, multiplication, and division extremely rapidly. It can also compare numbers, as well as characters, to see if they are equal to, less than, or greater than some other numbers or characters.

All numbers and characters (both letters and punctuation marks) are represented inside the computer by a special number system called *binary numbers.* Binary numbers are nothing more than a series of 1's and 0's, as we will explain in a moment.

The numbers and characters a computer processes are called *data.* This is the origin of the term *data processing.* What the computer does with this data depends entirely on what set of instructions or software is loaded into or stored in the computer. The computer cannot do anything but hum and consume electricity unless it has both data and software to tell it what to do.

The component parts of a typical personal computer system are not hard to understand, since we don't have to know exactly how they work—just where the data and the software go and what happens to them. Look at the diagram in Figure 2.1 and follow the arrows as we work through the computer system in the text.

HOW DATA MOVES THROUGH A
COMPUTER—FROM "A" TO "E"

No matter how large or small a computer is, it always consists of four basic hardware units—an input device, a central processing unit, one or more storage or memory devices, and one or more output devices. In Figure 2.1 the keyboard at "A" is the input element, the *CPU* at "B" is the processor, the storage devices are either temporary and internal (location "C") or semipermanent and external (at "D"), and the output devices at "E" are any one of several types. Let's look at what these do and see where the data goes.

Input. The simplest and most common way that data and programs enter the computer is through someone typing characters and numbers on a keyboard attached to the computer by a wire or other line. See the keyboard pictured at "A" in Figure 2.1; this is called an *input device.*

CPU. The data goes over the wire into the *central processing unit* (usually called a *CPU,* for short), located at "B". This complex unit, made up of many electronic components, understands that the electrical impulses

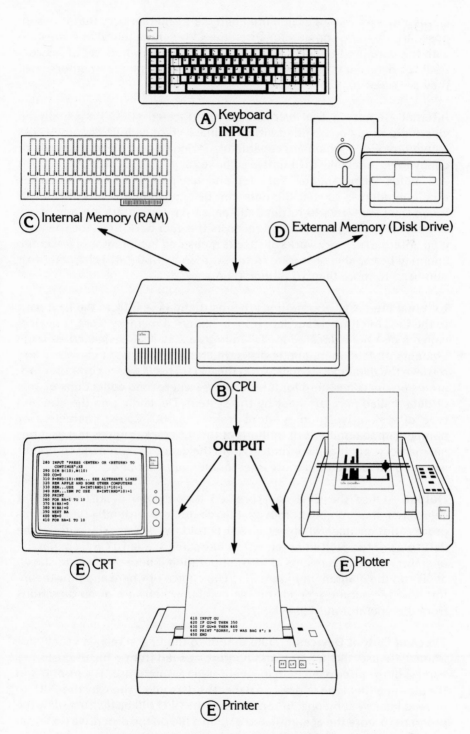

Figure 2.1.   Components of a Computer System.

coming in over the input line are characters and numbers that it is supposed to use to do something. Often the CPU cannot tell what it must do with the data until the operator finishes typing in a whole set of instructions (or data), so it temporarily stores them in its internal memory until they are ready for use.

Internal Memory.   The *internal memory* (located at "C") is usually an electronic circuit board filled with little black chips called *Random Access Memory* or *RAM,* which are capable of storing data in electronic cells or cubbyholes much like the numbered boxes at your local post office. Each cells holds one number or character, and, like post-office boxes, each has a unique address so that the data can be sent to and received from it. When the CPU wants to retrieve the data from temporary storage, it *addresses* (or "calls") the cell and receives the data back from the memory chip. Internal memory works at speeds measured in billionths of a second, and may be capable of storing from less than 64,000 (64K) characters (or numbers) to more than 16 million (16M).

External Memory.   Sometimes the instructions sent from the keyboard to the CPU tell it to obtain data from an external memory storage device, called a *disk drive,* located at "D" in Figure 2.1. This device stores large amounts of data on magnetic disks, in erasable form, and can store and retrieve the data upon request from the CPU. This is where computer programs are usually stored for later use, and where long collections or sets of data, called *files,* are kept by the system. Depending on the size and type of disk drive, it may store from 256,000 (256K) characters or numbers up to hundreds of millions of them. A disk is not as fast as internal memory, but it can continue to hold the data even when the computer is turned off, something most internal memory cannot do.

Output.   Once the CPU has received its program of instructions, it calculates the numbers, moves the characters around (as in word-processing), or does whatever else it is told. It then usually *outputs* the data to a printer, plotter, or television-like screen called a *CRT,* so that the operator can see the results of the computation. These devices are shown at "E" on the diagram in Figure 2.1. The choice of where and how the information is output depends on the computer software or on directions from the operator at the keyboard.

Types of Output Devices.   Data output to the CRT screen is usually for immediate use, like a name and address needed from a file of customer names, or the price of an item in inventory in a warehouse. The printer and the plotter either type or draw on paper the data given them by the CPU, to be read later by someone. In some cases, the CPU will be instructed by the program to store the accumulated data in a file on the disk drive (external memory) for subsequent use, as in the case of an updated mailing list intended to be printed out later.

WHAT DOES A COMPUTER PROGRAM LOOK LIKE?

To find out, let's look at an actual computer program, in several forms. By doing so, we will better understand what the courts are talking about when they refer to programs in "source code" and "object code", and to computer software in "ROM" or on diskette. When a programmer speaks of a computer program being in source code, he refers to the form of the original program he wrote in one of many computer languages, such as BASIC, COBOL, or PASCAL. Such a source program might look like this one, in BASIC:

```
REMARK     PROGRAM IN BASIC TO COMPUTE GAS MILEAGE

 4  PRINT
 5  PRINT
10  PRINT "TO COMPUTE GAS MILEAGE, TYPE TOTAL MILES
       TRAVELLED:   ";
23  INPUT MILES
25  PRINT
30  PRINT "HOW MANY GALLONS WERE USED:   ";
40  INPUT GALLONS
50  MPG = MILES/GALLONS
55  PRINT
60  PRINT "YOU AVERAGED    ", MPG   , "MILES PER
       GALLON."
70  END
```

In reading this program, note that it has a title, arbitrarily assigned line numbers down the left side, and a number of "PRINT" statements on lines by themselves. If you can ignore those distractions, you will see that the program merely prints out several lines of text, computes the mileage from data you type in, and then prints the results. If you were to run this program on your computer, your screen would look like this:

```
TO COMPUTE GAS MILEAGE, TYPE TOTAL MILES
TRAVELLED:   300

HOW MANY GALLONS WERE USED:   15

YOU AVERAGED       20.0000       MILES PER GALLON.
```

The computer would have typed out the material shown in capital letters, and you would have input the number of miles and gallons shown in boldface type. In line 50, the program tells the computer to divide the number of MILES by the number of GALLONS to obtain the MPG, which it is then told to print in the last line. The extra PRINT statements just cause the program to skip a line between the lines it prints out. That's all there is to a program in its simplest form. Now let's see what happens to this human-readable form of a program when it is stored in the computer.

HOW DATA IS STORED, MOVED, AND USED FOR COMPUTATION

The modern digital computer automatically converts all the data it receives into a series of binary digits—that is, either 0 or 1. Using a convention all manufacturers now adhere to, each decimal number, each alphabetical character (both upper and lower case), and each punctuation mark is given a binary code number. The computer instantly converts anything we type on the keyboard into a binary number, processes it in binary form, and then converts it back into a decimal number, alphabetical character, or punctuation mark so a human can read it.

In this way you and I need not even know how the things we type into the computer are represented internally. Unless we are working as programmers or electrical engineers, we don't care to know that the capital letter "A" is intepreted as "01000001" by the computer, as it actually is. The only important thing for us to know is that the character is converted, stored in this way, and moved from element to element of the computer system in this form.

For example, if an operator typed in the word "HELLO" the internal memory of a computer would contain this string of binary digits:

01001000   01000101   01001100   01001100   01001111

in each of the five memory cells where the five upper-case alphabetical characters are stored. Notice that each letter takes eight binary digits, called a *byte*. A single digit (0 or 1) is called a *bit*, or a BInary digiT.

Furthermore, if we were to look into the internal memory of our computer to see how it stored the source code of the BASIC program set out in the preceding section of this chapter, it would look like Figure 2.2, which is a listing of the source in binary, with line numbers on the left column, four characters in binary in the center, and the actual human readable source in the column on the right.

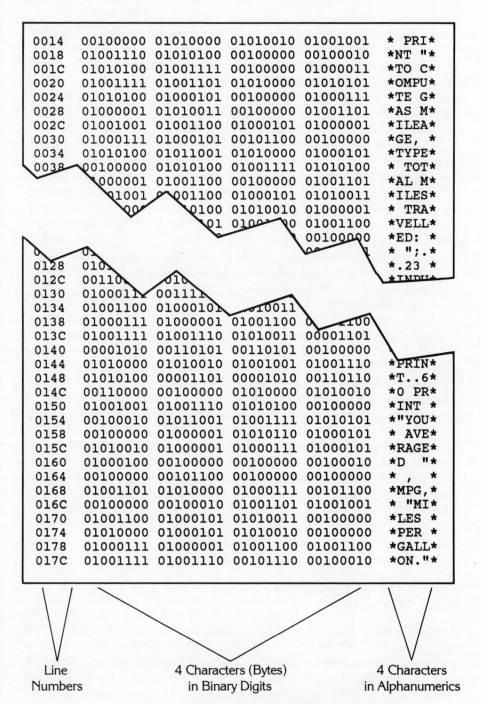

```
0014    00100000 01010000 01010010 01001001    * PRI*
0018    01001110 01010100 00100000 00100010    *NT "*
001C    01010100 01001111 00100000 01000011    *TO C*
0020    01001111 01001101 01010000 01010101    *OMPU*
0024    01010100 01000101 00100000 01000111    *TE G*
0028    01000001 01010011 00100000 01001101    *AS M*
002C    01001001 01001100 01000101 01000001    *ILEA*
0030    01000111 01000101 00101100 00100000    *GE, *
0034    01010100 01011001 01010000 01000101    *TYPE*
0038    00100000 01010100 01001111 01010100    * TOT*
        0000001 01001100 00100000 01001101      *AL M*
         01001  01001100 01000101 01010011      *ILES*
          00     0100 01010010 01000001         * TRA
           01 0100  00 01001100                 *VELL*
                       00100000                  *ED: *
                                                * ";.*
0128    010                                     *.23 *
012C    00110     010                           *INDH*
0130    0100011  001111
0134    01001100 0100010    10011
0138    01000111 01000001 01001100 0  1100
013C    01001111 01001110 01010011 00001101
0140    00001010 00110101 00110101 00100000
0144    01010000 01010010 01001001 01001110    *PRIN*
0148    01010100 00001101 00001010 00110110    *T..6*
014C    00110000 00100000 01010000 01010010    *0 PR*
0150    01001001 01001110 01010100 00100000    *INT *
0154    00100010 01011001 01001111 01010101    *"YOU*
0158    00100000 01000001 01010110 01000101    * AVE*
015C    01010010 01000001 01000111 01000101    *RAGE*
0160    01000100 00100000 00100000 00100010    *D  "*
0164    00100000 00101100 00100000 00100000    * ,  *
0168    01001101 01010000 01000111 00101100    *MPG,*
016C    00100000 00100010 01001101 01001001    * "MI*
0170    01001100 01000101 01010011 00100000    *LES *
0174    01010000 01000101 01010010 00100000    *PER *
0178    01000111 01000001 01001100 01001100    *GALL*
017C    01001111 01001110 00101110 00100010    *ON."*
```

| Line Numbers | 4 Characters (Bytes) in Binary Digits | 4 Characters in Alphanumerics |

Figure 2.2. Binary Representation of MPG. BAS.

For purposes of illustration only, the computer has been told to translate each line of four characters into English numbers or letters in the final column, so we can see how the binary numbers correspond to the original source code. There are dots for special characters like carriage returns and line feeds, which you can ignore. You can also disregard the first column on the left, which is a series of line numbers in a special mathematical notation used by the computer.

Likewise, if we were to look at the magnetic image of this same program stored on the tracks of a magnetic diskette (floppy disk), we would see the same series of binary digits. These digits are recorded on a series of concentric tracks, much like a phonograph record. The disk-drive electronics can then read the digits and send them to the CPU upon request. It can also record a new series of these binary digits on these or other tracks if the CPU tells it to store them.

In this way, the computer is able to send and receive characters and numbers from one part of the system to another, and to and from other computers. The system has encoded data that ultimately it will "decode" back into readable letters or numbers on the screen of the CRT or on the paper in a printer. It is this computer coding process that has caused such confusion in software copyright cases.

Once you see how everything that goes into and out of the computer is turned into binary digits, you can recognize why the court system has had such difficulty finding analogies between copyrights on printed material (like books) and computer software. A long string of 0's and 1's stored in a computer memory chip or on a magnetic disk doesn't seem to have much in common with printed words on paper—but it really does, for a human created the material in both cases. A computer translates the program into a binary code more useful for its purposes, while a book is printed by a machine directly in human-readable form. *That we, as humans, find binary code hard to read does not alter the fact of human authorship.*

WHY DOES A COMPUTER NEED SOFTWARE?

You might ask at this point, "If the computer is so damn smart, why does it need software?" There are, in fact, a number of technical reasons why a computer needs software, but the clearest answer is that the computer just isn't that smart. All it "knows" is how to add, subtract, multiply, and divide, plus compare characters and numbers. All the computer can do is step through sets of instructions, one by one, programmed in a language that it understands, until it has completed a task. It does not know how to think. It does exactly what it is told, and nothing more. A very fast but unintelligent machine.

USING PROGRAMMING LANGUAGES

The key to programming computers is through the use of specialized English words and invented terms meaning specific things to the computer. In order to write computer software, programmers have to learn a new vocabulary, as well as the various constructs and rules of the language, just as if you were to learn to speak and read, say, Chinese.

In the earlier example program, the term "INPUT MILES" tells the computer to wait for data, and when it receives them to proceed to the next instruction while remembering these data and storing them in internal memory in a place the programmer calls "MILES." The term "PRINT" means to print whatever follows enclosed in quotation marks, and then to skip to the next line.

Computer languages like BASIC are a form of coded communication between man and machine. They are themselves complex computer programs written by a software company, which are useable on a computer only if you have a diskette copy of that language program. BASIC was in turn written in another, even more complex but lower-level, computer language called "Assembly Language."

Assembly Language is a low-level language in that it uses cryptic mnemonic terms like "JMP" or "EQU" for instructions, instead of the whole words of BASIC. Assembly Language is very close to the actual binary numbers the computer understands directly as its most elementary instructions. A program written directly in coded binary-number instructions is called "machine language" and is almost impossible for a human to read and interpret.

For this machine language to work, some engineer or programmer had to design the CPU so that it would understand that receipt of the electrical impulses meaning "01000001 01000100 01000100" was an instruction for the CPU to add one number to another. In turn, the human who wrote the original Assembly Language had to know this and use these exact binary numbers to instruct the computer when he or she was creating the Assembly Language program. Once this was done, someone else could create BASIC in Assembly Language, and then I could use BASIC to write the program set out earlier in this chapter. In this way the higher-level languages are built from those a level below.

In short, computers must use languages to communicate, just as humans do. But since computers only understand languages based on (unreadable) binary numbers, programmers have created intermediate or high-level languages that allow both computers and programmers to more readily understand and communicate with each other.

SOURCE CODE AND OBJECT CODE—
COMPILERS AND ASSEMBLERS

How then do you fit machine-coded and machine-readable materials into a copyright system designed primarily to protect books and writings? Copyright laws protect only the "writings" of authors. It is at least arguable that the ultimate binary form of the computer program is "authored" by the computer and not by a human being. For this very reason a famous political scientist at MIT, Ithiel de Sola Pool, flatly predicts that our copyright system will no longer work in the environment of electronic creation of materials. It is this whole question of authorship that is behind all the confusion in recent copyright cases the world over.

This brings us to several final technical aspects of software that you have to understand if recent copyright cases and the current rules of the Copyright Office are to make any sense. The best I can do is explain these aspects quickly. You can accept them on faith until we get to Chapter 6 on copyright deposits, at which time you will see why you were exposed to this ultimate computer lore.

For the computer to use the high-level programming languages that programmers like to use, such as BASIC, there has to be a way to translate the human-readable source code into the final binary machine-language of the computer. Programmers call this lowest level of program code *object code* or *machine language*. The only instructions the computer can actually "execute" are those in binary machine-language form. To accomplish this translation from high-level source code to the lowest-level machine code, programmers make use of special software called *language compilers, interpreters* or *assemblers.*

These are very complex programs that take the human-readable words of, for example, my source program in BASIC and directly translate them into object code for the computer. The computer takes the intermediate binary representation of the source code you saw previously, processes it further, and turns the final program into another binary program called executable object code—code that is the object of all the prior programming work.

The translation process goes through a series of stages, the source code going from one form to another, then another, and finally emerging at the end as object code. Once source-code language is translated into object code, there is almost no way to reconstruct it exactly. The original source code contains not only instructions (which can be decoded by the computer, back to assembly-language source), but also addresses or locations in memory and *labels* (names given to locations in the memory). The *decompiler* or *disassembler* used to decode the object code can only guess whether the addresses and labels are instructions or numbers representing locations in memory.

Diagramatically, the process of translation from source to object code by a compiler would look like the process shown in Figure 2.3.

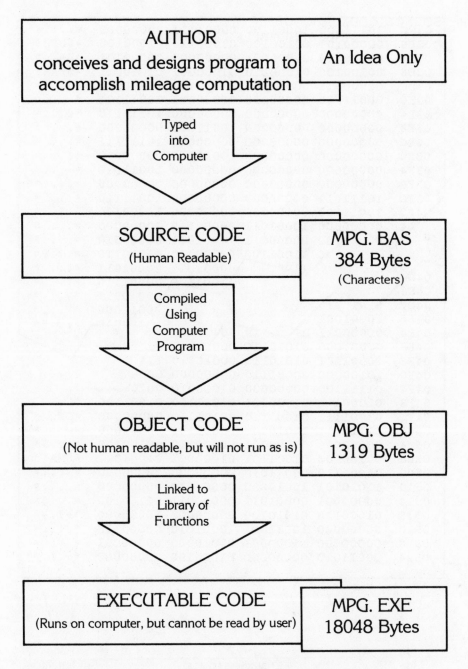

Figure 2.3. Evolution of the MPG. Gas Mileage Program.

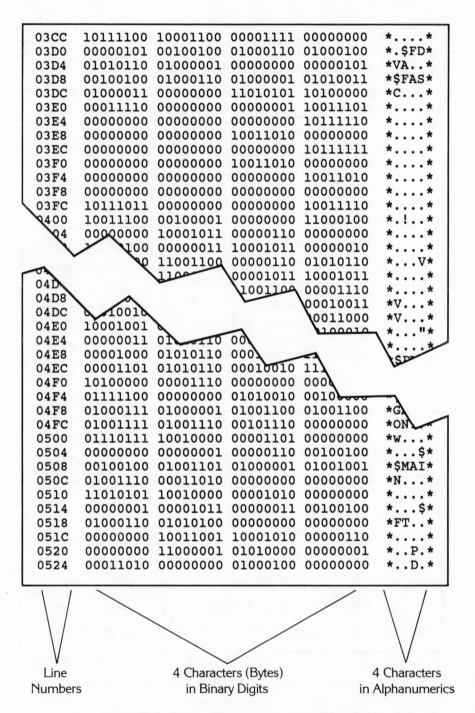

| Line
Numbers | 4 Characters (Bytes)
in Binary Digits | 4 Characters
in Alphanumerics |

Figure 2.4. Binary Representation of MPG. OBJ.

Decompilation or Disassembly

Object code consists of binary numbers, which are unreadable to all but the most highly skilled assembly-language programmers. The problem is that nothing but 1's and 0's on line after line of printout is extremely difficult to keep track of, or to separate into numbered instructions. It is possible, however, to develop an approximation of the original source code from the object code. This laborious reverse engineering process, as indicated above, is called *decompilation* or *disassembly*. This is one way of pirating software that has been previously marketed in object code.

The other way of pirating software is just to copy the object code diskette directly, but this is easier to detect, since most of the code is "fingerprinted" by serial numbers and other unique devices deliberately installed to detect copying.

To prevent pirating, most applications software, like WORDSTAR® and VisiCalc® , is only available to the end user in object-code form. However, some accounting software, written in BASIC, is available in source code, as is much of the software in the public domain of user groups.

Once the computer has compiled (translated) our BASIC program into object code that it can read and execute, the English words and punctuation now become binary gibberish that only the computer can interpret as is shown in Figure 2.4.

Notice that, unlike the translation back into English characters and numbers, which the previous printout had in the far right column, this column is now meaningless to us. This is machine language (not the human-readable source code) and is stored on the diskettes that are marketed to the microcomputer world as applications software.

THE ISSUE OF SUFFICIENT HUMAN AUTHORSHIP

As mentioned earlier, computer programs are usually marketed on diskette, but can also be stored in the computer on Read-Only-Memory (ROM) chips physically attached to the machine on a circuit board. In the case of video games, programs are also distributed in cartridge form. None of these forms of software are visible or readable in the normal sense of written human language. Is this then still human authorship? Or is the computer really the author?

In dealing with object code, the ultimate legal problem that has faced the courts is whether this unintelligible binary code is still *sufficient human authorship* to be protectable under the copyright, patent, and trade secret laws of the country. By now the courts have essentially concluded that since object code started out as a human-readable computer program, authored by a human, it should still be protected—even though what the consumer gets is a machine translation and machine-processed version of it. As we will see in later chapters, this raises numerous other, still partially unresolved, questions about software and computer technology.

By now you should have solutions to some of the riddles involved in understanding computer terminology. As a nontechnical person, remember that in this complex field it is imperative that you *say what you mean.*

3

Who Owns Ideas and Other Intellectual Property?

He who receives an idea from me, receives instruction himself without lessening mine; as he who lights his taper at mine, receives light without darkening me.

Thomas Jefferson, *Basic Writings of Thomas Jefferson,*
edited by Philip S. Foner, Willey Book Company,
New York, 1944, p. 712.

THE OWNERSHIP OF IDEAS

In a sense, this entire book is about the ownership of ideas. Learning how to protect ideas, as property, is a vital subject to you as a businessperson or computer professional and to everyone in the computer industry, since much of what is embodied in a computer program is merely the written expression of a programmer's ideas. If the program has commercial value, then the ideas behind it also have value, so we want to protect both the idea and the actual program. Our legal system has difficulty dealing with this duality, since it is hard to show a judge tangible evidence of the idea in the form of computer software when that idea is recorded in object code on a diskette.

Jefferson suggests that you cannot "possess" an idea if you disclose it, and he is correct in a literal sense. But under English and American law you can own legal rights in the application or expression of an idea such as an invention or the printed text of a book. These are known as "intellectual property rights." They are a special form of property and they are protected under some unique federal, state, and even foreign laws and treaties.

Basically, there are four separate bodies of law, each of which protects different aspects of intellectual property including computer programs. These are as follows:

- Trade-secret laws
- Copyright laws
- Patent laws
- Trademark laws.

In this chapter we will take a comparative look at hypothetical examples of ideas protected by each of these laws—laws that we can then explore more extensively in the rest of the book in a form more applicable to software.

PROTECTING IDEAS AS PROPERTY

An idea, in the context of this book, is the mental representation of an object or a process. When we develop an idea in our mind, we create an image or concept that often does not yet exist in a physical sense. We are the exclusive owner of that idea until we disclose it to someone else by discussing it with that person, by showing that person a physical model of it, or by letting others read a written description or expression of the idea in the form of a book or article. The act of disclosure of the idea to others is particularly important in patent and trade-secret law.

Each idea is an intellectual image that exists apart from the material object that is a copy of that idea: an artist's drawing would be a classic example. The idea is, nevertheless, a special kind of property capable of ownership in at least some forms. In the case of computer software we want to protect, if we can, both the idea and the program as a physical copy of it. The concepts (ideas) used to design the software may be protectable as a trade secret, while the written expression of those concepts in the form of a program are covered by copyright law.

Lawyers' shorthand for such mental concepts is "intellectual property," or in a broader sense "intangible property," to distinguish it from other physical forms of property. Historically, most law has related to the protection of tangible, physically existing property—like castles, horses, crops, or human slaves. We often do not recognize that *ideas are property.*

IDEAS MUST BE IN PHYSICAL FORM

Most forms of legal protection of ideas require that the idea be implemented in some tangible form or material object to be the subject of protection. What you end up owning as property in an idea is the physical manifestation of the idea, like a copy of the object code on a diskette. As one famous judge said, "A man's property in an idea is limited to the physical property which embodies his invention."

The only exception to the requirement that the idea be in at least semitangible form to be protected is found in trade-secret law (the subject of Chapter 4). Because trade-secret law is an exception to the general rule, it is of considerable value to the computer and electronics industry, which has to deal with both ideas in the abstract and those that have been implemented in physical objects.

There are several reasons why ideas generally have to be embodied in physical form before they can be protected. First, as long as they are still in someone's head they are subject to change from second to second, so that there is no way of determining the scope or extent of the idea. There is no reliable way of describing what is protected.

Second, if an idea like a mathematical formula were protectable, the owner of the formula could prevent the operation of anything that used or could be represented by the formula. This would give the owner too much of a monopoly. For example, if Einstein could have patented his discovery of the formula for the conservation of energy, $E = mc^2$, he would have been able to receive royalties on all devices like nuclear reactors and fusion and fission weapons. For reasons of public policy, nearly all exclusive ownership of intellectual property is restricted by law to a specified area or field or use of the idea and to a limited period of time. This is true of copyright, patent, and trademark law, but not trade-secret law, which is again an exception.

AN EXAMPLE OF A "NEW IDEA"

Consider the case of Ms. Shauna L. Scientist, who is full of great ideas and comes to us for advice on how to protect one of her latest ones. She is a jogger, bicyclist, and mountain climber who feels that there should be a better soft drink and that it ought to be packaged in a form more useable by active outdoor people. Watching the innovative feeding techniques carried out during a space shuttle mission inspired her to develop her new drink formula.

Shauna tells us, after we sign a confidential nondisclosure agreement for her protection, that she has developed a formula for a new drink, consisting of grape juice and tropical fruits together with vitamins and minerals. She feels it has great restorative powers for people who have been exercising hard and want a drink that will not make them more thirsty, nor cause them to be nauseated while still continuing to exercise. To make it more useable by active people, she has also designed a pressurized, biodegradable, flexible, plastic package with a small tube and valve that allows the user to drink while running, climbing, or cycling, without opening the container or spilling it. She wants to call the drink, for obvious reasons, "Computer Cola™—The Space Age Drink™."

Being an exceedingly clever young lady, she has also designed (but not yet built) a computer-controlled machine that mixes the drink in different forms, depending on the altitude at which it is to be used, fills the sterile package with a combination of inert nitrogen and the drink, seals it, attaches the valve and tubing, and adds a small strap so the package can be hung over the athlete's shoulder. The machine then labels the package and puts it in boxes—all under computer control so that it is never touched by human hands, only industrial robots.

Finally, after some research in her laboratory, Shauna has discovered that this drink is also an excellent form of diet food, so she wants to write a short book on how to use this drink with other food to lose ten pounds per week.

Unfortunately, she has lots of ideas, but no money and no business experience. She now wants to know if what she has done has any commercial value and how to protect what she calls her "great idea." Before we send her to a friendly and honest venture capitalist to help her out, we will need to examine with her what she can actually protect, at this and later stages.

COMPARING THE FOUR INTELLECTUAL-PROPERTY LAWS

Each of the four bodies of intellectual-property law protect a different aspect of Shauna's ideas and their practical applications; we will see what each law does and does not protect. But before we examine Shauna's ideas and inventions in this light, you should understand the basic intent and purpose of these unique laws and how they apply to your own ideas in the field of software.

Trade Secret Law.   This protects the unique and secret aspects of ideas, known only to the discoverer and his or her confidant(e)s. It is the only body of law that protects abstract information, such as the general knowledge of how to do something or the formula for Shauna's drink. Once disclosed generally, the trade secret is lost as a trade secret, although it might still be protectable under one of the other laws.

Patent Law.   This gives the owner the exclusive right to make, use, or sell articles that embody the ideas. The patent, however, covers only those specific claims that the inventor disclosed in his or her application, and protection lasts only for the term of the patent. It may cover processes or designs, as well. In Shauna's case, the patent might apply to her machine or to the process of packaging the drink, or both. The inventor must satisfy a series of legal tests before being entitled to the protection. The patent protects the application of the idea to some physical article or process.

Copyright Law. This protects only the written expression of the ideas, such as Shauna's book or her computer program. It does not prevent others from using the ideas expressed in the program, so long as they express them independently and without copying those of the author. Others may not copy, distribute, or derive other writings (without permission) from the original copyrighted work. Copyright occurs automatically, but may be lost through unintentional oversight or by intentional disclaimer.

Trademark Law. This is intended to identify the source of goods or services, so that the only thing that the law protects is the mark serving as the identifier. Shauna's proposed drink name, "Computer Cola™," is an ideal mark since it means little except as an identification for her drink. A trademark does not prevent others from making a similar article, as long as the maker does not attribute it to the trademarked source. Trademark rights arise upon first usage of the mark in commerce, and are lost when the mark is no longer used. In theory, the duration of trademark rights is perpetual, so long as the mark is in regular public use.

Using Trade-Secret Law to Protect Ideas

What, first of all, is a trade secret? It is any secret or information not generally available except under restrictions; information which, if made available to others without restriction would permit them to profit commercially, and which the owner has made a reasonable effort to protect from disclosure.

Until Shauna has implemented the idea of manufacturing and selling the drink on the public market, she can protect her ideas *in the abstract* as a trade secret. At this point, what she is trying to protect is her business plan, as well as her ideas about the design of the package, the machinery, the formula, and the name. Furthermore, the fact that the space program used plastic packages for food and drink does not preclude her from protecting her ideas, since they would be used in a different application and appear to use some unique techniques.

Shauna should not disclose her ideas in any detail to anyone unless they sign, as we did, a confidential nondisclosure agreement. Our joint act of signing an agreement was to illustrate that she could lose the trade secret protection by disclosure to anyone not bound by confidentiality.

Once fully disclosed, Shauna's trade secret would lose protection and the information would only be protectable under other legal principles, if at all. However, while her formula is protected as a trade secret, Shauna can obtain court orders (called "injunctions") directing people not to use or disclose the information, and might recover damages caused by improper disclosure of the information. Also, the source code of your computer program can be protected by this law. (See Chapter 4 for a detailed discussion of trade secrets.)

While Shauna's business plan, the package, and the packaging machinery will no longer be protected as a trade secret once the drink is marketed, the formula for her drink may, as with Coca Cola®, be a continuing trade secret protectable so long as she keeps it secret or permits others to use it only under a nondisclosure agreement. Properly handled, the formula could be a trade secret forever, whereas if Shauna chose to patent it protection would last only seventeen years.

Using Patent Law to Protect Ideas

Once Shauna has perfected her flexible plastic package and pressure valve, she must take steps to patent them within one year of disclosure, or she may lose her right to do so. In the meantime, she must rely on trade-secret law while the package and pressure valve are under design and until they have been completed. The same is true of her packaging machine and the process for manufacturing the drink by use of the machine and her computer. Her patent protection will date from the grant of the patent and run for seventeen years. During the patent application process her ideas and inventions are kept secret by the Patent Office. Once the patent is issued, the information becomes public and trade-secret protection is lost.

A patent is an agreement between the inventor and the federal government that, in return for full disclosure of the invention and all the claims made by the inventor, the government grants the patent applicant what amounts to a limited monopoly permitting him or her to preclude others from practicing or using the invention. Should people use the invention covered by the patent they must, during the term of the patent, pay royalties to the owner for the privilege of doing so.

There are several types of patents. Shauna might be entitled to file a claim for inventing an apparatus (machine) by reason of her bottling and mixing machine, a manufacture (article) patent on the plastic package and valve, a process patent for the mixing and filling aspects of the new machine, and perhaps even a patent on the composition of the drink itself if it could be shown to be a new food. Finally, she might even be able to obtain a separate design patent on the ornamental (or appearance) aspects of the plastic package.

Of particular interest to us in the field of computer programming is that Shauna's process patent might well be based upon the use of the computer program which determines the proper formulation of the drink for different altitudes and other conditions. In rare instances, although probably not here, the program itself might be patentable. (Chapter 9 of this book covers the subject of software and process patents in detail.)

In all of the above cases Shauna's inventions will not result in a patent unless the legal requirements of 1) novelty, 2) utility, and 3) nonobviousness are met, and unless other conditions in the patent law are complied with. (Again, Chapter 9 covers this ground.)

Using Trademark Law to Protect Ideas

A trademark is essentially any mark, name, figure, symbol, initials, or other distinguishing aspect of goods or services used in commerce which is intended to identify goods with their source. Registration of trademarks is one of the easier protective steps to take. It may be of considerable value to the publisher or distributor of software as a means of protecting a product from unauthorized duplication and distribution.

The owner of a trademark for a computer program, such as Visi-Calc®, can prevent others from marketing software under that or any similar name. Properly handled, the trademark is good for an initial term of twenty years and may be renewed as long as the trademark is in use and it qualifies as a registrable trademark. (See Chapter 10 for more on trademarks.)

Our young inventor would like to obtain a trademark on the name "Computer Cola" and the slogan "The Space Age Drink". While she can protect these names under both federal and most state laws, she cannot register these trademarks until they are actually in use; and until the actual trademarks can be registered, Shauna takes the risk that someone else will use and register them. There is the further possibility that someone else already has used and acquired ownership of these trademarks. For this reason, Shauna should have a trademark search conducted at once before spending money on advertising and labeling materials.

Once Shauna has registered her trademarks, she is entitled to the same type of damages and attorney fees for infringement that her patents would give her for her inventions. The cost of maintaining her trademarks is very low. But since she cannot register the trademarks until they are actually in use, she should start use of them at the earliest possible time.

Using Copyright Law to Protect Ideas

Essentially the only practical form of legal protection for mass-distributed computer software, the copyright laws of the U.S. provide that the owner of the copyright has the exclusive right 1) to reproduce or copy the work, 2) to prepare works derived from or based upon the original work, 3) to distribute the work or copies of it to the public by sale, rental, lease or lending, and 4) to display the copyrighted work. In the case of computer programs, the rightful owner of a copy of a program has the right to use it, to back it up, and to make adaptations of the program for his or her own use. The copies of the programs may be transferred only with the original copy, and the adaptations only with the permission of the copyright owner.

Until Shauna has actually written the book and the computer program to run the computerized bottling and mixing system, she has no protection for her naked ideas about doing them, except trade secrecy. The federal copyright laws (which preempt or supercede all state laws on the subject) require that Shauna's ideas be fixed or embodied in some tangible medium of expression before any protection starts. That medium may be paper in the case of the book, or a magnetic diskette in the case of the computer software. A copyright would last for the author's lifetime plus fifty years. The period would be seventy-five years if the program is created for a corporation. The useful life of a computer program is most likely to be much less than such periods of time.

Qualifying Shauna's book and computer program for protection under the copyright laws (steps discussed in detail in Chapters 5, 6, and 7) is generally fairly simple and straightforward. Shauna and computer-program authors have the right, once a copyright is registered with the Copyright Office of the Library of Congress, to bring suit for protection from copyright infringement. Relief available is in the form of injunctions, damages, and attorney fees and costs.

The biggest problem with software copyright infringement is catching the pirate. Since much of the piracy occurs at the individual level, infringement becomes nearly impossible to detect. It may also be difficult to prove copying unless the program author has followed some of the suggestions of this book.

A COMPARISON CHART
OF THE THREE AREAS OF THE LAW

During the 1970's, when Congress was considering revision of the federal copyright laws, including new laws to protect software, it created the National Commission on New Technological Uses of Copyrighted Works (CONTU). In the process of its studies, the Commission developed a cross-comparison chart showing the three major legal areas available to protect software, and listing the benefits and failings of each law.

This chart has been updated into the more complete and descriptive series of material that complete this chapter. You may wish to read through this material now, or refer to it later as you read through the book.

Comparative Characteristics of Copyright, Patent, and Trade Secrecy for the Protection of Computer Software

CHARACTERISTICS OF COPYRIGHT LAW

A. Copyright Protection is National. Protection under the copyright laws is available in each of the fifty United States through the federal courts. U. S. copyrights provide some level of international protection because of international agreements.

B. Copyrights Have a Long Life. For individuals copyrights may last for the life of the author plus fifty years, and for corporations copyrights may continue for seventy-five years.

C. Works Are Protected from Their Creation. The protection of a copyright attaches at the creation of the work. However it must be perfected by registration within ninety days of the work's publication to secure full statutory protection including various statutory remedies.

D. Copyright Protection Is Inexpensive. Initial protection attaches without cost, and the registration process is easy to comply with and inexpensive.

E. All Software May Be Copyrighted. Since the 1980 amendments to the 1976 Copyright Act, it has been clear that computer programs are copyrightable. (Some parties are arguing, in pending litigation, that some forms of computer programs may not be protected. This position is contrary to the clear language of the statute and seems to be without foundation.)

F. Copyright Survives Mass Distribution. Copyright protection is well suited for use with mass-distributed software, because the work may be publicly disclosed without a loss of the protection and rights granted by statute.

G. Copyrights Do Not Protect Ideas. A limitation of copyright law is that it protects the author from having works copied, but it does not protect the author's ideas and algorithms. Ideas disclosed in the published work may be learned by competitors and may be used in independently developed works.

H. The Law Provides Statutory Damages and Attorney's Fees. Once a work is properly marked with the required notices and a timely registration is made, the copyright holder has some powerful tools to use against an infringer. A registration certificate is prima facie evidence of the copyright's validity. The Act provides for substantial statutory damages or actual damages, and it provides for the recovery of attorney's fees and costs from infringers.

I. Protection May Be Lost by Neglect. The rights provided by the Copyright Act can be lost if the copyright holder fails to maintain the proper notices or through other neglect allows the work to go into the public domain.

J. The Cost of Maintaining Protection Is Low. The copyright owner must assure that authorized copies are properly marked with the required copyright notices and should take action against gross infringements.

K. The Cost of Enforcing Rights Is Moderate. Copyright infringement actions are moderately costly law suits; however if the plaintiff is successful and the defendant is not judgment proof the copyright owner can recover most of these costs.

CHARACTERISTICS OF TRADE SECRECY LAW

A. Trade Secret Protection Is a State Law Matter. Protection under the trade secret laws is a function of state statutes or common law. The scope of protection differs from state to state.

B. Trade Secrets Have an Indefinite Life. Trade secret protection may be terminated at any time by disclosure or independent development. However, as long as trade secrets are carefully protected they have the possibility of providing perpetual protection.

C. Works Are Protected by Nondisclosure Agreements. Trade secrets come into being when those developing them agree to regard and protect them as trade secrets. The proprietor must take all necessary steps to prevent the disclosure of his or her trade secrets to any one who has not contracted to protect them.

D. Trade Secret Protection Is Moderately Expensive. The cost of security, maintaining a record of who has had access to the secret, obtaining signed nondisclosure agreements, and the constant care it takes to protect trade secrets can add up to a substantial amount over time.

E. Only Limited Distribution Software May Be a Trade Secret. The requirement of continued security and signed nondisclosure agreements is workable for unpublished source code or limited distribution software but not for mass-distributed software.

F. Mass Distribution Destroys Trade Secret Protection.

G. A Trade Secret Protects Ideas. As long as a trade secret is maintained it protects the ideas and algorithms as well as the form of expression.

H. There Is No Provision for Statutory Damages or Attorney Fees. The general American rule is that in the absence of a statute or a contract to the contrary, each party pays its own legal fees and must prove its damages.

I. Protection Is Lost Upon Disclosure.

J. The Cost of Maintaining Protection Is Higher. The cost of protecting a trade secret is ongoing and must be incurred as long as the protection is desired, unlike copyrights.

K. The Cost of Enforcing Rights Tends to Be Higher. The proprietor has the burden of proving that there is a trade secret and that the defendant obtained it wrongfully. The law suit to enforce a trade secret may destroy the trade secret if the secret itself becomes part of the public record.

CHARACTERISTICS OF PATENT LAW

A. Patent Protection Is National. Protection under the Patent laws is available and enforceable uniformly in each of the fifty United States through the federal courts.

B. Patents Have a Moderate Life. Patent protection lasts for seventeen years.

C. Patents Must Be Applied for. The protection of a patent attaches on successful prosecution of a patent application. Applications must be made within one year of initial disclosure.

D. Patent Protection Is Moderately Expensive. The successful prosecution of a patent application is a fairly costly and time-consuming process requiring extensive legal and technical work.

E. Patents Are Available for Little if any Software. To date patents have largely been granted only for computer programs that were an intrinsic part of patentable processes, such as industrial control programs for machinery or processing systems.

F. Patents Survive Mass Distribution. Patent protection would be well suited for use with mass-distributed software, because the work may be publicly disclosed without a loss of the protection and rights granted by statute.

G. Patents Do Protect Ideas. Patents protect the ideas and algorithms they cover, even from independent development.

H. The Law Provides for Attorney's Fees and Treble Damages. Patents, once issued, have a presumption of validity, but often are attacked successfully. The patent holder must prove damages. However, the law does provide for the recovery of attorney fees and treble damages in cases of wilful infringement.

I. Protection May Be Lost by Unsuccessful Litigation. If the validity of a patent is challenged successfully, the patent is voided and protection lost.

J. The Cost of Maintaining Protection Is Low. Unless litigation is necessary, the cost of maintaining protection is low.

K. The Cost of Enforcing Rights Is Substantial. Patent infringement actions are fairly costly lawsuits. However, if the plaintiff is successful and the defendant is not judgment-proof, the patent holder can recover most of these costs.

4

How to Protect Software as a Trade Secret

'Trade secret' means the whole or any portion or phase
of any scientific or technical information, design,
process, procedure, formula or improvement which is
secret and is not generally available to the public, and
which gives one who uses it an advantage over
competitors who do not know of or use the trade secret;
and a trade secret shall be presumed to be secret when
the owner thereof takes measures to prevent it from
becoming available to persons other than those selected
by the owner to have access thereto for limited purposes.

California Penal Code Section 499c(a)(3).

A BACKGROUND TO TRADE SECRET LAW

Trade-secret law is the first line of defense for the software developer
intent on protecting his work and economic base. It is based on the law of
the individual states, as opposed to federal law, and is so important to the
economic health of business and industry that violation of it may be both
a civil and criminal matter. It is easily understood by anyone, and costs
very little to use. It may be the only real protection for source code and
flowcharts, and for the logic of programs, since competitive programs are
easily developed once the source code is available. Unfortunately, mass-
distributed object code ordinarily cannot be protected by trade-secret
law, but is covered by copyright law.

Trade secrets are protected by the law imposing upon employees
(and others who gain access to the secret information) an obligation not to
disclose or use that information for the benefit of themselves or
competitors of the owner of it. If they attempt to do so, the courts will

31

order them to stop, to return the trade-secret materials to their former employer or other owner of them, and to pay damages, if appropriate. To take advantage of this law, it is not necessary to register or disclose the trade-secret information to any government agency, but it is necessary to take a series of fairly simple steps to see that the information is properly treated. If you want the law to apply to your software, only you and the people who work in your business can take these steps. If you have not taken these steps from the beginning, there is little your lawyer can do at a later date to recover lost trade-secret status for software.

The California Penal Code section, quoted above, closely follows the accepted legal definition of the term "trade secret" under most civil and criminal statutes in the United States. Many states have adopted a uniform trade-secrets law, similar to the above definition, and many others are considering it. Because of its "high-tech" orientation, California has suffered an unusual number of recent criminal proceedings for theft of high-technology processes and ideas. Theft of computer designs and computer software may also be a serious federal crime, as the IBM-Hitachi Ltd. trade-secret cases attest. Private parties may also bring suit under the civil statutes for damages and injunctions.

Trade-secret law has been recognized in English and American law for the past 150 years under the assumption that it is unfair for an employee (or other person) to obtain commercial information while in a position of trust or confidence, and then to use this information to the detriment of the original owner. For this reason, the English, rather descriptively, call it the Law of Confidence which, if broken, becomes a form of theft of intangible property.

THE KEY ELEMENTS OF A TRADE SECRET

At least three, and sometimes four elements must be present for a trade secret to qualify for legal protection under the trade secret laws:

1. It must be information that is either a business secret or, at least, is not generally available without restrictions on its use or dissemination.

2. The information must have some commercial value to competitors or others in business.

3. The owner must have taken "reasonable steps" in the operation of the business to keep the information from becoming general knowledge through unrestricted disclosure.

4. The information must be something that the employer developed or obtained at his or her expense, such as through research and development (in the situation where a legal dispute arises between an employer and employee).

Each of these elements has been the subject of considerable litigation in most states. The next three sections illustrate these elements by reference to some of this litigation.

Secret or Confidential Information

The secrecy element is satisfied in nearly every case by the owner establishing that the information or process was developed in the business (or perhaps licensed from others), and that this information is something that others in the trade or business do not generally know or have available to them. The courts often require that the confidential information to be protected relate directly to the operation of the business. This is easily satisfied in the case of software, which is the primary product of the business.

The program logic, detailed file structure, and algorithms of an electronic spread sheet like VisiCalc®, as disclosed by the source code, is a classic illustration of a software trade secret. The owner or publisher or such a program will normally mass-distribute the program only in object-code form, and will usually restrict access to the source code to employees and manufacturers (OEMs) who have signed nondisclosure agreements.

While many people believe that a trade secret has to be unique in order to be protected, it does not. What is required is that it be information not readily available to competitors without considerable effort or research. Usually, it is something requiring "creative effort," like the development of a new program, new industrial process, or just a better way of doing something others have done for years. For this reason, lists of possible customers, which anyone could assemble from telephone or trade directories, would not normally be protected. On the other hand, the source code of almost any standard accounting program could be a trade secret, if the program runs faster or does things other programs do not readily do. For example, it might have a unique file-management structure.

An oft-cited example of a closely guarded trade secret is the formula for Coca Cola®, even though Coke® is certainly not the only cola drink. Another trade secret is the source code of Lotus' 1-2-3® integrated spread sheet, even though there are many other spread sheets. This remains a trade secret because the publisher does not make the source code available, only distributing object-code copies to the public and relying on copyright law to protect the object code.

The Requirement of Commercial Value

By this requirement you must be able to show that the confidential information gives you a competitive advantage over others. For example, the highly technical design details of IBM's next high-density disk-drive model would have obvious commercial value to any business manufacturing IBM-compatible disk drives for mainframes. In the 1973 Telex v. IBM case, IBM complained of the recruitment of its personnel by Telex for the purpose of gaining this technology, and prevailed in a multi-million dollar judgment against Telex. In the software field, Hitachi allegedly sought to obtain the IBM microcode for the then unreleased high-end computer IBM was developing. This act resulted in both a successful civil suit by IBM, and a federal criminal prosecution of Hitachi and some of its employees in 1983.

In a 1983 case, Sheridan v. Mallinckrodt, that involved a secret process for making plastic medical equipment, the court granted relief to the plaintiff, Mallinckrodt, because the trial judge found that Mallinckrodt "demonstrated the competitive edge afforded by use of the process." The court was impressed that no one else in the industry had been able to duplicate the particular design of the plastic instrument.

The Owner's Efforts to Protect the Trade Secret

The third requirement, that the owner treat the information as a secret and take "reasonable steps" to protect it, is where most trade-secret cases break down. If the owner does not act as though the information is valuable, and does not protect it by locking it up, marking it as "Confidential," and telling employees and visitors that it is valuable, then the courts will not consider the information a trade secret. Many software companies do not even take the minimal necessary steps of having employees sign nondisclosure agreements, or of having visitors sign-in and agree not to disclose confidential information they may learn.

How Not to Keep a Secret.   A recent software trade-secret case, Jostens, Inc. v. National Computer Systems, illustrates how your company can lose protection by failing to take "reasonable steps" to insist on secrecy concerning a program. Jostens had an employee-engineer and an outside subcontractor develop a unique Computer-Aided Design/Computer-Aided Manufacturing (CAD/CAM) process for making class rings, which it used to considerable competitive advantage. During his employment by Jostens, the engineer involved wrote and presented at a national conference a paper explaining in some detail the program and the procedures involved in development and use of the system. This was done with the express permission of the employer.

Moreover, Jostens never advised its employees that the system was a trade secret, nor that the program was "Company Confidential." Some years after the employee did the original work, he was asked to sign a general nondisclosure agreement. But when the employee left Jostens, the president of the company told him that his continued work in this area of technology "was fine with us." The employee then joined another company, which developed and eventually sold a similar system to Jostens' major competitor. When Jostens sued the other company and its former employee, the court denied any relief to Jostens on the grounds that it had never identified the program and system as a trade secret, and had not treated it as such, nor taken any reasonable steps to protect it. The court also said that Jostens' failure to identify the program as a trade secret had left the employee in an unfair situation, in which he had no way of deciding whether or not the information was a trade secret. The decision was upheld on appeal.

Protection from Non-Employee Use of Trade Secrets

A classic example of the limits on the "reasonable steps" doctrine was the case of E. I. DuPont de Nemours & Co., Inc., v. Christopher. The defendant, Christopher, had flown over a partially completed chemical plant under construction by DuPont for the purpose of photographing the secret equipment being installed. Although the defendant claimed it was up to DuPont to prevent disclosure, even from the air, the court said that while fences and ordinary roofs constituted reasonable protection, DuPont did not have to carry out its construction in an "impenetrable fortress" to protect its secret industrial processes. The court granted the injunction to prevent use of the defendant's photographs, even though the defendant was not an employee of and had no confidential relationship with DuPont.

In the context of the software business, software licenses assume a key role in the protection of software from non-employees. Since there is no pre-existing confidential relationship between the customer and the supplier of software, these licenses (special forms of software contracts) may be the only way to limit to whom and the manner in which the software technology is used. They create the special relationship that gives the owner the right to stop misuse of the trade secret. They are part of the important protective steps which the software author or publisher must take. The use of such licenses is dealt with in more detail in Chapter 11.

LIMITATIONS ON RESTRICTING
EMPLOYEE USE OF TRADE SECRETS

Obviously, if you do not treat the work done by your employees as commercially valuable, nor make efforts to protect that work as a trade secret, you will not be able to restrict that employee from later use of it. Furthermore, while an employer has the right to expect that work done by an employee belongs to the company (but not in the case of work done in the employee's spare time and with employee assets—an employee right upheld in states that include California, Minnesota, North Carolina, and Washington state) the courts are most reluctant to prevent an employee from using the normal skills and experience gained in a job in that employee's later jobs.

Moreover, the courts have consistently said that training gained in a job cannot be "wiped from the slate of the employee's mind," to quote a well-known trade-secret case. You can prevent a programmer from taking your source code and your manuals. However, you cannot prevent a programmer from using his or her skills later to devise similar programs, as long as this work is done from memory and over what would be a reasonable time for it to be performed independently.

THE RISK OF DISCLOSURE OF TRADE SECRETS IN MANUALS

A major hazard involved in relying on trade secrecy is that the material will be disclosed intentionally or carelessly by an employee, a customer, or in a publication. If the information enters general circulation, it is no longer protectable as a trade secret. In the software industry detailed user manuals for software are often distributed without restrictive licensing provisions or notices. In this case the protection may be lost if the manuals disclose too much of the logic or design of the product.

For example, Data General Corporation sued Digital Computer Controls for misappropriating the information contained in the Data General maintenance manuals distributed with each machine sold. From this material Digital Computer Controls had designed and was selling a minicomputer identical to that of Data General. While each set of the manuals contained a warning notice to the effect that the information in the form of drawings and specifications was the property of Data General, Digitial Computer Controls contended the requisite trade secrecy had been lost since almost 6,000 copies of the material had been sent out. In spite of this large number of copies of the information, the Court granted an injunction preventing Digital Computer Controls from using this information to compete with Data General, ruling that there had been only a limited dissemination of information which was reasonably necessary in order for users to maintain their computers.

Even closer to the point, disclosure of some of the logic of a computer program in user manuals has been held not to destroy the tradesecrecy protection for the program itself, especially where the owner released the manuals only under license and had registered the copyright for them as an unpublished work. The 1981 case of Warrington Associates v. Real-Time Engineering Systems involved a successful attempt by a former employer to forbid the use and sale of a competitive engineering program by former employees. The former employees had argued unsuccessfully that much of the logic of the program was known in the industry and that when the user manuals were issued to customers all trade secrecy elements were lost.

The court opinion points out that since the wrong voiced in most trade-secrecy cases involves a breach of trust or confidence arising out of employment or contract, the issue revolves not around the relative novelty or secrecy of the information, but around the "unique" commercial value of the information and the means by which the defendant obtained it.

These cases clearly illustrate the fact that a software house takes a serious risk anytime it discloses in its manuals what it considers to be trade secrets. For this reason it is vital that such materials carry some legend, throughout, that claims a proprietary interest in the information. Such a legend often reads, "The information contained herein is proprietary to ABC Software Company, and is provided to the user in connection with the use of the licensed software described herein. Reproduction of this manual in any form is prohibited." Where the manual is copyrighted, there are also some very complex issues about whether trade-secret law, copyright law, or both laws apply, a problem considered later in this chapter.

REVERSE ENGINEERING OF SOFTWARE FROM OBJECT CODE

Loss of trade secrecy by unintentional disclosure is a particularly troublesome issue in the case of so-called "reverse engineering" of software or hardware. It is well known in the industry that it is possible to acquire a copy of a program or a model of a computer device and to study it and its operation to the point that it is possible to construct a similar program or device. The new program or device then mimics or is a "look-a-like" of the original.

There is nothing in trade-secret law that prohibits "reverse engineering" as long as it is done fairly and with independent intellectual effort. Exceptions to this rule do exist, especially in the video-game field, when the code is protected under the copyright law. Two examples will demonstrate the possible alternative outcomes of reverse engineering under trade-secret principles.

Reverse Engineering—Example 1

Assume that you have just acquired a copy of the popular Digital Research operating system, CP/M®, signed the license agreement, read the warning not to open the package unless you agree to the license, and then broken the seal on the package. You then proceed to disassemble the object code into pseudo-assembly language in order to develop a competitive product. You should note that it is not uncommon for software license agreements, like these revised recently by IBM, to state flatly that disassembly of the code is prohibited. (See the Lifetree license form in Chapter 11.) This particular license does not, however, prohibit disassembly of the code.

Because your project is an important one to your company, you hire away from Digital Research one of its key programmers, who worked on the latest version of CP/M. This programmer had previously signed a nondisclosure agreement when he started at Digital Research. The two of you, using Digital Research manuals which state on every page that they contain proprietary information, proceed to complete your "look-a-like" program in two months.

Since the source code for CP/M® is not generally available except to manufacturers and others with a need for it, and then only under a stringent license, you have a serious problem—even aside from the copyright infringement that may have occurred. You and your programmer have intentionally misused a trade secret and are subject to an action for damages and an injunction being brought against you—an action that the owner of the information will undoubtedly win. These facts are very similar to those alleged by IBM in the Telex case, which IBM won.

Reverse Engineering—Example 2

Alternatively, let's assume that you obtain a copy of the equally popular word-processing program, WORDSTAR®, take it home, sign the license, use it for a while, and then decide that you can write and market a better program. You study the screen displays, cursor movement, screen messages, and all the external characteristics of the program as disclosed in the copyrighted user manual accompanying the package. You then set to work writing a better and faster program to accomplish substantially the same thing WORDSTAR does, with some better features and many similar ones. You even copy the well-known file structure and formats of the information in the files, since you want people to be able to use WORDSTAR files with your product. The project takes you six months, and you successfully start to sell the new program called "Super-Typer."

Unless you formerly worked for Micropro, publishers of WORDSTAR, or in some other way became subject to a nondisclosure agreement or confidential relationship, there is little Micropro could do about your product, even though you signed the license. You have reverse engineered, from publicly available information, a product competitive with WORDSTAR® by independent effort—hence the numerous word-processing packages today competing with WORDSTAR®.

The essential difference between Examples 1 and 2 is not that one is an operating system and the other applications software. In the first case there was a clear attempt to shorten development time by taking and using confidential information you and the programmer obtained under restrictions. In the second, you made use of publicly available information not obtained under any restrictions other than the use license.

A 1981 Illinois case, Colony Corporation of America v. Crown Glass Corporation, sums up the facts the courts will be looking for on the issue of reverse engineering of software. Since the logic and design of the program, which is what you really want to use, is not the product itself, you should have a good argument that what you did is lawful. As the court said:

Where a product is out on the market, and the secret is readily disclosed by the product itself, there is no trade secret. . . . If the secret is not easily ascertainable from the product itself, however, the sale of the products may be enjoined in order to protect the secret despite the fact that the products are not themselves trade secrets but are only the fruits of the use of the trade secret.

STEPS TO PROTECT YOUR BUSINESS UNDER TRADE-SECRET LAWS

Since it is up to you and your company to take steps to treat material as valuable and as a trade secret, the logical question is, "How, specifically, do you do that?" You must pay attention to three major areas of concern to meet your obligations as the owner of the information:

- You must provide reasonable security for the information.
- You must impose reasonable contractual limitations on your employees so they are aware of their obligations.
- When you disclose or distribute the information outside your organization, you must impose similar limitations on the users and possessors of the information.

The materials that follow provide specific actions you can take, and even some simple agreements as guidelines or checklists. These are not substitutes for adequate continuing legal advice from a competent attorney, but provide you with a starting point.

Physical Security for Information

Marking Information.   Insure that all source code, flow charts, detailed product specifications for unreleased products, and other like material is marked as "Company Confidential" or "Proprietary Information," and "Not for reproduction or removal from the premises without written permission." Put this or the more detailed notices described below on every few pages. Some companies, like IBM, overprint every page of secret manuals and listings with red cautionary legends. This concept of legends on critical information applies regardless of whether it is on paper or in magnetic form. Such notices should be put on diskettes or diskpacks as well. You may also want to assign numbers to each copy of really critical trade secrets and then log copies in and out to various people, just like the military does with secret items. Such a log is not only evidence that you did treat the material as a secret, but also useful in tracing possible leaks of proprietary information.

Locks and ID Badges.   Keep the above types of material, when not in use, in locked file cabinets in locked rooms. Do not permit removal of the material from the premises, and do not permit visitors to sit in or wander around the area where the material is being worked on. In larger companies, consider issuing ID badges to personnel. If you have ever visited an IBM installation, you know that you had to sign in, be escorted from place to place, and then sign out. This may not appeal to you in a small company, but there are less Draconian steps that have the same effect.

Computer Security.   See that computer systems that permit remote access do not have critical materials on the disk files. When the computer system is accessible only on the premises, use passwords and file locks to prevent unauthorized use or review of trade-secret materials. Some companies deliberately include harmless errors or programmer initials in programs, so they can be traced by the "fingerprint" this provides. Each file on the computer should also have a notice embedded at the beginning, in ASCII literal form, that it is a proprietary trade secret. Then, when it is printed out, the notice will also be on the printout.

Destruction of Materials.   Take steps to see that old listings of source code and other information that would disclose trade secrets are burned or shredded, and not just cut up for scratch paper.

Employee Training and Posters.   Consider conducting employee training seminars on the subject of trade secrets, as well as using posters or slogans on walls and bulletin boards reminding employees of the need to treat programming materials as confidential. Those of you old enough to remember World War II will remember posters with the legend "Loose Lips Sink Ships" in defense plants.

Break up the Project.   Finally, if the program is really valuable take a tip from the atomic bomb projects and break up work between programmers into modules. Don't let any one person except top people see the details about the whole program. This is rather drastic, but if the program has the potential for millions of dollars of revenue there is no point in taking risks.

Practical Steps to Take With Employees

There are all kinds of agreements that employees in information-critical businesses are asked to sign, but strangely enough the most obvious steps are often not taken:

Explain the Procedures.   First, when hiring programmers, secretaries, and even salespeople, explain to them at the outset how your business is based on valuable intellectual efforts that can be lost by careless disclosure to competitors, customers, or even the general public. Clearly identify the types of information you consider important to your business, and tell each employee what procedures he or she is expected to follow to protect trade secrets. A statement to the effect that everything the company does is confidential is not only counter-productive, it is dangerously untrue and dilutes efforts at protecting things that are really valuable. Show employees how source code and program design specifications are marked and how they are locked up when not in use. When an employee leaves, conduct an "Exit Interview" described below in conjunction with Form C.

Enforce the Procedures.   Once you have established security procedures, see that they are enforced, even to the point of disciplining employees who violate them. Consider bringing suit against former employees and their new employers, if you genuinely believe they are using your secret information. Review security procedures at least once a year in employee meetings, and see that some form of procedures manual describing the steps to be taken is available for the newer employees.

Employee Agreements.   Require that employees sign, *the first day they start work,* a simple confidentiality agreement, either as a separate document or as part of an employment agreement. It need not be any more complicated than the agreement set out as Form A at the end of this chapter. If the employee will likely be working on patentable inventions such as hardware, consider using Form B. Bear in mind that such agreements may not be enforceable unless signed at the outset, or when a raise or a stock option is given the employee.

Be very careful if you use Form B, since a growing number of states like California have restrictions on both employee non-competition agreements and the obligation of employees to assign inventions to their employer. The language in Form B is intended to take that into consideration. In states that permit more restrictive language, you may wish to include a restriction on competition with your company. This, however, is another area where advance legal advice may save you grief at a later date. Don't try to be overly restrictive, since agreements that are unfairly burdensome to your employees may be overturned by the courts. Such agreements can also build ill-will among employees, which sometimes goads them into starting competitive operations.

Exit Interviews.   When an employee leaves, either voluntarily or at your request, conduct an "Exit Interview" to determine whether he or she is taking away any materials used while working for the company, such as manuals, source or object-code listings, flow charts or unpublished product specifications. Have the employee turn in all keys to locked areas or cabinets, and promptly change combination locks to which the employee had access. Finally, ask the person to sign a statement (for both his and your protection) that he has returned such materials, and that the obligation of confidentiality is understood. A simple form for this purpose, like Form C at the end of the chapter, can be modified to suit your needs. You cannot force the signing of the form, but if the employee does not sign it you should immediately investigate the materials he or she had and should have returned on departure. If you know for certain that the employee has trade secret information, contact your lawyer at once and have him take steps to get it back. Failure to do so may be the most expensive action you never took, since timely legal action may be the only way to prevent disclosure that will destroy the trade secret status of the information.

You may feel a bit uncomfortable about asking your employees to do these things, which is natural when we would all like to think everyone is honest and good-hearted. However, if you take the time to explain that such steps apply to all professional employees and key clerical people, most employees can see that it is in their interest to conform, since their paycheck depends on the company's income.

Practical Steps to Take with Prospective Customers

The matter of protecting trade secrets from disclosure or use by customers and prospective customers is probably the most difficult of all steps, for you do not want to discourage sales or upset possible customers. Since you must disclose information to customers for them to buy or license it, you have to deal with the problem of nondisclosure agreements whether you want to or not. These suggestions present some simple forms and procedures; you should particularly note, here, the language intended for source-code protection. Some more complex licenses for use at the time of sale are presented in Chapter 11.

Product Discussion Agreements. Suppose, for instance, that you have set up a meeting with the XYZ Portable Computer Corporation to discuss your new, and as yet unreleased, electronic spreadsheet and data-base management program, which has unique features never before marketed. The XYZ computer has been rumored, but no pictures or details about it have been published in computer publications.

Do not disclose or discuss trade-secret information with your customer or prospective customer until a nondisclosure agreement is signed that protects your information. Such an agreement is set out at the end of the chapter as Form D. You will no doubt be asked to sign something that also protects XYZ information, so Form D contemplates that. Form D also deals with the fact that trade-secret information tends to become stale and no longer protectable, so provisions are made for this event.

Program Submission Agreements. Large companies like IBM are a special case, since it is a matter of policy for them not to sign anything that even looks like a trade-secret agreement. IBM contends that this protects their employees as well as the company from later claims that some new IBM project has become someone else's secret. There is some merit to their contentions, but it leaves you as a company wanting to do business with IBM in a very difficult position if you have not perfected your copyright or patent protection. The effect of the IBM form is to waive all trade-secret and confidentiality protection. You basically have two choices: sign IBM's rather shocking form either as is or with some slight modifications (if IBM really wants to deal with you), or don't deal with IBM at all. You and your lawyer will have to make that choice. Sometimes you can get around the situation by carefully giving IBM enough information for them to make a business decision, but not enough details to really compromise your information. In no case have I ever seen IBM accept materials for use or evaluation without deletion of all references to trade secrets. It's a tough problem to deal with. A form with language typical to that used by IBM is set out as Form E at the end of this chapter.

Form E demonstrates that when large companies take submissions or consider software from others they do so on their own terms, so you had best clearly understand what rights you and your company have before you deal with them. Large companies cannot afford to take the risk that another company will claim that its program was misappropriated or stolen by them, and they go to great lengths to avoid any such possibility.

There are two lessons in this. First, in dealing with a large company you need good legal advice. Second, if your company starts considering publication of software written by others, it too should have a similar but less one-sided form developed to protect your company from claims that you misused someone else's trade secrets.

Source Code Licenses.   When dealing with customers and prospective customers who are actually going to be given copies of your source code to a program, you had best utilize a much more detailed and stringent agreement form. Consult Chapter 11 for a discussion of language and concepts involved in a source-code license. IBM, for example, has become so concerned about the loss of trade secrecy of its programs, that its 1983 program licensing policy makes source code for operating systems and applications on the larger systems very difficult to obtain; virtually none of the applications software on the IBM PC is available in source-code form.

POSSIBLE LOSS OF TRADE SECRECY
BY PREEMPTION

The Conflict between Trade Secrets
and Patents or Copyrights

Before leaving the law of trade secrets, there is one other major concern of lawyers working in this field. This is the subject called "preemption", or the principle that one law may supercede or nullify another if the two come into conflict. This is a difficult legal issue that is still the subject of litigation in the courts, especially in the case of copyrighted software and user manuals.

Some but probably a minority of lawyers and courts believe that it is inconsistent to have patent and copyright laws protecting software or other intellectual property while at the same time permitting continuing protection of the information as a trade secret. The real issue here is whether these three bodies of law are mutually exclusive means by which software can be protected from misappropriation or unauthorized use by others. The answers may be different, depending on whether patent law or copyright law is in conflict with trade-secret law.

Patent Law v. Trade-Secret Law.   As a result of a number of recent cases, primarily a 1974 Supreme Court case, Kewanee Oil Co. v. Bicron Corporation, it is now believed that trade secrets, irrespective of their patentability, *may* be protected by state trade-secret laws since these laws are not inconsistent with the federal patent law. This makes a great deal of sense since there are many things that are not required to be disclosed in a patent application, which are nonetheless valuable commercial information that should still be protectable from unauthorized use by former employees or customers. If software is patentable (which is sometimes debatable, as we will see in Chapter 9), it should still be protected under state trade-secret laws.

Even if there is no preemption, if you do patent a particular computer program, you may be required in the course of the patent examination to disclose enough of the logic of the program that it will lose its trade-secrecy status—because the patent law requires disclosure, and trade secrecy is lost when the essential elements of a secret are disclosed. You should therefore consider carefully which method of protection is most likely to better protect your program. Most authors, on the basis of legal advice from competent attorneys, will elect the trade-secret route. However, where the information in the program would become available anyway, such as in an unlicensed machine that uses the program to run an industrial process, then the patent route may be the better alternative for your software.

Some lawyers today are still concerned that the issue has not been finally resolved, because two Supreme Court cases in 1964 (Sears, Roebuck & Company v. Stiffel Company, and Compco Corporation v. Day-Brite Lighting, Inc.) had held that the federal patent laws preempted (or superceded) state laws preventing copying of unpatented items like lamps. A theory of unfair competition or misappropriation was rejected in these cases on the basis that if an article was patented it was protected, but if it was not then there could be no such thing as an unfair copying under state law, because this would set up a potential conflict between the two laws. For a time after these cases, it was believed that this also meant the state laws regarding trade secrets were preempted, because some inventions or processes have been and still are protectable under *both* the patent laws and as trade secrets. I do not think there is or should be any preemption in this situation.

Copyright Law v. Trade Secret Law.   The real conflict may exist in the field of copyright law. Prior to the 1976 revision of the federal copyright laws, states could provide some protection for materials not otherwise copyrightable. Now, under the new copyright law (17 USC §302(a)), copyright automatically attaches to every original work from the moment of creation in tangible form. Furthermore, §301(a) of the new law specifically preempts "all legal and equitable rights that are equivalent to any of the exclusive rights within the general scope of copyright". This means that if trade secrecy is "the equivalent" of copyright, the two laws cannot protect the same thing. We presently have no authoritative cases under the new law, and thus no answer.

Let's see how this conflict between the two laws could arise. Suppose you treat the source code, logic, and detailed design of your program as a trade secret, access to which requires the signing of a license or non-disclosure agreement like those at the end of this chapter. You even insist that persons attending seminars on the use of the program sign agreements recognizing the trade-secret status of the material. However, behind the title page of the manuals describing the program and how to use it, you place as a precaution a standard copyright notice in the form "Copyright © 1984, ABC Software Company, All Rights Reserved," because you know that it is possible to lose trade-secret status for information if it is publicly disclosed. You fear that someone at the seminar will give your manual to others, who will copy it and develop similar programs. Now, which law applies, the new 1976 Copyright Law or state trade-secret laws?

Substantially this same situation occurred in two cases recently decided in the Midwest, one in a Wisconsin court and one in a federal court of appeals. Both cases held that the intent of the new copyright law was not to prevent reliance on trade secret laws and that state courts could still protect a trade secret even if a copyright notice was placed on some or all of the materials. In both of these cases, however, the copyrighted materials were prepared prior to January 1, 1978, the effective date of the new copyright law.

The Wisconsin case, M. Bryce & Associates v. Gladstone, involved a 1974 copyright notice on manuals and use in 1975 of the trade secrets. The Court concluded that there was no preemption intended in the 1976 copyright law, even if it were to apply to the acts in question.

Since these cases, there have been several federal trial courts rule the other way, as in the 1983 Nevada case of Videotronics, Inc. v. Bend Electronics. Here, use of a computer program in a video poker machine, which program was subject to copyright protection, resulted in state trade-secret law being held preempted. It is not possible to tell what the final law will be on this issue until a case reaches the U.S. Supreme Court.

Solving the Copyright–Trade Secret Dilemma.   These cases mean that in the software industry we may have an opportunity to protect trade secrets like source code by the confidentiality agreements discussed above; use of an additional escape hatch may help protect those same materials as "unpublished works" under the 1976 Copyright Law. Under this law, written materials not intended for general circulation, such as manuscripts, source code, design documents, and the like, are protected under the copyright law even when they are not registered with the Copyright Office. You may be able to claim the dual protection of trade secret and copyright law if you add the following notice to your source code, on the first and last pages, in both human readable and machine readable form. Then, should the trade secret protection in your unpublished work be lost through disclosure, copyright protection would take over. The dual notice would read as follows:

> *Notice:* This material is a confidential trade secret and proprietary information of ABC Software Company, which may not be reproduced, used, sold or transferred to any third party without the prior written consent of the Company. This material is also copyrighted as an unpublished work under Sections 104 and 408 of Title 17 of the United States Code. Unauthorized use, copying or other reproduction is prohibited by law.

Some lawyers recommend that the notice also contain a date, on the assumption that if the material is deemed to have been published the copyright notice will thereby be complete under the law. This may be dangerous since it has not yet been established whether use of a statutory notice with the date indicates publication, or only that publication may occur. There is a bill sponsored by ADAPSO pending in Congress in 1984, which would flatly state that, "Inclusion of a copyright notice with a date shall not be deemed to indicate publication of an unpublished work" for purposes of the copyright law.

Furthermore (as is explained in Chapter 5), the date is probably unnecessary in an unpublished work, since it can be added to all published copies. Under Sections 405 and 406, lack of a date in published copies is not fatal if the owner of the copyright makes a reasonable effort to correct this before too much time passes after first publication.

It should be clear, however, that you cannot "publish" source code, with or without a copyright notice, and still rely on obtaining trade-secret protection for your materials. "Publication" under the copyright law means to disseminate material generally without restrictions such as software licenses. If you have put a regular copyright notice on the source code, which you then distribute or publish, you have clearly elected to take your protection under the copyright laws. On the other hand, if you had no notice on the source code, you may, if you act quickly, correct that omission. However, if you do not act quickly enough you will have lost both copyright and trade-secret protection. Be sure you understand which laws you want to rely on, and treat your proprietary materials consistently. Discuss this matter with your lawyer if you are not clear what you want to do.

FORM A:
SIMPLE EMPLOYEE CONFIDENTIALITY AGREEMENT

I understand that I am being hired by *ABC Software Company* for the purpose of working on existing and future software projects of the Company, and that in the course of such employment I will be working with highly valuable, confidential trade secrets of the Company and other companies for whom and with whom the Company does programming work. I further understand that while most such trade secrets will be marked "Company Confidential" or some similar legend, the Company in general considers all unreleased software in source or object code form (including documentation, flow charts, logic diagrams, and product specifications) to be a trade secret, and that the source code of products released in object code form normally remains a trade secret. Furthermore, the Company's unannounced product plans, pricing, and similar marketing information is considered confidential, as is similar information which the Company receives in confidence from prospective customers about their products, equipment, or marketing plans.

In consideration of my employment and my continued employment by the Company, I agree not to disclose to anyone outside the Company, without the written permission of the General Manager of the Company, any aspect of such confidential trade secret information. This agreement will continue to restrict any disclosure by me of such information even after termination of my employment, until such information has been made public knowledge through no fault of mine. I further agree that any such trade secrets which I may work on or develop as part of my job as a programmer or manager are and shall continue to be the propery of the Company, as a "work for hire" under the Copyright Law.

Dated:_____ Employee:_____

FORM B:
MORE COMPLEX EMPLOYEE CONFIDENTIALITY
AGREEMENT

In consideration of my employment by *ABC Software Company,* and of the compensation paid to me from time to time while so employed, I agree to the following provisions of employment relating specifically to trade secrets, copyrights, patents, and other confidential information of the Company:

1. I acknowledge that during the course of my employment I will be exposed to secret and confidential business information of this Company and those of other companies with whom we do business on a confidential basis. While such information will normally be marked as such, I realize that all information about unreleased products, marketing plans, non-public financial information about the Company, and particularly the source code and related unpublished documentation of proprietary computer programs is a valuable trade secret of the Company, disclosure of which could severely damage the economic interests of the Company and my job. I therefore agree not to disclose any of such information to anyone outside the Company, nor to persons in the Company who have no reasonable need to know, without the written authority of management of the Company. This agreement not to disclose such information will continue to apply even after I am no longer working for the Company, until such time as the information becomes public knowledge through no fault of my own.

2. I further agree that all computer programs and documentation which I am asked to prepare or work on as part of my employment shall be considered "work for hire" under the terms of the Copyright Law of the United States, and shall belong exclusively to the Company.

3. Should I be asked to, or should I suggest that I work on development of inventions of any kind in the course of my employment, I will keep notes and other written records of such work, which records shall be kept on the premises of the Company and available to my supervisors at all times for the purpose of evaluation and use in obtaining patents or other protective procedures. Such records and notes shall belong exclusively to the Company. I will keep the Company informed from time to time about the progress of such work, and all improvements and inventions which I develop as part of my work.

4. I will upon request of the Company, both during and after my employment with the Company and at its expense, assist the Company in every way with applications for patents, trademarks, copyrights, or other forms of intellectual property protection for work on which I am involved during my employ-ment. I will sign all documents reasonably requested of me for the purpose of the Company establishing its right of ownership to such property, without any additional compensation to me.

[In those states that have similar laws, such as Minnesota, North Carolina, and Washington, include an appropriate sub-stitute for Paragraph 5. You may omit the paragraph in other states.]

5. I have been informed of the provisions of California Labor Code Section 2870, concerning inventions, which provides:

Any provision in an employment agreement which provides that an employee shall assign or offer to assign any of his or her rights in an invention to his or her employer shall not apply to an invention for which no equipment, supplies, facility, or trade secret information of the employer was used and which was developed entirely on the employee's own time, and (a) which does not relate (1) to the business of the employer or (2) to the employer's actual or demonstrably anticipated research or development, or (b) which does not result from any work performed by the employee for the employer. Any provision which purports to apply to such an invention is to that extent against the public policy of this state and is to that extent void and unenforceable.

Pursuant to Labor Code 2871, I agree to promptly disclose to the Company any inventions of mine which I believe are covered by the above Labor Code section, and I will offer the Company the right of first refusal as to the purchase or license of any patent resulting therefrom at its fair market value.

6. While I am not precluded from writing or working on com-puter programs similar to those worked on at the Company, once I leave its employment, I agree that while working here I will not do so for myself or third parties, in order to avoid possible disclosure of trade secrets of the Company. Once my employ-ment terminates, I am free to compete with the products of the Company but I agree that I will not use any of the confidential trade secrets of the Company or of third parties which I learned while employed here.

7. Upon termination of my employment with the Company, I will deliver to my supervisor or manager all books, equipment, computer programs, and documentation, notes, files, and other materials which I used or had access to during the term of my employment, which belong to or were loaned to the Company, and I will sign an acknowledgement that I have done so for the purpose of protecting both the Company and myself from claims

of theft or misuse of trade secret materials. Should such items turn up after my termination, I agree to return them promptly to the Company without retaining copies of any kind.

8. Finally, I represent to the Company, which relies on this representation, that I am free to enter into this Agreement in that I am not under any restrictions from a former employer or business which would preclude me from making these agreements. I understand that the Company does not want me to disclose to it any confidential information which I may have obtained from a former employer, although I am free to use my general knowledge and past experience in the performance of my job as a programmer or manager.

9. This Agreement shall be binding on my heirs, legal representatives and assigns, and shall inure to the benefit of any successors and assigns of the Company. This document supercedes any previous written or oral agreements relating to this subject which I may have made with the Company. It may not be changed orally.

10. This Agreement shall be governed by and construed under the law of the state of California. [Or your state.]

Dated:_____   Employee:_____

Accepted and acknowledged for the Company on the same date.

_____
Company Officer

FORM C:
Certificate On Termination As To Confidential Material

The undersigned Employee, recognizing his or her obligations with respect to protection of Company trade secrets and other confidential information, certifies under penalty of perjury that all notes, memoranda, reports, correspondence, files, manuals, equipment or hardware, documentation and flow charts, and software in both source and object code form belonging to or loaned to Company and used or possessed by Employee have been returned to the Company representative countersigning this Certificate. Employee agrees to return to the Company promptly any such materials which should subsequently turn up in Employee's possession, without further request from Employer. Employee acknowledges his or her continuing obligation to keep confidential all trade secrets of the Company and of others which came to Employee's attention or knowledge during employment, notwithstanding the fact that Employee is terminating his or her relationship with the Company on this date.

Date:_____ Employee:_____

Countersigned for the Company:_____

FORM D:
PRODUCT NON–DISCLOSURE AGREEMENT

ABC Software Company and *XYZ Portable Computer Corporation* desire to discuss the possibility of implementing ABC's new program, *DATA-SPREAD,* on the as yet unreleased XYZ Model 68000 computer to be manufactured by XYZ. Both parties are concerned about the protection of proprietary trade secrets of each which will necessarily occur in the process of discussion of this subject.

Either party may disclose such information to the other as is deemed necessary to carry out the purpose of this Agreement, and where the information is identified as confidential or as a trade secret, including but not limited to design specifications for products, source code, and future marketing plans, such information shall remain the property of the original owner and shall not be disclosed by the other except as permitted herein.

Where such material is in written form, the information shall bear a *Confidential* or *Company Proprietary* legend on its face, and copies given to a party shall be accounted and signed for upon request. Upon request of a party, a list of the general subject matter discussed orally will also be reduced to writing and attached to this form, as evidence of the nature of material discussed.

All confidential and trade secret information covered by this Agreement shall be protected, by the party receiving the same, in the same manner which it protects it own most proprietary trade secret information. When use of the confidential information is no longer necessary, the owner may request its return or destruction, and the possessor shall comply promptly with such request and so advise the other party.

The obligations imposed by this Agreement shall be continuing, and bind all employees and agents and legal successors in interest of each party, until such time as either (1) the information becomes public through no fault or act of a non-owner party; or (2) the information is furnished by the owner to others without restriction on disclosure; or (3) the information is hereafter furnished to a party by a third party as a matter of right and without restriction on disclosure.

Dated:_____   *ABC Software Company*   *XYZ PC Corporation*

_____   _____

FORM E:
SUBMISSION EVALUATION AGREEMENT

ABC Software Company and *Big Blue* are interested in discussing ABC's new program *DATA-SPREAD* which ABC has designed to run on the Big Blue Personal Computer. Big Blue has not solicited this discussion, and is willing to discuss the subject only if certain legal steps are agreed to in advance. It is therefore agreed:

1. Big Blue is in the business of developing and marketing software, so that it will evaluate other software only if:

a. the evaluation will not create any confidential or fiduciary relationship between the companies.

b. Big Blue has no obligation to treat the ABC software as confidential or secret.

c. no restrictive legends covering the software, except patent and copyright notices, will be effective against Big Blue.

d. Big Blue may market products or services that compete directly with ABC software.

e. Big Blue may use, publish, and market software similar to ABC's which it develops independently or obtains from others.

f. you agree to the foregoing provisions.

2. ABC warrants and represents that to the best of its knowledge and ability the ABC software in question does not infringe any copyright, patent, trade secret, or other intellectual property right, and it is not in the public domain. In addition, ABC represents that it is the sole owner of the software and that it has the full and exclusive rights to such software (including the right to disclose and license it to Big Blue), and that the officer signing this Agreement has the authority to do so on behalf of ABC.

3. Big Blue will evaluate the ABC software and tell ABC whether or not it is interested in licensing or using it, but will not give you its reasons for its decision. Although employees of Big Blue may discuss your software, nothing which they say will in any way change this Agreement, unless the change is made in writing and signed by an authorized Big Blue employee or officer.

4. Should any disagreement arise, the liability of Big Blue will be determined by the national copyright laws as to copyrights or the national patent laws as to patents. In all events the liability of Big Blue will be limited to $100,000.

5. ABC grants Big Blue the right to use, display, reproduce, and provide copies of the software to its employees and agents, for evaluation purposes only. We will put your copyright on any copies we make, if the original material had a copyright notice.

6. By signing this Agreement ABC agrees to the foregoing provisions, and further agrees that ABC and its employees will keep confidential any and all information which it receives from Big Blue in the process of the discussion, to the extent that such information is not already public or generally available without restrictions on disclosure.

Dated:_____   *ABC Software Company   Big Blue Computers*

_____   _____

CONCLUSION

Trade-secret laws, which vary from state to state, can form the basis for significant protection of computer software and related documentation, if the steps discussed in this chapter are followed *carefully* and *in detail* by you, your lawyer, and your company.

Once trade-secret status is lost for a particular item of software, there is little that can be done to recover or restore it. You must see that all reasonable precautions are consistently followed, and that everyone involved understands why these rules exist. Nondisclosure agreements with employees and prospective customers, licenses with customers, and exit interviews are all part of a shelter of protection that you must build.

To protect yourself and your company from the effects of loss of trade secrecy, you and your attorney should consider the possibility of obtaining patent protection, where available. (See Chapter 9 on Patents for software.) You should also consider the use of the unpublished work notice under the copyright laws. You may find, in the case of mass-distributed software, that the only really successful method of protection is a combination of trade secrecy for the source code and copyright for the object code. Adequate license agreements may also add to the protective web surrounding your valuable intellectual property.

All the votes are not in on the legal problems of protecting software, and only time, litigation, and congressional action will finally resolve these problems. While the preemption issues appear to be resolving themselves, case by case, you should keep in close touch with your lawyer to see what, if any, changes have occurred since this book was written. Finally, remember that there are other possible defenses to trade-secret protection which have not been considered by the courts yet, since the law is in a continuing process of development.

5

The Basics of Copyright Law

WHAT IS A COPYRIGHT?

My handy desk dictionary says a copyright is "the exclusive legal right to reproduce, publish, and sell the matter and form of a literary, musical or artistic work"—an excellent starting point for us on this subject.

Copyright protection in the United States is based exclusively on federal law, as set forth in Title 17 of the United States Code. While computer software is mentioned only twice in this law, it is now clear from court decisions that both source code and object code are protected from unauthorized copying and distribution. Computer programs fall into the "literary work" classification, as does other material you would not think of as "literary."

THE COPYRIGHT CHAPTERS IN THIS BOOK

This chapter and the three following chapters examine how copyright law applies to software and how you can take advantage of the provisions of this law in your software business. Specifically, this chapter covers the fundamentals of copyright law, while Chapter 6 provides information on how to file an application for copyright registration of a computer program and a software user's manual. Since there are considerable differences between video games and the more usual computer programs, Chapter 7 discusses the problems of protecting video games. Chapter 8 examines some of the unresolved problems caused by or involving software. Chapter 11 covers licensing software and Chapter 18 covers the specialized subject of copyright infringement (likely to be of most interest to lawyers). For international aspects of copyright law, consult Chapter 15.

Chapters 5 and 6 are the two that you should read thoroughly, because you will then be able to properly insert copyright notices and file copyrighted computer programs and manuals for copyright registration. You will be able to handle most of the routine copyright matters involving a software business. However, you should also read Chapter 8 very carefully for the unique problems created by the "High Tech" nature of software.

COPYRIGHT LAW
AND THE SOFTWARE INDUSTRY

The primary function of copyright law is to prevent unauthorized copying and to control distribution of copyrighted materials. Since most microcomputer software is mass-distributed on diskette or in cartridges, and since software on either of these media is easily copied, copyright law is the most effective means of protecting such material.

You will recall from the preceding two chapters that trade secret protection works only for information that can be kept secret, or at least for those items that are distributed under controlled circumstances. Obviously, when several hundred thousand diskettes of a popular computer program are marketed in hundreds of stores throughout the country, it becomes difficult to rely on trade-secret law as the primary basis for protecting the object-code version of such a program. (We will also see, in Chapter 9, that patent protection for software is, for a number of reasons, both generally unavailable and unsatisfactory.

While there are still unanswered questions about the exact nature of copyright protection for software, the software industry currently has no alternative but to rely on this area of the law. Copyright protection is inexpensive, easy to understand, and applies almost automatically to everything in written form. The law protects the program code, in source and object form, as well as the manuals and user documentation. Legal action against copiers (infringers) can be fairly swift and is relatively cost-effective.

THE HISTORICAL AND LEGAL BASIS
OF COPYRIGHT LAWS

Our current American Copyright Revision Act of 1976 became effective on January 1, 1978. It stems from a series of earlier laws enacted over the years since our national independence. All of these laws are based on the constitutional authorization to Congress found in Article I, Section 8, Clause 8, to secure "for a limited time to authors and inventors the exclusive right to their respective writings and discoveries."

Federal Law Replaces Common Law Copyright

As a result of the enactment of the current 1976 Copyright Act, the rights of an author of a computer program, along with the rights of authors of books and music, are based solely on federal, as opposed to state law. Until 1978 there existed a so-called "common law copyright," which relied upon some aspects of state law, but the new law effectively abolished that concept for all except the most unusual types of authorship (those items not fixed in any medium, like unwritten and unrecorded speeches). Because of the drastic changes brought into play by the new law, our discussion will be limited to computer programs and user manuals authored since January 1, 1978. (There are references in the Bibliography that discuss the provisions of the earlier law.)

While the immediate effect of copyright law is to protect the economic interest of the author in his work, the Founding Fathers had some higher purposes behind the law. As the Supreme Court said in Mazer v. Stein in 1954, the economic philosophy behind copyright and patent law "is the conviction that encouragement of individual effort by personal gain is the best way to advance public welfare through the talents of authors and inventors."

The theory was, and is, that if authors are encouraged to publish, they will add to society's fund of knowledge by disseminating useful information. This public policy explains why copyrights are protected so assiduously by the court system, and why infringements are punished with a regularity unusual in the law. It also explains why there are exceptions to what the law will protect, as we will see here and in Chapter 8.

THE FIVE EXCLUSIVE RIGHTS OF A COPYRIGHT OWNER

The rights of a copyright owner are presently spelled out in Section 106 of the Copyright Act (which section will be referred to throughout this book). This section says (subject to certain exceptions that will be touched on later) that the owner of a copyright has the exclusive right to do, and to authorize others to do, the following:

- To reproduce the copyrighted material in the form of copies in any media or format.
- To prepare derivative works based upon the copyrighted material.
- To distribute copies of the copyrighted work to the public by sale, or other transfer of ownership, or by rental, lease or lending.
- To perform the copyrighted work publicly in the case of works, unlike computer programs, where this would be useful.
- To display the copyrighted work publicly, in the case of literary and other types of works where this is appropriate.

It is illegal for anyone else to do any of these things with a copyrighted work, and if he or she does so he or she becomes a copyright infringer who may be fined, enjoined, or otherwise prohibited from violating the rights of the copyright owner. In the case of software protection, the first three rights of the owner are primarily the ones relied upon.

Exceptions. There are some exceptions to these rights, which are covered by Sections 107 through 118 of the Copyright Act, but for our purposes only Section 107 concerning "fair use" of copyrighted works and Section 117 concerning rights of the "owner of a copy of a computer program" have much relevance to software.

Fair use means that reproduction or use of reasonably limited quotations from copyrighted materials in book reviews, educational settings, and the like, is normally permissible without authorization or payment of royalties. (This concept is discussed further in Chapter 18 as a defense against copyright infringement. The scope and effect of Section 117 is referred to in Chapter 8.)

COPYRIGHT APPLIES TO ITEMS FIXED IN TANGIBLE FORM

Copyright does not apply only to books and periodicals. Section 102(a) of the 1976 Copyright Act explicitly says that copyright protection is for

> ... original works of authorship fixed in any tangible medium of expression, now known or later developed, from which they can be perceived, reproduced, or otherwise communicated, either directly or with the aid of a machine or device....

Original Works

Congress chose deliberately not to define the term "original works of authorship" in order not to preclude protection for future forms of authorship, as the House Committee Report points out:

> Authors are continually finding new ways of expressing themselves, but it is impossible to foresee the forms that these new expressive methods will take. The bill does not intend either to freeze the scope of copyrightable subject matter at the present stage of communications technology or to allow unlimited expansion into areas completely outside the present Congressional intent.

This was a very wise decision, particularly so when we consider the possible effect of new technology in Chapter 19.

Copies of Original Works

The law makes a conscious distinction between the "original work of authorship" and copies of it, which copies are merely the material objects in which the work is embodied. Since people in the computer industry are used to the concept of information as "data," it may help to consider these material objects as simply "data carriers," which transport or hold the data or work.

In other words, it is not the computer program source listing on paper that is protected, but the words shown on the paper. When the program is later embedded in computer memory chips or recorded on the magnetic diskette in object code, it is not the memory chip or the diskette that is covered by the law, but the original information or data recorded, as organized by the author with the help of his computer. The physical form in which the copyrighted data is currently embodied or "fixed" is, and should be, irrelevant.

COMPUTER SOFTWARE IS PROTECTED AS A LITERARY WORK

The Copyright Office has been accepting computer software for registration since late 1964, but there is no provision in the 1976 Act specifically stating that software is covered. In 1980 Congress added a definition of "computer programs" in Section 101, and made specific reference to the effect of copyright law on computer programs in Section 117. There is no question today, however, that computer programs in source code form *are* protected by the law. And subject to the open issues covered in Chapter 8, software in object code form *is* one of the forms of authorship intended to be included under the 1976 Act.

Separate Classes

Primarily as a matter of administrative convenience, the law divides copyrightable works into a series of seven categories of works. There is either a separate form for registration or some different registration rules that recognize the distinctive nature of each category. These classes also reflect new types of works created through the historical growth of the law. Since there is no separate class for computer programs, they were placed in the category of "literary works." Although video games are normally generated by a computer program, they are also protectable (with motion pictures) as "audiovisual works." (See Chapter 7.)

The term "literary work" is confusing, but it encompasses nearly all forms of written authorship except plays, music, and dance productions. Computer programs, in both source and object code form, and the manuals and other documentation that accompany software are considered to be "literary works," regardless of their lack of literary merit or character.

Copies in Physical Media

Copies of computer programs may be stored in the form of magnetically recorded disks, read-only memory chips (ROMs), or any other form, and they are still defined as literary works protected by the copyright laws. They do not have to be on paper, or even "human-readable." This issue has been, and will probably continue to be, the subject of considerable litigation for a few more years, because of the unique nature of software and a history of earlier cases to the contrary. Most lawyers, however, believe the current definitions in the law are clear as to congressional intent.

COPYRIGHT ATTACHES UPON CREATION, NOT REGISTRATION, OF THE WORK

Initial Creation

By definition in the law, a work is created when it is fixed in a copy for the first time. A program does not have to be registered to be protected, although there are major limitations on the scope of protection granted if the program is not registered promptly. The moment you have written a program on paper, it is copyrighted, and as soon as the original words I am writing now on a computer are recorded on the disk they are copyrighted. The fact that the paper or the magnetic image may later be destroyed, or that the original is never registered, does not preclude its being covered by the copyright law from the moment of its creation. (The effect of failing to register a computer program with the Copyright Office is discussed in Chapters 6 and 18.) This chapter assumes that the copyright owner has followed through with the registration process and that the work still exists.

Originality does not mean inventiveness, only lack of copying. It is not necessary that what you do be particularly creative, for in fact, you can write a program which almost entirely duplicates the ideas or processes of someone else's work, as long as you do it on your own. Many people (and courts) find it hard to see how this works and why it should be this way.

Progressive Creation

Where a work is created over a period of time, as in the case of a computer program, the part of the work existing in fixed form on a particular date is considered to be the created work as of that date. The work just grows from day to day, as it is created. Only when you elect to treat a program as a separate work, by designating versions or releases of a program, do you actually have different works. These different versions are considered "derivatives," a copyright term discussed below.

Fixation

A work is "fixed" in a copy when its embodiment in the copy "is sufficiently permanent or stable to permit it to be perceived, reproduced, or otherwise communicated for a period of more than transitory duration." It is fixed if it can be seen or heard in some repeatable form. The work doesn't have to be *readable* by a human being, only *perceivable* or *communicable*—a very important distinction in computer software and videogames cases tried in the courts during the past several years.

NO COPYRIGHT PROTECTION FOR IDEAS, PROCESSES, OR SYSTEMS

It is often said in copyright cases that copyright protection extends only to the form of expression, and not to the ideas, concepts, principles, systems, procedures, methods of operation, or discoveries involved. This limitation of copyright law is a critical principle, being the reason that other forms of intellectual property protection, like patents, trade secrets, and trademarks exist. This principle was also the core of the unsuccessful defense of the Franklin Computer Corporation in the Apple v. Franklin computer software case, discussed in detail in Chapter 8.

What this rule means, for example, is that if you develop a computer program to calculate the batting averages of your favorite National Baseball League players from each day's statistics, you can prevent someone else from copying or distributing your program, but you cannot prevent that person from independently writing a separate program to calculate the averages and then marketing it.

Limitations on Copyright Protection

Obviously, the fact that you cannot protect the raw ideas or procedures expressed in your software is one major limitation on the value of copyright protection. Without this limitation, once someone wrote a computer program to do double-entry bookkeeping and obtained a copyright on the idea of double-entry bookkeeping, that person could thereafter prevent anyone else from ever doing so—even to the point of preventing people from making up bookkeeping forms. This would be so untenable that it would cause the breakdown of all commerce.

The inability to protect raw ideas is also the reason that most software is distributed to the mass market only in object code form, it being harder for imitators to see how the program was written in the first instance. This limitation also explains why trade secrecy is a collateral form of legal protection, which software authors have to use to complete the web they create around their software.

If someone has to disassemble your object code in order to see what you did in the program, the effort involved in doing so will usually be more

costly than licensing a legal copy. Disassembly is a form of copyright infringement, but very difficult to prove. Thus, your efforts as an author or
publisher of software should be directed toward making it as difficult as
possible for imitators and potential pirates to see or have access to source
code in any form.

WHO IS THE AUTHOR ENTITLED TO PROTECTION?

Only the Author Can Claim the Copyright

Since it is the act of authoring that gives rise to the right, copyright protection attaches to a work of authorship from the time of its creation. For this
reason, only the author of a work is entitled to claim the protection.
However, the question of who the author is can be complex. The statute
tries to answer these questions at the outset.

If you are the sole author of a computer program, it is clear that the
copyright belongs to you unless you assign or sell it to someone else.
Similarly, when several people author a program, they are considered "co-
authors" unless they have agreed otherwise. Co-authors have equal rights
to their work, but this can create considerable problems if they have not
agreed in advance as to their respective claims on the work.

Generally speaking, all programming work done by an employee, as
part of his job, is considered to be authored by his employer, and the
employer is the owner of the copyright. This situation can be varied by a
written agreement between employee and employer. However, it is a bit
more complex than it appears.

"Works for Hire"—A Special Problem

When you are dealing with a computer program potentially worth millions
of dollars, it is of paramount importance to know who actually is the
copyright owner, for only the owner has the right to license its use and
distribution. For example, a consultant, who is not an employee of the
company that pays him to write a program, may in fact be the owner of the
program, and not the company itself.

Problems often arise when management and outside consulting programmers do not pay sufficient heed to Section 101. That section defines
a "work for hire" as a work prepared by an employee within the scope of
his employment, *or* a work specially ordered or commissioned for use as a
contribution to a collective work—as part of a motion picture or other
audiovisual work, as a translation, as a supplementary work, as a compilation, as an instructional text, as a test, as answer material for a test, or as
an atlas—*if the parties expressly agree in a writing signed by them that the
work shall be considered a work for hire.*

Consulting Agreements. Unless the work your company contracts to have prepared falls into one of the cases listed in the statute, it is not a work for hire. If it is not a work for hire, the consultant, and not the company, is the author and perhaps the owner of the program, notwithstanding anything that may have been said in an agreement. If you are fortunate, your company may be able to obtain ownership of the program by litigation, or you may have at least an exclusive license—but you also clearly have a problem.

In point of fact, many consultants and companies develop software without any contract in writing. However, in the event of a dispute over ownership, royalties, and other rights, a court may reach a decision completely contrary to the original intent of the parties. Since the purpose of legal agreements, whether prepared by laymen or lawyers, is to prevent later disputes and disagreements, it is important that mutual understanding be reached by both parties in the agreement under which the work is done.

How Not to Handle the Situation. A 1983 case involving the Select™ word-processing program is a classic example of failure to consider the effect of the law. Worst of all, one of the principal parties was a lawyer who should have known better. In Jerome Freedman v. Select Information Systems, the programmer sued Select and its president, Dean, to prevent the use and sublicensing of the Select program on the basis that it had been prepared before the corporation was set up and merely orally licensed to the company. Freedman claimed that he owned the program. Select contended that the work had been done "for hire" while Freedman was an employee-owner of the company. It also contended that it had an oral license that was still valid. While the case was eventually settled out of court (so we will never know the final outcome), Freedman was successful in obtaining a preliminary injunction against the company and Dean.

The Lesson: Never, never, rely on oral licenses or agreements concerning ownership of software. Resolve the issue of ownership in writing when you are starting the project, not after you start marketing the program.

Resolving the Consultant Issue. There is a simple solution: have the consulting agreement expressly provide that the program is intended to be a "work for hire" within the terms of the 1976 Copyright Act. But also specify that should there ever be any question as to program ownership, the consultant is obligated to execute an assignment of ownership to the company, upon request and without further cost. Some companies take the opposite approach and promptly register the program or other work in a manner clearly indicating that the author is the consultant, but that ownership has been assigned to the copyright claimant. This is specifically provided for in the box numbered 4 on the form TX—Application for Copyright Registration—at the end of Chapter 6. (For more information, review Chapter 6.)

Another approach, which I follow, is to have a formal copyright assignment prepared and signed by the consultant at the time the work is delivered, rather than to have to request a signature later from a consultant perhaps unwilling to cooperate. It is also wise to have the assignment acknowledged by a notary, since this is prima facie evidence of the execution of the transfer. Even if you have not registered the work in the name of your company, you should record the written assignment with the Copyright Office to give notice to third parties of your company's claim to ownership.

Don't Try to Be Overly Clever.   The foregoing steps are not necessary if the author is an employee of the software company in the true legal sense. It will not work, however, to call the consultant an employee in the agreement, if he is not treated as one. The legal tests for employment usually turn on whether or not the employer dictates the hours, place of work, work procedures, and the like. If the consultant is paid a fixed sum upon delivery of the program, the only control being specification of the contents of the program and the delivery date, then that person is not an employee.

You should also be aware that in some states, such as California, authors who are independent consultants are, nonetheless, required to be covered under your Disability Income, Unemployment and Worker's Compensation Insurance. So it may be better to make the consultant a real employee both for copyright and business reasons.

FOREIGN AUTHORS AND COPYRIGHT PROTECTION

Where computer programs are written outside the U.S. or by foreign nationals, consideration should be given to the provisions of Section 104 of the Copyright Act. It is easier than you may think to encounter this situation, because many translations of user manuals and program messages are done by foreign authors outside the United States. The situation is fraught with many unexpected dangers.

Copyright protection is available for all *unpublished works,* regardless of the nationality or domicile of the author. However, in order to complete the forms you still have to know who the author is.

Published works are eligible for copyright protection in the United States only if any one of the following conditions is met:

• On the date of publication, one or more of the authors is a national or domiciliary, or sovereign authority of a foreign nation that is a party to a treaty to which the United States is also a party, or is a stateless person wherever that person may be domiciled; *or*

- The work is first published in the United States or in a foreign country that, on the date of first publication, is a party to the Universal Copyright Convention; or the work comes within the scope of a presidential proclamation.

Effectively, this means that nearly any software, created by anyone in a nation with which the U.S. has normal commercial relations, will be covered by the copyright law. However, you should remember that other countries may not have the same "works for hire" rules as the U.S., and it will not always be clear who the author and copyright owner is. Your contract with the foreign national should make this clear from the outset, and you should include a choice of law paragraph stating that U.S. law applies.

You or your attorney can get help from the Copyright Office, for it maintains a list of copyright treaties and presidential proclamations. However, getting copies of the foreign copyright laws is much harder. (Chapter 15 of this book discusses international copyright problems in more detail.)

PUBLISHED VERSUS UNPUBLISHED WORKS

"Publication" of a work, the key to statutory protection under the 1909 Copyright Law, is no longer a critical concept. Current law requires neither publication nor registration with the Copyright Office, since protection attaches automatically upon creation. The 1976 Act defines publication as the distribution of copies of a work to the public by sale or other transfer of ownership, or by rental, lease, or lending. If you distribute a computer program through the use of signed licenses from each recipient, this is probably not deemed to be publication. However, it is not yet clear whether industry-standard "break open" package licenses constitute publication.

Nonetheless, there are distinctions between published and unpublished works in current law, and publication is still important because it has several consequences. Because of the potential conflict between copyright and trade-secret law, you may wish to take the position that your source code is a trade secret; in which case, when you file for registration you should claim a copyright for an unpublished work. If you do so, it is not yet clear under the law whether the mass-distributed object code is considered to be a separate published work or version; the 1982 GCA Corporation v. Chance case seems to indicate not. If you have carefully restricted distribution of your source code (as discussed in Chapter 4), you should be able to argue successfully that the source is still a trade secret but also rely on copyright protection for the object code.

The Effect of Publication

While neither unpublished nor published works have to be registered, if your work is considered to have been published you need to consider carefully the effect of publication. Once a work is published, all copies must bear the statutory copyright notice (discussed in more detail below). With some exceptions for microfiche and magnetically recorded works, you must deposit copies of published works bearing notices on them with the Copyright Office within three months of publication in the United States. In the case of works for hire, a seventy-five-year term of copyright begins from the date of publication, rather than the one-hundred-year term from creation applicable to unpublished works. Furthermore, the requirements for registration of published and unpublished works differ substantially.

The registration form (discussed in Chapter 6) specifically asks for the date of first publication. Be sure you understand the difference between published and unpublished works and that you have the facts straight when filling out your copyright application forms, since a wrong answer can create problems later.

DURATION OF COPYRIGHT PROTECTION

The term of copyright protection for software is of little significance due to the shorter useful life of software compared to books or other forms of copyrighted works. To date, most microcomputer software has had a commercial life of only five to ten years, before obsolescence sets in. There is some mainframe software that is approaching fifteen to twenty years of useful life; such longevity may become more critical as the industry matures. (Most of these provisions are in 17 USC § 302.)

Individual Authors. All copyrightable works created after January 1, 1978 are automatically protected from the moment of creation for the period of the author's life plus fifty years after death. Where there are co-authors, the term lasts for fifty years after the last surviving author.

Works for Hire. Works for hire, including those created by employees, have copyright protection of seventy-five years from publication or one hundred years from creation, whichever is the shorter.

Pre-1978 Works. Works created prior to January 1, 1978 that were neither registered nor published have been automatically brought under the new law and given protection. The term for these works is generally computed the same way, but will in all events have a term of not less than twenty-five years from the effective date of the new law, January 1, 1978. These works have special rules for renewal and extension, which should be reviewed carefully if you own a copyright on a work falling into this category.

DERIVATIVES AND COMPILATIONS UNDER COPYRIGHT LAW

A "derivative work," as defined in the 1976 Copyright Act, is a work based upon one or more preexisting works, such as a translation, abridgment, condensation, "or any other form in which a work may be recast, transformed, or adapted. A work consisting of editorial revisions, annotations, elaborations, or other modifications which, as a whole, represent an original work of authorship, is a 'derivative work'." This is a very important concept in copyright law as it relates to the software industry.

Modifying Public Domain Works

It is possible for a person to do enough work on a computer program presently *in the public domain* to entitle that person to register the new work with the Copyright Office. Since the original program has passed into the public domain, anyone has the right to create and register a derivative of it. The new author must simply add significant value or make material changes to the program in the form of original thought and effort. The author of the derivative work is entitled to derive royalties or economic benefit from his or her modification or supplementation of the public domain work.

In such cases, Section 103 of the Copyright Act provides that protection does not extend to any part of a derivative program in which preexisting material has been used unlawfully. For example, a programmer could not acquire rights in a derivative prepared from another person's copyrighted program by disassembly or by unauthorized access to the source code. Furthermore, the law limits the copyright in the derivative to the material contributed by the new author, and does not imply any exclusive right in the preexisting material. The copyright in the derivative work has no effect on the ownership of the earlier copyrighted work, nor its scope or duration, since the two are independent.

Program Improvements

Often an earlier copyrighted program is improved upon by someone else, such as a consulting programmer under contract to the copyright owner. The consultant may have the right to register the improved program as his derivative work, in the absence of proper contractual provisions limiting that right. Hence, any contract by which you or your company hire a consultant to work on an existing program should provide that the copyright to any derivative belongs to you and may not be registered by the consultant.

If the improved work is done by an employee within the scope of his employment, then the employer is deemed to be the author. Be sure that you use a properly drawn employment contract in this situation. Indeed, the original software development contract should always anticipate this issue, by specifying who will own any derivatives created at a later date.

Translations and Revisions

Occasionally, the question arises as to whether translation of a computer program from one computer language to another is a derivative work, or whether paraphrasing a program is prohibited as a derivative. From the language of the statute defining the term "derivative works," it would seem clear that both situations fall within this term. (Some of these issues are discussed further in Chapter 8.)

A 1983 District Court case in Idaho, Hubco Data Products Corporation v. Management Assistance Inc., indicates the extent of potential problems with software derivatives. MAI manufactures and sells the Basic Four minicomputer in several different versions, each faster and more expensive. Hubco allegedly discovered, by disassembling or comparing parts of the Basic Four operating system, that the lower cost systems could be made to perform at the higher speeds if part of the operating system code were changed. Hubco created a program which modified the object code in such way as to speed it up. MAI sued Hubco, claiming that any such code was a derivative of its copyrighted operating systems, which only it had the exclusive right to write and distribute. While the parties settled the case out of court during an appeal, it appears that MAI's argument was correct.

Manuals and Documentation

Any revision or major modification of computer user manuals and other written materials, which customarily accompany or supplement computer software, is deemed a derivative if the revision adds, revises, or significantly supplements the earlier version. Such revision should be registered with the Copyright Office, in the manner indicated in the next chapter. If you have merely corrected errors in printing or spelling, or inserted material accidentally omitted from the manual, this is not normally considered a registrable derivative.

New Program Releases

If a new program release differs enough as to carry a new number (such as going from Version 1.4 to Version 1.5), then it is a registrable derivative and should be registered as a precaution. Where there is a completely new version, such as Version 2.2 becoming Version 3.0, then it clearly should be considered a new and derivative work.

There is no universal test for what is *enough* to require registration as a derivative. But as in the case of manuals, if the only change is to correct a few errors and not to make any significant additions to the program, it probably should not be considered a derivative. Remember, however, the only thing which is protected by registering a derivative is the new, revised, or added material. (See Chapter 6 for specifying changes made in any derivative on the copyright registration forms.)

Compilations

You should be aware of the copyright terms "compilation" and "collective works". Most of the same rules that govern derivatives cover these terms. A compilation is any work formed by the collection and assembly of preexisting materials, or of data that are selected, coordinated, or arranged in such a way that the resulting work as a whole constitutes an original work of authorship. Databases are a classic compilation. A collective work, which is like a compilation, is work (like periodicals or encyclopedias) that contains the contributions of a number of separate and independent works assembled into a whole.

More than likely most computer programs will not fall into such categories, because they will be the products of employees of a software company, and thus works for hire. However, if a group of independent consultants collaborated to develop one larger program, that program would be considered a compilation or collective work. In such a case, Section 103 provides that the author of a part of the total work is entitled to claim the copyright only for his or her part, and not for the total work. It is imperative that conflicting claims in a collaborative work be avoided in advance by carefully worded contract provisions.

COPYRIGHT NOTICES AND SOFTWARE

Most people are vaguely aware of the copyright notices on books and other written materials, and of their legal effect. Prior to the 1976 Copyright Act, lack of a copyright notice on a published work caused the loss of the statutory copyright, which placed the work in the public domain. That is no longer the case, *if* the lack of notice is unintentional and *if* it is corrected promptly. (See the Innovative Concepts In Entertainment, Inc. case, discussed in Chapter 7.) Otherwise, prolonged failure to place a copyright notice on a work still causes loss of the copyright and entry into the public domain.

Copyright notices are covered in the Copyright Act by Sections 401 through 406 which, together with the detailed regulations of the Copyright Office, provide some very specific rules for placement of the notice, which you must follow carefully.

Notice Requirements

The purpose of a copyright notice is to provide a notice that someone claims a copyright on a particular work, to identify the copyright owner, and to give the publication date. The standard three-element notice, "Copyright 1984, XYZ Software Company" is familiar to most people. Its inclusion in all works published in the United States or elsewhere, by authority of the copyright owner, is required if the owner wishes to obtain protection of the work in this country. The law says the notice "shall be placed on all publicly distributed copies from which the work can be visually perceived, either directly or with the aid of a machine or device." This means that you must have a notice either on or in your software, regardless of the media on or in which it is distributed.

Permissible Forms of Copyright Notices

The form of the notice must consist of all three of the following elements:

- The symbol © (that is, the letter "C" in a circle), or the word "Copyright," or the abbreviation "Copr."
- The year of first publication of the work, and, in the case of derivatives or compilations the year date of the first publication of the derivative or compilation.
- The name of the copyright owner, or an abbreviation by which the name can be recognized, or a generally known alternative designation of the owner.

While there is a more detailed discussion in Chapter 15 of the use of the symbol © under the Universal Copyright Convention, that treaty is essentially the reason for most notices in copyrighted material to bear the © symbol. Under the UCC treaty, which governs most civilized nations, the use of the symbol will assure protection under the copyright laws of nearly every country if the type of material so marked is protectable in that particular country. (As is discussed in Chapter 15, copyright protection for software has not yet been established in all major foreign countries.)

For a similar reason, you will often see the notice with the added words, "All Rights Reserved." The Buenos Aires Copyright Convention, covering most South American countries, requires this language for protection in those countries. A fully protective notice will, therefore, often read:

Copyright © 1984, XYZ Computer Corporation.
All Rights Reserved.

Placement of the Different Elements.   There appears to be no legal reason the three elements have to be in this order, but usually you will see the word "Copyright" before rather than after the © symbol. The UCC requires only the symbol ©, the copyright proprietor's name, and the year. As long as you have the space on the labels of your software, in the program, and on the proper pages of manuals and other printed materials, it is a good idea to use this full form. Shorten the notice to "Copr." rather than omit the © or "All Rights Reserved." If you have only a tiny space, as in the case of notices on computer memory chips, select the symbol © and omit the other references to copyright.

Years. The rules on the inclusion of years are simple and should be followed carefully, since omission of the year can invalidate the notice. Where the material is changed year after year, do not bother to list every year, as this looks odd and takes extra space. Since the new editions are compilations or derivatives, use of the original year and only the most recent year of change will do, i.e. "1981, 1984."

Abbreviated Names. If your name is "International Business Machines," it is easy to rely on the name-abbreviation rules and use "IBM." It is not quite as simple if your company is not well known and the name is long, like "New York City Software and Computer Corporation," in which case the best you can probably do is to say "NYC Software" and hope that meets the law. Generally, you should use your full company name if you have the space. In the case of individuals, use whatever form of your name is commonly used, for it is important that people can identify you, the author/owner of the copyright, in case they want to look the copyright registration up in the Copyright Office or contact you to obtain a license to use the software.

Placing the Copyright Notice Properly

Where do you put the copyright notice on software distributed in magnetic or memory chip (ROM) form? The general Copyright Office rule for all notices is that they be placed in such a manner and location as to give reasonable notice of the copyright claim; such locations are, however, not to be considered the only ones you can use.

Where to Put the Notice. Acceptable methods of affixing the notice in machine-readable copies, or other copies from which the work cannot ordinarily be visually perceived without use of a machine, include any of the following methods:

1. A notice embodied in the machine-readable copies so that it appears with or near the title, or at the end of the work when the material is printed or listed on a printer.
2. A notice displayed at the user's terminal at sign-on time.
3. A notice displayed continuously on the terminal screen.
4. A legible notice reproduced durably, so as to withstand normal use, on a gummed or other label securely affixed to the copies, or to a box, reel, cartridge, cassette, or other container used as a permanent receptacle for the copies.

Combination Notices. It is best to use a combination of all these methods on all software to ensure there is no way that your copyright claim could not be seen by a user. If notices are only on labels and the software is copied onto another diskette, then there is no assurance there will be a label with the copyright notice on the second copy. If, however, the notice is in the software so that it prints out when the object code is dumped or listed, and if it is briefly displayed on the screen at sign-on time, it would be very difficult for a software pirate to argue that he did not see the notice on the second or subsequent copy. Typical notices in the software and on the actual label, together with notices of the licensed nature of the software, are set out as Examples A and B.

EXAMPLE A: TYPICAL COPYRIGHT NOTICE IN ACTUAL SOFTWARE

The following wording (or, in the event of space problems, *at least the first line*) must be inserted in each separate computer program, so that it will display on the screen for three to five seconds at sign-on time for view by the user. Many users object to this, so you may wish to use the wording only for the main module that first comes up:

(C) COPYRIGHT 1984 AMERICAN SOFTWARE, INC.

This software is licensed and not sold. All use of this software is subject to the terms and conditions of the ASI software license, which should be read carefully. Copyright infringement is a serious civil and criminal offense.

In addition, if you wish to treat the source code as a trade secret (as discussed above and in Chapter 4), you should have a short notice on all source listings in the form set out in the text toward the end of Chapter 4, concerning the unpublished nature of the work. In addition to the trade secret form, *always use the standard copyright notice shown above for object code,* so that you are protected if it is determined that the work has been published.

EXAMPLE B: TYPICAL SOFTWARE–LABEL COPYRIGHT NOTICE

This notice would normally be found printed on a stick-on diskette label, in the right or left upper-corner of end-user diskettes.

NOTICE OF COPYRIGHT LICENSE RESTRICTIONS

The software on this diskette is copyrighted and licensed for use only in accordance with the terms of the U.S. Software Corporation End-User Agreement. Title to the software remains with USSC at all times. It is serialized and may only be used by the registered user. It may not be transferred to anyone without the permission of the copyright owner. Disassembly of the code is prohibited. Unauthorized reproduction, transfer, or use of this material may be a civil and criminal offense under Federal Copyright Law.

Program Copyright © 1984 USSC, Monterey, California

I routinely recommend a combination of notices so that the notice appears on the diskette label, on the packaging (if possible), in the software in such manner that it displays on the screen at sign-on, and in the object code in what are called ASCII-literal characters. (ASCII-literal characters are those that print out exactly as set forth in the source code before assembly or compilation). It is very likely that a pirate would fail to change the notice embedded in ASCII-literals, even if he changes the messages on the screen and on the software labels. I have seen several cases in which exactly this happened.

Encoded Notices. Some programmers go even further and encode the screen copyright message so that it cannot be taken out of the object code, or modified in any way, without causing problems with the software. This entails use of a complex check-digit algorithm, which works on the numeric values of the characters in the message. It is a sound legal and technical approach with much to recommend it, since the copyright notice embedded in the code is often extremely effective evidence of software piracy.

Notices on Memory Chips. Read-Only-Memory (ROM) chips present another issue, relating to size and method of affixing the notice. Given the above rules, it is best to affix the notice, using white paint or silk-screening, on the top of the chip. As this is susceptible to obliteration, it is worth considering encoding the copyright notice in the special object code (sometimes called "ROMable code"), which is actually in the chip and can be read out by various electronic means. Using labels on ROM or other chips is not a good idea, since the heat can cause the glue to weaken and the label to come off.

Because chips are usually sold and not licensed like software on diskette, there are some other problems under the First Sale Doctrine, a copyright doctrine discussed in Chapter 11 that you should review if you are working with programs in ROM.

One of the earliest cases involving computer software copyrights, Data Cash Systems, Inc. v. JS&A Group, Inc., denied copyright protection to software in a ROM, on the basis that there was no copyright notice in or on the chip. Since this arose under the 1909 Copyright Law, lack of the notice was fatal to the infringement action and determinative of the case. This result is unlikely under current law, but is possible if no effort were made to mark the chips.

User Manuals. Location of the notice on computer software manuals or books may be almost anywhere on the title page, the page following the title page, on either side of the front or back cover, or on the first or last pages of the main body of the work.

As with this book, the notice will traditionally be found on the page following the title page, which is what I recommend. There are some further provisions concerning the nature of the software and the restrictions on it, which I prefer to have included on the copyright page. A typical page with this added language would look like Example C.

EXAMPLE C: TYPICAL COPYRIGHT AND RELATED NOTICES FOR USE ON COMPUTER SOFTWARE MANUALS

The following language is typical of the wording suggested for use on the back of the title page of the software manual:

COPYRIGHT NOTICE

Copyright © 1984 All American Software, Inc. All Rights Reserved. No part of this publication may be reproduced, transmitted, stored in a retrieval system, nor translated into any human or computer language, in any form or by any means, electronic, mechanical, magnetic, optical, chemical, manual or otherwise, without the prior written permission of the copyright owner, All American Software, Inc., Post Office Box 123, Monterey, California 93942. Copyright infringement is a serious matter under the United States and foreign Copyright Laws.

This manual is, however, tutorial in nature. Thus, permission is granted to the reader to include the example programs, either in whole or in part, in his or her own programs.

The copyrighted software that accompanies this

> manual is licensed to the End User for use only in strict accordance with the End User License Agreement, which License should be read carefully before commencing use of the software.
>
> This notice is often accompanied by others concerning warranties and trademarks of the products involved. The back of the title page is a good place for such information. Copyright notices should be the first things on the page in order to ensure their prominence.

If you have problems not covered by this discussion, the Copyright Office puts out a four-page circular, R96, on methods of affixing Copyright Notices, which is available free upon request. The address and phone number of the Copyright Office is listed in Chapter 6.

Notices on Source Code, As Unpublished Works. There is still considerable controversy in the courts and in the legal profession over whether copyrights and trade secrets are incompatible forms of intellectual-property protection. As Chapter 4 explains, I happen to believe strongly that the law and the few decided cases seem to consider the two perfectly consistent.

For this reason, it seems logical that the source-code version of software be kept secret and treated as an unpublished but copyrighted trade secret. In this way, you can seek double protection, and if one method fails the other should still apply. If you want to proceed in this way, the source-code listings should carry a special form of copyright notice indicating that they are not to be deemed published, but that should they become so you can claim copyright protection. To do this, you can use a notice form such as:

Unpublished Copyright © 1984, ABC Software Co.

or

Unpublished Work © 1984, LMN Computers, Inc.

It is not necessary to have a copyright notice on an unpublished work, except that it may be deemed to have been published by the fact you registered it or because it is mass-distributed in object-code form even though you consider it a trade secret. (See Chapter 4 as to the wisdom of including or excluding the year in the notice.) But you should be safe if you add the above form of notice to unpublished works and to all copies of source code—unless you want to take the postion that the source code has been published, in which case you must use the regular form of notice. Be sure, however, that you understand the consequences of whichever approach you take.

Correcting Defective Copyright Notices

While a defective or non-existent copyright notice on published software or user manuals caused the loss of all rights under the old 1909 law, this rule no longer applies. There are, however, steps you must promptly take on discovery of the error. Section 405 of the Act generally provides, that there is no harm if registration has been made before, or is made within five years after the publication without notice. However, a reasonable good faith effort must be made, promptly after the omission is discovered, to add the notice to all copies that are distributed to the public in the U.S. A recent case, however, holds that you must show the omission was unintentional and not purposeful in the first instance or even the current law will not save you.

Nor will you lose your copyright on software or manuals where the omission was only on a "relatively small number of copies." This exception will depend on the facts of your case, but much will probably depend on how many copies in total were published as against the number distributed without the notice. The time interval will, no doubt, also be an issue. For example, if you send out fifty copies without a notice in the first month or two, and then during the remaining ten or eleven months discover and correct the notice omission on the next one thousand copies licensed, you would doubtless retain your copyright under the "small omission" rule.

If you have failed to use a proper copyright notice, you should contact an experienced copyright or software attorney at once, since he or she may be able to correct the situation. Do not delay in such a case, though, for time may be critical.

Errors in Dates or Names in the Notice

The most common error in notices seems to be omission of the year date entirely, or use of a wrong year. A wrong year that is too early merely starts the term of the copyright earlier. But if your notice shows a year *later* than the correct year, you are deemed not to have included a year at all and Section 405 applies. Complete omission of the date is treated as though there was no copyright notice at all, and Section 405 specifies the corrections, if any, that are allowed in this case.

Complete omission of the copyright owner's name is considered so defective that the copyright notice is deemed not to have been given at all, and Section 405 again applies. More often, however, the wrong name is listed in the notice. Here Section 406 provides that if the name used is not that of the copyright owner (although the publication was authorized by the owner), the validity and ownership of the copyright is not affected. This typically occurs when software is licensed to a manufacturer (OEM) by a software house, and the manufacturer wishes to publish under its own name without referring to the real owner of the copyright. While this is, in effect, permitted by this section of the law, it is not a good idea. If a copyright is not registered in the correct name, an innocent third party has a defense against infringement if the third party was relying on a license from the named copyright owner.

If you have a business reason for permitting someone else to be listed as the owner in the copyright notice, you can protect yourself by either registering the work in your name at the same time any copies are distributed by the person named in the notice, or by recording a document with the Copyright Office showing that you are the true owner of the copyright but that you permitted the use of another's name in the notice. In all events, the person named in the notice must pay over any receipts for licenses that he grants without your authority.

Where my clients have agreed to this practice, I include a specific clause in the license to the OEM allowing his name to be listed in the copyright notice, but confirm in the agreement that the OEM gains thereby no ownership interest in the copyright. The license to the OEM should also state that the OEM has no authority to grant licenses beyond those authorized in the license to him. I then see that the copyright is promptly registered.

Use of (C) Instead of © in Notices

There is a problem unique to the users of computer printers and computer terminals which the Universal Copyright Convention and the Copyright Act did not contemplate. The Universal Copyright Convention requires the use of the © symbol in order to obtain coverage under that treaty. The 1976 Copyright Act permits the use of the same symbol, instead of the word "Copyright" or "Copr."

There are some lawyers who contend that if materials are printed or displayed on computer-terminal screens with the symbol (C) instead of the ©, then this is not in compliance with the law and the notice is therefore defective. While this strict construction of the law seems contrary to the intent of the 1976 Copyright Act, it may be more relevant to the requisites of the UCC. Only time and litigation will tell. There is pending in 1984 a bill, H.R. 6983, which among other things would permit use in the U.S. of the symbol (C) as an alternative to the © symbol.

Special Character Sets. The mechanical problem is that most computer printers and computer terminal screens do not have a character set that includes the standard form of the © symbol, so that it is literally impossible to comply strictly with the law. There are some daisy-wheel character printer wheels, like Diablo's Courier Legal 10A and special IBM character balls for typewriters, which do have the standard symbol, but the recently marketed Digital Equipment Rainbow™ Personal Computer is the only present computer terminal that can display the © symbol on the screen. There are now programs available that permit the user of a dot-matrix printer to create unique characters, and a few of the newest video terminals appear to have this same ability. You should use these special characters if they are available, since the issue could be decided adversely to a copyright owner.

Other Alternatives. Except for the problem under the Universal Copyright Convention, it would seem that there are several alternatives available to U.S. copyright owners. Use the "Copr." or "Copyright" form of notice if you don't have the proper symbol on your printer or available to display on the screen of a CRT terminal; or use some of the "Rub-On" artist transfer sheets that include the © symbol on the masters of any material to be printed.

Finally, in the case of screen notices, you would have a very strong case, unlikely to be overturned, if you used both the (C) symbol and the word "Copyright." While this does not strictly comply with the UCC treaty, under the circumstances it is surely the best notice you could adopt. Be certain there are proper copyright notices on the exterior of all diskettes containing software; since the screen notice should be only one of several displayed to the user.

Possible Legislative Solutions. H.R. 6983, the bill supported by ADAPSO, would make the (C) symbol the functional equivalent of the standard © symbol. Its fate is unknown at this time, but this would still not settle the issue under the UCC. The Copyright Office has also recently concluded, in the absence of legislation, that it has no authority to allow any substitution of the alternative form (C) for the © symbol; this position seems correct, both under U.S. laws and the various copyright treaties. However, a follow-on to the Videotronics case, cited in Chapter 4, held in 1984 that a C surrounded by a hexagon on a videoscreen is sufficient compliance with notice provisions of the law.

SUMMARY

The principles of copyright law can almost be reduced to a series of general rules:

- Nearly everything written, drawn, recorded, or in any way fixed so that it can be reproduced, is protected by the 1976 Copyright Act.
- Software is protected by copyright law in all forms, although there is still some residual argument about machine-readable forms of it. Computer manuals are books and are protected as such.

- Ideas, systems, and procedures are not protected by the copyright law, only the fixed expression of them.

- Copyright law gives the owner of the copyright a series of exclusive rights, which he or she may, in turn, license to others. In the absence of that license, people who exercise those rights are infringers.

- Employment contracts, consulting agreements, and software licenses need to be clear about who owns the program and derivatives of it.

- While publication is no longer a key element of copyright protection, registration is now more important than ever. Publication does have effects that have to be considered carefully.

- Notice of the copyright claim must be given in one of three forms, and must include all the elements, or the copyright may be lost if the work is considered published. There are still some unresolved problems about notice forms used on computers and in programs.

6

Copyright Registration and Deposits

PERFECTING YOUR RIGHTS BY REGISTRATION

Once you have placed the copyright notices in your software, you have accomplished only the first half of the job. Now you need to consider registering the copyright with the Copyright Office in the Library of Congress, in order to assure preservation of all the benefits of the law for your company. From reading Chapter 5 you have a background in the principles of copyright law, so it will be easier in this chapter to see the purposes, benefits, and procedures involved in registering your software and manuals.

Copyright registration is a legal formality, almost unique to the United States, intended to create a public record of information concerning each claim to a copyright. The entire process is covered by only six sections of the Copyright Act (Sections 407 through 412), but this whole chapter is needed to present it in detail as it relates to software. Since registration is not a legal requirement for copyright protection in most other countries, you may also want to review Chapter 15 on the international aspects of such protection.

Scope of this Chapter

When you have completed this chapter, you should be able to prepare, or assist in preparing, the requisite formal Application for Copyright Registration, which must be filed with the Copyright Office. The costs involved are nominal, but very valuable to your business. You will also have a clearer idea of some of the technicalities and special procedures, which can make this process one in which it is necessary to have competent legal advice available.

THE BENEFITS OF REGISTERING COPYRIGHT CLAIMS

Unlike the 1909 law, the current law does not *require* registration of a published work, except in two cases not particularly relevant to our purposes: any work published with a notice of copyright *before* January 1, 1978 must be registered and renewed during its original twenty-eight year term, if you wish to maintain protection for it; and in the case of a defective copyright notice, you may have to register the work in order to correct for the errors and preserve the copyright.

Reasons for Registering

The primary reasons to register each one of your computer programs are as follows:

- If you register your work within *three* months of publication or prior to an infringement of the work, you will be entitled to recover statutory damages and attorney's fees in any court action. Otherwise, you can recover only your actual damages and the profits of the infringer.

- Registration is normally required before you are permitted to file a copyright-infringement action in court.

- Registration, either before or within five years of publication, will establish prima facie evidence in court of the validity of the copyright and of the facts stated in the certificate of registration issued by the Copyright Office.

- Where there have been conflicting notices or claims to a copyright, lack of registration may preclude any recovery by you as the copyright owner if you did not register before an innocent third party relied on erroneous notices.

As a result of these provisions, it is clearly beneficial to routinely register any software which is being actively distributed to the public. On the other hand, registration is of less value where the software is used only in-house and a case of copyright infringement seems less likely. Furthermore, since in-house software is normally a trade secret, protected by employee confidentiality agreements, failure to register should minimize any question of the conflicts between trade secret and copyright law.

HOW COPYRIGHT DEPOSITS RELATE TO REGISTRATION

To assist in developing and maintaining the huge collection of books and other publications in the Library of Congress, Section 407 of the law requires that the owner of the copyright, or the holder of the exclusive right of publication, deposit with the Copyright Office two complete copies of the best edition of a published work. If the work carries a copyright notice, this must be done within three months of publication in the United States. Failure to make such deposits can result in fines and other penalties. Copyright deposits, however, are not necessarily the same as copyright registration.

Dual Purpose Filings

Fortunately, the deposit and registration schemes of the law overlap, and you may comply with the Library of Congress deposit rules by properly filing a copyright registration application with the required copies of the work. To qualify for this dual purpose filing, you must file the application form and the fee for registration with two copies of the work, at the same time and in the same package; if you don't send an application form and the correct fee, for example, your application, under Section 408, will either be rejected, or the copies sent will be given to the Library of Congress and you will later have to file more deposit copies with the proper application form and fees. Therefore, comply with the *deposit* rules by filing a copyright registration; and file the application form, the fee, and the required two deposit copies all in one package.

Exemptions from Deposit

The Copyright Office has the power to exempt entirely certain types of works (like valuable art work and sculpture) from deposit requirements, and to modify the deposit requirement where it deems appropriate. The latter has been done in the case of machine-readable works, like software. Usually a modified rule permits filing only one copy or allows deposit of so-called "identifying materials," which are portions or representations of the actual work. Videotapes, for example, are actually filed in single copies with other identifying material, while computer programs distributed on magnetic media must not be filed in this form but in the form of partial printer listings of the program, or on microform.

No Deposit of Unpublished Works

There is no requirement that you file *unpublished* works either with the Library of Congress or the Copyright Office. Therefore, most software companies do not feel it necessary or advisable to file software that is not being widely distributed, especially where the owner is primarily relying on trade-secret protection. Unfortunately, no one has yet resolved the issue of how much distribution to the public constitutes "publication" under the Copyright Act, even if distribution is under a license agreement.

How to Decide

The decision whether or not to register can be a difficult one. Because even trade secrets may inadvertently become "published" in the copyright sense, you should very quickly register your software, once it is published, to gain the benefits of registered works in case an infringement action is necessary. Many attorneys advise that valuable but unpublished software be filed for registration, as an unpublished work, which is permissible. Since an unpublished work that is registered does not have to be reregistered upon publication, there is never any question of timely registration. However, I would still not register software that is used strictly in-house as an unpublished work, there being no reason to expose it to the world unnecessarily.

TIMING AND EFFECTIVE DATES OF REGISTRATION

As noted above, if you do not register your published software or manuals within five years of publication, you lose the presumption of prima facie validity. If you do not register these within three months after publication or prior to an infringement of the work, you may lose the right to statutory damages and attorney fees. Despite these rules, the vast majority of software is probably not registered, even though copyright is claimed through use of the copyright notice.

You may register unpublished software or documentation at any time, yet registration isn't *necessary* unless you want to bring suit for infringement. Considering the very low cost of registration, it is foolish not to register software that is marketed in significant numbers, such as more than 100 copies.

Effective Date of Registration

Registration is effective on the date of receipt by the Copyright Office of all the required elements in acceptable form, regardless of the length of time it takes the Copyright Office to review and act upon your application form. This rule is quite significant, since the length of time taken by the Copyright Office may vary considerably. If the material submitted is in proper order, you should expect to receive a Certificate of Registration back within three to four months.

No Acknowledgement of Filing

You will not receive any acknowledgement of a filing, unless you send your packages via registered or certified mail and a return receipt is requested. Where the copyright examiner has questions or needs further information, you may receive a telephone call or a letter requesting clarification. Otherwise, you will receive either the Certificate of Registration, or a letter advising you of the Copyright Office's refusal to register your filing together with the reasons for that decision.

WHO IS ENTITLED TO FILE AN APPLICATION FOR REGISTRATION?

The author of computer software documentation will ordinarily sign the application and file it. In case of material prepared under the work-for-hire doctrine, the employer or other person for whom the work was done will sign and file it. In the latter case, the name of the person who actually wrote the program will not appear on the form—only the employer's name, whether an individual or a corporation. A corporate officer will normally sign for a corporation.

The Copyright Claimant

The law permits several other classes of persons to file the registration application, in lieu of the author. First, "a copyright claimant" may file. A copyright claimant is either the author of the work or someone who has obtained ownership of the copyright from the author by virtue of a contract or assignment of ownership. This could be a publisher, filing by virtue of a contract that gives the publisher the right to claim the copyright, or it could be an assignee of the right, who bought the copyright prior to or after first publication. An example of this is covered in the sample forms toward the end of this chapter.

The Owner of Exclusive Rights

The owner of "exclusive rights" to a copyright may also file. Under the present law the rights of the author may be split up such that one person may own the exclusive right to publish the software in the United States, while someone else may own rights for the rest of the world. A licensee with one of these rights may file for registration in the United States without the need for the other licensee or owner joining in the same application. This division of rights is not unusual in the case of software, which is often distributed worldwide, as in the case of the book and movie-script businesses, where screen rights are often separated from stage-play rights and book rights.

Agents of the Author

The most common person to file a copyright registration (other than the author) is an agent—who may be an attorney, literary agent, or anyone else acting with the authority of the author, copyright claimant, or owner of exclusive rights. An agent does not have to prove his or her authority in order to sign and file the application. Of course, if the agent does not have any authority to do so, this could affect the validity of the registration.

There is no legal requirement that applications be prepared or filed by lawyers. Even though preparation of an application form is fairly easy, it may be wise to obtain the help of an attorney the first few times, or in complex cases. You should also understand that not all lawyers are familiar with copyright law, and fewer still are knowledgeable in the area of computer software. (See Chapter 20 about selecting a lawyer for your software business.)

REGISTRATION PROCEDURES

Before looking at specific examples of typical Registration Application Forms, let's discuss the mechanical details of registering your software and manuals. There are basically three elements involved in a registration:

1. The properly completed application form.
2. A non-refundable filing fee of $10 for each application.
3. The required deposit for the particular class of work being registered.

All three components have to be sent to the Copyright Office in the *same* package, or the package will be rejected.

Use the Proper Form. The proper form of application for both software and the related manuals is Form TX, Application For Copyright Registration for a Non-dramatic Literary Work. Video games are covered by different provisions in the law, discussed in Chapter 7. You must use the official Copyright Office form, which is on archival bond paper, or the application and filing will be rejected. Because everything is microfilmed, you must complete the forms with either black pen or with a typewriter with dark ink. Pencil or excessively light original applications will be rejected.

Manuals and Software. The Copyright Office instructions allow user manuals and related written materials to accompany software filings under the same registration application. To do so, you must send two copies of the manual with the special identifying program materials. While this can save a separate filing fee, it is not common practice, since the manuals are often published at a different time and revised less frequently than the software releases or versions. If you do so, you may later be faced with separate filings, which is confusing to everyone.

Obtaining the Forms. The application forms for registration and all the other Copyright Office materials mentioned in this book may be obtained by using the Forms Hotline maintained by the Copyright Office. You may call, 24 hours a day, (202) 287-9100, if you know the name or number of the forms or information you want. This is a tape recorded message system, from which the Copyright Office fills orders for forms, quite promptly. The Copyright Office has a number of informational sheets or brochures on various subjects, which they will send free, if you know what to ask for.

Other Information. If you do not have the needed information, you can call, (202) 287–8700 during business hours of 8:30 through 5:00, Eastern Time and talk to one of the Public Information Officers in the Copyright Office. The Copyright Office personnel are among the most helpful people in Federal government. However, they cannot, and will not, provide legal advice on copyight matters.

Where to Send the Application. Packages containing the complete registration, and letters requesting information or forms, should be sent to:

Register of Copyrights
Copyright Office
Library of Congress
Washington, D.C. 20559

No street address or box number is necessary.

DEPOSIT REQUIREMENTS FOR REGISTRATION

Books and Manuals

Except for the actual computer software, which has different deposit requirements, books, user manuals, and similar written materials are subject to the following deposit requirements under the Copyright Office regulations:

- If the work is unpublished, one complete copy must be deposited together with the copyright registration application and fee.

- If the work was first published in the United States on or after January 1, 1978, two complete copies of the best edition of the work must be filed.

- If the work was first published in the United States before January 1, 1978, two complete copies of the work as first published must be filed.

- If the work was first published outside the United States, one complete copy of the work as first published should be filed, regardless of the date of publication.

- If the work is a contribution to a collective work (such as series of programs by different authors, published together), and published after January 1, 1978, then one complete copy of the best edition should be filed.

Computer Programs

Most computer programs are distributed only in machine-readable, magnetic form, rather than on paper like books. Because of this the Copyright Office has established separate rules for deposits of machine-readable works. These deposit rules apply to all computer programs, whether they are unpublished literary works fixed in machine-readable form or published works distributed only in machine-readable form. Machine-readable copies are defined as those copies distributed on magnetic, chemical, paper or plastic, or optical media such as diskettes, tapes, punched cards, bar codes, or laser disks, which cannot ordinarily be perceived except with the aid of a machine or other device. In other words, they cannot normally be read directly by a human being.

Identifying Materials. In order to provide the Copyright Office examiners with something that they can actually see to examine, 37 C.F.R. § 202.20(c) of the Copyright Office rules provides for the deposit to be in the form of "identifying portions of the program." These are required either to be printouts of the first twenty-five and last twenty-five pages of the source program, or the same data in microform, together with the page (or equivalent unit) containing the copyright notice (if any). The Copyright Office will not accept computer programs in ROM, on diskette, tape, punched cards, or any other form that the examiner cannot visually perceive without a machine (except microforms, which obviously need an optical reader).

REGISTRATION—SOME UNRESOLVED SOFTWARE ISSUES

Object Code and the Rule of Doubt

The Copyright Office does not want you to use object code for deposits because its examiners cannot read such materials to determine if they are copyrightable. Software companies would rather not file source code as a deposit because it discloses the actual code and compromises the argument that source code is a trade secret. This presents software companies with some difficult decisions.

First, object code will not be accepted as identifying material, unless you insist that the Copyright Office file your deposit in object code form, under what it calls the "Rule of Doubt." If you do so, your application will be specially noted, which could create legal problems later. The Rule of Doubt is a practice of the Copyright Office of accepting, with the reservation that the filing is accepted "for whatever value it has," deposits and registrations for items or in forms it would rather not accept. The law is not clear what effect, if any, a filing under the Rule of Doubt has. Therefore, if you are unwilling to file source code as your deposit, you should read Chapter 8 carefully for some alternatives and presently pending changes in the rules.

Be Careful What You File

A second practical issue is that the rules do not define what a "page" of a program is, nor what constitutes the first and the last pages of a program. In absence of these definitions, nearly any twenty-five consecutive printer pages of program code should do for the required "first" twenty-five pages, and nearly any additional twenty-five consecutive pages should suffice for the "last twenty-five pages." The starting point in a long program can probably be determined, but where the program goes from there will depend entirely upon which routines and subprograms are called by the demands of the user.

Since most programs contain a number of subprograms, it is not at all clear what is required to be filed as a deposit. Because of this, and the practical reason of not wishing to disclose data structures and program logic any more than necessary, it is important to chose carefully what you file. The Copyright Office seems to recognize this and will generally accept anything that discloses authorship of any substantial amount of code.

Short Programs

If your program is less than fifty pages long, file whatever is available. In this case, however, file the object code only, subject to the Rule of Doubt; but you must accompany your filing by a letter explaining that filing the whole program would unnecessarily disclose the entire program and that you specifically elect to file only the object code.

The Copyright Office will normally file any complete program even if the program is just a few pages long, but it might reject a program of less than two or three pages, on the basis that the work lacks originality. Their position overlooks the fact that while a one-page program in BASIC could be almost trivial, one full page of a program in APL could be the functional equivalent of ten or fifteen pages of BASIC code. Most examiners are not programmers and many cannot read or interpret programs, although they can usually tell what computer language is used.

FILING SOURCE CODE—THE CONCERN ABOUT DISCLOSURE

The concern about having to file source code copies of your program is based on the fact that this discloses all of the actual code and logic to anyone who requests the right to examine your copyright deposit. Any member of the public, including your competitor, has the right to do this at the Copyright Office. Admittedly, it is not particularly easy to gain access to deposits, since the Copyright Office normally requires several days to a week's notice to obtain a deposit for examination, and deposits are often not available for examination until all work on registration and indexing is complete.

Furthermore, the Copyright Office requires that you look at the deposit in a study carrel, near some of their clerical staff, and that you sign a statement agreeing not to copy the material you examine. But an experienced programmer could learn a great deal about the logic of the program from the source deposit, just by reading it, or someone could photograph it with a pocket camera. If this should happen, you would have difficulty maintaining your argument that the source code is a trade secret.

Another serious concern some lawyers have is the fact that it is not the source code version of the program which is actually being distributed to the world. The software you are distributing is only in object code, which is what you expect the copyright law to protect. It seems likely someone will eventually make this argument to a court in a copyright infringement case. The infringer in GCA v. Chance presented this argument and lost the case, but who wants to take that chance?

Possible Deposit Rule Changes

Most lawyers who work with software authors and publishers are concerned about the present copyright rules for software deposits. There are several possible interim solutions, identified by the Copyright Office, which are being used by those few who know about them. These are described in Chapter 8, under the subject of "Source v. Object Code Protection." The present "identifying material" deposit rules are currently under examination by the Copyright Office. These rules may be revised in the future, so you should watch for possible announcements of changes.

SECURE TESTS AND SPECIAL RELIEF FOR SOFTWARE DEPOSITS

It is possible that, by written request, you could convince the Copyright Office to give your source code deposit special treatment similar to that for a "secure test" like bar examinations, but the Copyright Office has been extremely reluctant to do so in the past. For example, in National Conference of Bar Examiners v. Multistate Legal Studies, Inc., a 1982 case, the rules of the Copyright Office which provided that bar examination questions could be examined and returned to the registrant were upheld. There the Copyright Office retained only a small identifying portion of the test on a permanent basis, under its rules found in 17 C.F.R. § 202.20(b) and (c). Some similar provisions might be appropriate for software.

The Copyright Office rules have provisions in § 202.19 and 202.20 for "special relief" from the normal deposit requirements, where standard treatment would be burdensome, expensive, or otherwise unjustified. Under these rules, solely in the discretion of the Copyright Office but authorized by Section 408 of the Copyright Act, you can request special relief from the deposit rules. To qualify, you must show facts which justify special treatment, such as a desire to maintain trade secrecy. If you qualify, the Office will accept something other than the usual deposits called for by the rules, such as source code with critical routines blacked out on the listings. Recently this procedure has been granted for software in a few special cases, but the secure test rules have never been applied to software.

It would seem well worth the trouble to apply for relief under these rules if you have source code you believe would be compromised by depositing the material normally required. New permanent rules for software deposits may be issued in the near future that will obviate the need for these special rules.

SPECIAL HANDLING OF REGISTRATIONS FOR LITIGATION

Although normal registration takes three to four months for processing, the Copyright Office has a special handling procedure for filing registrations that must be completed in order to file a copyright infringement action. This service, which costs an extra $200 above the regular filing fee of $10, usually takes about ten working days to accomplish. You must accompany any application for special handling with either a special form (reproduced below) or a letter explaining the need for expedited treatment, including the name of the proposed plaintiff and defendant, the court where the action will be filed, and other information from which the Copyright Office can ascertain that the request is valid. You must also certify that, to the best of your knowledge, the information contained in the request is correct.

Such a request should be sent in an envelope marked "Special Handling Request," together with payment for both the special handling and the registration fees ($210 total), and it should be addressed to, "Library of Congress, Department DS, Washington, D.C. 20540, ATTN: Acquisitions and Processing Division." You may also file the request in person at the Public Information Office, Room LM-401, James Madison Memorial Building, Library of Congress.

FILING FEES FOR COPYRIGHT REGISTRATION

The registration fee, which must accompany your application, is $10 per application or supplementary registration application. Renewal fees, if applicable, are only $6 per application. Under current rules, these fees will not be refunded if you withdraw your application. Certified copies of

Copyright Office • The Library of Congress • Washington, D.C. 20559

request for special handling

1

NOTE: The special handling of a claim severely disrupts the entire registration process. It is, therefore, granted only in the most urgent of cases. A request for special handling is subject to the approval of the Chief of the Acquisitions and Processing Division, who takes into account the workload situation of the office at the time the request is made. A minimum period of five working days is required to process a claim under our special handling procedures.

Why is there an urgent need for special handling?

_____

_____

_____

2

If special handling is needed because of litigation, please answer the following questions:

_____

a. Is the litigation actual or prospective?

_____

b. Are you (or your client) the plaintiff or defendant in the action? Please specify.

_____

c. What are the names of the parties and what is the name of the court where the action is pending or expected?

_____

_____

_____

d. What is the latest date on which the certificate(s) or other requested item(s) could be furnished to you and still be of use in this matter?

_____

_____

I certify that the statements made above are correct to the best of my knowledge.

_____
(Signature)

_____
(Address)

_____
(Phone)   (Date)

FOR COPYRIGHT   Information Specialist handling matter
OFFICE USE ONLY _____

remarks

registrations may be obtained for $4 per registration, and certification of any other document is $4 per document.

Transfers.   Should you be recording a transfer, as discussed toward the end of this chapter, the fee is $10 for each document of less than six pages that includes transfer of no more than one copyrighted title, and 50¢ per page for each additional page and for each additional copyrighted title.

Searches.   If searches are necessary to find information you request, a $10 per hour fee (or fraction thereof) is charged for such services. Be sure to provide the registration number and year of anything your request or you will be charged this search fee, since works are microfilmed sequentially by number and year.

RETENTION OF COPYRIGHT DEPOSITS

Until recently the Copyright Office retained copyright deposits almost indefinitely, but now it is running out of space. It therefore discards at the end of five years almost all deposits not turned over to the Library of Congress. This practice of the Copyright Office means that you or your attorney will have to maintain your own master copies of all deposits made with the Copyright Office, in case you need to produce the original or a duplicate copy of a program or manual in an infringement claim. This is not a simple problem, since many infringements do not occur until a product has been on the market for some time, and even then a trial could take place years later.

Requesting Permanent Storage

The other alternative is to pay the extra fee of $135 for permanent storage of the work until the 75 year term runs out. If you wish to do this, you should contact the Records Management Division of the Copyright Office for the necessary information. Generally speaking, you must adequately identify the deposit to be retained by providing details on the original filing, and must clearly indicate that full-term retention is desired. The request must be signed by or on behalf of the depositor or the copyright owner of record. The Copyright Office will then decide if your request is to be granted and will notify you, after which you have 60 days to pay the storage fee.

SUPPLEMENTARY COPYRIGHT REGISTRATIONS

As a general rule, only one basic copyright registration may be made for the same version of a particular work. One exception is the right of the registrant to register a copyright as an unpublished work and then later as a published work. Another exception is where someone other than the author is identified as copyright claimant in the earlier registration, in which case the true author may subsequently file an application in his or her own name as the correct copyright claimant.

The law permits the filing of an application for a supplementary registration to correct or amplify the information set forth in the original registration. Such a supplementary registration does not supercede the earlier registration, but augments it.

The supplementary registration should be filed on Form CA, reproduced below. The form is largely self-explanatory. It may be filed by anyone who could have filed the original registration. It may not be used for renewals, however, nor to record transfers of ownership or rights in the copyright itself. It is filed with the Copyright Office, and the fee is also $10 per application.

RECORDING TRANSFERS AND OTHER COPYRIGHT-RELATED DOCUMENTS

The primary reason for recording a document with the Copyright Office is to transfer ownership of a copyright. Such transfer might occur as a result of a sale, purchase, or merger of a business, or for many other reasons. Section 205 of the Copyright Act, as supplemented by the regulations under 37 C.F.R. § 201.4, provides a mechanism for effecting such a transfer.

If you anticipate such a transfer, you should either call the Copyright Office for information and a copy of Circular R96 on the subject of recording transfers, or consult your attorney, since the rules are very technical concerning the requirements for such filings.

What May Be Recorded

In general, you may record any document relating to a copyright, if it is in writing, signed legibly, is complete, and is accompanied by the filing fee noted above for recording transfers and other documents. It must be totally legible and capable of being reproduced on microform, since it will be filmed. If the document is a copy, it must be certified as to its authenticity by a notary or other appropriate goverment official.

If the document refers to other documents as exhibits or schedules, these must be attached unless you can explain why they are missing. You may, however, incorporate other documents by reference.

The transfer or other documents are deemed filed on the date on which all necessary requirements for recording are met with the Copyright Office, regardless of the date on which the Office acts on it. The original document is returned to the sender with a certificate of recording.

FORM CA
UNITED STATES COPYRIGHT OFFICE

REGISTRATION NUMBER

TX	TXU	PA	PAU	VA	VAU	SR	SRU	RE

Effective Date of Supplementary Registration

. . . .
MONTH   DAY   YEAR

DO NOT WRITE ABOVE THIS LINE. FOR COPYRIGHT OFFICE USE ONLY

Ⓐ

Basic Instructions

TITLE OF WORK:

REGISTRATION NUMBER OF BASIC REGISTRATION: | YEAR OF BASIC REGISTRATION:

NAME(S) OF AUTHOR(S): | NAME(S) OF COPYRIGHT CLAIMANT(S):

Ⓑ

Correction

LOCATION AND NATURE OF INCORRECT INFORMATION IN BASIC REGISTRATION:

Line Number . . . . Line Heading or Description . . . .

INCORRECT INFORMATION AS IT APPEARS IN BASIC REGISTRATION:

CORRECTED INFORMATION:

EXPLANATION OF CORRECTION: (Optional)

Ⓒ

Amplification

LOCATION AND NATURE OF INFORMATION IN BASIC REGISTRATION TO BE AMPLIFIED:

Line Number . . . . Line Heading or Description . . . .

AMPLIFIED INFORMATION:

EXPLANATION OF AMPLIFIED INFORMATION: (Optional)

EXAMINED BY..........	FORM CA RECEIVED:	FOR COPYRIGHT OFFICE USE ONLY
CHECKED BY..........		
CORRESPONDENCE: □ YES	REMITTANCE NUMBER AND DATE:	
REFERENCE TO THIS REGISTRATION ADDED TO BASIC REGISTRATION □ YES □ NO	DEPOSIT ACCOUNT FUNDS USED: □	

DO NOT WRITE ABOVE THIS LINE. FOR COPYRIGHT OFFICE USE ONLY

CONTINUATION OF: (Check which) □ PART B OR □ PART C

(D) Continuation

DEPOSIT ACCOUNT: If the registration fee is to be charged to a Deposit Account established in the Copyright Office, give name and number of Account

Name.. Account Number....................

(E) Deposit Account and Mailing Instructions

CORRESPONDENCE: Give name and address to which correspondence should be sent:

Name... Apt. No...................

Address...
      (Number and Street)   (City)   (State)   (ZIP Code)

CERTIFICATION ✱ I, the undersigned, hereby certify that I am the: (Check one)

□ author □ other copyright claimant □ owner of exclusive right(s) □ authorized agent of:
                                                          (Name of author or other copyright claimant, or owner of exclusive right(s))
of the work identified in this application and that the statements made by me in this application are correct to the best of my knowledge.

Handwritten signature: (X)....................................

Typed or printed name.......................................

Date:...

(F) Certification (Application must be signed)

✱ 17 USC §506(e) FALSE REPRESENTATION—Any person who knowingly makes a false representation of a material fact in the application for copyright registration provided for by section 409, or in any written statement filed in connection with the application, shall be fined not more than $2,500.

	MAIL CERTIFICATE TO	**(G) Address for Return of Certificate**
.... (Name)		
.... (Number, Street and Apartment Number)		
.... (City) (State) (ZIP code)	(Certificate will be mailed in window envelope)	

U.S. GOVERNMENT PRINTING OFFICE 1983—381-278/502

OBTAINING COPIES
OF COPYRIGHT RECORDS

With very few exceptions, all of the records of the Copyright Office are open to the public. They may be inspected in person or copies obtained by mail. Most records can be obtained in certified copy form. Searching for and locating these records can be a problem if you do not know exactly what you are looking for. The Office charges for search time and for copies.

Generally, your best bet is to call the Certifications and Documents Section of the Copyright Office or to write them at: Certifications and Documents Section, LM-458, Copyright Office, Library of Congress, Washington, D.C. 20559. The Public Information Section also puts out a free Circular R6, entitled "Obtaining Copies of Copyright Office Records and Deposits." It is very helpful, and lists other departments and related information.

RENEWAL OF COPYRIGHTS

Current Law. Due to the provisions of the 1976 Copyright Act, which grants initial copyright terms for the author's lifetime plus fifty years for individuals and seventy-five or 100 years in the case of works for hire, renewal of software copyrights is no longer an issue. It seems very unlikely that software will have a useful life of more than ten to fifteen years.

Pre-1978 Law. Under the old 1909 law, the copyright term lasted twenty-eight years, with a right of renewal. If you have pre-1978 software copyrights, you should discuss the matter with your attorney or call the Public Information Office of the Copyright Office to request Circular 96, which relates to regulation 202.17 of the Copyright Office and provides detailed information on renewing copyright terms. The rules are fairly complicated, but understandable once you have read Circular 96.

EXAMPLES OF COPYRIGHT
REGISTRATION APPLICATIONS

The following example forms are completed for a typical individual author and then for a work for hire. Since each case is different, it is important that you not just copy them, but that you read your own Form TX instructions carefully and then complete the form in the fashion necessary to fit your set of facts. Form TX provides an information sheet with both basic information for filing registrations and line-by-line instructions. These are helpful but do not always apply to your situation, especially when you are filing a computer program.

Following each form are comments intended to help you understand exactly why the blanks are filed in as they are. Those comments are keyed to the space numbers on the Form TX.

Step by Step through the First Form TX

Item 1. Whatever you put here will be the name under which the computer program is indexed. If it is a book, just use its title. Where, as here, the name is short, it is best to add things like a qualifier and a version number. If you add version numbers, be sure to explain why it is not version 1.0, if it is not.

Item 2. The instructions call for your full name, but you may give it as usually written. It is in your interest to provide the most detail you can, since this is also indexed, and "J. Smith" doesn't tell anybody much. Your birth date is helpful for identification years later. You must answer the "work for hire" question and the citizenship/domicile one. Unless applicable, check "NO" for the other questions on that line. The final question is intended to tell the Copyright Office what you contributed, so that it can evaluate the nature of authorship. It is most important if there are co-authors, in which case you may so state. This is also where you make clear that the filing is a computer program, if that is the case. If there are co-authors you must complete the form for each author involved.

Item 3. Every form must have a creation date, but the publication date only applies if it is, in fact, published. To protect your trade secrecy, if you want to take the position that your program is licensed only, and therefore is not published, this box must state that it is an unpublished work. No date is needed in such a case. If it is published, however, you must disclose the country of publication, since this defines the rights you have.

Item 4. This will usually be the same person as Items 1, 9 and 11, if the author is an individual. However, this need not be the case, as you can see in the second example Form TX, which has several addresses and persons.

Item 5. This presupposes that this is Version 2.0 of a substantially modified program, so you must provide the earlier registration information.

Item 6. Here you need to specify how you did enough work to qualify this as a registrable derivative, and how it differs from the earlier work.

Item 7. It is not clear how this line applies to computer programs, since it usually applies only to books and other nondramatic literary works in English, and programs aren't really in English. Complete it anyway to help the Copyright Office.

Item 8. Not likely to be applicable to programs, but could be for user manuals. Read the instructions carefully on this.

FORM TX
UNITED STATES COPYRIGHT OFFICE

REGISTRATION NUMBER

TX	TXU

EFFECTIVE DATE OF REGISTRATION

Month	Day	Year

DO NOT WRITE ABOVE THIS LINE. IF YOU NEED MORE SPACE, USE A SEPARATE CONTINUATION SHEET.

1

TITLE OF THIS WORK ▼

SUPERTYPER WORD PROCESSOR, VERSION 2.0

PREVIOUS OR ALTERNATIVE TITLES ▼

SUPERTYPER WORD PROCESSOR, VERSION 1.0

PUBLICATION AS A CONTRIBUTION   If this work was published as a contribution to a periodical, serial, or collection, give information about the collective work in which the contribution appeared.   **Title of Collective Work ▼**

If published in a periodical or serial give: **Volume ▼**   **Number ▼**   **Issue Date ▼**   **On Pages ▼**

2

a

NAME OF AUTHOR ▼

HUNT N. PECK

DATES OF BIRTH AND DEATH
Year Born ▼   Year Died ▼
1940   --

Was this contribution to the work a "work made for hire"?
☐ Yes
☒ No

AUTHOR'S NATIONALITY OR DOMICILE
Name of Country
OR { Citizen of ▶ USA
{ Domiciled in ▶

WAS THIS AUTHOR'S CONTRIBUTION TO THE WORK
Anonymous?   ☐ Yes ☒ No
Pseudonymous?   ☐ Yes ☒ No
If the answer to either of these questions is "Yes," see detailed instructions

NATURE OF AUTHORSHIP   Briefly describe nature of the material created by this author in which copyright is claimed. ▼
AUTHOR OF ENTIRE COMPUTER PROGRAM AND ALL REVISIONS

NOTE

Under the law, the "author" of a "work made for hire" is generally the employer, not the employee (see instructions). For any part of this work that was "made for hire" check "Yes" in the space provided, give the employer (or other person for whom the work was prepared) as "Author" of that part, and leave the space for dates of birth and death blank.

b

NAME OF AUTHOR ▼

DATES OF BIRTH AND DEATH
Year Born ▼   Year Died ▼

Was this contribution to the work a "work made for hire"?
☐ Yes
☐ No

AUTHOR'S NATIONALITY OR DOMICILE
Name of country
OR { Citizen of ▶
{ Domiciled in ▶

WAS THIS AUTHOR'S CONTRIBUTION TO THE WORK
Anonymous?   ☐ Yes ☐ No
Pseudonymous?   ☐ Yes ☐ No
If the answer to either of these questions is "Yes," see detailed instructions

NATURE OF AUTHORSHIP   Briefly describe nature of the material created by this author in which copyright is claimed. ▼

c

NAME OF AUTHOR ▼

DATES OF BIRTH AND DEATH
Year Born ▼   Year Died ▼

Was this contribution to the work a "work made for hire"?
☐ Yes
☐ No

AUTHOR'S NATIONALITY OR DOMICILE
Name of Country
OR { Citizen of ▶
{ Domiciled in ▶

WAS THIS AUTHOR'S CONTRIBUTION TO THE WORK
Anonymous?   ☐ Yes ☐ No
Pseudonymous?   ☐ Yes ☐ No
If the answer to either of these questions is "Yes," see detailed instructions

NATURE OF AUTHORSHIP   Briefly describe nature of the material created by this author in which copyright is claimed. ▼

3

YEAR IN WHICH CREATION OF THIS WORK WAS COMPLETED   This information must be given in all cases.
1983   ◀ Year

DATE AND NATION OF FIRST PUBLICATION OF THIS PARTICULAR WORK
Complete this information ONLY if this work has been published.   Month ▶ August   Day ▶ 2   Year ▶ 1983
United States   ◀ Nation

4

See instructions before completing this space.

COPYRIGHT CLAIMANT(S)   Name and address must be given even if the claimant is the same as the author given in space 2.▼

HUNT N. PECK
1222 OFFICE PARKWAY
DALLAS, TEXAS 74422

APPLICATION RECEIVED

ONE DEPOSIT RECEIVED

TWO DEPOSITS RECEIVED

REMITTANCE NUMBER AND DATE

DO NOT WRITE HERE OFFICE USE ONLY

TRANSFER If the claimant(s) named here in space 4 are different from the author(s) named in space 2, give a brief statement of how the claimant(s) obtained ownership of the copyright.▼

MORE ON BACK ▶ • Complete all applicable spaces (numbers 5-11) on the reverse side of this page.
• See detailed instructions.   • Sign the form at line 10.

DO NOT WRITE HERE

Page 1 of _____ pages

EXAMINED BY	FORM TX
CHECKED BY	
☐ CORRESPONDENCE Yes	FOR COPYRIGHT OFFICE USE ONLY
☐ DEPOSIT ACCOUNT FUNDS USED	

DO NOT WRITE ABOVE THIS LINE. IF YOU NEED MORE SPACE, USE A SEPARATE CONTINUATION SHEET.

PREVIOUS REGISTRATION Has registration for this work, or for an earlier version of this work, already been made in the Copyright Office?

☒ Yes ☐ No If your answer is "Yes," why is another registration being sought? (Check appropriate box) ▼

☐ This is the first published edition of a work previously registered in unpublished form.

☐ This is the first application submitted by this author as copyright claimant.

☒ This is a changed version of the work, as shown by space 6 on this application.

If your answer is "Yes," give: Previous Registration Number ▼ TX 1-038-989   Year of Registration ▼ 1982

5

DERIVATIVE WORK OR COMPILATION Complete both space 6a & 6b for a derivative work; complete only 6b for a compilation.

a. Preexisting Material Identify any preexisting work or works that this work is based on or incorporates. ▼

WORD PROCESSING PROGRAM FOR ORIGINAL MODEL IBM P.C. WITH FLOPPY DISK ONLY

b. Material Added to This Work Give a brief, general statement of the material that has been added to this work and in which copyright is claimed. ▼

ADDITIONAL FEATURES ADDED AND CONVERTED TO RUN ON IBM MODEL XT P.C. WITH HARD DISK

6

See instructions before completing this space.

MANUFACTURERS AND LOCATIONS If this is a published work consisting preponderantly of nondramatic literary material in English, the law may require that the copies be manufactured in the United States or Canada for full protection. If so, the names of the manufacturers who performed certain processes, and the places where these processes were performed must be given. See instructions for details.

Names of Manufacturers ▼   Places of Manufacture ▼

DISK COPY CORPORATION   DALLAS, TX.

7

REPRODUCTION FOR USE OF BLIND OR PHYSICALLY HANDICAPPED INDIVIDUALS A signature on this form at space 10, and a check in one of the boxes here in space 8, constitutes a non-exclusive grant of permission to the Library of Congress to reproduce and distribute solely for the blind and physically handicapped and under the conditions and limitations prescribed by the regulations of the Copyright Office: (1) copies of the work identified in space 1 of this application in Braille (or similar tactile symbols); or (2) phonorecords embodying a fixation of a reading of that work; or (3) both.

a ☐ Copies and Phonorecords   b ☐ Copies Only   c ☐ Phonorecords Only

8

See instructions.

DEPOSIT ACCOUNT If the registration fee is to be charged to a Deposit Account established in the Copyright Office, give name and number of Account.

Name ▼   Account Number ▼

9

CORRESPONDENCE Give name and address to which correspondence about this application should be sent. Name/Address/Apt/City/State/Zip ▼

HUNT N. PECK

]222 Office Parkway

Dallas, TX. 74422

Area Code & Telephone Number ▶ (706) 244-8888

Be sure to give your daytime phone number

CERTIFICATION* I, the undersigned, hereby certify that I am the

Check one ▶

☒ author

☐ other copyright claimant

☐ owner of exclusive right(s)

☐ authorized agent of _____

Name of author or other copyright claimant, or owner of exclusive right(s) ▲

of the work identified in this application and that the statements made by me in this application are correct to the best of my knowledge.

Typed or printed name and date ▼ If this is a published work, this date must be the same as or later than the date of publication given in space 3.

HUNT N. PECK   date ▶ 8/4/83

Handwritten signature (X) ▼ *Hunt N. Peck*

10

MAIL CERTIFICATE TO

Certificate will be mailed in window envelope

Name ▼

HUNT N. PECK

Number/Street/Apartment Number ▼

1222 OFFICE PARKWAY

City/State/ZIP ▼

DALLAS, TEXAS 74422

Have you:
• Completed all necessary spaces?
• Signed your application in space 107
• Enclosed check or money order for $10 payable to Register of Copyrights?
• Enclosed your deposit material with the application and fee?

MAIL TO: Register of Copyrights, Library of Congress, Washington, D.C. 20559.

11

* 17 U.S.C. § 506(e): Any person who knowingly makes a false representation of a material fact in the application for copyright registration provided for by section 409, or in any written statement filed in connection with the application, shall be fined not more than $2,500.

★U.S. GOVERNMENT PRINTING OFFICE: 1983: 381-278/101   April 1983—100,050

Item 9.   The deposit account is explained is Chapter 7. The important thing here is to provide an alternative address if someone other than the author is to respond to inquiries, such as your lawyer.

Item 10.   You must check this box carefully or the application will be returned, unless it is crystal clear who the signer is. Many people forget the date or put in a date before the publication date, which you cannot do. Don't forget to sign it.

Item 11.   This is for the address to which the certificate will be mailed in a window envelope. Be sure, therefore, that your typing stays in the box so the address shows or it may never arrive.

Step by Step through the Second Form TX

Item 1.   Note the explanation provided on the form, which will save later questions by the examiner. You could provide the same information in your cover letter.

Item 2.   Since this is a work for hire, the employer is listed as the author. You could also list the human author, as an employee, but this is not usually done and can be confusing. Remember that the employer is deemed the author of a work for hire. Check the work-for-hire box and the citizenship, but you don't have to check the other boxes since there is no human author listed.

Item 3.   Same as the previous form.

Item 4.   Here the claimant is not the author, so you list the employer's name and provide a simple explanation as to who the claimant is and how the claimant obtained the right to file for registration.

Item 5.   Once you check "NO," there is nothing else to say here or in Item 6.

Items 7 & 8.   Same as the previous form.

Item 9.   Same as the previous form.

Item 10.   In this case the attorney is an authorized agent, so he signed and indicated his capacity. He also put his name and address in Item 9 so that questions on the form could be directed to him.

Item 11.   Whoever the registered certificate is returned to should be careful not to lose it. You can get replacements, but it takes time and is a nuisance.

FORM TX
UNITED STATES COPYRIGHT OFFICE

REGISTRATION NUMBER

              TX   TXU
EFFECTIVE DATE OF REGISTRATION

Month   Day   Year

DO NOT WRITE ABOVE THIS LINE. IF YOU NEED MORE SPACE, USE A SEPARATE CONTINUATION SHEET.

1

TITLE OF THIS WORK ▼

TYMKEEPER ACCOUNTING SYSTEM, VERSION 1.1

PREVIOUS OR ALTERNATIVE TITLES ▼

NONE - EARLIEST VERSION NOT PUBLISHED

PUBLICATION AS A CONTRIBUTION If this work was published as a contribution to a periodical, serial, or collection, give information about the collective work in which the contribution appeared. **Title of Collective Work ▼**

- - -

If published in a periodical or serial give: **Volume ▼**   **Number ▼**   **Issue Date ▼**   **On Pages ▼**

2

NAME OF AUTHOR ▼

a ACCOUNTING SOFTWARE, INC.

DATES OF BIRTH AND DEATH
Year Born ▼   Year Died ▼
--   --

Was this contribution to the work a "work made for hire"?
☒ Yes
☐ No

AUTHOR'S NATIONALITY OR DOMICILE
Name of Country
OR { Citizen of ▶   USA
{ Domiciled in ▶ _____

WAS THIS AUTHOR'S CONTRIBUTION TO THE WORK
Anonymous? ☐ Yes ☐ No
Pseudonymous? ☐ Yes ☐ No
If the answer to either of these questions is "Yes," see detailed instructions.

NATURE OF AUTHORSHIP Briefly describe nature of the material created by this author in which copyright is claimed. ▼
COMPLETE ACCOUNTING PROGRAM WRITTEN IN PL/I FOR CP/M SYSTEMS

NAME OF AUTHOR ▼

b

DATES OF BIRTH AND DEATH
Year Born ▼   Year Died ▼

Was this contribution to the work a "work made for hire"?
☐ Yes
☐ No

AUTHOR'S NATIONALITY OR DOMICILE
Name of country
OR { Citizen of ▶ _____
{ Domiciled in ▶ _____

WAS THIS AUTHOR'S CONTRIBUTION TO THE WORK
Anonymous? ☐ Yes ☐ No
Pseudonymous? ☐ Yes ☐ No
If the answer to either of these questions is "Yes," see detailed instructions.

NATURE OF AUTHORSHIP Briefly describe nature of the material created by this author in which copyright is claimed. ▼

NAME OF AUTHOR ▼

c

DATES OF BIRTH AND DEATH
Year Born ▼   Year Died ▼

Was this contribution to the work a "work made for hire"?
☐ Yes
☐ No

AUTHOR'S NATIONALITY OR DOMICILE
Name of Country
OR { Citizen of ▶ _____
{ Domiciled in ▶ _____

WAS THIS AUTHOR'S CONTRIBUTION TO THE WORK
Anonymous? ☐ Yes ☐ No
Pseudonymous? ☐ Yes ☐ No
If the answer to either of these questions is "Yes," see detailed instructions.

NATURE OF AUTHORSHIP Briefly describe nature of the material created by this author in which copyright is claimed. ▼

NOTE
Under the law, the "author" of a "work made for hire" is generally the employer, not the employee (see instructions). For any part of this work that was "made for hire" check "Yes" in the space provided, give the employer (or other person for whom the work was prepared) as "Author" of that part, and leave the space for dates of birth and death blank.

3

YEAR IN WHICH CREATION OF THIS WORK WAS COMPLETED This information must be given in all cases.
1982 ◀ Year

DATE AND NATION OF FIRST PUBLICATION OF THIS PARTICULAR WORK
Complete this information ONLY if this work has been published.
Month ▶ May   Day ▶ 15   Year ▶ 1983
USA ◀ Nation

4

COPYRIGHT CLAIMANT(S) Name and address must be given even if the claimant is the same as the author given in space 2.▼

AMERICAN SOFTWARE, INC.
82 WAREHOUSE ROW
LOS ANGELES, CA. 90001

See instructions before completing this space.

APPLICATION RECEIVED

ONE DEPOSIT RECEIVED

TWO DEPOSITS RECEIVED

REMITTANCE NUMBER AND DATE

DO NOT WRITE HERE
OFFICE USE ONLY

TRANSFER If the claimant(s) named here in space 4 are different from the author(s) named in space 2, give a brief statement of how the claimant(s) obtained ownership of the copyright.▼

TRANSFER OF ALL RIGHTS BY CORPORATE AUTHOR

MORE ON BACK ▶ • Complete all applicable spaces (numbers 5-11) on the reverse side of this page.
• See detailed instructions.   • Sign the form at line 10.

DO NOT WRITE HERE

Page 1 of _____ pages

EXAMINED BY   **FORM TX**

CHECKED BY

☐ CORRESPONDENCE
   Yes   FOR
                                               COPYRIGHT
☐ DEPOSIT ACCOUNT   OFFICE
   FUNDS USED   USE
                                               ONLY

DO NOT WRITE ABOVE THIS LINE. IF YOU NEED MORE SPACE, USE A SEPARATE CONTINUATION SHEET.

PREVIOUS REGISTRATION Has registration for this work, or for an earlier version of this work, already been made in the Copyright Office?
☐ Yes ☒ No If your answer is "Yes," why is another registration being sought? (Check appropriate box) ▼
☐ This is the first published edition of a work previously registered in unpublished form.
☐ This is the first application submitted by this author as copyright claimant.
☐ This is a changed version of the work, as shown by space 6 on this application.
If your answer is "Yes," give: **Previous Registration Number** ▼   **Year of Registration** ▼

5

DERIVATIVE WORK OR COMPILATION Complete both space 6a & 6b for a derivative work; complete only 6b for a compilation.
a. **Preexisting Material** Identify any preexisting work or works that this work is based on or incorporates. ▼
--

b. **Material Added to This Work** Give a brief, general statement of the material that has been added to this work and in which copyright is claimed. ▼
--

6

See instructions
before completing
this space.

MANUFACTURERS AND LOCATIONS If this is a published work consisting preponderantly of nondramatic literary material in English, the law may require that the copies be manufactured in the United States or Canada for full protection. If so, the names of the manufacturers who performed certain processes, and the places where these processes were performed **must** be given. See instructions for details.
Names of Manufacturers ▼   • **Places of Manufacture** ▼
AMERICAN SOFTWARE, INC.   LOS ANGELES, CA. USA

7

REPRODUCTION FOR USE OF BLIND OR PHYSICALLY HANDICAPPED INDIVIDUALS   A signature on this form at space 10, and a check in one of the boxes here in space 8, constitutes a non-exclusive grant of permission to the Library of Congress to reproduce and distribute solely for the blind and physically handicapped and under the conditions and limitations prescribed by the regulations of the Copyright Office: (1) copies of the work identified in space 1 of this application in Braille (or similar tactile symbols); or (2) phonorecords embodying a fixation of a reading of that work; or (3) both.
a ☐ Copies and Phonorecords   b ☐ Copies Only   c ☐ Phonorecords Only

8

See instructions.

DEPOSIT ACCOUNT If the registration fee is to be charged to a Deposit Account established in the Copyright Office, give name and number of Account.
Name ▼   SCHROEDER & DAVIS INC.   **Account Number** ▼   X34567-2

CORRESPONDENCE Give name and address to which correspondence about this application should be sent. Name/Address/Apt/City/State/Zip ▼
G. GERVAISE DAVIS III, ESQ.
P.O. BOX 3080
MONTEREY, CA. 93942
                    Area Code & Telephone Number ▶ (408) 649-1122

9

Be sure to
give your
daytime phone
◀ number.

CERTIFICATION* I, the undersigned, hereby certify that I am the
                                        Check one ▶
☐ author
☐ other copyright claimant
☐ owner of exclusive right(s)
☒ authorized agent of AMERICAN SOFTWARE, INC.
of the work identified in this application and that the statements made   Name of author or other copyright claimant, or owner of exclusive right(s) ▲
by me in this application are correct to the best of my knowledge.

Typed or printed name and date ▼ If this is a published work, this date must be the same as or later than the date of publication given in space 3.
G. GERVAISE DAVIS III   date ▶ June 1, 1983

👉 Handwritten signature (X) ▼ _[signature]_

10

MAIL CERTIFI-CATE TO
Name ▼
G. GERVAISE DAVIS III, ESQ.
Number/Street/Apartment Number ▼
P.O. BOX 3080
City/State/ZIP ▼
MONTEREY, CALIFORNIA 93942

Certificate will be mailed in window envelope

Have you:
• Completed all necessary spaces?
• Signed your application in space 10?
• Enclosed check or money order for $10 payable to Register of Copyrights?
• Enclosed your deposit material with the application and fee?
MAIL TO: Register of Copyrights, Library of Congress, Washington, D.C. 20559.

11

* 17 U.S.C. § 506(e): Any person who knowingly makes a false representation of a material fact in the application for copyright registration provided for by section 409, or in any written statement filed in connection with the application, shall be fined not more than $2,500.

☆ U.S. GOVERNMENT PRINTING OFFICE: 1983: 381-278/101   April 1983—100,050

Send A Covering Letter

Every time you file Form TX or another document with the Copyright Office, it is very important that you accompany it with a letter of explanation, together with the filing fees and deposits. The examiners, sitting in Washington, D.C., have no way of knowing the background of what you are filing. For example, if you file a program in COBOL for a mainframe or a fairly short microcomputer program written in the C language, you should tell the examiner very precisely what you have sent them to look at in the way of deposits. They must be able to tell what you wrote and how much you have contributed as an author. If you do not send source code or if there are not a total of fifty accompanying pages, explain why.

Compiled Programs

If your program is compiled by a compiler produced by someone else, it is not uncommon for other copyright notices to appear. These notices are generated by the compiler. Should you be filing source and object or just object code, which has other notices in the object code, explain this is in the covering letter. Anything that might be confusing or look strange should be explained, so the examiner does not have to write or call you for clarification.

SUMMARY

You should register your copyright for programs and user manuals within three months of publication. The costs are nominal compared to the benefits. Remember that you cannot bring a copyright infringement case until the copyright has been registered.

Be very careful what you select and send in the way of copyright deposits for your programs. If you want to protect the source-code secrecy, consider filing only object code, or using the special relief provisions described in detail in Chapter 8.

Read the instructions with the various forms carefully, since failure to use the official forms and to provide the exact information requested will result in delays or rejection of your filing. Send all the elements to the Copyright Office together in one envelope.

Be sure you understand how to apply the work for hire rules which cause many rejected applications because the authorship is not clear.

7

The Rules
for Copyrighting
Video Games

Skeptical citizens might do well to pay attention to a
peculiar clinking sound audible across the land. The
noise is made by the estimated 20 billion quarters that
poured last year into the arcade monsters. . . . $5 billion
is exactly twice the reported take in the last fiscal year of
all of the casinos in Nevada. It is almost twice the $2.8
billion gross of the U.S. movie industry. And it is three
times more than the combined television revenues and
gate receipts last year of major league baseball,
basketball and football.

> "The Craze That Won't Quit,"
> *Time*, January 18, 1983, page 51.

MAKING THE VIDEO-GAME
PIRATES WALK THE PLANK

Video games have come upon the world with a vengeance, as well as a
suddenness, almost equal to the speed and force of the rockets and space
ships represented on the color screens at your local video-game arcade.
As the daily clink of millions of quarters rack up profits for the game
owners and operators, modern-day pirates seek their share of the bounty
through the manufacture and sale of what the industry calls "knock-

---

I am indebted to David A. Gerber, Esq. of Loeb and Loeb, Los Angeles, California, for use of
his research notes and for his suggestions concerning this chapter. David has litigated many
of the important video-games cases, on behalf of his clients.

offs"—identically operating video games that duplicate the currently popular models.

Neither patent law nor trade-secret principles are feasible or useful for the protection of visual images and sounds in this fast-moving industry. To stop the video-game pirates, virtually all video-game manufacturers are currently relying on some unique and successful legal theories under the copyright laws. As a result of some very extensive and very expensive litigation by the major suppliers of such games, these theories have developed more rapidly even than the market for the games themselves. Bally-Midway and Atari are estimated to have spent more than $15 million in legal fees over the past five years to accomplish such a task. This chapter discusses these theories and other practical steps to be taken to protect your video games.

WHAT IS INVOLVED IN A VIDEO GAME?

Arcade Games

The typical arcade video game consists of a brightly colored wooden or plastic box frame with sides, back, top, and on the front a player's control area at waist height. At eye level there is a color television-type screen on which the action is displayed as the game is played. The player manipulates a multi-directional joystick together with a panel of several buttons to control other functions.

Home Games

Home video games use the family television set for the screen and have a separate control panel connected by wires to the television, but they are otherwise similar to the arcade games. There are also numerous video games that run on home and office computers and that may use the computer keyboard and cursor controls to manipulate the game. All follow the same general principles.

Game Objectives

Depending on the game and its rules, the player guides an airplane, rocket, or spaceship through various battlegrounds or hostile territory. The objective is to rack up the highest possible number of points in a given time, in a game that usually gets harder and harder as the time passes and as the points add up. During the play, strange sounds, flashes, and color changes occur with increasing frequency. The famous PAC-MAN™ game involves maneuvering odd little colored characters through a maze—gobbling up "power pills," and avoiding hazards in the form of monsters, rocks, and other items—with the objective of getting the most points by avoiding errors and by the cleverest manipulation of the characters. The scores are displayed in flashing lights on the screen.

Attract Mode and Play Mode

Attract Mode. When no one is actually playing the game, the screen often displays moving objects and emits sounds of battlefields and crashes, flashing colored lights, and lists of instructions. This condition is known as the "attract mode." It repeats over and over again until someone puts a coin in the machine to start the second phase.

Play Mode. The second phase is called the "play mode." During the time a player actively uses the game, one of a hundred or so scenes or one of only a few scenes could appear on the screen, depending on the complexity or the design of the game. Which one of the different displays actually appears is a direct function of the predetermined decisions (known to programmers as "branches") built into the computer program, the graphics capability of the screen and its circuitry, and the actions taken and decisions made by the player. In most of these games, there are potentially tens of thousands of variations on a theme that could develop, but the variations are not infinite since the rules are integral to the computer program controlling the game.

Program Design and Storage

To design and market these games someone has had to decide on the theme of the game, has had to set the rules ahead of time and has had to write and debug the source code for the computer program. Debugging is a form of trouble-shooting by a programmer, who tests and corrects errors that show up in a completed program. Once the program is debugged, it is reduced to binary object-code form and loaded into a series of integrated circuit chips, called ROMs or PROMs, which are then plugged or soldered into the circuit boards of the actual game. It is this software that causes the circuitry to react to the actions of the player by changing the audiovisual effects on the screen. While the player can vary the action by his or her decisions, there are a series of fixed images that must appear from time to time because of the way the program was written.

Access to the Program. Unlike word processors or other more sophisticated personal and business computers, there is no disk drive or keyboard in a video game, nor any other way for the user to directly read out the program on the screen; the user never has direct access to the software. The program is therefore relatively "safe" from pirates—unless they open up a game and remove the ROMs or PROMs and duplicate them. Unfortunately, duplication of such chips is fairly easy using a device known as a PROM programmer, an electronic machine available to nearly all engineering and technical personnel. If and when the contents of chips are copied, the pirates have then infringed the copyright of the designer and manufacturer of the machine.

For example, in a precedent setting case, the JS&A mail-order company was enjoined in late 1983 from selling a device called PROM BLASTER, which was being sold for the express purpose of making copies of videogame cartridges. The company had contended that the device was sold only to permit users to make "backup copies" of games, as authorized by § 117 of the copyright law, but the trial judge concluded that its only significant use was to permit users to copy other game cartridges. The case was on appeal in late 1984.

THE ISSUES INVOLVED
IN PROTECTING VIDEO GAMES

Whether the video game is an arcade coin-operated version, the main target of litigation, or a home video cartridge, there are three basic legal issues involved in disputes over video-game protection:

- Can the visual and aural aspects of these games be protected as audiovisual works under the copyright law?
- Can the computer programs that create the game rules and the visual and aural effects be protected as literary works under the law?
- Is copyright protection precluded because many of these devices are primarily electronic machines, where the program is stored in ROM and is inaccessible to the user?

Another issue, of considerable importance to the whole field of computer programming, is the question of how close you can come to copying the ideas in a video game without infringing its copyright.

VIDEO GAMES AS AUDIOVISUAL WORKS

New Technology Is Covered

The 1976 Copyright Act defines audiovisual works in 17 USC § 101 as "works that consist of a series of related images which are intrinsically intended to be shown by the use of machines, or devices such as projectors, viewers, or electronic equipment, together with accompanying sounds, if any, regardless of the nature of the material objects, such as films or tapes, in which the works are embodied."

As a result of a series of court cases (Stern Electronics, Inc. v. Kaufman; Midway Manufacturing Co. v. Dirkschneider; and most recently, Midway Manufacturing Co. v. Artic International), it is now clearly established under the copyright laws that a video game is an audiovisual work, as such term is defined in 17 USC § 102(a)(6). The Midway-Artic case expressly recognized that video games may not have been anticipated by Congress when it passed the new Copyright Law in 1976, but concluded that the law had to be flexibly interpreted to cover new technology as it develops.

The "Fixation" Argument

The defendants in each of the above cases contended that video games could not be protected as audiovisual works, since all of the "play modes" were not fixed in a tangible medium of expression as required by § 102(a). They argued that since the scenes in the games varied with different plays; there was no *fixation* in the sense that a video tape or movie film is fixed. The courts did not agree. One of the cases, Stern, held that since there were constants in the game, such as sounds and actions that repeated over and over again, this fact alone was sufficient for copyright protection. Interestingly enough, none of the defendants ever contended that the "attract mode" was not protected as an audiovisual work, but concentrated their attack on the "play mode."

There are a finite number of scenes possible in a video game, although the number of variations may be in the hundreds of thousands or even millions. If someone played long enough, all possibilities would eventually be exhausted. Yet, some scenes are fixed and appear with regularity as part of the game. The 1983 appellate court decision involving Midway's PAC-MAN recognized this and concluded that the fixation requirement meant only that there had to be a series of images fixed in the machine. The fact that they could appear in a different order or sequence was not deemed important to their protection. The sounds are also fixed in certain sequences, tied to the appropriate visual image, and are protected under the same law.

The Player as the Author

The defendants also argued, imaginatively, that the intervention of the player, who determined which images appeared by virtue of his or her actions at the controls, meant that the player was the author of each session. They claimed that the game actually played was not the same as that stored in the machine—especially since each session with the game was different, depending on the decisions made by the player each time he or she moved the joystick or pressed a button.

The Stern court rejected this argument by pointing out that someone first conceived what the visual and aural effects would be, and that this was where originality and authorship occurred. This conclusion was further supported in the Midway-Artic decision, which likened the decisions of the player to the television viewer who sees what he or she does by changing channels, but who cannot change the television signals available. In other words, subsequent decisions by the player do not matter, since the player's decisions cannot change the original range of possible audiovisual effects.

As a result of these decisions, it is highly unlikely that subsequent cases will be able to overcome the consistent conclusions of the federal courts that video games are audiovisual works protected by the copyright statutes.

VIDEO GAMES AS COMPUTER PROGRAMS

Video games also include computer programs, which are classified as protectable "literary works" under 17 USC § 101(a)(1). Thus, both the Stern case and the more recent case of Williams Electronics, Inc. v. Artic International, Inc. have concluded that the making of copies of the ROMs and PROMs, in which the programs are electronically embedded, are infringements of those programs, which the copyright owner can protect by injunctive relief and, if applicable, money damages.

Fixation of the Program

Furthermore, the Williams case and Midway Mfg. Co. v. Artic International, Inc. also established that the requirement of 17 USC § 102(a) for fixation of the computer program in tangible form is satisfied by the necessary program instructions being electronically embedded in the ROM or PROM. Moreover, Williams holds that object code is a copy of the source-code program, is fixed in a tangible medium of expression (the ROM or PROM), and is protectable under the 1976 Copyright Act. This same conclusion was reached in Midway Mfg. Co. v. Strohon in 1983.

Derivative Works

An additional issue in the Midway-Artic case, in the 7th Circuit Court of Appeals decision, was whether or not "speed-up kits" sold by Artic were "derivative works" of the original game, which could not be sold without infringing Midway's copyright. Speed-up kits are replacement or add-on boards that make the original game run faster, and thus make it harder for the players and more profitable for the arcades who have the games. A similar issue was involved in Strohon, where the defendant made plug-in ROMs to change the characters from the PAC-MAN "gobblers" to other characters.

Since the Copyright Act defines a derivative work as "a work based on one or more preexisting works," the Midway-Artic court had no difficulty in finding that a speeded-up video game is a substantially different product—although based on the original copyrighted game, which new product the original copyright owner has the exclusive right to exploit. This conclusion may also have value for stopping pirates of computer software who "reverse engineer" existing programs by disassembling or decompiling them, and then market faster and slightly different programs under a different name.

COPYRIGHT NOTICES ON VIDEO GAMES

If your video game is to be protected under the copyright laws, you will have to take the same steps discussed earlier—namely, place copyright notices on it, and then register the game as both an audiovisual and a literary work. Notices on video games may vary from those on other types of computer programs.

Required Copyright Notice

First, be sure to place a copyright notice in the standard form, "© Copyright 1984, Video Games of America, All Rights Reserved," on the screen display of the game while it is in the "attract mode." Such a notice is usually placed at the bottom of the screen, and may go on and off as the various states of the attract mode change. The 1984 Videotronics case held that it cannot appear randomly, and must always display under the same conditions. It does not have to be there constantly, however. If your game is a fixed handheld device such as some of the recent Japanese imports, it is sufficient to affix the notice permanently on the frame of the screen.

Optional Copyright Notices

In addition, you might want to have the initial stage of the "play mode" display the copyright notice on the screen for a few seconds after the game begins. Some authors have this notice appear on the screen every time the play mode reaches a new level of difficulty. There really is no ironclad rule, other than the fact that it is better to be safe than sorry by displaying notices adequately, yet discreetly.

Copyright Notices on the Chips

If your game is embedded in a ROM or a PROM, it is important that you also place the copyright notice on the top of the chip, usually by white-stamping ink or silk-screening paints. Because of the size of the chip, you may have to abbreviate the notice to "© 1984 Video Games," which is perfectly legal so long as the notice is reasonably clear and the name or abbreviation you use is sufficient to identify your company. It is unwise to use a stick-on label. The law requires that the notice be in a permanent form, and a removable label does not meet that rule.

Copyright Notices inside the Program

Finally, place an abbreviated copyright notice in your game in ASCII literal characters in the actual binary code at the beginning of the contents of the chip. ASCII literals are a form of data that remain as alphanumeric characters even when compiled or assembled into object code. While placement of this notice is not absolutely necessary, it will prevent software pirates from arguing that they did not know the program contained in the chip was copyrighted since all they saw was the program "dumped" out onto a typewritten page in object code. It may also help at a later date in the event your notice on the outside of the chip is removed by someone.

Even if you start distributing your video game without proper copyright notices, you may nevertheless be able to correct this error if you act promptly.

Copyright Notices in Source Code

If you wish to treat the source code of the video-game computer program as a published work, it is important that at least the beginning page of the source listings always has the standard copyright notice printed on it. Where you wish to treat the source code as an unpublished work (which I think is the better alternative), then you should use an unpublished work copyright notice that includes a trade-secret notice. Bear in mind that very few people will ordinarily see this source code, so that you will have an excellent case for trade-secret protection if you follow the suggestions in Chapter 4.

REGISTERING A VIDEO GAME

It is important that you take the precaution of registering the video game with the Copyright Office both as a computer program/literary work and as an audiovisual work.

Register the Program as a Literary Work

First, protect the actual program by preparing a Form TX for the computer program. All the registration procedures in Chapter 6 apply to the computer program, including preparation and filing of the program listing. Whatever you do, don't fail to take this simple step, since the computer program for your game is so easily registered under the copyright laws. Choose whether to register the actual source or the object code, complete the Form TX, and send it in to the Copyright Office with the standard fee and your actual pages of program listings.

Videotape the Audiovisual Work

Equally important, prepare for the second step of registering the video game as an audiovisual work on Form PA, by setting up a video camera and video-taping system using standard VHS or Beta cartridges. Proceed to tape all of the visual and aural effects on the screen in the "attract mode." Then record a representative sample of ten or more minutes of the "play mode." Start with the beginning and then tape a few minutes of play in each stage of difficulty. The important thing is to have a good solid video-tape record of what the game looks like as a player works through all the normal stages. Then make a copy of the videotape for yourself (so you have one for possible future litigation), and send the videotape itself to the Copyright Office as your deposit.

The Copyright Office will not have your actual game, so what you are doing is giving them enough identifying portions for them to determine the originality and scope of the game, as well as all of the characters, sounds, important scenes, and stages involved. They will not return your tape after examination, since it becomes part of their permanent records. The value of keeping a complete tape of all stages of the game is that you will have evidence, in case of a later infringement, of exactly what the game does as it progresses, so you can fight copiers who only used parts of your game.

Prepare a Synopsis of the Events

Once you have made the tape, you must also prepare a written synopsis of the audiovisual events depicted on your tape, for the purpose of helping the examiner understand what he or she is looking at and hearing. The synopsis must give the examiner a reasonable indication of what is going on in the game, as depicted on the tape. Alternatively you may record a running commentary on the tape, as long as this does not block out the aural effects. However, the Copyright Office prefers the written synopsis explaining the audiovisual scenes.

Preparing to File Form PA and Deposits

Once you have prepared the tapes and the synopsis, you must complete Form PA, based on the instructions set forth below and the sample forms provided. No book can anticipate every question or fact that may apply to your registration, so you must think carefully about the suggested forms, read the directions provided by the Copyright Office with Form PA, and insert the appropriate information.

Request Special Relief.   Because your tape is not a copy of the entire game, you must request, in your letter of transmittal, that the Copyright Office accept the filing under the provisions of their "Special Relief From Deposit Requirements" rule, which is found in § 202.20(d) of their regulations. This bureaucratic requirement may be eliminated in the future by modification of the deposit regulations, since all video games require special relief. Your request for special relief will nearly always be granted, since there is no other way you can comply with the deposit requirements.

Unlike movies, books, and other written material, the Library of Congress does not normally receive and retain the video game tape deposit from the Copyright Office for its reference library. Under present rules, your deposit will be destroyed in five years unless you request it be held longer. There is apparently some possibility that this will change in the near future, since both video games and computer programs are part of the cultural history of our country, which should be placed in permanent historical collections like the Library of Congress.

Filing Forms TX and PA with Deposits

After you have completed Form PA, the video tape, the written synopsis of the tape, and your letter requesting special relief from the deposit requirements, send them all in the same package with the ten dollar registration fee to the Copyright Office. The Copyright Office takes about three months to complete the registration process, but much depends on how well you have filled in the form and the explanation you provide about the game in your transmittal letter. (Where speed is important, see Chapter 6 for possible special handling.)

While you may include in the same package Form TX, an additional ten dollars for filing it, and the program listing for the computer program, it is best not to do so. The computer program is examined by the Literary Section and the tape and other material by the Performing Arts Section of the Copyright Office.

Modified Video Games
and Derivative Works

If you change your video game materially, so it looks, sounds, or operates differently from the original game, you should file a subsequent registration for it on both Form TX and Form PA. If your changes are primarily in the computer program, you would only file Form TX; but if the changes are mainly audiovisual, you would only file Form PA.

Remember that you need to explain clearly to the examiner in your covering letter how the game is changed and what aspects, in particular, are different. Keep in mind that the subsequent filing covers only the changes and that you must rely on the original registration for protection of the earlier portions of the work.

If you have a derivative work, because of new features, characters or other reasons, the preparation of the tape, synopsis, and program listings should be easier, since your second tape and your new program listings would normally only cover the changed parts. This tape might only last for three or four minutes, and you might have only ten pages of new program. However, you will still have to complete the forms, request special relief, and perform all the other steps, just as if you were filing originally for registration.

Can You Prevent Copies in Another Media?

You may be able to prevent others from using your video-game sequences, arrangements, characters, or sounds in another medium, such as books illustrated with the characters of your game. Technically, what is being protected is the pictorial expression of the character, and not the character itself—in other words, how it customarily looks. For example, in Publications International, Ltd. v. Bally Mfg. Corp. the book publisher was held to have infringed the PAC-MAN copyright by copying elements of that game, which included the images of the characters.

On the other hand, the Atari vs. Amusement World case held that where similarities are unavoidable, given the idea of a particular game, use of these elements does not constitute infringement. Amusement World developed a space game called "Meteors," which was very similar to that of Atari's "Asteroids" game, yet the court held it could not preclude the new game even though "to put it bluntly, defendants took plaintiff's idea." Since ideas are not protected by the copyright laws, a work may not be protectable where the expression and the idea are so close as to be one and the same.

The case of Atari v. North American Philips Consumer Electronics is even more instructive. Philips attempted to develop a PAC-MAN look-a-like called K.C. Munchkin, which had many similarities and some differences. Atari and Midway successfully stopped Philips from distribution of this game because of what the appellate court called "the substantial appropriation of the PAC-MAN characters." The decision says that it is the "audio component and the concrete details of the visual presentation" that constitute the copyrightable expression of the game. The decision concluded that it was the "total concept and feel" of PAC-MAN™ repeated in K.C. Munchkin that caused the problem, and made the latter substantially similar to PAC-MAN. The court prohibited the sale of the competitive program.

FILLING OUT FORM PA—
A FAIRLY SIMPLE EXAMPLE

A completed Form PA registration for an audiovisual work in the form of a video game might look like the following:

Step by Step through Form PA

The above form assumes that the video game was co-authored by two individuals, is the original work, and that there are no special problems. Now let's go through the form, item by item.

Item 1. The Copyright Office requires that you give any work you register a name of some sort, so it can be identified. Form PA also requires information about previous names for the same work, if any exist; you may omit answers where that information is not relevant, as here. You must describe the nature of the work so the examiner can instantly see whether you have used the correct form, and so it can be classified.

FORM PA
UNITED STATES COPYRIGHT OFFICE

REGISTRATION NUMBER

	PA	PAU

EFFECTIVE DATE OF REGISTRATION

Month	Day	Year

DO NOT WRITE ABOVE THIS LINE. IF YOU NEED MORE SPACE, USE A SEPARATE CONTINUATION SHEET.

1

TITLE OF THIS WORK ▼

SPACE STATION SEVEN

PREVIOUS OR ALTERNATIVE TITLES ▼

NONE

NATURE OF THIS WORK ▼ See instructions

AUDIOVISUAL WORK IN VIDEO GAME

2

a **NAME OF AUTHOR ▼**

I. M. Martian

DATES OF BIRTH AND DEATH
Year Born ▼ 1940   Year Died ▼

Was this contribution to the work a "work made for hire"?
☐ Yes
☒ No

AUTHOR'S NATIONALITY OR DOMICILE
Name of Country
OR { Citizen of ▶ _____
Domiciled in ▶ __USA__

WAS THIS AUTHOR'S CONTRIBUTION TO THE WORK
Anonymous?   ☐ Yes ☒ No
Pseudonymous? ☐ Yes ☒ No
If the answer to either of these questions is "Yes," see detailed instructions

NATURE OF AUTHORSHIP Briefly describe nature of the material created by this author in which copyright is claimed. ▼
Visual effects

NOTE

Under the law the "author" of a "work made for hire" is generally the employer, not the employee (see instructions) For any part of this work that was "made for hire" check "Yes" in the space provided, give the employer (or other person for whom the work was prepared) as "Author" of that part, and leave the space for dates of birth and death blank.

b **NAME OF AUTHOR ▼**

A. Lotta Noise

DATES OF BIRTH AND DEATH
Year Born ▼ 1945   Year Died ▼

Was this contribution to the work a "work made for hire"?
☐ Yes
☐ No

AUTHOR'S NATIONALITY OR DOMICILE
Name of country USA
OR { Citizen of ▶ _____
Domiciled in ▶ _____

WAS THIS AUTHOR'S CONTRIBUTION TO THE WORK
Anonymous?   ☐ Yes ☒ No
Pseudonymous? ☐ Yes ☒ No
If the answer to either of these questions is "Yes," see detailed instructions

NATURE OF AUTHORSHIP Briefly describe nature of the material created by this author in which copyright is claimed. ▼
Aural effects

c **NAME OF AUTHOR ▼**

DATES OF BIRTH AND DEATH
Year Born ▼   Year Died ▼

Was this contribution to the work a "work made for hire"?
☐ Yes
☐ No

AUTHOR'S NATIONALITY OR DOMICILE
Name of Country
OR { Citizen of ▶ _____
Domiciled in ▶ _____

WAS THIS AUTHOR'S CONTRIBUTION TO THE WORK
Anonymous?   ☐ Yes ☐ No
Pseudonymous? ☐ Yes ☐ No
If the answer to either of these questions is "Yes," see detailed instructions

NATURE OF AUTHORSHIP Briefly describe nature of the material created by this author in which copyright is claimed. ▼

3

YEAR IN WHICH CREATION OF THIS WORK WAS COMPLETED This information must be given in all cases.
1983 ◄ Year

DATE AND NATION OF FIRST PUBLICATION OF THIS PARTICULAR WORK
Complete this information ONLY if this work has been published.
Month ▶ 3   Day ▶ 17   Year ▶ 83
USA ◄ Nation

4

COPYRIGHT CLAIMANT(S) Name and address must be given even if the claimant is the same as the author given in space 2.▼

I. M. Martian and A. Lotta Noise
c/o G. Gervaise Davis III, Esq.
P. O. Box 3080, Monterey, CA. 93942

See instructions before completing this space

TRANSFER If the claimant(s) named here in space 4 are different from the author(s) named in space 2, give a brief statement of how the claimant(s) obtained ownership of the copyright.▼

APPLICATION RECEIVED

ONE DEPOSIT RECEIVED

TWO DEPOSITS RECEIVED

REMITTANCE NUMBER AND DATE

DO NOT WRITE HERE OFFICE USE ONLY

MORE ON BACK ▶ • Complete all applicable spaces (numbers 5-9) on the reverse side of this page
• See detailed instructions.   • Sign the form at line 8

DO NOT WRITE HERE

Page 1 of ___ pages

EXAMINED BY	**FORM PA**
CHECKED BY	
☐ CORRESPONDENCE Yes	FOR COPYRIGHT OFFICE USE ONLY
☐ DEPOSIT ACCOUNT FUNDS USED	

DO NOT WRITE ABOVE THIS LINE. IF YOU NEED MORE SPACE, USE A SEPARATE CONTINUATION SHEET.

PREVIOUS REGISTRATION Has registration for this work, or for an earlier version of this work, already been made in the Copyright Office?
☐ Yes ☒ No If your answer is "Yes," why is another registration being sought? (Check appropriate box) ▼
☐ This is the first published edition of a work previously registered in unpublished form.
☐ This is the first application submitted by this author as copyright claimant.
☐ This is a changed version of the work, as shown by space 6 on this application.
If your answer is "Yes," give: **Previous Registration Number** ▼   **Year of Registration** ▼

DERIVATIVE WORK OR COMPILATION Complete both space 6a & 6b for a derivative work; complete only 6b for a compilation.
a. Preexisting Material Identify any preexisting work or works that this work is based on or incorporates. ▼

b. Material Added to This Work Give a brief, general statement of the material that has been added to this work and in which copyright is claimed. ▼

See instructions before completing this space

DEPOSIT ACCOUNT If the registration fee is to be charged to a Deposit Account established in the Copyright Office, give name and number of Account.
Name ▼   **Account Number** ▼

CORRESPONDENCE Give name and address to which correspondence about this application should be sent.   Name Address Apt City State Zip ▼

     G. Gervaise Davis III, Esq.
     Box 3080
     Monterey, California 93942

Be sure to give your daytime phone ◄ number

Area Code & Telephone Number ▶   408/649-1122

CERTIFICATION* I, the undersigned, hereby certify that I am the
Check only one ▼
☐ author
☐ other copyright claimant
☐ owner of exclusive right(s)
☒ authorized agent of   I. M. Martian and A. Lotta Noise
     Name of author or other copyright claimant, or owner of exclusive right(s) ▲

of the work identified in this application and that the statements made
by me in this application are correct to the best of my knowledge.

Typed or printed name and date ▼ If this is a published work, this date must be the same as or later than the date of publication given in space 3.

     G. Gervaise Davis III   date ▶ March 25, 1983

Handwritten signature (X) ▼   *G. Gervaise Davis III*

MAIL CERTIFI-CATE TO		
MAIL CERTIFI-CATE TO	Name ▼ M & C Video Games, A Partnership	**Have you:** • Completed all necessary spaces? • Signed your application in space 8?
Certificate will be mailed in window envelope	Number/Street/Apartment Number ▼ 24 Galaxy Way	• Enclosed check or money order for $10 payable to Register of Copyrights? • Enclosed your deposit material with the application and fee?
	City/State/ZIP ▼ Sea Beach, California 99999	**MAIL TO:** Register of Copyrights Library of Congress Washington D.C. 20559

* 17 U.S.C. § 506(e) Any person who knowingly makes a false representation of a material fact in the application for copyright registration provided for by section 409, or in any written statement filed in connection with the application, shall be fined not more than $2,500.

Sept. 1982—300,000

Item 2.   Where the author is a natural person, you must provide his or her name, date of birth (and death, if deceased), citizenship or domicile, and a description of the nature of the author's contribution. Since registrations are indexed by name, it is important to use the author's full name for best identification. The dates of birth and death are again for identification, since the life of the copyright depends, in the case of natural persons, on these dates. As a condition of obtaining U.S. protection, the author must meet certain citizenship requirements; or be covered by treaty; or a publication have occurred in the U.S.

Where there is more than one author, specifying the nature of the contribution assists in classifying and separating the rights of authors. This classification may have little significance in a single-author video game, but might in a movie where there are often many authors of parts of the movie. Do not include anything relating to the computer programming aspects of the game here, for these belong only on the Form TX. The "work made for hire" section concerns works created for an employer or specially created for particular uses belong to the employer. (The next example form deals with this in more detail.) Note that you must provide all this information for each co-author involved.

Item 3.   The year of creation is when the work was completed in the form you are presently registering it. This would be when you first had a working version ready to sell or license out to others. Do not consider earlier versions that may have already been registered, or perhaps were abandoned. The date of first publication is when you first distributed the game to the public, or offered to do so. This date is important since if you register within three months of first publication you get protection dating back to the creation date. If you wait beyond that point, the protection only dates from the "Effective Date of Registration," which is when you filed it with the Copyright Office in proper form. You must also also state the country in which the game was first published, since this affects rights under copyright treaties.

Item 4.   This question ascertains whether the original authors are now claiming the copyright, or whether others are doing so on the basis of a transfer of ownership after creation of the work. The address is required so that others can later reach the claimant to obtain permission, for example, to license the work. If there was a transfer, the explanation of the transaction would be shown here (as it is in our second example form that follows). It might read, "By transfer of all rights in written assignment." In such a case, you must file the assignment for record with the Copyright Office in order to bring an infringement action based upon that assignment, but not otherwise.

Item 5.   This information tells the Copyright Office whether this work is claimed as an original work, or whether there is prior material that should be referred to, such as an earlier work.

Item 6.   Since the previous answer was negative, this does not apply. If you were registering a new version, you would explain here how this one differs from the previous one.

Item 7.   This is usually applicable only to companies and law firms. It is not usually applicable for individuals filing only occasionally. The second section tells the Copyright Office who to direct any questions or problems to, in this case, the attorney. You may file your own registration application without an attorney, but most people enlist the help of an attorney the first few times.

Item 8.   This certification must be completed and manually signed by one of listed persons, or it will be rejected by the Copyright Office. Be sure you fill in the date.

Item 9.   It is to this address that the Copyright Office sends your completed, filed registration. Since the Copyright Office uses a window envelope, be certain the address is within the boundaries of the window. That office will send the registration wherever you designate, so carefully consider this address. The certificate is valuable and easily lost or misplaced, so you may want it sent to your place of business, or to your attorney. However, you can always get a certified copy from the Copyright Office at a later date.

Miscellaneous Information

Use Only Official Forms.   You absolutely have to use the Copyright Office forms and cannot use photocopies. The forms are printed on specially processed paper that is supposed to last for 100 years or more. The Copyright Office will reject any registration application prepared on copies of the forms. You can obtain forms free from "The Copyright Office, Library of Congress, Washington, D.C. 20559." It usually takes at least a week to get them, and sometimes up to three or four weeks.

Additional Information; Correcting Errors.   Should you run out of space on the form itself, and you wish to provide additional information, there is a continuation form attached to the official instruction form blank, called Form PA/CON. If you discover errors or omissions after you have filed Form PA, there is also a Form CA, Application for Supplementary Copyright Registration, which can be used for the purpose of correcting or supplementing the original registration form. Do not, however, use Form CA to file a new application for a new version.

What Happens to the Application Form?

Processing Procedures.   Once the Copyright Office receives your Form PA, with the proper fee ($10.00), the video tape, the written synopsis of the tape, and your letter with any additional information, it is logged in and assigned a processing number, briefly checked over for completeness, and then assigned to an examiner from the appropriate section of the Copyright Office to see that it meets all legal requirements.

Registration Numbers.   If the form is entirely correct and the examiner believes the work is appropriate for registration, a registration number is assigned to it, the seal of the Copyright Office is affixed on the top left corner, it is officially filed and indexed, and eventually a permanent copy will be returned to the person listed in the window box at item 9. This usually takes three or four months.

Deposits Not Returned.   Your videotape will not be returned to you. Most deposits will be disposed of at the end of five years. You may, however, request that the Copyright Office maintain your deposit for the full term of the copyright, if there is some reason to do so. It was suggested earlier that you maintain a duplicate of the videotape you file. It is possible to obtain a certified copy of the deposit tape, which you can later use to prove what the game looked and sounded like in the event of an infringement action.

Filing Delays.   Where you have followed our advice and registered both the audiovisual work and the computer program, do not be surprised if the two registrations do not come back at the same time, since they are processed by different groups of examiners. If you haven't heard from them after three or four months, you should write to them.

FILLING OUT FORM PA— AN EMPLOYER OR A BUSINESS

The next example of a Form PA Application assumes that the owner of the copyright is the employer for whom the work was prepared by its employees, and that the work being registered is a new version of an older work that has been significantly upgraded. It also assumes the application was filed by in-house legal counsel for the employer, whose former company has just been acquired by a larger one. Few applications would have all these complications, but they are included here for purposes of illustration.

Step by Step through Form PA

Item 1.   This lists the name of the work and the fact it is an audiovisual work in the form of a video game. It is also necessary to give the name under which the work was originally registered since this filing is for a derivative work, as is indicated in more detail on the second page of the form. This is important because of the cross-indexing system used for filing copyrights.

FORM PA
UNITED STATES COPYRIGHT OFFICE

REGISTRATION NUMBER

PA	PAU

EFFECTIVE DATE OF REGISTRATION

Month	Day	Year

DO NOT WRITE ABOVE THIS LINE. IF YOU NEED MORE SPACE, USE A SEPARATE CONTINUATION SHEET.

1 TITLE OF THIS WORK ▼

WAR OF THE WORLDS

PREVIOUS OR ALTERNATIVE TITLES ▼

STAR TRACK

NATURE OF THIS WORK ▼ See instructions

AUDIOVISUAL WORK IN VIDEO GAME FORM

2 a NAME OF AUTHOR ▼

Small Town Software, Inc.

DATES OF BIRTH AND DEATH
Year Born ▼   Year Died ▼

Was this contribution to the work a "work made for hire"?
☒ Yes
☐ No

AUTHOR'S NATIONALITY OR DOMICILE
Name of Country
OR { Citizen of ▶ US
Domiciled in ▶

WAS THIS AUTHOR'S CONTRIBUTION TO THE WORK
Anonymous? ☐ Yes ☐ No
Pseudonymous? ☐ Yes ☐ No
If the answer to either of these questions is "Yes," see detailed instructions

NOTE
Under the law, the "author" of a "work made for hire" is generally the employer, not the employee (see instructions). For any part of this work that was "made for hire" check "Yes" in the space provided, give the employer (or other person for whom the work was prepared) as "Author" of that part, and leave the space for dates of birth and death blank.

NATURE OF AUTHORSHIP Briefly describe nature of the material created by this author in which copyright is claimed. ▼

b NAME OF AUTHOR ▼

DATES OF BIRTH AND DEATH
Year Born ▼   Year Died ▼

Was this contribution to the work a "work made for hire"?
☐ Yes
☐ No

AUTHOR'S NATIONALITY OR DOMICILE
Name of country
OR { Citizen of ▶
Domiciled in ▶

WAS THIS AUTHOR'S CONTRIBUTION TO THE WORK
Anonymous? ☐ Yes ☐ No
Pseudonymous? ☐ Yes ☐ No
If the answer to either of these questions is "Yes," see detailed instructions

NATURE OF AUTHORSHIP Briefly describe nature of the material created by this author in which copyright is claimed. ▼

c NAME OF AUTHOR ▼

DATES OF BIRTH AND DEATH
Year Born ▼   Year Died ▼

Was this contribution to the work a "work made for hire"?
☐ Yes
☐ No

AUTHOR'S NATIONALITY OR DOMICILE
Name of Country
OR { Citizen of ▶
Domiciled in ▶

WAS THIS AUTHOR'S CONTRIBUTION TO THE WORK
Anonymous? ☐ Yes ☐ No
Pseudonymous? ☐ Yes ☐ No
If the answer to either of these questions is "Yes," see detailed instructions

NATURE OF AUTHORSHIP Briefly describe nature of the material created by this author in which copyright is claimed. ▼

3 YEAR IN WHICH CREATION OF THIS WORK WAS COMPLETED This information must be given in all cases.
1982 ◀ Year

DATE AND NATION OF FIRST PUBLICATION OF THIS PARTICULAR WORK
Complete this information ONLY If this work has been published.
Month ▶ 2   Day ▶ 22   Year ▶ 83   ◀ Nation

4 COPYRIGHT CLAIMANT(S) Name and address must be given even if the claimant is the same as the author given in space 2.▼

Conglomerates of America, Inc.
One World Way
New York, New York 10001

See instructions before completing this space

TRANSFER If the claimant(s) named here in space 4 are different from the author(s) named in space 2, give a brief statement of how the claimant(s) obtained ownership of the copyright.▼
Transferred by operation of law as result of acquisition of author company in statutory merger on March 25, 1983

APPLICATION RECEIVED

ONE DEPOSIT RECEIVED

TWO DEPOSITS RECEIVED

REMITTANCE NUMBER AND DATE

DO NOT WRITE HERE
OFFICE USE ONLY

MORE ON BACK ▶ • Complete all applicable spaces (numbers 5-9) on the reverse side of this page
• See detailed instructions • Sign the form at line 8

DO NOT WRITE HERE

EXAMINED BY _____

CHECKED BY _____

☐ CORRESPONDENCE
   Yes

☐ DEPOSIT ACCOUNT
   FUNDS USED

FORM PA

FOR
COPYRIGHT
OFFICE
USE
ONLY

DO NOT WRITE ABOVE THIS LINE. IF YOU NEED MORE SPACE, USE A SEPARATE CONTINUATION SHEET.

PREVIOUS REGISTRATION Has registration for this work, or for an earlier version of this work, already been made in the Copyright Office?

☒ Yes ☐ No If your answer is "Yes," why is another registration being sought? (Check appropriate box) ▼

☐ This is the first published edition of a work previously registered in unpublished form.

☐ This is the first application submitted by this author as copyright claimant.

☒ This is a changed version of the work, as shown by space 6 on this application.

If your answer is "Yes," give: **Previous Registration Number ▼**   **Year of Registration ▼**

          PA 23456   1982

5

DERIVATIVE WORK OR COMPILATION Complete both space 6a & 6b for a derivative work, complete only 6b for a compilation.
a. **Preexisting Material** Identify any preexisting work or works that this work is based on or incorporates. ▼

Original game published by Small Town Software involved two space stations, six kinds of Klingons, four types of spaceships and was in three colors.

b. **Material Added to This Work** Give a brief, general statement of the material that has been added to this work and in which copyright is claimed.▼

New audiovisual effects represented by six colors, additional space stations, additional playing objects in form of laser driven rockets, and totally new mother ship.

See instructions before completing this space

6

DEPOSIT ACCOUNT If the registration fee is to be charged to a Deposit Account established in the Copyright Office, give name and number of Account.
Name ▼   **Account Number ▼**

Conglomerates of America, Inc.   007007

7

CORRESPONDENCE Give name and address to which correspondence about this application should be sent. Name/Address/Apt/City/State/Zip ▼

James P. Legal, Esq.
Legal Department, Mail Stop 34
One World Way
New York, New York 10001

Area Code & Telephone Number ▶   212/555-0002

Be sure to give your daytime phone ◀ number

CERTIFICATION* I, the undersigned, hereby certify that I am the
Check only one ▼

☐ author

☐ other copyright claimant

☐ owner of exclusive right(s)

☒ authorized agent of _Conglomerates of America, Inc._
          Name of author or other copyright claimant, or owner of exclusive right(s) ▲

of the work identified in this application and that the statements made by me in this application are correct to the best of my knowledge.

Typed or printed name and date ▼ If this is a published work, this date must be the same as or later than the date of publication given in space 3.

James P. Legal, VP-Legal   date ▶   4-1-83

8

Handwritten signature (X) ▼

James P. Legal

MAIL CERTIFICATE TO

Name ▼ Conglomerates of America, Inc.
Legal Department, 88th Floor, Mail Stop 34-57

Number/Street/Apartment Number ▼
One World Way

City/State/ZIP ▼
New York, New York 10001

Certificate will be mailed in window envelope

Have you:
● Completed all necessary spaces?
● Signed your application in space 8?
● Enclosed check or money order for $10 payable to Register of Copyrights?
● Enclosed your deposit material with the application and fee?

MAIL TO: Register of Copyrights Library of Congress. Washington DC 20559

9

* 17 U S C § 506(e) Any person who knowingly makes a false representation of a material fact in the application for copyright registration provided for by section 409, or in any written statement filed in connection with the application, shall be fined not more than $2,500

Item 2.   Since this is a work for hire, prepared by employees of the corporate author, the names of the actual persons who worked on the program and the video game are not listed. As is explained in more detail in the other copyright chapters, the person or entity who commissioned or paid for the work is deemed to be the owner of a work for hire. Under § 302(c) of the Copyright Law the term of a copyright on a work for hire is either seventy-five years from the date of first publication or one hundred years from first creation, so that the dates of birth and death of the human authors are irrelevant. You must however list the "citizenship" of the corporate author, which is "U.S." if the corporation is incorporated in the United States.

Item 3.   This information is given to determine the term of the copyright. You must list the creation date in all cases, and the publication date if the work is published. Any video game in public use or on sale is, of course, a published work of the audiovisual category. You might claim that the computer program was not published, if it is a trade secret. (See Chapter 4.)

Item 4.   Notice that here the claimant of the copyright is different than the author, so a different name is listed. For this reason, the explanation in the "Transfer" box must be given. It is best to provide full information here, continuing on the Copyright Office Form PA/CON if there is not enough room on the basic form, and to supplement the form in the accompanying correspondence. In this example, the acquisition of the copyright-owner company occurred after the publication, so that a formal assignment document or some indication of transfer (like merger papers) will be necessary if the chain of title to the work is to be complete. The law requires that documents of assignment be in writing to be valid, and that these be recorded with the Copyright Office in order to maintain a legal action on the copyright.

Item 5.   Since there is an earlier registration here, the proper boxes must be checked; the earlier registration number and year must be given so that the examiner can find and verify the original information quickly.

Item 6.   As stated in the text, the registration of the original work covers all material in it, and this new registration of the derivative work covers only the changed material. The information set out here is necessary for the permanent records of the Copyright Office. From this explanation, both the examiner and the public can tell just what type of things were changed or added. It is possible that the examiner might decide that the work is not sufficiently different to merit a new filing and reject the work for lack of orginality. It is important, for this reason, to make clear in this space exactly what changes or additions were made to the original work.

Item 7. Because the claimant files many registrations with the Copyright Office it maintains a "Deposit Account," which is simply a fund held by that office against which filings may be made. This procedure is very convenient for law firms and large companies. The box for correspondence is, again, used by the Copyright Office as the source of information in the event of problems with the registration.

Item 8. As with the previous example form, this is being filed by an agent of the author or claimant, the attorney for the company, so the proper box must be checked and the blank filled in with the name of (in this case) the claimant. It must always be signed by the person listed, and dated, or it will be rejected at the Copyright Office in the preliminary examination stage.

Item 9. This is self-explanatory. Do not forget to complete this box since it will list the place to which your valuable certificate of registration will be mailed.

SUMMARY

If you bear the above information in mind and if you keep close tabs on the rapidly developing case law, then protecting video games under the Copyright Law becomes a fairly easy process. However, since the law is still developing there will be new questions and answers from time to time, so you may want to discuss protecting your games with an experienced and competent attorney.

It is especially critical that you remember to register both the actual computer program and the audiovisual work as separate works, since from a legal standpoint two separate works are involved here.

The law is definitely not settled on the issue of how much protection is accorded by copyright registration to work threatened by later look-a-likes. The cases we have discussed suggest that the sequences, arrangements, characters, and sounds are all protected, but each case will always have different questions of fact and the final result will depend on the impression on the user.

There is continuing legal argument over the extent to which the expression of ideas can and should be protected. For example, it is unlikely that the creators of PAC-MAN could now protect the concept of a "maze" or even the idea of gaining power from eating "power pills." However, the unique characters in the game probably are protectable since they are pictorial expressions of the idea, just as the Mickey Mouse character is the clear property of Walt Disney Studios, at least until the copyright runs out. If you are writing a video game, originality in appearance, sound, and concepts is not only a better legal approach, but also more likely to be more commercially successful.

While this chapter has not discussed the legal steps that your attorney can take to protect your video game once it is registered, the subject is covered in Chapter 18 in this book. You should also consider the additional protection accorded by use of trademarks and trade names associated with your game. If your game becomes well known, imitators will try to copy the name as well, and you may have the right to stop them on this basis alone. On the subject of trademarks and computer programs, you may wish to read Chapter 10.

As you can see, there are many ways in which you can take the vital first steps toward the protection of your programming efforts. But be watchful for changes in the law, since the law cannot and does not stand still in an industry as dynamic as the video-game bonanza.

8

Unresolved Problems with Copyrights and Software

There is nothing more difficult to plan, more doubtful of
success, or more dangerous to manage than the creation
of a new system. For the initiator has the enmity of all
who would profit by the preservation of the old
institutions and merely lukewarm defenders in those who
would gain by the new ones.

Nicolo Machiavelli, 1513.

NEW SYSTEMS, NEW TECHNOLOGY, AND NEW LAWS

The software publisher or author of today is faced with a new 1976
Copyright Act that became effective on January 1, 1978; a microcomputer industry that only really got started in about 1978; a technology that
seems to change dramatically every year at an ever-increasing rate; and a
slow-moving legal system that cannot match the pace of such swift
change. It is a recipe for turmoil. Add to this a society that is in the process
of converting from an Industrial Age based on the printed word to an
Information Age based on the electronic word. In light of this it seems
only fitting to note the timing of Machiavelli's words, coming shortly after
the invention of movable type and the printing press. Human beings seem
to change very little.

Fortunately, in late 1983 and during 1984 a series of critically
important court cases interpreting the copyright laws were decided.
These decisions form the basis of some of this analysis, and allow us to
catalog some of the major open questions that still remain in this field.

THE OPEN ISSUES CONCERNING
SOFTWARE COPYRIGHTS

A number of unresolved legal issues remain in the field of copyright protection for software. While some are highly technical questions, any one of them could have a substantial dollars and cents effect on your software business. There are also some issues that depend almost totally on the course of future computer and communications technology and not the law, and these are dealt with in Chapter 19.

When you have completed this chapter, you will have a better idea of the probable answers to the following legal questions and of a number of related issues:

- What forms of computer software (source code, object code, ROM, Microcode, etc.) are protectible under the present copyright law, as interpreted by recent cases?

- How far does copyright law go toward protecting systems, procedures, and formats, notwithstanding the language of the new copyright law and some of the cases?

- How far can you go in copying algorithms, structures, and the general appearance of another's program?

- Does the Copyright Act preempt trade-secret protection, and if not, what effect does registering source code have on trade secrecy?

- What alternatives exist to depositing source code with the Copyright Office, and what are the consequences of using such alternatives?

- Can anything be done about software "rental" and similar schemes?

Some other major issues, concerning the licensing of software, are dealt with in Chapter 11, including the enforceability of "break-open" package licenses.

THE ELECTRONIC WORD
VERSUS THE PRINTED WORD

Most of the software copyright questions facing courts and lawyers today are brought about by the abrupt change from working with a copyright law intended to protect the *visible* written word into a law stretched to fit an invisible, electronic world—a world where knowledge, information, and these same printed words are *invisibly* transmitted, stored, and retrieved.

In the new Information Age the legal issues of society are focusing more clearly on the ownership of knowledge, information, processes, and systems, such as software. Since these highly valuable assets are almost entirely intangible, they are instantaneously communicable from point to point. Much of their value is dependent upon timely distribution and use before they become obsolete. If these intangible properties cannot be protected readily from misappropriation, there is little economic incentive to develop them. Furthermore, their intrinsic value per copy is much greater than books, music, and even motion picture films, while their cost of reproduction is insignificant compared to their inherent economic value. Worst of all the means of their instant reproduction is available to almost anyone.

STRIKING A BALANCE— THREE BASIC LEGAL ISSUES

The Information Age seeks to encourage the flow of information and knowledge while at the same time protecting and compensating authors and originators of that knowledge in order to encourage such activity. Striking a socially acceptable balance here means compromising and finding an existing legal theory to shelter these new forms of wealth. The new Copyright Act was an attempt by Congress to deal with these questions. It has not yet been entirely successful, and may require the assistance of a number of interpretive court decisions.

Three underlying legal issues need to be addressed in order to answer the questions posed at the outset of this chapter:

1. Was software intended to be protected by the new copyright law, and if so, how far should such protection extend?
2. How to reconcile the fact that software, which makes a machine work, is protected by copyright law with the principle that copyright does not protect ideas, processes, and systems?
3. How far does copyright law go toward permitting the copyright owner to control distribution and use of the copyrighted software?

DID CONGRESS INTEND TO PROTECT SOFTWARE BY COPYRIGHT?

Yes. No one has ever seriously contended that Congress, after its 1980 amendment of the Copyright Act, did not intend to protect software under the copyright laws. This amendment, which added a statutory definition of a computer program to § 101 and revised § 117 to permit certain uses of programs, was added as a direct result of the 1978 study and recommendations of the National Commission on New Uses of Technology (CONTU). CONTU recommended making the copyright law "explicit that computer programs, to the extent that they embody an author's original creation, are proper subject matter of copyright." In 1984 even stronger language concerning software protection by copyright was proposed in Congress.

Source Code Versus Object Code Protection

The argument in recent video-game and software cases that only source code was intended to be protected by copyright was based on a 1908

Supreme Court case, White-Smith Music Publishing Co. v. Apollo Co. There a paper piano roll was held not to be a copy of a musical composition because it was not readable by, nor could it directly communicate with, a human being.

The Apple Computer Software Cases.   The position of Franklin Computer in Apple Computer, Inc. v. Franklin Computer Corp. was that, because of this principle, it was not possible to obtain a copyright on a computer program in object-code form, since it was not "human readable." The 1983 opinion of the U.S. Third Circuit Court of Appeals in Apple-Franklin entirely rejected this line of argument.

Apple had sued Franklin in 1981 to stop the distribution of the Franklin computer with software that Franklin had admitted copying from object code versions of Apple's operating system and applications software, in both ROM and diskette form. The trial court refused to grant a preliminary injunction because of its uncertainty as to the copyrightability of the software in question. This case was virtually the only decision in the federal trial courts after 1979 that denied copyright protection to software. In 1979 a trial court had ruled, in Data Cash Systems, Inc. v. JS&A Group, Inc., that software in object code, in ROM, could not be protected under the 1909 Copyright Act, since it could not be visually perceived.

Object Code Is Protected.   Protection of object code was definitively established in Williams Electronics, Inc. v. Artic International, Inc., a 1982 video-game case, after an exhaustive analysis by the court of the legislative history of changes intended in the law. The defendant in Williams had argued that material had to be intelligible to humans to be copyrightable. Quoting the language of the statute itself, § 102(a), to the effect that works were protected if they could be communicated, either directly or with the aid of a machine or device, the court rejected any distinction between source and object code under the copyright law. The same conclusion had been reached in several other cases, GCA Corp. v. Chance, Midway Mfg. Co. v. Strohon, and Apple Computer, Inc. v. Formula International. (See discussion below.)

Is Object Code In ROM Protected?

The second issue raised in Apple-Franklin was whether ROM-based software was protected, since there is no way any human can "read" or directly use the object code embedded in ROM chips. Franklin argued that such chips were not intended for human use, but rather were part of the machine itself, and as such were "utilitarian objects" or machine parts. Under long-established law, such parts would not be copyrightable.

ROM Programs Are Protected.   Citing its own opinion in the Williams-Artic case, the Apple-Franklin Court summarily rejected this argument.

The Williams-Artic Court had pointed out that to protect source code but not object code in ROM would make copyright protection meaningless. It had said that the new copyright law had made clear that it made no difference what media was used to copy the work. The Apple-Franklin decision concluded this issue with the statement, "we reaffirm that a computer program in object code embedded in a ROM chip is an appropriate subject of copyright."

A number of other recent cases have come to the same conclusion. See, for example, the cases of Midway Manufacturing Co. v. Strohon, Tandy Corp. v. Personal Micro Computers, Inc., and Stern Electronics, Inc. v. Kaufman. Chapter 7 discusses some other video-game cases reaching the same result. The logic behind these decisions seems irrefutable for, as the trial judge said in Midway-Strohon, there is "no basis for concluding, in effect, that object code stored on a silicon chip may be freely copied while the same code stored on a tape or disc may not be."

New Forms of Program Storage.   We may now assume that when software is distributed in new forms of storage media, such as bubble memory, laser discs, or anything else the electronics industry can think of, it will also be protected under the copyright law. Such media is but a "data carrier" utilized to transport the object code in a form more useable by the computer. To preserve the copyright, however, it is still necessary to comply with the notice and other requirements of the copyright laws. (See Chapter 5.)

Silicon Chip Masks.   The concept of protecting silicon chip masks under the copyright laws is in no way related to protecting software, since these masks are only used in a mechanical process for the production of the actual physical chips, such as microprocessor and memory chips. After three years of industry disagreement over the form of protection to be granted chip masks, Congress in 1984 passed new sections 901 through 912 to Title 17, thus creating a unique form of semiconductor mask protection by registration with the Copyright Office, and requiring use of a new notice symbol, the letter M in a circle. The term of protection is only ten years, but is otherwise similar to a copyright.

Is Operating System Software Protected?

Having reached the conclusion that object code, in any form, is protected under the copyright laws, the courts in both the Apple-Franklin and Apple-Formula cases had before them the final argument that operating system software should not be protected. The defendants, Franklin and Formula, both asserted that an operating system is a process or system expressly excluded from protection by § 102(b) of the copyright law.

Formula, which had already lost in the trial court, contended that operating system software was not protected since it merely controlled the internal operation of the computer, which made it a "process" or an idea. It argued that such software did not communicate with the user, but with the machine, and that to be protected the software had to provide expression to the computer user. Both courts rejected the infringers' positions, on the basis that there was no support for this theory in the CONTU Report, the legislative history, decided cases, nor in the Copyright Act itself. Apple prevailed in both cases. Let's see why.

Protecting Ideas, Systems, and Processes

There has always been a conflict in the law between protecting raw ideas and their practical applications. Congress decided to protect computer programs under the Copyright Act, but did not authorize this law to be used to protect the idea or process standing alone. As Section 102(b) of the copyright law says:

> In no case does copyright protection for an original work of authorship extend to any idea, procedure, process, system, method of operation, concept, principle, or discovery, regardless of the form in which it is described, explained, illustrated, or embodied in such work.

The intent of this section was explained in the House Committee Report, which accompanied the new law in 1976:

> "Some concern has been expressed lest copyright in computer programs should extend protection to the methodology or processes adopted by the programmer, rather than merely to the 'writing' expressing his ideas. Section 102(b) is intended, among other things, to make clear that the expression adopted by the programmer is the copyrightable element in a computer program, and that the actual processes or methods embodied in the program are not within the scope of the copyright law.

In the CONTU Report mentioned earlier Commissioner John Hershey argued, in a minority report, that when the purpose of a computer program was to communicate with a computer, it should no longer be protected, *once in that form.* The majority rejected his arguments, stating that the fact "the words of a program are used ultimately in the implementation of a process should in no way affect their copyrightability." The majority report explains:

> All that copyright protection for programs, videotapes, and phonorecords means is that users may not take the works of others to operate their machines. In each instance, one is always free to make the machine do the same thing as it would if it had

the copyrighted work placed in it, but only by one's own creative effort rather than by piracy.

Congress accepted the CONTU recommendations by amending the Copyright Act in 1980 almost word for word, as suggested by CONTU, without further comment.

What the Two Apple Cases Mean

The two appellate court decisions in these cases should lay to rest the argument that a computer program has to communicate directly with the human user to be protected. Both cases made clear that the copyright applies only to the particular set of instructions, and not to the underlying computer process or even to the ideas expressed in the program. As the Apple-Formula opinion stated, "The distinction between ideas and expression is intended to prohibit the monopolization of an idea when there is a limited number of ways to express that idea."

All that the software copyright owner should have to demonstrate to overcome this issue is that there are other ways of expressing the same idea or process. However, a copyright case in 1984, involving a book about the Scrabble game, raises some doubts, which may have to be resolved in future software cases. The Franklin court had pointed out that Apple "does not seek to copyright the method which instructs the computer to perform its operating functions but only the instructions themselves."

Protecting Machine Dependent Code.   Relying upon this law, IBM in early 1984 successfully concluded a number of infringement cases against manufacturers of IBM PC "look-a-like" systems, such as Corona Data, Eagle, and Handwell, precluding each from using the Basic Input-Output System (BIOS) developed by IBM and used in the PC operating system. The BIOS software is about as close to the line dividing idea and expression as you can come, since it is totally machine dependent in the sense that the functions are the same from machine to machine but implemented differently in each computer.

Summing Up the Cases.   The entire subject can now best be summed up in this quotation from the Apple-Formula case:

Formula provides absolutely no authority for its contention that the 'expression' required in order for a computer program to be eligible for copyright protection is expression that must be communicated to the computer user when the program is run on a computer. The Copyright Act extends protection to 'original works of authorship fixed in any tangible medium of expression, now known or later developed, from which they can be perceived, reproduced, or otherwise communicated, either directly or with the aid of a machine or device.' 17 U.S.C. § 102(a). The computer program when written embodies expression; never has the Copyright Act required that the expression be communicated to a particular audience.

The courts have now spoken definitively.

HOW FAR DOES THE IDEA-VERSUS-EXPRESSION PRINCIPLE GO?

No one is yet certain how far the copyright law goes toward preventing paraphrasing, translating, and creating look-a-likes, since this gets into another aspect of the area of protecting ideas, systems, and processes. Unlike the concepts reviewed to this point, these answers are less clear.

Expressing Ideas

If I express an idea, process, or system in writing in the form of a computer program, it should be protected by the present copyright laws regardless of the use to which it is put or the form it takes in order to be used. The eligibility of computer programs under copyright law should turn only upon the originality of the work, not upon how good it is nor how it is intended to be used. As the appellate court said in Alfred Bell & Co., Ltd. v. Catalda Fine Arts, Inc.:

> All that is needed to satisfy both the Constitution and the statute is that the 'author' contributed something more than a 'merely trivial' variation, something recognizably 'his own.' . . . No matter how poor artistically the 'author's' addition, it is enough *if it be his own.* [Emphasis added.]

Originality means only that the work originated with the author. The fact the computer program includes instructions to the computer on how to do something (a process or a system) should no more preclude copyright protection for software that it does in the case of a book on how to build furniture or bake cakes. In both cases, it is the product of human authorship. On the other hand, protection of that particular program does not preclude others, who work independently, from making use of the same system or process. But they must have done this work on their own, and not lifted it from other works.

Reverse Engineering and Disassembly

One of the more interesting issues is how far one software house can go toward duplicating the appearance and functionality of another's software. Technically, there are several ways of accomplishing this objective.

One way is to disassemble an existing program to determine its logic. Hubco Data Products Corp. v. Management Assistance, Inc., involved what is sometimes called "reverse engineering." MAI manufactures and distributes an operating system containing "governors" that prevent the system from running faster than a set speed, unless the customer pays for a more powerful system. Hubco developed a program known as the Nilsson Method II, which in effect locates the governors in the MAI operating system and changes them so that it will run faster. The trial judge granted a preliminary injunction in favor of MAI, precluding Hubco from using this method or any similar method that in any way accesses or copies the MAI operating system. In effect, the court held that reverse engineering object code by reading it into a computer, in order to modify it, is an infringement of the copyright owner's rights. The ruling is clearly correct, and augurs a future method of preventing indirect piracy of software. The case was appealed but settled in 1984.

Translation from One Language to Another

Several similar or related cases are pending in the federal courts concerning the legality of translating a program from one computer language into another. For example, the case of IBM v. NCR Comten, Inc. involves alleged paraphrasing and translation of IBM's assembly-language code into the assembly-language code of NCR's subsidiary in the form of a series of communications programs. Cases like this will set precedents needed to determine the boundary between the use of an idea, not protected by copyright, and the theft of a work by paraphrasing or translating it into another computer language. As several earlier cases in the field of book publishing have ruled against the translator, the final outcome would seem favorable to prevention of this type of activity. Toksvig v. Bruce Publishing Co. and Margaret Hubbard, a 1950 case, involved translations of materials from Danish into English. This activity was enjoined.

Formal Derivatives of Programs

Chapter 6 on copyright registration discusses a related problem—namely, when a new version or release of a program becomes so different or includes so much new material that it is a derivative that should be registered as a separate work. This often arises in the context of a licensee who is permitted to create a special version of a program for a specific machine, and when the license agreement has not dealt with the derivative ownership question. Since the copyright owner is the only one permitted to create derivatives, this should not be an issue, but it often is. No one should ever grant a software license without first agreeing upon who owns any adaptations or derivatives of the licensed work. Care should be taken to see that such derivatives are in fact registered, if they have any commercial value.

Copying Appearance, Formats, and Data Structures

There is one consistent area of frustration and misunderstanding about software copyright protection. This involves the degree to which, if at all, computer formats and the order of data may be protected by copyright.

Synercom Technology Inc. v. University Computing Co., a 1978 Federal District Court case that arose in Texas, is a classic case. Synercom, the plaintiff, had spent nearly $500,000 in developing software and training customers in the use of a structural engineering program known as STRAN. It relied on copyright to protect its product, which was later substantially duplicated in form and substance by the defendant, University Computing. Synercom contended that University infringed the manuals and the input formats of the program. While concluding that the manuals were infringed, the court held that the input formats were essentially a matter of the order and sequence of data, which was not protectible. An alternative holding was that forms, in general, are not covered by the copyright laws.

Copying Ideas. This again illustrates that ideas cannot be protected, only the expression of them. It is a most difficult concept to grasp in the context of computer programs, particularly since the major value of the expression is often the exact order in which the things are done, or the form in which the data is collected, processed, and output. The painful history of the cases in this area is one of unsatisfactory answers and unresolved, perhaps even unresolvable, definitional problems. Judge Learned Hand expressed it well when he said, in the Peter Pan Fabrics case, "Obviously, no principle can be stated as to when an imitator has gone beyond copying an 'idea,' and has borrowed its 'expression.' Decisions must therefore inevitably be *ad hoc*."

In the context of computer programs, one of the arguments of Franklin in Apple v. Franklin was that operating systems and particularly the Boot ROM could not be protected by copyright, since there were only a limited number of ways of expressing the rules and systems involved in operating an Apple computer. This argument did not prevail on appeal, having been expressly rejected in several other recent cases cited above, and surely would not have been considered by the court in the recent IBM BIOS case. It is, however, another aspect of the idea-versus-expression dichotomy inherent in copyright law.

Ideas Expressed in Software. This struggle to reconcile protection of works of authorship without inhibiting the use of ideas may be seen from the fact that Microsoft's MS-DOS™ operating system was, in its initial implementation, extraordinarily similar to the design and functionality of the copyrighted CP/M® operating system of Digital Research; yet no litigation ensued. Similarly, it is obvious that nearly all the "Calc" spreadsheet programs are based on the original model of VisiCalc®, which was the first microcomputer program of this type. Under the copyright laws, there is no way to protect such an idea from use by others since it consists of a screen format and a particular way of manipulating data, neither of which are protectible as a copyrightable expression.

This distinction is difficult and becomes a serious practical problem given the necessary similarities of word processing, spreadsheets, accounting and data-base management programs. Under the principles of the earlier cases, there would seem no reliable way of protecting either a screen, input, or output format forming part of a program. Perhaps if the program were to do more than just format the data, such as analyze, extract, and project data, then some aspect of the output might be protected, but even this would be unusual. It is also frustrating to software authors who take the time and trouble to develop the program, only to have the concept borrowed by someone else. Watch for the development of further case law in this area. One argument that might be made is that the screen or other format is a "display" of the work, protected by the copyright laws.

COPYRIGHT PROTECTION AS PREEMPTING TRADE–SECRECY PROTECTION

At the end of Chapter 4 we discussed how the enactment of the 1976 Copyright Act arguably resulted in the preemption (or loss) of the right under state laws to protect software or other intellectual property by the principles of trade secrecy. If a federal law preempts state law, it supercedes it by virtue of greater coverage or by an express declaration of Congress. In Chapter 4 there are some suggestions about how you could potentially use trade-secret law and still remain consistent with copyright law. This chapter considers the matter from the vantage point of copyright law.

Section 301 does, in fact, state that after the effective date of the new copyright law, January 1, 1978:

> [A]ll legal or equitable rights that are equivalent to any of the exclusive rights within the general scope of copyright as specified by section 106 in works of authorship that are fixed in a tangible medium of expression and come within the subject matter of copyright as specified by sections 102 and 103, whether created before or after that date and whether published or unpublished, are governed exclusively by this title. Thereafter, no person is entitled to any such right or equivalent right in any such work under the common law or statutes of any State.

Thus, to use the words of the statute, the question is whether the legal principles of trade secrecy and copyright are "equivalent." Congress did not seem to think they were, since its own House Committee Report stated:

> The evolving common law rights of 'privacy,' 'publicity,' and *trade secrets* . . . would remain unaffected as long as the causes of action contain elements, such as an invasion of personal rights or a breach of trust or confidentiality, that are different in kind from copyright infringement.

The Issue Of Equivalency

"Equivalent" means virtually identical in force or function, or equal in value or purpose. Since trade secret law is intended to protect specific ideas, and systems based on the ideas, from disclosure and dissemination without permission, and copyright law is intended to encourage disclosure of the expression of an idea but to prevent copying or use without permission, any overlap would seem small. There does not seem to be any equivalency here.

The courts continue to have difficulty with this issue, however, as illustrated by a 1983 Nevada Federal District Court case, Videotronics, Inc. v. Bend Electronics. Videotronics contended that Bend Electronics had developed a competing electronic game through misappropriation of Videotronics' trade secrets. No effort had been made to copyright the program developed by Videotronics. Citing Apple Computer v. Formula International for the proposition that software in ROM is protected under the copyright laws, the court denied an injunction to Videotronics on the theory that the state law of trade secrecy had been preempted by the passage of the new copyright law. The court reached this conclusion even though it called the facts of the case "a classic case for application of the law of misappropriation," were it not for the new copyright law. Without the opportunity to review the record of evidence in the case, this decision seems to be wrong.

How Can We Seek Trade Secret
and Copyright Protection Simultaneously?

Many attorneys believe trade secrecy and copyright are not equivalent, and that they may coexist in the same work, especially when that work takes several forms. On this issue the law is in a state of flux, however, and I can only hazard my own opinions here.

Protecting Different Things. You will remember that there is a distinction in the copyright law between published and unpublished works. There is no requirement for registration of unpublished works. It is also possible to register a work in unpublished form, and then later in published form. The form of the two types of works may be different too, such as unpublished source code and published object code, in which case there are really two different types of things being protected.

The source code discloses logic, data structures, processes, and systems—all things that copyright does not protect. While the object code discloses very little except the literal expression of the program, which is exactly what copyright law is supposed to protect. If the object code is disassembled or decompiled, in order to examine the logic of the program, this should also constitute an infringement since the code is being copied for an improper purpose. Reverse engineering of trade secrets in a computer program was held in a 1984 Delaware case to be improper.

Disclosure by Distribution. In considering this issue, the argument has been made, as by the trial judge in Videotronics, that once the object code version of the program is distributed there is no longer a "secret," since the information is then available to the public. Trade secret cases have limited this view where it takes extraordinary efforts to discover the secret information from the publicly available item.

In Videotronics the source code was the secret the plaintiff was trying to protect. Source code cannot be reconstructed from object code without considerable difficulty and programming skills. Availability of object code only is a far cry from the source code being accessible. Since this is the case, there is no reason why Videotronics could not have treated the unpublished source code as a trade secret, and the published object code as protected by copyright law. The two forms of protection are not equivalent and subsequent cases should recognize this.

Protecting Both Forms of the Program

Just as it was suggested in Chapter 4 that you could *mark* the source code as a trade secret and an unpublished work protected under the Copyright Act, so you can *register* the source code as an unpublished work. If you do, however, you will want to take care to ask for the "Special Relief," described in Chapter 6 on registering copyrights, so that you do not have to disclose all of the key, secret source code. You may be permitted to file only portions of the code, or to delete any part you feel is the essential part of your "secret." You may also request (although this will probably be denied you) that the material be treated the same as "secure test materials," and not made available to the public for examination.

File as Both an Unpublished and a Published Work. If you register the source code as an unpublished work, you can then follow up by filing the object code as a published work when you actually release the object-code version of the program. You will need to explain in your cover letter that you are doing this to protect your claim to trade secrecy in the source code. To avoid problems under the Copyright Office's "Rule of Doubt," you will, however, have to follow the suggestions in the next part of this chapter.

ALTERNATIVES TO SOURCE CODE AS A COPYRIGHT DEPOSIT

To simplify the examination process, the Copyright Office would prefer that you file source code as identifying material for your software copyright deposit. But you may not want to file and disclose large portions of your source code, which you consider a trade secret. Until recently, the Copyright Office would only accept object code deposits under their "Rule of Doubt," which meant that they were not making any determination of the copyrightability of the work. While there is no statutory basis for the Copyright Office Rule of Doubt, it raises unnecessary questions and probably should be avoided. Are there some other alternatives?

The Copyright Office has received many inquiries and complaints about its inflexible formal rules for depositing computer software. Recognizing the special problems of software, it recently adopted a set of unofficial alternatives for source code as identifying material. These rules will be included in the 1985 version of its Compendium of Copyright Office Practices.

Alternative Deposit Rules

In lieu of the first twenty-five and last twenty-five pages of source code together with the page with the copyright notice on it, you may at the present time use *one* of the three following alternatives as a deposit:

- The first twenty-five pages of object code, the last twenty-five pages of object code, the page with the copyright notice, and at least ten full, consecutive pages of source code selected from any part of the program with no lines blocked out.

- The first and last twenty-five consecutive pages of source code, from which you have blocked out any lines of code (up to about half the material submitted) that you consider a trade secret; together with the page with the copyright notice.

- As little as the first and last ten pages of the source code, with no deletions, and the page with the copyright notice.

You must specifically request the right to use these alternatives under the "special relief" provisions of the registration deposit rules, stating that you are doing so to protect your trade secret claims.

My own preference would be the first of these alternatives, which is best used when registering a published work. This alternative discloses almost nothing in the way of trade secrecy if you carefully select the ten pages of source code.

Deposits When Registering Source Code and Object Code

If you are registering source code as an unpublished work, you may have to adopt the last alternative, which can be dangerous to trade secrecy claims if those pages disclose data structures and other details about the program. Once the source is filed, don't hesitate to register only object code for the published work. Under Section 408(e) of the Copyright Act once an unpublished work is registered, you do not have to register the later published work to be covered for both versions. You *may,* however, register both, and I would do so just to be sure of the added rights for timely registered works.

Logically, there are other things that would accomplish the same objective. But the Copyright Office has refused to accept such things as actual ROMs, object code diskettes, and other physical objects that contain what is actually "published". It contends that examiners cannot tell from those objects whether the material is copyrightable. This position seems questionable, since it must be equally hard to review Sanskrit, microfiche, or comparable material that the Copyright Office does accept.

Object Code Contains Different Things from Source Code. The Copyright Office position that source code is the best evidence of authorship has a fundamental technical flaw, which has been overlooked. Software is almost always distributed in object-code form, since the author wishes to keep the source-code version a trade secret. Because object code is what is actually distributed, it is usually object code that is copied by an infringer. Unfortunately for the copyright system, object code contains a number of elements that are not in the source code, so that the source-code deposit is not representative of what is copied.

When source code is assembled, compiled, or linked in the process of creating object code that will run on a machine, the process results in large portions of code being brought in or added to the original source code. Thus, the two versions are not the same. If the deposit is to be meaningful, the Copyright Office should ask for ten pages of random source code and the actual diskette, tape, or other physical object that includes the object code. Then in case of infringement, there would be something available to compare with the infringing copy. Note, too, that most other countries do not even require copyright deposits, and still manage to have functional copyright laws.

Pending Legislation. In the long run it may take changes in the actual copyright laws to achieve full resolution of the trade secrecy issues as they relate to the deposit requirements. Several bills introduced in Congress over the last few years are intended to clarify the continued viability of trade secrecy laws, even after the new Copyright Act, while others direct the Register of Copyrights to provide regulations for the secure deposit of confidential material, like software. It is likely that some clarification of these issues will be contained in any amendment to the law that passes in the near future.

SOFTWARE RENTAL AND ELECTRONIC SOFTWARE DISTRIBUTION

Rental Companies

The recent prominence of so-called "software rental" companies, who "rent" commercially distributed microcomputer software to end users for a seven or ten-day period, parallels developments in the videotape and cassette-tape fields where such practices are rampant. It is probable that this practice will be stopped either by litigation, such as recent suits filed by MicroPro International and Management Science Associates (MSA) against United Computer Corporation, or by legislation. Congress passed in 1984 several provisions to make commercial rental of videotapes, phonorecords, and cassette tapes subject to payment of royalties. Legislation seems inevitable, since software rental companies are tempting and assisting users to pirate software, causing large revenue losses to software publishers.

Disk Formats and "Down-Loading"

The proliferation of different diskette sizes and formats for microcomputers has also created a group of potentially profitable businesses engaged in "down-loading" or "up-loading" of software. Most microcomputer software is distributed in a limited number of disk sizes and formats, such as the IBM PC format on five and a quarter-inch disks and the CP/M format on eight-inch disks. As more and more new computers hit the market with three, three and a quarter, three and a half-inch disks, unusual five and a quarter-inch formats and the like, it is necessary to provide a form of compatibility by which computers can be equipped with software in their particular size and format. Businesses are now (legally and illegally) engaging in transferring software from one format to another or one size to the other, as a convenience to users. Without permission from the owner of the copyright, or unless § 117 should be interpreted to allow this as a "back-up copy," this activity is clearly copyright infringement.

Electronic Distribution

An obvious solution is for copyright owners to license distributors to do this. Some companies are in fact actively engaged in setting up large computer systems, accessible over phone lines, which will down-load the software from its hard-disk memory to the specifications of local stores and selected machines. Documentation will be stocked by the computer stores locally.

If this practice becomes widespread, it has the potential for increasing the availability of software in different formats and sizes, but also for increasing the problem of controlling the licensing of software and the use of trademarks. When the dealer or customer, dealing directly with the electronic distributor, receives the software on his machine, there is no assurance he will place the necessary software license notice and trademark notice on the diskette. This makes it even more important for the copyright owner to embed such notices in the software in the form of screen notices and serialized copyright warnings. Without this practice, there is a substantial danger that the software will not meet the requirements of the copyright law notice provisions, nor of the trademark laws. This could result in loss of protection under either or both laws. Other possible abuses in this form of distribution are readily apparent.

SUMMARY

This completes a series of four chapters on the protection afforded computer software by the United States Copyright Act of 1976, and the various unresolved issues created by the new law. Chapter 19 provides some final thoughts on the effects of changing technology on software protection, where there may be no answers at all to some questions.

Overall, it seems likely that the software industry will somehow blunder through the next few years of uncertainty, while various issues are litigated, some are compromised, and others are legislated out of existence. The flexibility of the American legal system is always amazing, and a tribute to the ingenuity of the legal profession and trial and appellate judges. But as Machiavelli said in 1513, the creation of any new system has never been easy.

9

Patent Protection for Computer Software

Whoever invents or discovers any new and useful
process, machine, manufacture, or composition of
matter, or any new and useful improvement thereof, may
obtain a patent therefor . . . .

35 U.S.C. § 101.

The term 'process' means process, or method, and
includes a new use of a known process, machine,
manufacture, composition of matter, or material.

35 U.S.C. § 100(b).

THE PROS AND CONS OF SOFTWARE PATENTS

In Chapter 3, which compared the different legal methods of protecting
computer software, we saw that the patent laws are theoretically available
for the protection of software. This chapter will examine the patent
system in more detail. In the process, you will learn the checkered history
as well as the present shortcomings and pitfalls of software patent
protection.

The patent system is often ill-suited to serve as the primary mode of
protection for software for a number of reasons. Preparation of a patent
application is beyond the capabilities of nearly all programmers and most
lawyers, unless they are specially trained. The time and cost involved in
obtaining a patent make it unattractive in the case of most microcomputer software, although it may be worthwhile in major mainframe software projects. One other disadvantage is that, in return for protecting the
application of the ideas and methods disclosed, issuance of a patent

necessarily results in disclosure and loss of trade-secret status for the program.

There are also instances in which software patent protection really can work, and some specific situations where it has advantages over copyright law. In general, the state of software patent law is presently unsettled and not always predictable.

THE BACKGROUND TO THE PATENT SYSTEM

While the United States patent system was formalized and created by Article I, Section 8 of the U.S. Constitution in 1787, there is evidence of the grant of patents to persons in Colonial America. As early as 1641 one was granted to Samuel Winslow for a new method of making salt, and another was granted in South Carolina in 1732 for a rice-cleaning machine.

On a worldwide basis, other legal histories show the grant of patents as early as 1469, when John of Speyer was issued a patent by the Republic of Venice for a form of typography or printing. Venice thus sought to encourage its infant publishing industry. Current interpretations of the U.S. patent laws have not been as encouraging to the youthful American software industry.

What Is a Patent?

A patent is no more than a grant by the Federal Government, to the inventor or discoverer, of what is sometimes referred to as a "monopoly" on the application of an idea to a particular solution. That solution may be a process, a machine, an item of manufacture, or the composition of matter or materials, or even an improvement to an earlier invention. A patent does not give the patent owner the right to produce anything, only the right to exclude others from making, using, or selling products incorporating the invention.

Grants of Exclusive Rights

Since the word "monopoly" has bad connotations, patent lawyers prefer to say that the patent system gives the owner of the patent a set of *exclusive rights* to benefit from the invention. Whichever way you put it, these exclusive rights, usually limited to a period of seventeen years, are given to the inventor or discoverer in return for disclosure of the art (skills used) or technique. The Founding Fathers believed that without the incentive of exclusive rights, inventors would be unwilling to explain the technology behind new processes and machines; thus the progress of science and of society as a whole would be impeded and the sum of useful knowledge restricted. Because of these rights the inventor can usually demand and receive royalties for the use of his invention or for the privilege of infringing the patent. In theory, this provides the inventor with a strong financial incentive to make full disclosure in order to protect the full scope of the invention.

While patent protection is available to many classes of inventions, there are limitations on what may be patented. Numerous rules determine when and how a patent will be issued, which we will now examine in the context of software and computers.

LEGAL REQUIREMENTS FOR OBTAINING A PATENT

Statutory Subject Matter

To qualify for a patent, the inventor must show that the invention or discovery is within the class of inventions and discoveries intended by Congress to be covered by the patent law. This class is usually referred to as "statutory subject matter." In examining a patent, the first step taken by the Patent and Trademark Office (PTO) will be to determine if the claims are within this class. If the examiner or the courts conclude that the application covers "nonstatutory subject matter," then the application will be rejected entirely or all the claims falling into that classification will be rejected. It is here that most computer programs fail to qualify, as will be discussed in more detail below.

Ideas Are Not Patentable. It has long been established that an idea in and of itself is not patentable, and that the discoverer of a scientific principle or a mathematical formula may not patent the principle or the formula. We saw earlier how Einstein, who formulated and first proved the formula for the conservation of matter, $E = mc^2$, could not patent his discovery nor the formula. Moreover, the Supreme Court held in the Gottschalk v. Benson software case quoted below that newly discovered principles of nature, mental processes as such, and abstract intellectual concepts are not patentable, since they are the basic tools of scientific and technological work. However, the Supreme Court earlier held in Mackay Co. v. Radio Corporation, a patent case involving radio antennas, that "while a scientific truth, or the mathematical expression of it, is not a patentable invention, a novel and useful structure created with the aid of knowledge of scientific truth may be."

Specific Applications of Ideas Are Patentable. For example, Samuel Morse was granted a patent for the process of using electromagnetism to produce distinguishable signals for telegraphy (Morse code telegraphy), but was denied a patent on his more general claim to the use of electromagnetism for marking or printing letters at a distance. The latter claim was determined to be too broad, since he did not show in his patent application how the principles of the latter claim were actually applied. In essence, the distinction between patentability and "nonstatutory subject matter" seems to turn on making a claim based on a *specific application* of a scientific principle or use of a mathematical formula. This is more readily seen in the discussion of computer software cases that follows.

Three Further Elements Required for a Patent

For an inventor to succeed in his quest for a patent, he must demonstrate three further elements. These are:

1. The invention must be novel.
2. It must be nonobvious.
3. It must have sufficient utility to make it worth protecting.

The "novelty" requirement is met by showing that the same or similar invention was not previously known or used by others in the U.S., nor patented nor described (disclosed) in a publication in the U.S. or elsewhere.

"Nonobviousness" means that a person of ordinary skill *experienced in the subject of the invention* could not have developed the invention without the element of additional insight brought to bear on the existing technology by the inventor. Even where the invention is significant, it may be rejected as obvious. For example, merely increasing the speed of a machine would not normally meet this test, while inventing an entirely unanticipated use for the machine at the higher speed might be considered nonobvious. Nonobvious seems to be harder and harder to demonstrate as the technology of industry grows more complex.

The "utility" requirement simply means that the invention must work and that it must not be frivolous or immoral.

APPLYING FOR A PATENT

Patent Applications

To obtain a patent an inventor must prepare and file a Patent Application, requesting the grant of a patent by the U.S. Patent and Trademark Office (PTO). This application is normally prepared with the assistance of a trained and licensed patent lawyer, or by a patent agent who is not a lawyer. The application consists of a general description (sometimes called "the specification") of the invention claimed, together with a list of detailed claims which delineate (or "claim") precisely what is new in the invention or process. The application must be accompanied by a drawing of the device or a flowchart of a process.

All this must be done in the stilted, formal language of patent applications, which has established meaning to the patent practitioner. The application must be filed within one year of first public disclosure, use, or sale of the invention in the U.S., or all rights may be lost. In cases where timeliness is or may be an issue, the determination of the surrounding facts by a competent patent lawyer is vitally important.

Algorithms

In the case of a computer-program patent application, the claims normally list the logical steps involved (often referred to as an "algorithm"), as well as a detailed description of what the program is to do. There will almost always be a detailed flowchart of the algorithms and block diagrams of the elements of the program. For example, in the first U.S. Supreme Court case expressly ruling on software patents, Gottschalk v. Benson, one of the patent application claims sought (unsuccessfully) to protect this algorithm:

> 8. The method of converting signals from binary-coded decimal form into binary which comprises the steps of
>
> (1) storing the binary-coded signals in a re-entrant shift register,
> (2) shifting the signals to the right by at least three places, until there is a binary '1' in the second position of said register,
> (3) masking out said binary '1' in said position of said register,
> (4) adding a binary '1' to the first position of said register,
> (5) shifting the signals to the left by two positions,
> (6) adding a '1' to said first position, and
> (7) shifting the signals to the right by at least three positions in preparation for a succeeding binary '1' in the second position of said register.

A Software Patent Example

By way of comparison with Claim 8 in the Benson case (which is discussed in more detail later), there follows as an example three randomly selected pages from a recently granted software patent. This patent covers elements of the well-known "Easytrieve" data-base management program for mainframe computers. While the patent describes the functions and logic of the program, it does not actually list the source code of the program. According to its Manual of Patent Examining Procedure and other publications, the PTO expects either the source code of the actual computer program or (as here) a reasonably detailed flowchart delineating the sequence of operations that the program must perform. Note also that this particular patent was first applied for in 1971 and only granted in 1982, a period of eleven years during which the law swung back and forth over the issue of patentability of computer programs.

United States Patent [19]

Beckler

[11]   **4,309,756**

[45]   **Jan. 5, 1982**

[54]   **METHOD OF AUTOMATICALLY EVALUATING SOURCE LANGUAGE LOGIC CONDITION SETS AND OF COMPILING MACHINE EXECUTABLE INSTRUCTIONS DIRECTLY THEREFROM**

[76]   Inventor: Robert I. Beckler, 654 Kennebec Ave., Takoma Park, Md. 20012

[21]   Appl. No.:   **419,496**

[22]   Filed: **Nov. 28, 1973**

Related U.S. Application Data

[63]   Continuation of Ser. No. 116,160, Feb. 17, 1971, abandoned.

[51]   Int. Cl.³ G06F 3/00
[52]   U.S. Cl. **364/300**
[58]   Field of Search 444/1; 340/172.5; 364/300

[56]   **References Cited**

PUBLICATIONS

Graham, R. M., "Bounded Context Translation," in AFIPS Conference Proceedings, vol. 25; 1964, Spring Joint Computer Conference, pp. 17–29.
Cheatham, T. E., Jr. and Sattley K., "Syntax–Directed Compiling", in AFIPS Conference Proceedings, vol. 25; 1964, Spring Joint Computer Conf., pp. 31–57.
Halpern, M. I., "XPOP: A Meta-Language Without Metaphysics" in AFIPS Conference Proceedings, vol. 26; 1964, Fall Joint Computer Conference, pp. 57–68.

Primary Examiner—Leo H. Boudreau

Attorney, Agent, or Firm—Larry S. Nixon

[57]   **ABSTRACT**

A method for use under program control in a digital computer for automatically evaluating compiler level language logic condition sets and for compiling machine executable instructions directly therefrom is disclosed. More specifically, a unique method of constructing an array of novel logical linkages is described which permits an especially rapid direct compilation of an efficient and optimum-sized set of machine executable instructions without constructing the usual logic decision tables or going through an extra assembly level language step as is the case with most prior compilers. Rather, the method described generates an array of so-called primary link codes representing logical interrelationships or links between successive source deck cards in a condition set while also generating an associated array of so-called secondary link codes representing logical interrelationships or links between successive entries on the same source deck card in a condition set. These arrays are formed in such a manner that a simple analysis in terms of increasing/decreasing values of the primary and secondary link codes permits direct compilation of machine executable instructions from a computed array of incremental addresses for each term of the condition set. Further, the resulting set of machine instructions is near optimum in terms of both the core storage area utilized and the object program execution time.

24 Claims, 5 Drawing Figures

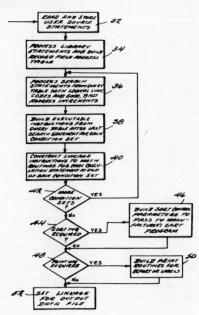

4,309,756

1

2

METHOD OF AUTOMATICALLY EVALUATING
SOURCE LANGUAGE LOGIC CONDITION SETS
AND OF COMPILING MACHINE EXECUTABLE
INSTRUCTIONS DIRECTLY THEREFROM

This is a continuation, of application Ser. No. 116,160
filed Feb. 17, 1971, now abandoned.

This invention generally relates to a method of programming digital computers for automatically evaluating high level language statements and compiling a set of machine executable instructions therefrom. Such methods are usually in the form of computer programs called compilers or assemblers and permit a computer programmer to code a desired complex machine operation in a form approaching that of the English language (or other accepted human level language) without being forced to laboriously code each and every necessary minute and incremental machine operation in a detailed machine language form.

As those in the art will appreciate, the task of generating a desired set of machine language instructions for digital computer execution is one that has received a god deal of attention. All general purpose digital computers are designed to perform several fairly simple tasks such as comparing the contents of one set of storage locations with another, adding, subtracting, moving data from one storage location or register to another, etc. In addition, each of these simple tasks is designated by a predetermined code structure or "machine language" instruction code and the computer is designed to sequentially scan at least a portion of its storage locations and to sequentially execute the simple tasks represented by coded machine instructions previously stored therein. The further ability to break the sequence of this scan by programmed jumping or branching of machine control to another programmed storage location (either unconditionally or conditionally as based on the results of some previous compare operation or the contents of a certain register, etc.) makes possible rather complex computer operations wherein complex logical conditions can be evaluated with particular predetermined programmed machine operations occurring in dependence upon the outcome of logical functions.

However, as those in the art will realize, hand coding these elemental machine operations in machine language codes and keeping track of absolute core storage addresses etc. is a very laborious task.

The earliest computers required just such a laborious manual coding process and were therefore programmable only by highly trained personnel with the permissible overall program complexity being limited both economically and conceptually by the laboriously detailed work involved.

Later, the persons responsible for manually generating such machine language programs recognized that many of the steps they were performing were repetitious, readily predictable and therfore themselves machine programmable. As a result, so called assembly level programming languages were developed for use with an "assembler" or a special computer program designed to generate the necessary machine language instructions or codes from the assembly level language statements. For instance, the actual set of machine instructions for performing "$X + Y = Z$" might involve moving the contents of a storage location (assigned to represent X) to a certain register, moving the contents of another storage location (assigned to represent Y) to

another register, combining the two register contents in an add operation, and moving the result from the proper register to yet another storage location (assigned to represent Z). The assembly level language permits the programmer to effectuate all these operations by coding a single simple entry such as, "ADD X, Y, Z". The assembler program then interprets this assembly language statement and generates all the necessary machine language instructions.

While assembly level languages were closer to the more usually understood English language, programmers were still required to learn quite a bit about the computer's more elemental operations before becoming an adept programmer even in the assembly level language. For instance, skill in the use of index registers, and knowledge of input/output devices and the interrelationships between compare switch settings and branch instructions, etc. were still necessary for the programmer. Thus, new higher level "compiler" languages were developed (i.e. FORTRAN, COBOL, etc.) to permit efficient programming with a minimum of knowledge concerning elemental machine operations. For instance, the previous computation example would be written exactly as "$Z = X + Y$" in FORTRAN. However, these compilers usually involve a two-step process. First, the compiler language is analyzed and an assembly level coding structure is generated. Then, this assembly level coding is analyzed to generate the actual machine language instructions. Thus, the compiler consumes more total time in processing the higher level language to result in at least one disadvantage that accompanies the desired result of realizing a higher level source language.

Further, since most compiler languages have been designed to satisfy a broad spectrum of end uses (computation, data base maintenance, report generation, on line control, etc.) the resulting generalized compiler does not always generate the most optimum machine language program in terms of size or execution speed, as will be appreciated by those in the art.

A new specialized compiler for directly generating machine language instructions (without an intermediate assembly language level step) has now been developed and is being sold under the name EASYTRIEVE. This compiler is specifically directed towards easy and efficient manipulation of and report generation from existing data files although it also permits limited creation of new files from input data. The EASYTRIEVE language is very close to the English language in form and is utilized in a free-flow form that is easily understood by managers and others having little or no previous programming experience.

The subject of this invention is a particularly advantageous and unique process employed in the EASYTRIEVE compiler for evaluating source language logic condition sets and for directly generating machine language instructions therefrom. Of course, since similar logic condition sets must often be analyzed in other compiler systems as well, the process of this invention will also find advantageous use in such other compiler systems; however, for purposes of explanation, it will be described hereafter as it relates to the EASYTRIEVE compiler.

This invention is directed to a unique method of constructing an array of novel logical linkages which is then used to rapidly and directly generate an array of incremental addresses which are, in turn, used to result in the desired machine language instructions. The link-

4,309,756

-continued

FIG. 4	Program Instruction		Explanation
End of con- dition set?	CLC	FRSTWRD,AND	Compare the first word on the newly read card to "AND"
	BE	AND/OR	Branch if equal to instruction at location AND/OR.
	CLC	FRSTWRD,OR	Compare the first word on the card to "OR".
◎	BNE	C	Branch if not equal to instruction at location C.
First word on card	AND/OR CLC	FRSTWRD,AND	Compare first word to "AND".
	BE	SETAND	Branch if equal to instruction at lo- cation SETAND.
LINK 1(n)= Link 1(n−1) Link 2(n)= Link 2(n−1)	SETOR MVC	LINK1, LINK1−16	Set present LINK1 value to previous LINK1 value.
	MVC	LINK2, LINK2−16	Same for LINK2
Ⓐ	B	A	Unconditional branch to the instruction at location A.
LINK1(n)= LINK1(n−1) + 1 LINK2(n) = 1	SETAND MVC	LINK1, LINK1−16	Set present LINK1 value to previous LINK1 value.
	AP	LINK1,PAK1	Add +1 to LINK1 where +1 is stored in lo- cation PAK1.
	ZAP	LINK2,PAK1	Zero LINK2 and add +1 thereto.
Ⓐ	B	A	Unconditional branch to instruction at location A.

Of course, if higher level programming languages are used fewer separate program instructions may be necessary to implement the program segments as will be appreciated.

Although only one exemplary embodiment of this invention has been described in detail, those skilled in the art will readily appreciate that many modifications of the exemplary method are possible without materially changing the structure of the resulting logical linkage array or the corresponding good and bad incremental addresses which may be so advantageously employed in efficiently compiling an almost optimum set of machine instructions for evaluating a condition set. Accordingly, all such modifications are intended to be included within the scope of this invention.

What is claimed is:

1. A method to be carried out within a digital computer under programmed control for automatically evaluating a logic condition set composed of query statements connected by logical connectors and expressed in high level computer program source statements and for automatically compiling a compact and efficient set of machine executable instructions corresponding thereto, said method comprising the steps of: constructing an array of logical linkage codes having at least one entry for each query statement in the condition set with the value of successive entries in the array being assigned in dependence upon the particular type of logical connector adjoining the respectively associated query statement, scanning the resulting array of logical linkage codes in a predetermined order and comparing the values of adjacent entries to determine relative ordering therebetween, and

computing the necessary addresses for insertion in branch instructions included within said set of machine instructions in dependence upon said relative ordering.

2. A method as in claim 1 further comprising the steps of:

performing said set of machine executable instructions in skeleton form with a subset of at least one compare, one conditional branch and one unconditional branch instruction corresponding to each query statement and with address arguments for the branch instructions being intialized to correspond to the address of the compare instruction of its associated subset, and wherein said computing step comprises:

constructing an array of good incremental addresses with each entry corresponding to a particular subset of instructions and with the value of each entry being calculated in dependence upon said relative ordering of corresponding adjacent linkage array entries,

constructing an array of bad incremental addresses with each entry corresponding to a particular subset of instructions and with the value of each entry being calculated in dependence upon said relative ordering of corresponding adjacent linkage array entries,

incrementing the address arguments of said conditional branch instructions with the value of the corresponding entry in the array of good incremental addresses, and

incrementing the address arguments of said unconditional branch instructions with the value of the corresponding entry in the array of bad incremental addresses.

Information as to "Prior Art"

The patent application or accompanying papers should also include a list of references to the most similar prior patents granted, and disclosures of other inventions that the inventor and his attorney believe to be similar to but different from the claimed invention. The information on "prior art" may consist of non-patent publications such as periodicals, technical journals, sales brochures, and the like. The inventor is thereby disclosing how his invention differs from others, and assisting the examiners in the search of the "prior art" to establish that the new claims are indeed novel and patentable.

Patent Searches.   While not required to do so, the inventor and his or her lawyer will often have conducted a patent search, either by themselves or through the services of one of many search companies, in order to study the claims of prior patents. In many situations, the search will disclose prior patents which include elements (or similar aspects) of the invention claimed by our inventor. The patent application cannot claim inventions known to have been covered by earlier patents, so it should list references to the prior related patents found.

Patent Application Fees.   The current PTO application filing fee for most patents is $300, but small businesses and non-profit organizations only have to pay half the scheduled fees. There are numerous other fees for processing the application and issuing the patent, which your patent attorney will be able to explain. (See Usual Legal Fees.)

FINDING A PATENT LAWYER TO HELP YOU

Because of the detailed requirements for a patent application, you as the inventor really should retain a competent patent lawyer experienced with the computer industry, to draft the application and to handle the processing of the application and the correspondence. This can take two or three years of communication with the PTO.

Where to Look and What to Expect

You should select your patent lawyer the same way you would a doctor— by recommendations from friends, your personal attorney, or business associates who have used that patent lawyer's services in the past. Due to the length of time the process takes, a patent lawyer will usually ask for a retainer fee, and then will bill you from time to time as the case proceeds. At the outset you should discuss with the patent lawyer the estimate of probable legal fees and out-of-pocket expenses, and reach an understanding on how this will be billed to and paid by you.

Usual Legal Fees

Depending on the style and practice of the patent lawyer, you may be quoted a fixed fee for preparing and filing the application, but usually the work of processing the claim through the PTO will be done on an hourly fee basis. There is no way of anticipating how much work will be involved in this process of negotiation with the patent examiner handling the case. As of this writing, you can expect to pay a minimum of $2,500 for a software patent application, and the cost could be up to as much as ten times that amount.

THE PATENT–PROCESSING PHASE

Timing

It usually takes several years to obtain a patent because there is a backlog of literally hundreds of thousands of patent applications pending at any one time. Furthermore, a great deal of negotiation may go on between the PTO examiner and your patent attorney over what claims are valid, whether the description and disclosure of the invention is adequate, and whether the invention is obvious or was anticipated by earlier inventions. It is important that this be handled correctly, since intentional failure to disclose known similar inventions, or making misleading claims, may result in the patent being held invalid in later litigation.

Examining "Prior Art"

In the case of software there is a great deal of "prior art" that may be in technical publications and papers from all over the world, which material is not on file with the PTO. The PTO is hiring some 600 more patent examiners over the next three years, to reduce the lengthy time presently taken to process applications. One qualification may be familiarity with computers and software.

"Patent Pending" and Other Notices

While a patent application is pending, the owner may include the customary notice "Patent Pending" to indicate that a patent application has been filed covering the invention. However, one of the major differences between patent and copyright protection is that the owner of a patent has no legal protection until the patent is issued, and cannot recover royalties for use of the patented software during the application period. Conversely, since copyright attaches upon fixation in a copy, there is little delay in copyright protection. If the software copyright is registered within three months of first publication, the protection starts with the date of first publication.

A specific patent number is assigned at the time the patent is formally issued. Thereafter, any patented article should carry a legend show-ing the actual patent number, such as "U.S. Patent No. 5,789,432," in order to provide notice of the extistence of the patent. Multiple patent notices often read, "This device utilizes one or more of the following U.S. Patent Numbers, 5,678,890, 5,789,765," etc. Notice of all applicable patents is necessary, since, under 35 U.S.C. § 287, failure of the patent owner to give notice, or to prove that the infringer had actual notice of the patent, can preclude the owner from recovering damages.

THE EFFECT OF THE GRANT OF A PATENT

The value of patenting software is that the patent protects the owner from anyone using the claimed method or process without paying royalties. Unlike copyrights that only protect the owner from copying and help con-trol distribution, patents can be used to prevent use of the idea, as dis-closed and applied in the patent application. While patent protection is gained by disclosure, at least for the term of the patent, remember that trade-secret protection is lost by such disclosure. There are obvious trade-offs.

Patent Owner Rights

Once the patent has been granted, the owner has the exclusive right for a period of seventeen years (with certain exceptions not relevant here) to make, use, or sell the patented invention, or to authorize others to do so. Anyone who does so without authority is guilty of patent infringement under 35 U.S.C. §271. In such an event, the owner may obtain an injunc-tion to prevent further infringement, and may recover damages in the form of a royalty or license fee. These damages may be trebled if the in-fringement is shown to be wilful.

While there is no requirement that the infringer have knowledge of the patent to be an infringer, there can be no recovery of damages unless the infringer received notice of infringement and continued to infringe, or unless the infringer copied patented goods marked with a patent notice. Lack of notice does not prevent the patent owner from obtaining an in-junction to stop further infringement. All actions for patent infringement must be brought in the U.S. District Courts, which means you need a lawyer experienced in federal trial practice as well as patent law.

The Cost of Patent Infringement Suits

Many patents issued are honored as valid and royalties are paid by users. But where users ignore the patent, or treat it as invalid, it must be en-forced through a patent infringement action. Unfortunately, patent suits are likely to blossom into long and protracted litigation, which can be ex-tremely expensive. Some lawyers may be willing to handle an infringement action on a contingent fee basis, but otherwise very few individuals can afford to engage in patent litigation. It is not uncommon for legal fees incurred by the patent owner to exceed $100,000. Most cases are settled before trial, even by large corporations, because of the high costs involved. Recently, Congress changed the patent laws to permit arbitration in some patent disputes, which may prove less expensive than court trials.

Patent Invalidity

A danger in bringing an infringement action is that the alleged infringer will raise patent invalidity as a defense. Statistically, there is a nearly even chance that the patent will be held invalid after a long trial. In such event, the inventor will have spent a great deal of money and will recover nothing. Worse yet, the inventor will no longer have a patent for which to collect royalties. The inventor will also have disclosed the principles of his or her invention, and will have rendered them unprotected from use by others.

Centralized Appeals

Until 1983, appeals from patent infringement trials went to twelve different federal courts, depending on where the case arose. This led to extreme variences in results and uncertainty as to validity of many patents. To resolve this problem, all appeals now go to one centralized court, the United States Court of Appeals for the Federal Circuit (CAFC), in Washington, D.C. The CAFC is more likely to provide more consistent results for patent appeals.

THE PROBLEM WITH SOFTWARE PATENTS

The history of efforts to obtain U.S. patents on software is a zig-zag of inconsistent case law brought about, in part, by uncertainty on the part of the Patent Office and by industry as to whether or not they wanted software to be patentable. The courts have since concluded that *some* software is patentable in *some* cases; the problem is in deciding which software and in which cases. (By comparison, the European patent convention, discussed in Chapter 15, flatly states that computer software is not patentable. But even in Europe that is not always true.)

In terms that you and I, as non-patent lawyers, can understand, the reason most software cannot be patented is that it is often merely the "computerization" of a *series of steps* that have been and still can be done by a human being. Neither mental steps nor mathematical formulas are patentable. The courts and the PTO have couched this problem in a series of rules and exceptions that make the problem nearly incomprehensible to any normal mind. This is not to say that there are not some good reasons for the principles established in this area over the years. It is almost impossible, however, to understand them, without examining the history of the more recent cases, which this next section does.

If all you want to know is what kinds of programs are likely to be patentable, you can skip to the end of the chapter and use the intervening materials merely as a reference. But if you would like to understand *why* certain software is or is not patentable, you should read this section, especially if you are a lawyer or work closely with patent lawyers.

THE RECENT HISTORY OF SOFTWARE PATENTS

The Problem in a Nutshell

The legal problem is that the claims of invention in many computer programs cannot meet the initial test of being "statutory subject matter" under 35 USC § 101, because they involve mathematical formulas or *a series of mental steps,* which only perform work previously done by hand or in the human mind. A classic example of such non-patentable subject matter would be almost any program that computed amortization schedules for mortgage payments or kept a running inventory for a merchant.

Formulas or Obviousness

The constant argument in nearly every contested computer-software patent case is that the program is no more than the application of a known mathematical formula to the solution of a well-known problem. Or, as in the recent Paine Webber-Merrill Lynch case discussed in detail below, the software is questioned on the basis that it is merely a computerized "business system," which is not patentable subject matter. Many applications programs will also fail the obviousness test. In Dann v. Johnston, a 1976 Supreme Court case, a patent was denied for a computerized bookkeeping system that categorized and classified expenditures for check writers, something that has been done manually for years by every bookkeeper.

The Dawn of Software Patents

In the cases before 1968, the courts viewed computer programs as nothing more than a recitation of "mental steps" to be performed by a machine as opposed to a human. Such steps, taken alone, were not patentable. Then in 1968, following considerable controversy in patent circles, the Court of Customs and Patent Appeals (CCPA) decided one of the first cases to consider the suitability of a computer program for patent protection. This case, called In Re Prater, held that an improved method for processing spectrographic data, which used a newly discovered equation in a computer program, could not be denied patent protection under the "mental steps" doctrine. This broader view of software patentability was followed by several other cases that concluded that since the program in effect configured a machine, even for a short moment, a software patent should be allowed because this constituted invention of an apparatus or a machine.

The Patent Office and the CCPA, as the then principal court for patent appeals, engaged in a tug-of-war for a few years over software patentability. The Patent Office's position was that it did not have the facilities to deal with software patents, so it did not want software to be patentable. It found a number of reasons to reject software.

The Supreme Court and Software Patents

The Benson Case.   Patent lawyers were discouraged, however, when the Benson case (mentioned earlier) was considered by the Supreme Court in 1972. This was the first major Supreme Court case involving the subject of patents and computer programs. In a decision widely claimed at the time to deny a patent to any computer program, the court concluded that granting a patent for an invention on the basis of the use of a mathematical formula could completely preempt the use of the formula under other circumstances. This would, in effect, be the equivalent of granting a patent on the mathematical algorithm itself. The Benson process involved a mathematical algorithm for converting binary-coded decimal numbers to binary.

Software Algorithms versus Mathematical Algorithms.   It is important to realize that a mathematical algorithm is not necessarily the same thing as a software algorithm. Most program algorithms involve mathematical computations by a computer, but they do not have to. For example, a word-processing program may use math, but its primary purpose is not to compute numbers nor to reach a mathematical result. Benson, on the other hand, sought a patent on a mathematical algorithm—but not the program itself—that merely computed a new number from the number with which it started.

The Benson court decided that a patent on a mathematical algorithm was the same as allowing a patent on an idea. It therefore held that the mathematical formula was not patentable. The court was concerned that this formula had sufficient general application that, if patented, it could not have been used in any other computer program where it was later needed. It did not want this result.

The Public Policy Aspect.   The Supreme Court made two significant statements in the case, which were largely overlooked at the time: first, the patentability of computer programs was a public policy issue, which should be addressed by Congress and not the courts; second, it might be possible to patent algorithms and computer programs if they were only part of a particular application of a process. This was not so in the case of

Benson, but it set the stage for the next Supreme Court case, Parker v. Flook, in 1978.

The Flook Case.   Flook had applied for a patent on a method for updating "alarm limits" during the catalytic conversion process, such as in oil refining. (Alarm limits are numbers controlling an industrial process that indicate something is about to go, or has gone, wrong.) The only novel feature of the application was the use of a mathematical formula in the process, which formula could be used in a computer program to automatically compute alarm limits.

The Supreme Court in the Flook case, looking back to Benson, rejected the patent application, because merely using data for some constructive purpose, after they had been computed by the formula, was not enough to make the method patentable. It was not the fact that a computer program was involved that caused this result, but the *lack of novelty* or genuine inventiveness. All the process did was provide a new or better method of computing alarm limits. The court said, however, that the decision was not to be taken as a blanket denial of patent protection to "novel and useful" computer programs. It once again stated that most of the issues in the case were better addressed in Congress.

The Open Door—Diamond v. Diehr.   Congress did not take up the issue, and in 1981 the Supreme Court decided the most recent high-court case, Diamond v. Diehr. Here the court approved patent protection for an industrial process for curing rubber that utilized a computer program as an integral part of the process. The program, in turn, used a well-known mathematical equation in order to recompute, as necessary, variables such as temperature and pressure. Its unique feature was that it used this equation and the pressure/temperature data to determine when to open the tire-mold automatically. While some of these steps had previously been used together, lack of an integrated system had left much of the decision to human guesswork as to when the rubber had been properly cured.

Contrary to what was written up in many newspapers and journals, this conclusion did not firmly establish computer programs as a patentable class of invention. All the case really showed was that an industrial process will not be denied patent protection merely because it includes a computer program as part of the process. This was a big advance from the earlier cases, however, and represents some signs of progress for the patent system in the computer age.

THE ALGORITHM PROBLEM
AND RECENT CASES

Since the Diehr case a number of other software patent cases have reached the appellate courts. Most of them have struggled to reconcile the language of Diehr with the rules of the earlier Benson and Flook cases. The questions about patentability of mathematical algorithms has remained especially troublesome. Finally, in a 1982 case, In re Pardo, the CCPA ruled that since an "algorithm" was merely the name for a set of rules used to achieve a particular result, some distinction needed to be drawn between mathematical algorithms and computer program algorithms. It concluded that the two were not necessarily the same.

Algorithms versus Mathematical Steps

The In re Pardo case involved an attempt to patent a claim protecting a very complex series of steps used in a computer-language compiler. The patent had been denied by the lower court because the claim used the word "algorithm" in describing the steps. The CCPA ruled that the steps in the program were not mathematical in nature, stating that:

> Appellants' method claims are directed to executing programs in a computer. The method operates on any program and any formula which may be input, regardless of mathematical content. That a computer controlled according to the invention is capable of handling mathematics is irrelevant to the question of whether a mathematical algorithm is recited by the claims.

The Two-Step Test

The CCPA ruled that the claim involved patentable subject matter. In so doing, it reiterated *the two-step test* now applied to all patent applications that seek protection for mathematical algorithms but run into a problem on the statutory subject-matter rules: first, the claim is analyzed to see if a mathematical algorithm is directly or indirectly used to describe the process claimed; second, the claim as a whole is analyzed to determine whether the algorithm is applied to physical elements or process steps. If both steps meet the test, the claim is considered suitable subject matter for a patent, even though a mathematical algorithm has been claimed as part of the invention.

The Whole Greater than the Parts Test

Based upon this test, the subsequent case of In re Abele reveals that even a mathematical formula may be part of a patentable process or a patentable apparatus (a machine), if it is part of an invention in which the *whole* appears to be substantially greater or more useful than the *parts*. Abele involved a patent on a computerized, axial tomography (CAT) scanner device. This is a highly specialized x-ray machine that allows physicians to x-ray soft tissues like internal organs, which could not be done without the scanner. It was the computer and the specialized equations in the program that made the machine unique and patentable.

Process Patents

Another case, In re Taner, involved a seismic exploration patent, which had recited a mathematical algorithm used in a computerized geophysical application (oil exploration). While the Patent Office had rejected the claims as being merely a method of calculating or summing numbers, CCPA upheld the patentability of the claims. It said that where the algorithm is used to obtain a number, which number is then converted into another form, the claims constitute a "process" that is within the statutory subject matter. (Under this interpretation, the Benson conversion process of binary-coded decimal numbers to binary might have been patentable.)

Use of mathematics in a computer program or process is not fatal to patentability, if the program permits the machine or process to do something it could not have done without the program. Note, however, that none of these recent cases involve a computer program alone, and all of them allow a machine or process to operate more effectively as a direct result of the use of the program.

On the other hand another 1982 case, In re Meyer, concluded that unless the mathematical algorithm is applied to a *specific process that achieves a unique result,* as opposed to a mere claim of the general principle, it will not be patentable. Meyer claimed use of a complex mathematical formula for testing and determining probability, used to draw inferences from facts provided to the system. One possible application given in the opinion was to a form of computerized diagnosis by a physician, but the inventor however, did not claim this as a process or machine. The court denied the patent, stating:

> . . . [W]e conclude that appellants' independent claims are to a mathematical algorithm representing a mental process that has not been applied to physical elements or process steps and is, therefore, not limited to any otherwise statutory process, machine, manufacture, or composition of matter.

THE CURRENT STATUS OF THE LAW

Based upon all of this litigation, the Patent Office is now actively processing and issuing software patents on a much broader scale. Most software patents are still for very complex industrial processes in which the software is but a part of the whole procedure. But there have been a number of patents granted recently on software, during the past several years, for database-management systems, information-retrieval techniques, and even cash-management systems for use in the stock-brokerage business.

The latter subject has not only involved issuance of patents, but recent litigation over their validity.

Business Cash-Management Systems

In 1980 the Merrill Lynch brokerage organization filed for a patent on its proprietary computer program, which was designed to handle securities brokerage and customer cash management. It was essentially a financial and business system intended to provide better control over unused cash for brokerage customers who wanted to leave their money with Merrill Lynch, but have it accessible for checking and credit-card use. Such systems are now very common in the marketplace.

The patent was issued in 1982 after considerable negotiation with the PTO, and in the same year Paine, Webber, Jackson & Curtis, Inc. filed suit in District Court to have the patent held invalid, and to prevent Merrill Lynch from bringing infringement actions against other brokerage houses using similar systems. Merrill Lynch had notified brokerage houses using similar systems that it expected to receive $10 per customer per year as royalties for its patent. (A second patent has since been issued for improvements on the earlier system.) Paine Webber ultimately lost its suit, which shows how far things have recently developed in the area of software patents.

Paine Webber had argued that the Merrill Lynch patent was nothing more than a familiar business system, combining a brokerage account, a money-market fund, and a checking/charge account. It cited cases holding that business methods and systems were not patentable. It also claimed that Merrill Lynch's patent was invalid since it merely recited a mathematical algorithm. After reviewing the history of the same mathematical-algorithm cases reviewed in this chapter, the court rejected both contentions. It held that the patent "claims a methodology to effectuate a highly efficient business system and does not restate a mathematical formula as defined by Benson."

The court further concluded that while the business system would be unpatentable if done by hand, the program was patentable subject matter since "the claims allegedly teach a method of operation on a computer to effectuate a business activity." This is all that is required, since the product of the computer program is irrelevant as long as there is no Benson algorithm. The law is clearly changing in favor of software patents.

WHAT THEN IS PATENTABLE SOFTWARE?

The case law still does not establish definitively what software is and what is not patentable. We can, however, draw some general principles as guidelines for the software author or software attorney.

First, it is not possible to obtain a patent on an idea, mathematical formula, scientific principle, or discovery unless the inventor has reduced the idea to some *specific application* in the form of a manufacturing process or a useful device. However, one recent exception was the Diamond v. Chakrabarty case involving genetic engineering, where the Supreme Court upheld a patent on a live, human-made organism without tying its issuance to any particular application. Nonetheless, the more specific, novel, and useful the application of an idea, the more likely it is to be subject to a patent. General principles are never patentable, no matter how inventive or novel.

Second, it is highly unlikely that any computer program that merely automates something that has been done manually, or does something more quickly than some other existing machine, will receive a patent. However, an innovative improvement in an existing computer program that provides a whole new function might be patentable; such an invention could qualify as an improvement patent if it meets the other tests for patentability. Keep in mind, though, notwithstanding the Merrill Lynch patents, that the automation of mental processes, such as a bookkeeping system, is rarely patentable.

Third, the fact that a computer program involves the use of a mathematical algorithm is not necessarily fatal to its patentability. The real issue is whether the mathematical computation is an end in and of itself, or whether the computation is then used, as in Diehr, to do something to or with a machine or a process. Algorithms are patentable if they do something other than merely calculate numbers. For example, if the calculation allows doctors to take x-rays in a form not available without the use of the computer (as in the Abele CAT scanner invention), then the machine or process should be patentable.

Finally, computer programs are themselves algorithms, since they are methods for solving particular problems, and in some cases they, alone, should be patentable. For example, a complex data-base management scheme, which is novel, useful, and can manipulate information in a new way, could be the subject of a patent. Another likely area for software patents is in the field of industrial process controls, such as processes controlling factories and machines, and making commodities like alcohol or gasoline. Another good possibility is that "firmware" (also known as "microcode") will be patentable since it is really part of the design of the computer architecture, and the PTO may consider it similar to software.

SUMMARY

If your program is important enough or has a long enough useful life, there can be benefits in patenting it. Firstly, patent coverage is broader than the prohibition on copying found in copyright law. It covers the functions and ideas inherent in the process or method, and is not limited to the specific instructions used or the specific implementation involved. Secondly, patent coverage extends more broadly than copyright or trade-secret principles, since the infringer may be stopped even though innocent of any intent to copy or without prior knowledge of the patent. Thirdly, a patent is not lost by disclosure, as is the case with a trade secret, nor is it limited to the exact expression of the program, as is a copyright. Fourthly, if broadly enough based, a patent may lead to further patents for improvements, which can create an even tighter monopoly for the patent owner.

For a number of reasons patent law cannot serve as the primary means of software protection. It has the following limitations, important in today's fast-moving microcomputer market. First, it takes over two years to obtain most patents. Second, it costs between $2,500 and $25,000 to obtain a patent. Third, issuance of a patent will result in disclosure of most of what was previously treated as a trade secret. Fourth, no protection is available until a patent has been issued, and even then a high percentage of patents are declared invalid in litigation. Fifth, even when a patent is issued, it is unlikely that you can obtain a preliminary injunction, so legal resolution may take two to three years or more. Finally, the cost of patent litigation is very high compared with copyright litigation, and there are no provisions for recovering attorney fees.

In the final analysis, the decision to pursue software patent protection will be a business judgment in which you will weigh the risks and costs against the probable benefits. The law is still developing in this area, and it looks more interesting each year. For example, Apple Computer obtained, in August 1984, a patent on the mouse used with the Lisa and Macintosh computers, *and* on the pull-down menu process used in its software. You should explore the law carefully if your program has major commercial value over time.

10

Trademarks as a Form of Software Protection

Twoallbeefpattiesspecialsaucelettucecheesepicklesonionsonasesameseedbun.

U.S. Registered Trademark No. 1,253,001,
owned by the McDonald's hamburger chain.

HOW TRADEMARKS CAN PROTECT SOFTWARE

You, as a software author, may not select quite as fanciful a mark to identify your software as McDonald's did its hamburgers. However, you should not overlook the business benefits available under the various federal and state trademark and trade name laws. Trademark law, and related statutes, can provide you with a whole arsenal of legal weapons to fend off software pirates. Trademarks are another part of the legal web you can weave around your software. In the next few pages you will learn how to select, use, register, and protect the names you associate with your software products.

Since the purpose of a trademark is to identify a specific product with a particular source of supply, you can, if you do it carefully, select and use a trademark to prevent others from selling copies of software with your trademark, but copied by them. You can also stop them from marketing software in a manner that confuses the public because of similarity of names, symbols, packaging, or other characteristics. The cost of obtaining a trademark is usually less than $1,000 and the protection can last for twenty or more years, if you comply with the law. However, registering a trademark and understanding some of the applicable law requires professional help from a trademark attorney, so this chapter will also explain how to get further help in establishing and registering your trademarks.

WHAT IS A TRADEMARK?

Bombarded as we all are by print and television media advertising, nearly all of us see dozens of familiar trademarks in the course of a single day. Within ten feet of my word processor, I can see ten or so trademarks related to the computer industry alone—IBM®, Televideo®, Dysan®, Altos®, CP/M®, WORDSTAR®, Volkswriter®, TI®, 3M® and on and on. Some of these are merely words, while others are letters and symbols in special forms.

All of these marks help me connect the product I have with the manufacturer or supplier of the product. All of them are valuable evidence of the good will created by expensive advertising by the owners. You and I select products on the basis of these marks, yet most of us do not consciously think of these marks as being trademarks until they are called to our attention.

Formal Definitions

Some formal definitions, with examples, should help us get started on this interesting subject. Since trademarks are a legal concept, the law and the legal profession depend on the use of these terms in a consistent manner. There are several types of marks expressly recognized by the federal trademark law (known as the Lanham Act).

A *trademark* includes any word, name, symbol, or device, or combination of them, adopted or used by a manufacturer or merchant to identify goods it makes or sells as its own, and to distinguish them from those manufactured or sold by others. The mark selected is such that customers will identify the seller or provider as the source of the goods. Kodak® film, IBM® computers, and Scotch® brand transparent tape are typical examples. Trademarks are only properly used as adjectives or adverbs, and never as nouns or verbs. For example, you may be using "the CP/M® operating system" on your computer, not "CP/M," and you do not "xerox" something but rather you copy it on a Xerox® copying machine.

A *service mark* is a mark used in the sale or advertising of services to identify the services of one person and distinguish them from the services of others. Since there are often no goods involved in services, the mark will normally be placed on advertising or literature, or perhaps on the vehicles providing the transportation service, as in the case of TWA® or Greyhound®. Other familiar examples are Hertz® car rentals, Allstate® insurance, or GE® or Sorbus® computer maintenance.

A *certification mark* is a mark used upon or in connection with products or services of one or more persons other than the owner of the mark to certify regional or other origin, material, mode of manufacture, quality, accuracy, or other characteristics of such goods or services, or union labor certifications. In the electronics field, the Underwriters Laboratories "UL® " label is a classic example. There is now a class of computer programs called "DEC Certified Software" with a silver seal of approval, just like the Good Housekeeping Seal, where the manufacturer has approved something done by others as meeting certain objective standards.

Finally, the term *collective mark* means a trademark or service mark used by the members of a cooperative, an association, or other collective group or organization, and includes marks used to indicate membership in a union, an association, or other organization. Thus, electrical engineers belong to IEEE, oranges and lemons come from Sunkist®, and persons who have passed certain tests in data processing may use the mark DPMA or CDP. These marks may or may not be formally registered, but they are collective marks.

Trade Names Distinguished from Trademarks

To distinguish the above formal definitions from similar terms, you should also note that a *trade name* or *commercial name* means individual names, firm names, and trading names adopted by manufacturers, industrialists, merchants, growers, and others to identify their businesses, vocations, or occupations. These trade names also include the entity names of companies, unions, and others engaged in commerce, who may sue in or be sued under such names.

There are no provisions in the Lanham Act expressly authorizing registration of trade names, although a trade name may be registrable if it is used as a trademark. For example, the Xerox Corporation has a trademark "Xerox," but its trade name is the company name, just as "IBM" is a trademark of the International Business Machines Corporation, and "DEC" and "Digital" are trademarks of the Digital Equipment Corporation. Where a trademark becomes almost synonymous with a company name, that company may change its name, as happened when Personal Software, Inc. changed its name to "Visicorp, Inc." because its product, "VisiCalc®," became so well-known.

SOURCES OF TRADEMARK LAW

The original idea of unique marks on products came from the craft guilds in the late middle ages, each of whom stamped its gold, silver, and china goods with a mark signifying the origin. English and American common law then adopted this idea, and today in the U.S. we have both a federal trademark statute, commonly called the Lanham Act, 15 U.S.C. §1051, and a series of state trademark laws which are very similar to each other. Your rights as a trademark owner today stem directly from these statutes. The Lanham Act provides for a registration procedure, and also creates a federal law of unfair competition in § 43(a), which is discussed in more detail below. The state laws may also protect trade names. This chapter is based on those laws and the cases interpreting them.

SELECTING TRADEMARKS

Most computer software trademarks will be fairly mundane things like words, initials, numbers, or distinctive designs involving animals and words. But a trademark can be any word, name, symbol, or design, or combination of these, and there are many unusual marks which you would not ordinarily think of as being trademarks. The shape of the Haig & Haig pinch bottle, for example, is a registered trademark, as is the yellow McDonald's arch.

Often the mark is a simple combination of letters, written in a particular form, such as "CP/M," "VisiCalc," or even "1-2-3." It may also be a common word or name applied to an uncommon item, such as "Apple Computers" or "Verbatim®" floppy disks. Or it could be a graphic, multicolored representation of an apple with a bite taken out of it combined with the word "Apple®," a mark that any computer user would instantly recognize today, but which was never heard of before 1978.

The Three Types of Trademarks

Trademarks are often grouped into three types, based on their inherent strength and registrability: arbitrary or meaningless marks, suggestive marks, and descriptive marks. If you are looking for a trademark for your new software package, you will want to adopt the strongest mark available. A strong mark is easier to register, and over the years the stronger the mark the easier it will be to protect it from infringement by others.

Arbitrary Marks.   This first type of trademark is the strongest of all, because it is "made-up" or arbitrarily used with the product, and it usually says nothing about that product until consumers begin to associate a particular source with it. The best-known mark of this type is "KODAK", which was coined by its owner precisely because it meant nothing at the time. In the microcomputer software field, "LOTUS" is a perfect example of an arbitrary mark. Arbitrary marks also include letters like "IBM" or "CP/M," symbols like McDonald's yellow arches, numbers like the Control Data "7600" computer, common words like "Standard®" for oil, and imaginary or fanciful characters and names like "PAC-MAN®." The value of these marks lies in the fact that they quickly come to be closely identified with one product and its source of supply.

Suggestive Marks.   These are marks that literally suggest something about the product, like the "1-2-3" spreadsheet software of Lotus, or the term "VisiCalc." Suggestive marks are stronger than descriptive marks, but not as good as arbitrary marks. A term like "Volkswriter" does not describe its product, but the term does make it easy for the consumer to identify the brand desired because of the suggestion of some desirable characteristic of the product.

Probably one of the more clever marks in this group is "MEOW MIX®" cat food, and its accompanying slogan, "Tastes so good cats ask for it by name®." The name MICROSOFT, on the other hand, is a clever combination of words, but it is a poor trademark since it is a contraction of the words "microcomputer software." The difficulty of a trademark in this class is that if it is too suggestive of the product itself, it may be held as merely descriptive. If so, it is not registrable until it becomes so identified with the product and its source that it has acquired a "secondary meaning." The "EVEREADY" brand flashlight battery faced this problem until the name became sufficiently well-known.

Descriptive Marks.   Trademarks in this group are the poorest marks, since they cannot ordinarily be registered until they have acquired a strong secondary meaning. For example, the Singer® sewing machine was named after its inventor, but was so closely identified with him that it was not granted a trademark registration for many years until the secondary meaning was established. The words "FAST" or "QUICK" would be poor marks for a microcomputer since they are standard English words and descriptive, while "COMPAQ™" is an excellent, suggestive mark by virtue of its unusual spelling but clever application to a portable microcomputer. While "HERTZ®" and "Hershey®" are proper names, they acquired the necessary secondary meaning long ago to qualify them as trademarks. Proper names or geographical terms are not usually good trademarks, unless they are suggestive—such as "Kilimanjaro" for safari and mountain gear.

Unavailable Marks

There are a number of items that cannot be registered as trademarks because of public policy against such use. These include immoral words or obscene symbols, national flags or coats of arms and seals, and names of public figures (unless they consent).

As a general rule no mark that is solely descriptive or that is generic to the item(s) in question can be registered, and if the mark becomes generic the owner may no longer protect it. Thus, "Sticky glue" is purely descriptive and would be a poor choice for a trademark. This rule can be disastrous in some cases, as in a 1983 case where Parker Brothers lost its right to prevent the use of the term "Monopoly" in a game title, called "Anti-Monopoly," on the basis that "Monopoly" had become the generic term for any game of this type in the minds of consumers. Similarly, years ago the term "Aspirin" was a registered trademark of the Bayer Company, but was lost when it became the descriptive term for any similar drug, regardless of its source.

Desirable Qualities in Trademarks.™

The U.S. Trademark Association Handbook suggests a series of things to look for in a trademark:

- Brevity—short names like "Coke®."

- Easy to Remember—like "1-2-3."

- Easily Readable and Pronounceable—XEROX® is an example of a case where the opposite principle worked well.

- No Unpleasant Connotations—BURP seems like a great name for a soft drink, but probably would not make it commercially.

- Suitable for Export—The trademark must be pronounceable and acceptable in other languages. This is reportedly why the trademark EXXON® was chosen after a long and expensive computer search.

- Lends Itself to Pictorialization—Here Apple Computer did a great job with both its original name and the subsequent symbol, as well as with follow-on products like the MacIntosh™.

In short, you need to give considerable thought to the selection of any trademark you attach to your software. A good one can add value to the product, while a poor one invites litigation and lack of clear identification with your company.

HOW YOU OBTAIN RIGHTS TO A TRADEMARK

Just because you have thought up a great trademark for your software does not mean you own it or can use it right away. First, you should have a search conducted to see that no one else is currently using that trademark for a similar or confusing purpose. Then, in order to obtain rights to the mark you select, you actually have to *use* it "in commerce" on a product or in connection with services you render. Generally, the first person or company to use a mark widely is the one entitled to register and use it. In the U.S. you can only establish your rights to the trademark by use, unlike in Japan and many South American countries where it is possible to register a mark without having used it.

Order a Trademark Search before Marketing

Before you spend any money on advertising, literature, or manuals using the chosen trademark, have a trademark search conducted by one of the several firms that do so. This might include Thompson and Thompson of Boston, Massachusetts, or other firms that advertise in the American Bar Association Journal and in publications like Popular Mechanics Magazine. Most such firms use computerized databases, as well as conducting manual searches. The cost of a search of U.S. records is currently about

$200, depending largely on the scope of what you order. A complete search usually takes three or four weeks to complete.

The trademark search should cover not only registered marks in the U.S. Patent and Trademark Office (PTO), but also trade journals, trade registers, telephone books, and in important cases the various state trademark and trade name registration systems. It should also include all classes (categories used by the PTO) which might be applicable to the products planned. To reduce the amount of searching necessary, trademarks are grouped into classes of similar goods by the PTO and other foreign trademark offices. Software (except video games) normally falls into International Class 9, and printed publications, like manuals or books, into Class 16. If you expect to market in foreign countries, you will need to search those records as well. Foreign searches take more time and often cost considerably more. They are best handled directly by your attorney.

It is not uncommon to find that the proposed trademark name is already in use in several places in the U.S. and that various forms of it have been already registered in similar classifications with the PTO. In cases where a potential conflict arises, your trademark attorney can help you evaluate the results of the search and suggest alternative ways of using the mark. You will not be able to register (or use) the mark if the proposed mark is "likely to cause confusion" with an existing mark. If you are careful at this stage, you can save yourself a lot of wasted advertising and printing costs, as well as possible litigation over alleged conflicts.

Establishing First Use in Commerce

To register a trademark under the Lanham Act you must be able to show the PTO that you used it in commerce. If you expect to hold the exclusive right to the mark throughout the U.S., you must also demonstrate that your use was the *first* such use in commerce. Sometimes there are conflicts where someone has used a mark only in a small part of one state, in which case your ownership registration may be exclusive, except for that area. Since Congress cannot constitutionally legislate in the intrastate field, the Lanham Act only applies to those areas like interstate and foreign commerce and where the commerce affects interstate commerce (such as a business on a large interstate freeway). This differs from copyright law, where the federal law has preempted state copyright laws.

Under the law, you have met the use requirement if the mark is on goods, "when it is placed in any manner on the goods or their containers or the displays associated therewith or on the tags or labels affixed thereto and the goods are sold or transported in commerce." 15 USC § 1127. A similar rule applies to services and "service marks," which is what trademarks are called when they identify the source of services.

Typically, software trademarks are printed on the label of the diskette, may appear in screen messages, and are usually on the cover of the user manual as well as on the slipcase package. Use of the trademark in advertisements alone does not establish use under the law. Furthermore, it is not sufficient to place the trademark on the user manual only. The PTO has recently started to reject applications for registration that rely on such limited use. The manner in which the mark is used can have a significant adverse effect on your ability to register it.

The example of the title page of a manual in use by Digital Research with one of its popular products, illustrates how to display a number of registered and some as yet unregistered trademarks. Where the registration of the mark has not yet been completed by the PTO, the "TM" symbol is used by Digital Research to indicate a claim to the mark. The symbol " ® " (sometimes called the Circle R) is used to indicate status as a registered mark. In this case a trademark of another company, International Business Machines, is used and the term "IBM" is shown with the ® symbol to indicate that it, too, is a registered mark of someone.

Obtaining Evidence of Use in Commerce

Suppose that you have selected your own new trademark for an appointment scheduling program, to be called "Making Time," and you have already determined through a search that it does not conflict with other marks. You and your attorney have decided that all the other similar marks are not likely to be confused with your product, and you have the artwork done, including one version with an hourglass between the words. What do you do now? Take an early, and perhaps *beta* test copy of your program for shipment to an early customer, and place the selected brand name on the label as well as in the screen display, so that you have a label like this:

MAKING TIME™—Appointment Scheduler

Version 1.0   Serial Number—12233444

© Copyright 1984   Hometown Software Ltd.

NOTICE: This software is licensed only under the terms of your Agreement. Please read it carefully and return the registration card before using it.

The trademark name can actually be typed, unless you are claiming unique lettering or artwork as part of the mark. Your screen notice might use similar language at sign-on time, but have an hourglass displayed between the words. Perhaps you could even arrange for the sand to shift

Figure 10.1.   (Courtesy of Digital Research Inc. Reproduced with permission)

from the top to the bottom of the glass while it displays. Now you have a trademark in several forms (and you may need several drawings for the different versions). Even though the software is intangible and invisible to the licensee except when in use, you have complied with the law by placing the mark (the brand name) on the physical container of the product. Here the actual diskette, the screen, and the user manual are all embodiments of the product.

When you first ship the diskette and manual in commerce, which should be to a customer in another state, keep copies of the shipping invoice with the date, showing the sale, the price, the customer, and the product shipped. This is your permanent evidence of the first registrable use of the trademark. If you had used the mark on the product within your own state earlier, keep those invoices too, since this was technically the first date of use, a date which is also needed for your trademark registration.

Do not try to establish your first use in commerce by advertising, shipping to your brother in Las Vegas, or by giving copies away. These schemes may work as long as no one contests your mark, but if someone else really makes a sale in commerce under the same mark in the meantime, you may have lost your trademark. Only legitimate business transactions, even though prearranged, will satisfy the law.

You should, if possible, follow up with a few other actual sales over the next few weeks using the mark on your software, in order to establish a course of transactions in commerce. You must also keep copies of the labels or other materials that contain the mark, since you or your attorney will need to send five copies of them in to the Patent and Trademark Office (PTO) when you apply for registration.

Once you have evidence of shipments in commerce, you can temporarily stop shipping until you get the rest of the bugs out of the software, but even at this point you may want to start the registration process described below. Remember, however, you must continue using the mark over a period of time in order to meet the continued use requirement of the trademark law. If you stop using the mark during the first five years, or for two continuous years thereafter, you may permanently lose it to someone else who adopts it for a similar product. Non-use for two years is presumed by law to indicate an intent to abandon the mark.

REGISTERING THE MARK—HOW AND WHY

Why Register?

The Choice to Register.   You have a choice between registering your mark or not, and whether to rely on a state registration if your sales will be local only, or proceeding with a federal registration under the Lanham Act. Software sales tend to be national in scope, so a state registration probably would not be your choice. You may elect to spend the money for the national registration.

Not everyone needs to register his or her trademarks, because some products never achieve enough success to make it worthwhile financially. You have to make that decision. Even if you elect not to register the mark, you still have what are called "common law" rights to the mark and may be able to prevent others from using a confusing or similar mark by bringing a lawsuit in state court. About all you would need to prove under state law is that the mark was first used by you and that it would tend to confuse the consumer. It is much easier if you have a registration under the Lanham Act. So long as you still have the legal basis for doing so, you can apply to register a federal trademark at any time after it went into use, but you may have to prove that you were first to do so, as against other claimants, and that the claimed mark was in continuous use.

The Benefits of Registration.   Let's assume you are going ahead with federal registration. The Lanham Act provides a procedure for registration of marks that qualify, and they are placed on either the Principal Register or the Supplemental Register. Everyone tries to have a mark placed on the Principal Register since it provides three benefits not available to marks on the Supplemental Register: 1) the ability to use the registration notice, usually the ® symbol; 2) the ability to sue in federal court based on your Certificate of Registration; and 3) the right to have your mark used as a reference against registration of confusingly similar and subsequent marks. Registration on either register also allows you to register the same mark more readily in foreign countries.

The Supplemental Register is used for those marks that do not qualify, for one reason or another, for the Principal Register. These are often marks involving surnames, slogans, numerals, or other things that are adequate to distinguish the goods, but which have not been in use long enough to have acquired a secondary meaning. For example, the federal trial court in San Francisco recently (1984) dismissed a trademark infringement suit brought by Computerland against Microland Computer Corporation. The decision was based on the conclusion that "Computerland" is not presently legally protectible, since it is either generic or descriptive and lacks secondary meaning. This kind of mark belongs on the Supplemental Register, since it cannot qualify as a trademark until (if ever) time and advertising expenditures give it the necessary secondary meaning.

The Term of Protection.   Once the registration is issued on either register, the mark is protected for an initial term of twenty years, so long as it is continuously in use, and so long as the owner files an affidavit of use during the sixth year of the term. The mark will be deemed abandoned, and cancelled by the PTO, if the affidavit is not timely filed. Otherwise the term will continue and the registration may be renewed for a series of successive twenty-year terms so long as it is still in use. You may sell the trademark along with the goodwill built up with it, and you can bring suit to protect the mark, when necessary. You lose all the benefits of the Lanham Act if the registration expires or is cancelled. Remember, however, that a trademark lasts only as long as it remains in use—whether or not it is registered.

The Registration Process

To apply for a trademark registration you must properly complete a registration form, supply five copies of the mark as actually used, a drawing of the mark in a very specific format, and pay the filing fee of $175.00 per class of goods or services. An illustrative completed form with the drawing page is shown as Figures 10.2 and 10.3. The form may be entirely typewritten, or on the printed forms available from the PTO. You mail it to Commissioner of Patents & Trademarks, Washington, D.C. 20231, for filing.

If all goes well, the form is processed by the PTO, the mark published in the PTO Official Gazette, the mark registered on the Principal Register, and a Certificate of Registration is issued by the PTO to you as the appli-. cant. You then have all the benefits described in the preceding section. If it were only that simple!

What actually happens is that once the application arrives in Washington, D.C. it is assigned to an examination section of the Trademark Office, and after many months it is looked at by someone who notices something missing, or who has some question about the application or the drawing. Months later you receive a form letter inquiring about the problem, which you answer and then you wait. The process takes on average from eighteen months to two years and can be very frustrating. If you have done anything wrong, your application may be rejected, and you will have to start all over again. If you fail to answer within six months of the letter to you, the file is closed.

Unlike patent law, any attorney can theoretically prepare and file your trademark application with the PTO, but in practice most attorneys consider this a specialty and will refer you to a law firm that routinely handles trademark matters. You may prepare and prosecute the application yourself, if you have the time and energy. Most people find the experience not worth the $600 to $1,000 legal fee, which includes the filing costs and a great deal of correspondence with the PTO.

Doing it Yourself.   If you want to prepare and file your trademark application yourself, you can obtain the forms and a pamphlet on trademark registration, free, by writing to the Director of Trademark Examining Operations, Patent & Trademark Office, Box 5, Washington, D.C. 20231, (or you can telephone the office at (703) 557–3881). This office will not give you legal advice nor any significant help in filling out the forms. Be sure you follow the detailed rules concerning preparation of the drawing showing the mark, since most of the correspondence with laymen turns

TRADEMARK APPLICATION, PRINCIPAL REGISTER, WITH DECLARATION (Individual)	MARK *(identify the mark)* Making Time
	CLASS NO. *(if known)* Intl. Class 9

TO THE COMMISSIONER OF PATENTS AND TRADEMARKS:

NAME OF APPLICANT, AND BUSINESS TRADE NAME, IF ANY

Fred Programmer d/b/a Hometown Software Ltd.

BUSINESS ADDRESS

777 Lucky Lane, Suite A, Monterey, California 93940

RESIDENCE ADDRESS

888 Scenic Drive, Carmel, California 93923

CITIZENSHIP OF APPLICANT

United States

The above identified applicant has adopted and is using the trademark shown in the accompanying drawing[1] for the following goods: __computer programs recorded on magnetic tape and__ diskettes and accompanying instructional materials

and requests that said mark be registered in the United States Patent and Trademark Office on the Principal Register established by the Act of July 5, 1946.

The trademark was first used on the goods[2] on ___March 17, 1983__ ; was first used on the goods[2] in
(date)

___interstate___ _____ commerce[3] on __April 1, 1983__ ;
(type of commerce)   *(date)*
and is now in use in such commerce.

4

The mark is used by applying it to[5] ___tags and labels affixed to the goods and__ on the containers for the goods

and five specimens showing the mark as actually used are presented herewith.

6

Fred Programmer

(name of applicant)

being hereby warned that willful false statements and the like so made are punishable by fine or imprisonment, or both, under Section 1001 of Title 18 of the United States Code and that such willful false statements may jeopardize the validity of the application or any registration resulting therefrom, declares that he/she believes himself/herself to be the owner of the trademark sought to be registered; to the best of his/her knowledge and belief no other person, firm, corporation, or association has the right to use said mark in commerce, either in the identical form or in such near resemblance thereto as may be likely, when applied to the goods of such other person, to cause confusion, or to cause mistake, or to deceive; the facts set forth in this application are true; and all statements made of his/her own knowledge are true and all statements made on information and belief are believed to be true.

Fred Programmer

(signature of applicant)

__April 13, 1983__
(date)

Form PTO - 1476 **(Rev. 10-82)** *(Instructions on reverse side)*   Patent and Trademark Office - U.S. DEPT. of COMMERCE

(over)

Figure 10.2

APPLICANT: Fred Programmer, dba Hometown Software Ltd.

ADDRESS: 777 Lucky Lane, Suite A, Monterey, California 93940

FIRST USE: March 17, 1983

FIRST USE IN COMMERCE: April 1, 1983

GOODS OR SERVICES: Computer programs recorded on magnetic tape and diskettes and accompanying instructional materials.

MAKING TIME

Figure 10.3. Attachment to Trademark Application

on this piece of Bristol board and india ink. The PTO is very picky about this aspect of things.

The biggest problems in trying to file your trademark application yourself lie in the areas of evaluating existing marks which might conflict, selecting the proper class or classes of goods for registration, and then defending your application if the examiner rejects or questions it on various legal or factual grounds. If you get into the latter situation, you should immediately seek help from an attorney who has handled trademark applications before.

As Figure 10.2 indicates, most computer software falls into International Class 9 with other scientific and electrical equipment. User manuals (to the extent the trademark is valid in such a case) are in Class 16. Video games are now in Class 28. There are thirty-four trademark classes and eight service mark classes. There is also an older U.S. classification system which is still used for some searches and which uses different numbers. You should use the international classes.

The description on the form, of the items to which the mark is affixed, can often be broader, like "Computer programs recorded on magnetic and other media or in computer components," or perhaps just "Computer programs in machine readable formats, and related promotional materials." The broader form is better for you, if you can get it approved. However, the examiners handling electrical equipment (Class 9) tend to require that you be more specific.

Other Procedural Matters. The purpose of publishing your proposed registered trademark in the Official Gazette is to give other companies a thirty-day opportunity to object to the registration. There are several procedures that can be used to consider these objections, which can result in administrative hearings similar to trials. During such trials the parties have a chance to present their views and evidence, after which a judge or hearing officer will decide the case.

If your application results in a trial, you will need an experienced attorney to represent you in the proceedings. You may also need legal help if the application gets bogged down in technical arguments, or if you wish to object to actions taken by the PTO. Most attorneys who work with computer law have some expertise in this field, although they may or may not be licensed patent attorneys. Any qualified attorney can appear in trademark matters for you, but most general practitioners will refer you to a specialist.

The Certificate of Registration

A typical Certificate of Registration is set out as Figure 10.4 (pages 1 and 2). You can see that it contains only minimal information, but this document is important to you in that it may be used by your attorney to bring a trademark infringement action against anyone misusing your registered

N⁰ 1242679

THE UNITED STATES OF AMERICA

CERTIFICATE OF REGISTRATION

This is to certify that the records of the Patent and Trademark Office show that an application was filed in said Office for registration of the Mark shown herein, a copy of said Mark and pertinent data from the Application being annexed hereto and made a part hereof,

And there having been due compliance with the requirements of the law and with the regulations prescribed by the Commissioner of Patents and Trademarks,

Upon examination, it appeared that the applicant was entitled to have said Mark registered under the Trademark Act of 1946, and the said Mark has been duly registered this day in the Patent and Trademark Office on the

PRINCIPAL REGISTER

to the registrant named herein.

This registration shall remain in force for Twenty Years unless sooner terminated as provided by law.

In Testimony Whereof I have hereunto set my hand and caused the seal of the Patent and Trademark Office to be affixed this twenty-first day of June, 1983.

Donald J. Quigg

ACTING COMMISSIONER OF PATENTS AND TRADEMARKS

Figure 10.4 (page 1)

O

Int. Cl.: 9

Prior U.S. Cl.: 38

United States Patent and Trademark Office

Reg. No. 1,242,679
Registered Jun. 21, 1983

TRADEMARK
Principal Register

VOLKSWRITER

Lifetree Software Inc. (New York corporation)
Suite 342
177 Webster St.
Monterey, Calif. 93940

For: COMPUTER PROGRAMS RECORDED ON CARDS, TAPES, DISKS AND DISKETTES, in CLASS 9 (U.S. Cl. 38).
First use Mar. 5, 1982; in commerce Mar. 5, 1982.

Ser. No. 375,084, filed Jul. 16, 1982.

DONALD B. AIKEN, Examiner

Figure 10.4 (page 2)

trademark. It is, alone, sufficient evidence to the court that you are the owner of the mark and that the facts stated in it are correct, unless the other side can refute them. The right to use the mark becomes uncontestable in later legal actions, once five years of continued use have been completed, and if you file several affidavits permitted under the law. There are some technical exceptions to this rule, but your attorney can explain these and help you with the filing of these forms, as well as setting up a calendar reminder.

USING AND ADMINISTERING TRADEMARKS

Registered trademarks can be lost if they are improperly used or if they become "generic." In other words, if they come to mean the goods themselves and not the particular brand. Trademark lawyers could list for you proprietary marks which have, over the years, lost their identification with the source—such as aspirin, cellophane, escalator, kerosene, lanolin, linoleum, shredded wheat, thermos, and most recently the term MONOPOLY for games. All of these were at one time registered trademarks.

Some companies like Xerox, DuPont, and Coca Cola spend millions of dollars annually in advertising trying to prevent their brand names XEROX, NYLON, and COKE from becoming generic. Other companies like Merriam-Webster, Inc. have sued (1984) software companies like Cornucopia Software, Inc. for using the term "Electric Webster," and words, designs, and trade dress which look like the Webster's dictionary cover. Failure on its part to take such action could easily result in the term Webster becoming synonymous with all dictionaries.

Adequate protection through proper use will take the combined efforts of you, your attorney, your employees, and your advertising and marketing people. You and your attorney can see that necessary filings for renewal and continuation are made. But there are some general rules for proper trademark use which everyone can follow, as suggested in a very useful handbook, Trademark Management, put out by the U.S. Trademark Association. That book sets forth, in more extended form, the following five rules, to which I have added some computer industry examples:

- Always use the generic name of the product in association with the trademark. Thus, use "the CP/M operating system," not "CP/M;" "XEROX copying machines," not "a xerox."

- Use one of the three statutorily acceptable notice forms with the trademark to remind the public that it is a registered trademark. Most people prefer to use the Circle R form "®." So you will see the forms, 3M® brand diskettes, or ALTOS® computers. With an asterisk (*), a footnote, or a dagger symbol, you can also use the terms "Registered in U.S. Patent and Trademark Office" or the shorter form "Reg. U.S.

Pat. & Tm. Off." at the bottom of the page. If the mark has not yet been registered, you should *never* use these forms, but you can use the informal "™" or the term "A trademark of Lifetree Software, Inc." following the mark or at the bottom of the material.

- Always display the trademark with some form of special typographical treatment, such as script, italics, boldface, or at a minimum, capital letters. Everyone in the computer industry is familiar with the IBM logo, consisting of the letter IBM made up of narrow horizontal bars, one on top of the other.

- Never allow the trademark to appear in an incorrect grammatical form, especially as a noun. Do not say your store carries "a whole line of IBM's." Never use the mark as a verb; XEROX gets upset at writers who "xerox a set of documents."

- Finally, do not create other word forms from the original trademark, either by coining new words or splitting the original. Use the form the same way all the time, although you may vary its size to fit the neighboring text.

You should not permit other people to use your trademarks improperly, either. Write to them if they do, and object. Sue them if they continue. But do remember that you cannot prohibit them from referring to your trademark in advertisements, as long as they do not create confusion or mislead the consumer. Several recent trademark cases have confirmed this principle.

WHAT TO DO ABOUT MISUSE OF YOUR TRADEMARK

The most important right that you have once the trademark is registered is the power to obtain, with the help of the federal courts and marshals, injunctions and court orders preventing others from using the mark on any goods similar to yours, including copies of your programs. According to Section 32(1) of the Lanham Act, it is illegal for any person to do the following without your permission:

- (a) use in commerce any reproduction, counterfeit, copy, or colorable imitation of a registered mark in connection with the sale, offering for sale, distribution, or advertising of any goods or services on or in connection with which such use is likely to cause confusion, or cause mistake, or to deceive; or

- (b) reproduce, counterfeit, copy or colorably imitate a registered mark and apply such reproduction, counterfeit, copy, or colorable imitation to labels, signs, prints, packages, wrappers, receptacles or advertisements intended to be used in commerce upon or in connection with the sale, offering for sale, distribution, or advertising of goods or services on or in connection with which such use is likely to cause confusion, or to cause mistake, or to deceive . . .

In plain English, a software pirate cannot use your trademark on diskettes or software which is not your product and which did not originate from your company or persons authorized by you to distribute it. If the pirate, as often happens, copies your label or your trademark onto his diskettes and makes copies of the software, he is in violation of this law and you can bring suit against him under federal law.

Filing Suit

If this should occur, you will need to collect some evidence of the facts and take that evidence to your attorney for assistance. Legal action can then be filed in the appropriate U.S. District Court where the defendant resides or does business, so that you may seek injunctive relief and damages for the infringement. The trial of the case and the preliminary steps leading to an injunction are very much like those described in Chapter 18 on Remedies for Copyright Infringement. Your attorney will probably have combined a copyright infringement action with the trademark action in any case in which you own a trademark involved. This gives you two shots at the defendant, and a better chance of stopping him. Trademark infringement cases involving software are often easier to prove than copyright infringement, since the pirate either copied the trademark or he didn't.

Other Remedies

Besides the injunctive relief, you may obtain recovery of all your damages in the form of lost profits, all the profit made by the defendant, and the court costs of your legal action. In exceptional cases, the trial judge may award attorney fees, but this is not as common as in copyright cases, where they are almost always awarded. The best part of collecting damages in a trademark case is that all you have to do is prove what the defendant's sales were. It is then up to him to prove what his allowable costs were, in order for the judge to decide what his profit was.

If you win your case, the court can order the destruction of all offending labels, advertising materials, and the means of making them. If the trademark cannot be separated from the goods, as in the case of counterfeit or copied software, the court may order the destruction of the actual software, too. If you succeed, you will be able to have the marshal or sheriff seize the bank accounts and assets of the defendant and sell them, in order to pay the money damages you will probably have been awarded. This result creates a strong inclination on the part of the pirate not to do this type of thing anymore!

There are a number of other technical rules as to trademark infringement procedures, but, if applicable, those are best left to a discussion with your lawyer. The losing party has a right to appeal the case to the United States Court of Appeals for the federal circuit in which the trial took place. If this happens, the final outcome may not be known for years, because these courts are sometimes three or more years behind. But to forestall enforcement of the judgment, pending outcome of the appeal, the losing party will have to file an appeal bond to protect you. Since these bonds are costly, you will often have the benefit of injunctive relief during this time. Because of this, the preliminary injunctions that are granted in trademark cases often prove to be the end of the case, since once a mark is taken out of use by the defendant he will normally have selected a new name and advertised that in the meantime.

Remedies against Imported Infringing Goods

As computer-related products become more and more international in scope and marketing, the international aspects of protection become more important. There are remedies available in case of international infringements. You should also review some of the related information in Chapter 15 on the international problems of software protection.

Importation of Goods with Infringing Marks.   Under Section 42 of the Lanham Act the importation of goods bearing infringing marks or names is forbidden. To implement this section of the law, the U.S. Customs Service maintains a register of trademarks, copyrights, and trade names that have been in use for more than six months. Once a name or mark is recorded on this register, at the request of its owner, Customs Inspectors have the authority to detain for thirty days any imported article that bears a mark or name which might be "confusingly similar" to that of one on the register. Unless the importer is able to show that the mark is either authorized for use in the United States or that it is not likely to confuse, the goods are subject to seizure and forfeiture under federal law.

The dual benefit of this procedure is that not only do you have the government working for you, but the burden of proof also shifts to the importer. In the meantime, the goods do not enter the stream of commerce, where tracing them down and impounding them becomes very difficult. An injunction against trademark infringement runs primarily against the defendant, so you must actually find the infringing goods in order to have them seized and destroyed. This system works equally well for copyrighted goods, and has been used very successfully by the Bally and Midway video game manufacturing companies to prevent the importation of Pac-Man and other infringing games. Apple Computer has also used this system.

Only trademarks registered on the Principal Register are eligible for recording with the Customs Service. The procedure is fairly complex, so you should ask your attorney to assist you. The filing fee is currently $190 for each trademark and each additional class of goods, so the process can become expensive. It is also possible to record business names and trade styles which have been in use for at least six months. Current Customs Service rules should be consulted for details.

False Descriptions.   There are also provisions in Section 43(b) of the Lanham Act which prohibit the importation of goods marked with false designations of origin or false descriptions that would mislead consumers. Under Section 43(b) such goods may be stopped at the customhouse at the port of entry, subject to hearings on behalf of the owner or importer similar to those authorized under Section 42, described above.

The International Trade Commission.   Another way of stopping the importation of goods that misuse trademarks (and even unregistered trade names) may be through the United States International Trade Commission. Under the provisions of 19 USC § 1337 unfair methods of competition and unfair acts in the importation of articles into the United States, or in their sale by the owner, importer, consignee, or agent of either, is unlawful, and the Commission may exclude items from entry into the United States under this law. If an item is found to be part of such activity, the Commission issues an order of exclusion, advises the Secretary of Treasury of such order, and then the U.S. Customs Service enforces the order whenever the goods show up at a port of entry.

   Detailed rules for this remedy are found in 19 CFR Part 210, which provide the means for causing the Commission to start an investigation into claims of unfair competition or unfair acts. While the provisions of the law often are applied to patented items, there is no reason that other types of unfair activities could not be stopped in this manner. In fact, the video game manufacturers have used this law most effectively against Japanese imports that are "look-a-likes". A similar proceeding was instigated at the behest of Apple Computer as a reaction against the numerous Apple look-a-like microcomputers being made in Taiwan and Hong Kong, and shipped into the U.S.

Section 43(a) and Private Actions for Unfair Competition

In recent years considerable legal activity has arisen under Section 43(a) of the Lanham Act, which contains a federal action for unfair competition against competing manufacturers. This increasingly important remedy is based on the principle that it is illegal to distribute or sell goods in interstate commerce which have marks that falsely designate the origin of the goods or falsely describe the goods. The plaintiff need not have a registered trademark to begin his suit, but he is required to show that the defendant's acts of falsely marking or designating his goods will likely injure the plaintiff or his business.

   Where there is direct competition or a substantial likelihood of confusion, the courts have been increasingly willing to grant injunctive relief, and in some cases damages, under this section. The law is very favorable to owners of trademarks, so that if you believe a competitor is selling a software or hardware product which is falsely marked or misleadingly like your own, you should discuss the matter promptly with your attorney. A number of recent cases provide substantial help in this area, especially when combined into a copyright and a trademark cause of action.

PROTECTING TRADEMARKS UNDER INTERNATIONAL LAW

As Chapter 15 on the International Aspects of Software Protection indicates, there are trademark conventions similar to the copyright conventions and treaties, but they do not provide as automatic a protection as those concerning copyrights. Instead, trademark registration is a local matter dependent on the law of each country. Since the Lanham Act does not extend trademark protection outside the United States, it is necessary, with few exceptions, to separately register a mark in every country of the world where protection is sought. In other common law countries, like Great Britain and Australia, an unregistered mark may have some protection, but in most countries only registration affords any basis for protection.

Under international treaties, there are some areas of the world where there are simplified procedures for obtaining national registration in a group of countries at one time, such as under the Madrid Convention which covers most of Europe. These rules are complex and changing, so that you and your attorney will want to discuss the subject with an attorney practicing in the country or countries in question. Almost all foreign trademark applications are handled by corresponding attorneys in the actual country of desired registration, acting under a power-of-attorney.

The rules differ drastically from country to country, so you must do some advance planning if you think your trademark may become important in foreign countries. Because some countries allow registration prior to actual use, you may have to register your trademark abroad to avoid someone else preempting it during the several years time it may take for your software product to get into the international marketing arena.

This step is especially critical in Japan and the Common Market countries, which are the logical international markets for American software. Unless you are willing to risk finding at a later date for example, that a distributor selling the product in Japan has filed for your trademark, you may have to act before you would otherwise have been ready to proceed. If you do not, you may not be able to terminate the distributor and still use your own product name in Japan. Pre-use registration must be planned carefully, since even countries permitting this practice require that use commence in commerce in the country within three to five years of first registration.

On the international level, you need, more than ever, good legal advice from an attorney with competent contacts in these countries. Lawyers in foreign countries do not necessarily operate in the same manner as in the U.S., and the costs of international legal help can be high. It is still cheaper to do advance planning with an attorney, than litigation or cancellation of an international advertising program because of trademark conflicts.

ASSIGNING AND LICENSING TRADEMARKS

There are many serious and potentially disastrous problems involved in assigning (selling) or licensing the use of your trademarks to others. The subject could fill a whole book, so a few comments are in order here. The most critical point to remember is that if you do not handle transactions of this type correctly, you may well lose the trademark entirely.

The assignment of a trademark (or trade name) means the complete transfer of all rights to the mark and the goodwill associated with it. Under Section 10 of the Lanham Act, any attempt to transfer only the trademark, without the goodwill, may result in complete loss of all prior rights to the mark. The form of the assignment document is, therefore, critical, the drafting of which should be handled by an attorney skilled in such matters.

All trademark assignments must be in writing and signed by the parties, and should be acknowledged before a notary public and recorded with the PTO. An assignment is void as against purchasers without notice, unless recorded in the PTO within three months after the date of assignment or prior to the innocent purchase and assignment. Since trademarks and trade names are part and parcel of the goodwill of a business, it is rarely possible to transfer them to a third party after the business has ceased to operate for a period of time.

Conversely, a trademark license is a contract in writing which gives a third party the right to use a trademark and to benefit from the goodwill. It is not a transfer of the ownership of the mark itself. Trademark licenses are not required to be recorded in the PTO to be valid. There are, however, a goodly number of anti-trust and other legal problems involved in trademark licenses, which should be discussed with your attorney in advance of your agreeing to such licenses. Violations of the anti-trust laws through the improper use and licensing of a trademark can result in loss of the right to the mark, as well as awards for money damages.

Monitoring Trademark Use by Licensees

Many software licenses permit the licensee (usually an OEM making computers) to use and reproduce software and the trademark of the licensor.

Where this is the case, unless the trademark licensor retains control over the manufacture and/or distribution of the product using the mark, there is a good possibility the trademark will be lost. By law, the licensor must control the "nature and quality" of the goods and services sold under the mark by related companies, or risk the loss of the mark. If the licensor does not have *and exercise* this control, prohibition of use of the mark by others may be unenforceable, and the mark will be lost as a trademark.

This situation most often occurs in franchising, such as McDonald's or ComputerLand, where the essential element of the franchise is the use of the well-recognized name which is a trademark or service mark. However, where distributors or OEM's are authorized to reproduce software for distribution, the licensor must have, at a minimum, strong contractual controls on the conditions under which the product is produced. The licensor should also make it a point to check on the quality and consistency of the product reproduced, to protect the associated goodwill and the trademark.

This legal principle is based on the idea that if the licensor does not take these measures, the level of quality may fall or be inconsistent, but no one will be able to tell the true source of the product, which is the purpose of trademarks in the first place. Make sure, therefore, that all licenses authorizing use of a trademark in connection with software reproduced by others have this element of control built into the license.

SUMMARY

A federal trademark registration for the brand name of a software product can be of considerable value in protecting the author or publisher from unauthorized use of the copyrighted software or the trademark.

Infringement of the rights of the owner of the trademark subjects the defendant to the jurisdiction of the federal courts and a body of reasonably well-developed law, which law includes injunctive relief as well as damages, costs, and perhaps attorney fees. Since the cost of obtaining federal trademark protection is relatively low, it would seem foolish to ignore the possibilities for protection offered by the Lanham Act.

The process of obtaining a federal trademark is not particularly complex or expensive, but is best left to trained legal personnel experienced in the field. Errors in obtaining or transferring the trademark may be fatal, resulting in complete loss of rights to the mark. Businessmen and women can, however, take many of the steps themselves, and they should understand the basic principles of trademark and trade name law. Since both federal and local law may apply, and many changes may occur from time to time, it is important to select an attorney who works in this field on a continuing basis.

11

Why Software is Licensed and Not Sold

THE SCOPE OF THIS CHAPTER

Software Licenses

Software licenses are unusual legal documents, which are not well understood by either the computer industry or the legal profession. A license is the grant of a right by the "licensor" to a "licensee" to do something that the licensee could not do without the permission of the licensor. The grant is almost always in writing. The licensee has only those rights granted in the license and can only exercise them under the precise conditions set in the grant. In the case of a copyright license, the grant involves one or more of the rights otherwise exclusively reserved to the copyright owner by 17 USC § 106.

The document granting a software license does not have to be a formal, signed contract to be enforceable. It is usually a hybrid document that consists of *both* a license grant (subject to various conditions) and a contract (which is created either by express agreement or by the conduct of the parties). The legal concepts involved are quite different than many of the principles that business people usually work with. It is therefore important to examine them in detail in the context of a real-life situation.

I have chosen to do this through presenting a typical end-user object-code software license form, and then exploring the reasons for the grant of copyright licenses, by reference to the applicable law. Without commenting on the example license form on a paragraph by paragraph basis, I have nevertheless used it as the fulcrum of this discussion. We will come to this example form in a moment.

Copyright Licenses Only

The licenses we will examine here relate exclusively to copyrights. Trade secret, patent, and trademark law could also be used to license the technology or information found in software, but for one thing, it is not practical to license mass-distributed *object* code under trade secret principles, since it cannot be deemed "secret" under these circumstances. This chapter is a follow-on from Chapters 5–8 on Copyright law, which you should have read in advance. The final key will be Chapter 18 on Remedies For Copyright Infringement.

Most software copyright licenses in use today blindly copy existing licenses and are confusing and inadequate. It is not easy to make a software license short and clear, but at least it should be consistent.

The explosive growth of the microcomputer software industry is now going to force both the legal profession and the computer industry to take a second, more careful look at software copyright licenses.

What is not Covered Here

Readers hoping to find copies of software copyright licenses at all the various levels of distribution—developmental license agreements, escrow agreements, and Original Equipment Manufacturers (OEM) source and object-code distribution agreements—may be disappointed. To include even portions of such other licenses would have taken too many additional pages in a book intended for a diverse audience. I decided that it was more important to provide you as a reader with a breadth of coverage. The bibliography provides you with other sources for such license agreements.

AN END-USER OBJECT-CODE LICENSE FORM

The End-User Object-Code License Form that follows is an adaptation of a copyrighted license, prepared by my law firm and currently in use by a client engaged in distribution of one of the better-known, international word-processing programs available for use on the IBM Personal Computer. It covers all the issues discussed, and more. It is used with permission of Lifetree Software, Inc., Monterey, California. (Note that most of the warranty provisions are omitted here, because they are included in Chapter 12.)

LIFETREE SOFTWARE, INC.
SINGLE–SYSTEM END USER
OBJECT CODE SOFTWARE LICENSE AGREEMENT

DO NOT OPEN THE ACCOMPANYING SEALED DISKETTE PACKAGE UNTIL YOU HAVE READ THIS LICENSE AGREEMENT. MAKE SURE

THIS SOFTWARE PRODUCT IS DESIGNED FOR YOUR COMPUTER.
IF THE SOFTWARE IS NOT MEANT FOR USE ON YOUR COMPUTER
OR IF YOU DO NOT AGREE TO ABIDE BY THE TERMS OF THIS
LICENSE, YOU MAY RETURN THE COMPLETE SOFTWARE PACK-
AGE TO YOUR DEALER FOR EXCHANGE OR A REFUND WITHIN
FIVE (5) DAYS OF PURCHASE, SO LONG AS THE SEAL ON THE
DISKETTE ENVELOPE HAS NOT BEEN BROKEN.

* *

Please fill in the following information for your records:

Name of Licensed SOFTWARE . . . .   VOLKSWRITER® DELUXE
Version Number. . . . .   V. 2.1
Serial Number. . . . .   _____
Date You Received The SOFTWARE. . . . . . .   _____
Where You Acquired The SOFTWARE .   _____

* *

    LIFETREE SOFTWARE, INC. and LICENSEE have agreed, by LI-
CENSEE's act of opening the sealed diskette package or by LICENSEE's
use of the SOFTWARE, that LICENSOR's grant to LICENSEE of the right
to use and possession of this SOFTWARE shall be subject to all the following terms and conditions:

1. Definitions of Terms Used

    A. "LSI" means LIFETREE SOFTWARE, INC., a California corpora-
tion with its principal office located at the Pacific Professional Building,
Suite 315, 411 Pacific Street, Monterey, California 93940, the owner of
the copyright on the SOFTWARE or its licensed publisher.

    B. "LICENSEE" means the individual or the business entity licens-
ing this copy of the SOFTWARE and includes those persons in
LICENSEE's immediate organization, such as business associates, partners and employees who are authorized to use this copy on the COM-
PUTER under the terms of this Agreement.

    C. "COMPUTER" is the single microcomputer system, utilizing a
single processor or a co-processor, on which LICENSEE is licensed to use
this SOFTWARE. Multiple CPU systems, use on networks, or emulations
on mainframe or minicomputers require supplementary licenses.

    D. "SOFTWARE" is the set of copyrighted, object-code computer
programs provided in the accompanying sealed package, regardless of

the form in which LICENSEE may subsequently use it, and regardless of any modification which LICENSEE may make to it.

E. "DOCUMENTATION" means LSI's published SOFTWARE manual and any written or printed technical material provided by LSI with the SOFTWARE to explain its operation and aid in its use.

F. "LICENSE" means this LICENSE Agreement and the rights and obligations which it creates under the United States Copyright Law, foreign treaties, and the laws of California.

G. "REGISTRATION CARD" means the LICENSEE information card provided with the SOFTWARE, which LICENSEE should complete and return to LSI so that LSI can provide newsletters, product notices and other support services.

H. "DERIVATIVE" means any other or related computer program which may be developed that contains all or any part of the SOFTWARE, regardless of the form of the code, the media it is carried on, or its intended use.

2. Grant of License and Licensee's Agreements

2.1 In consideration of LICENSEE's payment of the license fee and of LICENSEE's agreement to abide by the terms and conditions of this LICENSE, LSI grants LICENSEE a nonexclusive right to use and display this serialized copy of the SOFTWARE on a single COMPUTER at a single location, so long as LICENSEE complies with the terms of this LICENSE. If the COMPUTER on which LICENSEE uses the SOFTWARE is a authorized multi-user system, then the LICENSE covers all users on that single system, without further license payments. LSI retains the right to terminate this LICENSE, at any time, by notice to LICENSEE should LICENSEE violate any of its provisions. LSI reserves all rights not expressly granted to LICENSEE.

2.2 LICENSEE agrees to comply with the terms and conditions of this LICENSE and agrees to take all reasonable steps to protect LSI's SOFTWARE from theft or use contrary to the terms of the LICENSE. LICENSEE agrees to pay LSI for additional licenses if LICENSEE intends to use or does use the SOFTWARE on more than one COMPUTER or in any way beyond the scope of this LICENSE. LICENSEE agrees not to disassemble, decompile, or otherwise reverse engineer the SOFTWARE. LICENSEE agrees either to destroy or return the original and all existing copies of the SOFTWARE to LSI within five (5) days after receiving notice of LSI's termination of this LICENSE.

3. Ownership of Software

LICENSEE shall be deemed to own only the magnetic or other physical media on which the SOFTWARE is originally or subsequently recorded or fixed, but an express condition of this LICENSE is that LSI shall at all times retain ownership of the SOFTWARE recorded on the original diskette copy(ies) and all subsequent copies of the SOFTWARE, regardless of the form or media in or on which the original and other copies may subsequently exist. This LICENSE is not a sale of the LICENSEE'S copy or of any subsequent copy.

4. Possession and Copying of the Software

LICENSEE agrees that the SOFTWARE will only be displayed or read into or used on the licensed COMPUTER. LICENSEE agrees to make no more than three (3) copies of the SOFTWARE for backup purposes only, all of which copies (with the original) shall be kept in the possession or direct control of LICENSEE. LICENSEE agrees to place a label on the outside of each backup copy showing the serial number, program name, version number, and the LSI copyright and trademark notices, in the same form as they appear on the original licensed copy. Transfer of a copy to one hard disk on the licensed COMPUTER shall count as one backup copy.

5. Transfer or Reproduction of Software

5.1 LICENSEE is NOT licensed to rent, lease, transfer, network, reproduce, display, or otherwise distribute this SOFTWARE, except as specifically provided in this LICENSE agreement. LICENSEE understands that unauthorized reproduction of copies of the SOFTWARE and/or unauthorized transfer of any copy of the SOFTWARE may be a serious crime, as well as subjecting LICENSEE to suit for damages, injunctive relief, and attorney fees.

5.2 The SOFTWARE may only be used on one COMPUTER at a time. LICENSEE may change the COMPUTER on which LICENSEE is authorized to use the SOFTWARE to another computer within LICENSEE's immediate organization. In such case, neither LICENSEE nor anyone else may continue to use the SOFTWARE on the former computer.

5.3 LICENSEE may not transfer any copy of the SOFTWARE to another person or entity outside LICENSEE's immediate organization, on either a permanent or a temporary basis, unless LICENSEE obtains the prior written approval of LSI and pays the then current license transfer fee. Approval will not unreasonably be withheld if LICENSEE advises LSI in writing of the name and address of the proposed license transferee, the license transferee returns a copy of the REGISTRATION CARD, and the transferee agrees to be bound by the terms of this LICENSE. LSI will provide an additional copy of this LICENSE and a new REGISTRATION CARD for this purpose upon request, at the time the license transfer fee is paid. If the license transfer is approved, LICENSEE must transfer all copies of the SOFTWARE including the original. LSI retains the right to terminate the LICENSE, to trace serial numbers, and to take legal action if any of these conditions are violated.

6. Derivatives, Adaptations, and Modifications to the Software

Should LICENSEE make any DERIVATIVE of the SOFTWARE, LICENSEE shall have a nonexclusive royalty-free license to such adaptations or modifications which LICENSEE may create, but shall have no ownership interest in the SOFTWARE or the DERIVATIVE. LICENSEE may not distribute or make any copies of the DERIVATIVE contrary to the provisions of this LICENSE or LICENSOR's exclusive rights to distribute or copy the SOFTWARE without the prior express written consent of LSI. If the LICENSE is terminated for any reason, LICENSEE may not continue to use any part of the SOFTWARE, or any derivative thereof, contained in any DERIVATIVE work.

7. Limited Warranty and Disclaimer of Liability

LSI HAS NO CONTROL OVER THE CONDITIONS UNDER WHICH LICENSEE USES THE SOFTWARE, THEREFORE LSI DOES NOT AND CANNOT WARRANT THE PERFORMANCE OR RESULTS THAT MAY BE OBTAINED BY ITS USE. HOWEVER, LSI PROVIDES THE FOLLOWING LIMITED WARRANTY:
[Text of Warranty Omitted—See Chapter 12]

8. Diskette Replacement Policy

After expiration of the sixty (60) day warranty period, and for one (1) year from the date of delivery, the original diskette(s) provided by LSI may be returned to LSI for replacement if it (they) become damaged. The damaged diskette(s) must be returned with the proper Diskette Replacement Form and the then current diskette replacement fee, to the address on the form. LSI will replace the diskette, on an exchange basis, with the same or similar SOFTWARE, provided that LICENSEE has returned the REGISTRATION CARD to LSI.

9. General Conditions

9.1 The validity and performance of this LICENSE shall be governed by California law, except as to copyright and trademark matters which are covered by United States laws and international treaties. This LICENSE Agreement is deemed entered into at Monterey, California.

9.2 The failure of either party to enforce any of the provisions hereof shall not be construed to be a waiver of the right of such party thereafter to enforce any such provisions.

9.3 The expiration or termination of this LICENSE shall not affect provisions of this LICENSE which by their terms and meaning are of a continuing nature.

9.4 This LICENSE sets forth the entire understanding and agreement between LSI and LICENSEE as to the subject matter hereof and merges all prior advertising, discussions, proposals, purchase orders, agreements, communications, and representations between them, whether written or oral. Neither of the parties shall be bound by any conditions, definitions, warranties, or representations with respect to any of the terms or conditions hereof other than as expressly provided in this LICENSE. This LICENSE may only be modified by a written agreement made subsequent to commencement of this LICENSE and signed by an officer of LSI and LICENSEE or his authorized representative.

9.5 Notwithstanding any failure of LICENSEE to sign and return the REGISTRATION CARD to LSI, LICENSEE shall be considered to have agreed to all the terms of this LICENSE if LICENSEE opens the sealed SOFTWARE envelope or if LICENSEE uses the SOFTWARE.

9.6 If any provision of this LICENSE agreement shall be held by a court of competent jurisdiction to be contrary to law, the remaining provisions of this Agreement shall remain in full force and effect.

9.7 Headings included in this Agreement are for convenience only and are not to be used to interpret the agreement between the parties.

9.8 This LICENSE shall be deemed effective from the date LICENSEE receives the SOFTWARE, and shall be valid only so long as LICENSEE uses or possesses the SOFTWARE, unless cancelled by LICENSOR for a violation of its terms.

LIFETREE SOFTWARE, INC.
By: CAMILO WILSON, President
Authorized Officer

VOLKSWRITER is a registered trademark of Lifetree Software, Inc.

SAVE THIS COPY OF THIS LICENSE FOR FUTURE REFERENCE

* *

FIRST STEPS IN UNDERSTANDING WHY SOFTWARE IS LICENSED AND NOT SOLD

If you *sell* a copy of copyrighted software, you lose all legal right to control the terms and conditions of its use, and the right to prevent its subsequent sale, transfer, or other disposition. Conversely, if you properly grant a written nonexclusive, nontransferable object code *license* for the use of the software, you can continue to control substantially all the conditions of its use and distribution.

Owner's Rights

By virtue of your ownership of the copyright on a computer program, Section 106 of the Copyright Act gives you the sole right to authorize others to use and distribute the software. By granting a license you are sharing those exclusive rights with another who would, in absence of your grant, not be able to use the material. As the grantor of rights to someone, you have the legal right to set the conditions under which that person may exercise those rights. If the grantee (licensee) fails to comply with those conditions, he or she has no legal basis for exercise of the rights and becomes an infringer against whom you may bring legal action.

Sharing These Rights

As the court concluded in Lawlor v. National Screen Service Corp., copyright law confers upon the owner of the copyright a limited monopoly as to the copyrighted material. You, the copyright owner, may license others to share parts of that monopoly. You may grant others exclusive or nonexclusive rights; if you grant exclusive rights, such a grant has the effect of excluding others (including you as the owner) from exercising those granted rights. The conditions and scope of use may be set by the owner in his grant, and any use by the licensee outside of the limits set in the license becomes an infringement.

Example of Infringement

The most graphic illustration of infringement through use beyond the conditions set in the license grant is found in the famous "Monty Python" case, Gilliam v. American Broadcasting Companies, Inc. The English comedy group complained that ABC, in editing their videotaped show down to a shorter running time, had destroyed the character of the performance and thereby infringed the license granted. The court said "the ability of the copyright holder to control his work remains paramount in our copyright law." It concluded that, in spite of a valid license to use the material, such unauthorized editing was an infringement of the owner's copyright "similar to any other use of a work that exceeded the license granted by the proprietor of the copyright."

Control of Copying

Do not lose sight of the fact that, aside from any licensing or sale that may have occurred, you can still prevent software from being copied without your permission. Naturally, you will need to know that it is being copied, and who is copying it, and you have to be willing to bring suit for copyright infringement. (See Chapter 18 on Remedies for Copyright Infringement.)

Before we can fully answer the question, "Why is software licensed and not sold?", we need to understand a number of other legal concepts.

OWNING A COPYRIGHT
VERSUS OWNING A COPY

There is a vital distinction between owning the copyright itself, which is based on the original work, and the ownership of a copy of the original work. As I write this book, I am creating an original work of authorship, for which I hold the copyright ownership. This right is granted to me by Congress, by authority of the Constitution. When I print out a paper copy of the original text, presently only in magnetic form on the disk, I am exercising my right as the owner of the copyright to make copies. If I then sell you a copy of that paper printout, I have exercised my right as the copyright owner to distribute copies of the work.

Once you own a "copy" of my book, you have an absolute right to sell, transfer, or otherwise distribute *that particular copy* on any terms and for any use you wish—as long as you and your purchaser do not copy it. However, by the mere fact of selling you a copy I have not given you permission to copy it. You do not own any interest in my copyright by the fact of owning a copy of the book; you own only that copy and a license to use it. This is the crux of the distinction.

COPYRIGHT ASSIGNMENTS
VERSUS COPYRIGHT LICENSES

Copyright Assignment—Transferring Ownership

Since I own the copyright on this book, I have the right to sell or otherwise transfer ownership of that copyright to anyone of my choosing, on whatever conditions I may set. Such a transfer is called an "assignment" of a copyright. Once I assign my copyright to another person or company, that person (called the "assignee") owns all the rights and privileges that go with the grant I formerly held.

Under 17 USC § 204, this assignment must be in writing and signed by me as the owner of the copyright. It will normally also be acknowledged before a notary public. The assignment may be recorded in the Copyright Office if I or the assignee want to do so, and under 17 USC § 205 it must be recorded there if the new owner wants to bring suit for copyright infringement. Recording the assignment also provides notice to third parties of the legal owner's claim. I no longer have any rights to the copyright after the assignment is made.

Exclusive Copyright Licenses—
Transferring Less Than Full Ownership

Should I want to transfer less than all my rights in the copyright, I can grant to others an exclusive part of the ownership, which is limited in some manner—in time, place, or scope. This is called an "exclusive license," which might be a grant of the exclusive right to publish and distribute this book in Asia or Europe. Or it might be an exclusive right granted to a software publisher, valid only during the years 1985 and 1986, to reproduce and distribute worldwide a microcomputer program that I wrote. An exclusive license must also be in writing, signed by the copyright owner, and may be recorded. Where the owner grants exclusive rights in a copyrighted work, these are subtracted from his larger rights and become the rights of the licensee.

Nonexclusive Copyright Licenses

Finally, I may want to grant rights to someone that do not preclude me and others from using the same rights under the copyright. These rights are still based on, and derived from, my ownership of the copyright, and I have the power to set the conditions binding on my licensee. Such a grant is called a "nonexclusive license," and it does not make the licensee the owner of any part of the copyright. Furthermore, the nonexclusive licensee does not have the right to stop others from doing what he is authorized to do, nor to transfer the license to others unless given that right by the owner. A nonexclusive license does give the licensee the privilege to exercise one or more of the rights that are otherwise the exclusive province of the copyright owner.

Different Kinds of Software Licenses

Since software can be distributed in both source and object-code form, the owner of the copyright can license either or both. The earlier example license covers only the object code because this is what normally is licensed in the mass market. Were the license to cover source code, as well, the form would have to deal with possible trade secret aspects of the code and many other issues involving physical security and protection, warranties, indemnities, taxes, the effects of bankruptcy, etc. Distribution and reproduction licenses permit the licensee to duplicate and distribute the software, usually upon payment of royalties, for a period of time or based on a limited number of copies; unfortunately, these licenses are beyond the scope of this book, except where mentioned in passing.

WHAT ARE THE EXCLUSIVE RIGHTS OF THE COPYRIGHT OWNER?

You will remember that Section 106 of the law gives the copyright owner the exclusive rights "to do and to authorize" any of the following things:

1. To reproduce the copyrighted work in copies in any media.
2. To prepare derivative works based upon the copyrighted work.
3. To distribute copies of the copyrighted work to the public by sale or other transfer of ownership, or by rental, lease, or lending.
4. To perform the copyrighted work publicly.
5. To display the copyrighted work publicly.

In the case of software, we are mainly interested in the first three rights. The right of performance (4) is not applicable to software, although the right to display (5) might be. When licensing software, our major concerns are to control its subsequent distribution (sale or transfer), to prevent copying, and to limit the conditions under which it is used. With a well drafted nonexclusive license we can, by very specific provisions, control the rights granted to the licensee out of the exclusive rights of the copyright owner; the Lifetree Software, Inc. End-User License is an example of a very explicit license, which attempts to do just that.

Limitations On The Copyright Owner's Exclusive Rights

Limited Monopoly. Because of the principles of intellectual property law, and the fact that these exclusive rights of the copyright owner are a form of monopoly granted by the Government, there are some limitations on the exercise of these exclusive rights. It would be ridiculous, for example, to try to prevent anyone from briefly quoting from a book in the process of teaching, broadcasting, or newspaper publishing, so 17 USC § 107 creates the right of "fair use." This right gives other people reasonable rights to quote from a copyrighted work for teaching, research, and other similar publicly oriented uses.

Library Use.   There are exceptions to the copyright holder's exclusive right to copy and distribute his work. For example, nonprofit libraries and archives may copy limited portions, or not more than one whole copy, or may distribute a copy for traditional library purposes. Neither this exception nor the previous "fair use" exception are of much concern to us in the software business.

Disposition Once Sold.   Section 109 provides that, notwithstanding the exclusive rights given the copyright owner under § 106, *"the owner of a particular copy . . . lawfully made under this title, or any person authorized by such owner, is entitled, without the authority of the copyright owner, to sell or otherwise dispose of the possession of that copy. . . ."* Even this exception is limited by subsection (c) of § 109, which says that these privileges do not, unless authorized by the copyright owner, "extend to any person who has acquired possession of the copy . . . from the copyright owner by rental, lease, loan, or otherwise, *without acquiring ownership of it."* Section 109 is the basis for the "First Sale Doctrine," discussed below.

Archival Copies.   Finally, in late 1980 the current language of Section 117 was adopted in order to recognize the existence of computer software and its special problems. This law says that it is not an infringement *"for the owner of a copy of a computer program* to make or authorize the making of another copy or adaptation of that computer program," if the new copy or adaptation is created as an essential step in the utilization of the computer program in conjunction with a machine and that it is used in no other manner; or that such new copy or adaptation is for archival purposes only, and that all archival copies are destroyed in the event that continued possession of the computer program should cease to be rightful. Section 117 concludes:

> Any exact copies prepared in accordance with the provisions of
> this section may be leased, sold, or otherwise transferred, along
> with the copy from which such copies were prepared, only as part
> of the lease, sale, or other transfer of all rights in the program.
> Adaptations so prepared may be transferred only with the au
> thorization of the copyright owner.

Notice that § 117, in the text above, refers to "the owner of a copy." The original draft of this section referred to "rightful possessors of a copy," but this was changed by Congress in the final bill. This has created some confusion, since the original wording was the correct way to phrase it. These exceptions make it critical to know who is the owner of a copy (that is, someone who has *purchased* a copy), who is the owner of the copyright, and who is merely a licensee with more limited rights (as in the case of most software). A 1984 case, Micro-Sparc v. Amtype, says even the *owner* of a copy may not permit others to make copies for his use. From this, you can see why the concept of licensing software is so crucial to control of the use and distribution of software.

THE "FIRST SALE DOCTRINE" AND CONTROL OF DISTRIBUTION

In the context of software protection, the "first sale doctrine" is one of the more esoteric, but important, principles of copyright law. It has been the subject of much litigation, especially in those industries (like the movie industry) where it is desirable to control distribution of the copyrighted product after it reaches the hands of the user. It is the flip side of the right to license copyrighted material.

Motion Pictures as an Example

Virtually all motion pictures are licensed to theaters on condition that the particular copy of the film is to be shown only on specified dates, that royalties (rents) are to be paid for its use, and that it is to be returned to the distributor by a particular date. Similarly, when films are distributed in eight or sixteen-millimeter sizes, they are restricted to home, as opposed to commercial, use. Both types of licenses attempt to preclude subsequent sale or rental of the film copy by the licensee. However, these restrictions may not be enforceable if the transaction is deemed to be a sale, because of the provisions of § 109 of the law, which denies the right of the copyright owner to control distribution of copies that have been sold.

Exhaustion of Rights by Sale

The first sale doctrine initially became an issue at the Supreme Court level in 1908 in Bobbs-Merrill Company v. Straus. In order to protect the rights of the copyright author, the court said that the copyright law granted the author the exclusive right to make the first sale of each copy of his copyrighted works, but once this sale occurred and the author received his revenue, his right to control use and resale of the copy of the work was exhausted. (There is a similar principle in the field of patent licensing.) From this and earlier cases at lower court levels, the current statutory and case law has developed an established position, expressed in some detail in several recent court cases. However, when and under what conditions a "first sale" occurs is usually a major issue in the litigation.

Current Law

Since the exact language of the statutes creating and implementing the copyright law has changed with the adoption of the 1976 Copyright Act, all of first sale cases are now governed by Sections 106, 109 and 117. We must base the enforceability of the distribution restrictions in any software license on these sections. In addition, revised § 117 gives the owner of a copy of a computer program certain other rights previously described.

Effect of a First Sale
On Continuing Restrictions

The 1978 case of American International Pictures, Inc. v. Foreman is particularly helpful to an understanding of the effect of a first sale. As the opinion states:

> Even if the copyright holder places restrictions on the purchaser in a first sale (such as specifying the permissible uses of the article), the buyer's disregard of the restrictions on resale does not make the buyer or the person who buys it in the secondary market liable for infringement. . . . The first sale thus extinguishes the copyright holder's ability to control the course of copies placed in the stream of commerce.
>
> Conversely, even an unwitting purchaser who buys a copy in the secondary market can be held liable for infringement if the copy was not the subject of a first sale by the copyright holder. . . . Thus unless title to the copy passes through a first sale by the copyright holder, subsequent sales do not confer good title. . . .

Software and the First Sale Doctrine

Given this court's conclusions, which represent current law, every software company should critically examine its current method of licensing and the license-agreement language. In my judgment, not more than ten percent of the microcomputer software licenses in use today properly take the first sale doctrine into consideration.

Don't forget, however, that the occurrence of the first sale does not relieve the possessor of the software from a charge of copyright infringement if he or she copies it. Although the first sale deprives the copyright owner of the right to stop subsequent *transfers* or to impose conditions upon use of the software, it does not exhaust or limit the exclusive right to make copies of the copyrighted software. A 1963 case, Platt & Munk Co. v. Republic Graphics, Inc., specifically ruled that the copyright proprietor can prevent possessors, and even owners of copyrighted objects from making copies of them. Section 202 of the Copyright Act confirms this principle by stating that ownership of the media does not imply ownership rights in the copyright itself.

OEM Licenses.   Your software license, however, can permit limited or unlimited copying by the licensee, or anyone else you chose to permit. Thus, software publishing houses may grant distribution licenses to manufacturers, under which the manufacturer is given the unlimited right to serialize, copy, and distribute specific software for a particular type of hardware made by the manufacturer. Such a document is referred to in the trade as an "OEM license." It is a very complex and important legal document, yet it is often negotiated and prepared by non-experts who may have no comprehension of the consequences, if it is not drafted correctly, of its effect on the ability of their company to protect the software. There are, for example, different warranty and indemnity issues involved in OEM licenses, income and sales tax consequences, and many problems in defining the scope of distribution rights granted.

THE OWNER'S OBJECTIVES ARE REALIZED ONLY THROUGH LICENSING

The objective of the software owner must, then, be to control the use and future transfer of the software through a carefully drafted nonexclusive copyright license, which spells out the conditions of the license grant. The range of possible restrictive conditions and rights to be exercised through the license granted to the licensee is essentially unconstrained by the law, except for the three or four statutory limitations described above. For example, in the Lifetree license, the publisher imposes various conditions upon the licensee, such as not using the software on more than one computer at a time, not renting or further transferring it without the permission of the owner, and expressly authorizing the making of a limited number of backup or archival copies.

Negating a First Sale

To avoid application of the First Sale Doctrine, the terms of any license must, at an absolute minimum, negate any idea on the part of the licensee, or any court examining the agreement, that a sale occurred. This issue was examined in several Federal appellate cases, the most recent of which was United States v. Wise, a criminal prosecution for copyright infringement by the sale of licensed motion pictures. In Wise, the court

looked at the language of the licensing agreements for all the films involved and at the actual conduct of the distributors and film producers to
see if the contracts were, in fact, treated as licenses. It concluded they
were in all but one film.

Referring to an earlier case, the Wise court pointed out that even
where a motion picture exhibition license contains no limitation as to
time, requires a flat lump-sum payment, has no requirement that prints
and negatives be returned, places no limitation on the right to abridge or
alter the film, and where the contracting party is given the same
geographical territory as the copyright owner, the transaction will still be
treated as a license and not a sale.

Apply the Law to Software

It is clear from these two cases that software licenses, drafted in the manner of the Lifetree example, should be construed as being a license and
not a sale, since it makes clear that title has not passed. If so, then all the
other conditions imposed in the license should also be enforceable on the
licensee. There are, however, no software licensing cases yet which either
agree or disagree with this analysis.

It is likely that future cases will turn on the need for a mechanism to
differentiate software from books, and to enlarge upon the analogy to
movies that I earlier provided. Perhaps decisions will turn on matters like
the Lifetree license permitting what might be called "commercially
reasonable" uses, and prohibiting those things that would cost the software author and publisher revenues. The aim in drafting a license should
always be to give the user/licensee the maximum leeway, but to anticipate
as much as possible changes in reproduction technology that could ruin
the copyright owner if not restricted. The results may also depend, in part,
on the language in the intermediate distributors' agreements, should they
refer to *sales* instead of licenses.

Software Rental

The current rage of "software rental companies" is a perfect example of
the need of an adequate license agreement. These companies advertise
that you can "rent" or "try" software for a week for about 20% of the list
price of the software package, in order to "try out" the product. It is clear
that these are mostly transparent efforts to help users copy software instead of buying it. Several suits have been brought by major software
houses to stop this practice, and all have resulted in consent judgments
where the renter agreed to stop the practice unless the software was adequately "copy protected." Provided that the license agreement is clear
that the software is licensed and not sold, the software companies should
always prevail in these cases. (Note that Sections 3 and 5.1 of the Lifetree
license specifically deal with this issue.)

THE EFFECT OF OWNERSHIP OF THE STORAGE MEDIA

A related question, dealt with in the Lifetree license, is what effect the ownership of the media (on which the copy is recorded, embedded, or printed) has on the first sale doctrine and the right to copy. Compared to book publishing or even the movie industry, the software industry is faced with a unique situation, since its licensed product is distributed on magnetic media that can be copied or even moved from one form of media to the other in a few seconds, with no effect on the source media and at very minor cost compared to either film or paper media. If the licensee either owns the media from the outset or copies the program onto media owned by him or her, what effect does this have on the rights of the copyright owner or the licensee?

Two earlier cases, Harrison v. Maynard, Merrill & Co. and Independent News Co. v. Williams, suggest that if the ownership of the media on which the copyrighted material is printed is transferred to a third party, even in violation of contractual obligations of the second party-seller not to make further sales, then a first sale has occurred and the copyright holder cannot stop or control subsequent sales. In the Harrison case, damaged sheets and copies of a book were sold to a wastepaper dealer under an express agreement that they would not be used for anything else. The defendant acquired them and started selling them. When the publisher tried to obtain an injunction to stop the sales, he was rebuffed by the court, which held that the sale of the paper was a first sale. It agreed that the copyright owner had a breach of contract action against the initial licensee, but, because the first sale had occurred, the owner could not bring either a breach of contract action nor a copyright infringement action against the third party.

Similarly, in the Independent News case, comic books with covers removed were resold in violation of an agreement to use them only for wastepaper. The court held that the seller of the comics was not infringing the rights of the copyright holder to distribute and sell the comics, because a first sale had occurred when they were acquired without restriction from the wastepaper dealer. These two cases seem erroneous and inconsistent with the more recent American International Pictures decision discussed above.

Downloading Software

There are growing signs of businesses in the software industry that will "download," or transfer software from the media distributed by the licensing company onto different sizes or formats of customer media, either in the store or by telephone.

Transactions of this type are occurring daily in computer stores, albeit with the parties probably unaware of the possible legal consequences. If such transactions were to occur with any frequency, the argument might eventually be that since the software was delivered on customer-owned media, that therefore a first sale occurred, regardless of the terms of the license agreement. If the downloading is not authorized by the copyright owner, however, this is a clear case of copyright infringement by copying. Where it has been authorized by license, it raises the issue of media ownership and the first sale doctrine.

Furthermore, if the Harrison and Independent News cases were correct, when a customer acquires software under a license on an eight-inch diskette, title to which diskette and software is expressly retained by the licensor, all the licensee would have to do to create a first sale would be to load the software onto his or her own hard disk or even another floppy, and then sell either media to a third party. The third party would then be free of any restrictions on sale or use, even though the licensor would have a breach of contract action against the original licensee. There seems no question that media ownership will be held to be irrelevant, in the future, in spite of these two earlier cases.

The Present Law

In my judgment, the correct answer is found in § 202:

> Ownership of a copyright, or of any of the exclusive rights under a copyright, is distinct from ownership of any material object in which the work is embodied. *Transfer of ownership of any material object, including the copy or phonorecord in which the work is first fixed, does not of itself convey any rights in the copyrighted work embodied in the object . . . .* [Emphasis added].

If that were not enough, the discussion about the problem in the Platt & Munk case, in the context of a first sale argument, is even more to the point:

> [I]t would seem exceedingly odd that copyright protection should turn on which party has furnished the physical stuff to which the copyrighted conception is affixed—with the protection lost if the author does not . . . [provide the media or acquire it as part of the printing process].

To clarify this problem, section 3 of the Lifetree license specifies the effect of this situation, and attempts to anticipate subsequent issues, like loading software into ROM or bubble memory from the distribution media, or onto a hard disk.

ENFORCING SOFTWARE LICENSE AGREEMENTS

Now that we have seen the purpose of license agreements, it is time to explore potential issues relating to their enforceability. No one has ever seriously contested the validity or enforceability of mainframe software licenses, because all of them were signed before the software was delivered or as part of the purchase of the computer system itself. The advent of microcomputers, software stores, and mail-order sales has raised new questions. Most of today's licenses are packed with the software and are never signed by the user/licensee. Are they enforceable? The answers that follow are largely my theories about this subject, since there is very little existing law on the subject.

The Unsigned License Argument

In the introduction and at section 9.5, the Lifetree license deals with the possible argument that the license agreement is not binding on the licensee since it has not been signed. This is one of the two arguments the software "rental" companies rely on as the legal basis for their whole business of loaning software, for a price, to individuals and companies. The other argument is that the software was really sold to them and not licensed. It is clear from advertisements and public statements of some of the participants that at least one purpose of such rental businesses is to permit people to make illegal copies of copyrighted software.

Analogy to Videotapes.   Apparently the prerecorded videotape industry failed to consider these issues when it started, with the result that a whole subindustry of videotape rental stores has grown up in the past few years. Videotapes are not normally accompanied by any license agreement, beyond a copyright notice prohibiting copying. This has created such an adverse effect on that industry that Congress is presently considering legislation which would impose compulsory licenses on film and videotape rentals. A similar bill to prohibit unlicensed rentals of phonograph records and other forms of sound recording was passed by Congress in 1984, amending Sections 109 and 115 of the Copyright Act.

Economics of the Industry.   Suppose that the end user who acquires one copy of Lifetree's word-processing package, Volkswriter®, could use it or transfer it without restriction onto every machine in the company, onto networks, onto multiterminal systems, and onto mainframes. LSI's revenue base would melt away so rapidly that after the first distribution of a few hundred packages there would simply be no market left. In order to survive in this situation it would have to price microsoftware at the level of mainframe software—in the tens of thousands of dollars per copy.

What Makes Software Licenses Enforceable?

Interestingly enough, the LSI license is really a hybrid of a license and a contract. Of all the hundreds of software licenses I have seen, I cannot think of one that was not. Yet the language of most software licenses is not consistent with this situation. It seems to me, again without any specific software case supporting the theory, that this fact should support the validity and enforceability of these instruments. Only a future case will decide this issue for certain.

Licenses Are Grants.   A nonexclusive copyright license grant to the end user from LSI is simply a *grant* of a license. Such licenses do not need to be signed by the licensee to be enforceable, since they are the unilateral act of the licensor granting the license. If the licensee abides by the conditions, he or she has a license without having signed anything. As the owner of all rights in the copyrighted work, LSI has almost total authority to determine who may use the software and under what conditions it may be used. While these conditions must be reasonable and must be communicated clearly to the licensee, the scope of the grant of rights is up to LSI. It is only limited by the exceptions in the copyright laws, and to some extent by the American antitrust laws.

The License Determines the Scope.   Once the conditions under which the licensee may use the software have been set by the language of the license, the licensee who fails to meet them has no rights under the license and becomes an infringer. If the licensee complies with the conditions, he or she has a valid license to do what the license says he can. But the licensee has only the rights granted in the license, and no more.

Violating the License Terms.   Once the conditions are violated, the licensee is an infringer and all the rights either revert to the owner, or the owner may have legal authority to cancel the grant made to the licensee, depending on the severity of the failure. If there are no contract terms or covenants involved, the licensor cannot base any claim on contract law. Note that in the LSI license there are a number of conditions (sections 2.1, 5.3, 6) which, if broken, allow LSI to cancel the license. In section 2.1 LSI also reserves all rights not expressly granted to the licensee.

The License Is Also a Contract.   To the extent that the LSI license seeks to have the licensee agree to specific terms of the agreement, this makes it a contract. Contracts are based on one or more terms to which the parties are bound if they reach an agreement, either expressly or by implication. Most of us think of contracts as formal written documents, signed by two or more parties. But contracts don't have to be written, and they don't always have to be signed by both parties to be enforceable.

Here LSI has stated in a printed license form, packaged with the software, that the software may be used on certain specified terms and conditions. The agreement also clearly says several times that the licensee does not have to accept the terms of the license, but that if the licensee does so *by his or her conduct,* then he or she will be deemed to have agreed to such terms and conditions.

Opening the accompanying sealed diskette envelope or using the software (if the envelope happens to have been left open) is the one act that irrevocably obligates the licensee to the contract terms. As the Uniform Commercial Code (the law in every state except Louisiana) § 2-204(1) says, "A contract for sale of goods may be made in any manner sufficient to show agreement, including conduct by both parties, which recognizes the existence of such a contract." If someone can be held to have bought something, based on his conduct, surely he can assume lesser obligations by conduct.

Agreement by Conduct

We can all think of situations where we have agreed, by implication, to pay for something or to conduct ourselves in a certain way. Both the acknowledged legal authority, the Restatement of Contracts, Second § 69, and many state laws specifically so provide. For example, there are a number of California cases that follow the rule in California Civil Code § 1589 to the effect that "A voluntary acceptance of the benefit of a transaction is equivalent to a consent to all the obligations arising from it, so far as the facts are known, or ought to be known, to the person accepting."

In those cases, our conduct in the face of an obvious obligation about to be imposed on us makes a contract out of our actions. Cases throughout the U.S. hold that conduct is sufficient to result in a contract, as in an early New York case, United Merchants Realty & Improvement Co. v. Roth, which refers to "an overt act" of a party as making a contract. Some consumer laws modify these rules, but they would not appear to apply in situations where the consumer has an opportunity to inspect and read the license before opening the diskette package. A contract might *not* arise, however, if the consumer had to open the sealed diskette package in order to read the terms of the actual license, which is why I have suggested below a means of packaging the software to avoid this trap. Louisiana now has a law making break-open licenses enforceable.

Examples. If you drive your car into a service station with posted gasoline prices of $1.50 per gallon, and you either permit the attendant to fill your gas tank, or do so yourself, you have agreed *by conduct* to a contract to pay $1.50 per gallon for the fuel you put in your car.

The next time you go to the dry cleaners, a parking garage, or a theater, look at the ticket stub which you get back. The dry cleaner stub says that there are certain conditions under which your clothes are accepted, so that if the dye in your blouse runs or your drapes split, there is little or no remedy available to you. There are some exceptions, but most turn on reasonableness of the specified conditions and adequacy of the notice.

Likewise, your parking ticket disclaims liability and obligates you to pay for parking based upon posted costs, including rates that may vary from day to day or parts of the day and night. Your theater ticket licenses you to see the picture, but not to take photographs of it while it is running.

All of these are forms of reasonable contracts, and in the latter two cases licenses combined with contracts, which you did not sign but under which you have a legal obligation to pay or conduct yourself in a particular manner.

How Can Licenses Be Enforced If They Are Hybrids?

The license grant portion of the Lifetree Software license document creates conditions; while the contract portion of the document creates terms or covenants and some conditions; all of which gives rise to legal rights in both parties.

Terms and Conditions.   Lawyers are fond of using the words "terms and conditions" in contracts, which they do both because of habit and because of sound historical legal reasons. Contracts and licenses have conditions in them, which, if not met, permit the party who specified the conditions to cancel or rescind the contract or license for failure of those conditions. Failure of the conditions means that the rights vanish. Or the rights may not arise until an event occurs. For example, if I grant you the right to use my software exclusively for nonprofit educational purposes, on condition that you set up and maintain a college or school, your rights begin as soon as you comply with these conditions. The rights will end the day your school closes.

Termination of Conditions.   Rights may be granted so they only exist so long as a set of specific conditions is met. The Lifetree license says the license is only valid under certain conditions of use, such as use of the software on one machine at a time, and it provides for cancellation if this condition is violated. When the conditions are no longer being met, the license no longer exists and the licensee becomes an infringer at the instant the condition fails. Finally, there are grants with conditions that are bound to occur, such as a license to use software until the end of calendar 1985, at which time the license automatically terminates.

Effect of Violation of Conditions.   Because software licenses are derived from the copyright owner's statutory rights, the conditions in a license agreement are enforceable by bringing an infringement action in the Federal courts; the related contract issues can also be heard at the same time. This right to sue is known as "a tort action," which means that a civil wrong has been committed that a court will correct since the infringer had some legal duty.

Breach of Contract. Your remedy against people who violate the "terms" or "covenants" of your software license is an action for a breach of contract. A covenant or term of an agreement is a promise one party has made, the breach of which entitles the other party to seek damages, or in some cases the termination of the agreement. LSI, for example, obtained the agreement of the licensee not to transfer the software to a third party without prior permission of LSI, and not to use it on more than one machine at a time. While these might be considered conditions of the license, they are also terms or covenants, and LSI can elect to sue for breach of contract or for copyright infringement, or both.

Combined Remedies. Typically, suits against infringers will contain allegations of the existence of both an agreement and a license. For this reason, most copyright license cases are brought in Federal court since you can sue there for *both* breach of contract and copyright infringement. In state court, however, you can only bring suit for breach of contract.

Reasonableness and the Importance of Notice to the User

Before listing some ideas for packaging software in a way that will enhance the enforceability of your license, we need to consider the importance of reasonable contract language and the need for adequate notice of the provisions imposed on the licensee by his or her conduct. Unless you have taken these factors into consideration, your license may not be enforceable. Chapter 12 describes the legal problems of warranties and the consumer, so this material assumes you will consider that aspect separately.

Registration Cards. It is not always possible to obtain the licensee's signature on a license agreement, as is the case in the current microcomputer software market. Obviously, a signed agreement would add further legal basis for enforcement of the license. For this reason, some software companies include a registration card for the user/licensee to sign, which states that the licensee agrees to be bound by all of the terms and conditions of the license. However, only about 20% of these cards are usually returned. The LSI card does *not* require the signature or state the signer agrees, because failure to sign could be taken as a refusal to agree. LSI's card only says the user acknowledges having read the license form.

Reasonableness of the License. Reasonableness is a subjective consideration based on all the facts and the experience of the parties. The LSI example license contains a number of terms and conditions, which, taken collectively, seem to me to be reasonable in the *current* microcomputer software market. These conditions also take into consideration that this particular software package is licensed for less than $300 in the mass market. Each test of reasonableness has to be judged on its own merit.

Unconscionable Agreements. American law abounds with cases stating the basic principle that "unconscionable" contracts will not be enforced. These are contracts containing terms and conditions that offend the court's sense of fairness and reasonableness. (See, for example, the FMC tomato-packing equipment case discussed in Chapter 12 on warranties.) The requirement that contracts and software licenses be reasonable is also important, since under copyright law every contract contains an implied covenant of good faith and fair dealing.

The Requirement of Notice. The element of notice is, in essence, part of the fairness element, since if you are to be held to a contract by your conduct, quite obviously you have to be on notice of the terms and conditions of it. In the material that follows, there are a number of suggestions on how best to present the license and the warranty language so that the licensee will be on notice of the provisions of the license.

Freedom to Reject the Agreement. Where contracts are held to arise from conduct, the court will usually conclude this is the case only if the party whose conduct acts as an acceptance of an offer has the freedom to reject the agreement. Thus, if software is sent by mail or delivered to you, a contract will not exist from merely accepting delivery of the software, since until the software has been examined in some reasonable manner there is no way an intelligent acceptance of it can occur. For this reason, a license agreement would not be enforceable that said you were deemed to have agreed to all its terms *by the fact of payment* for the software, where you could not read it until you opened the package. In this "Catch 22" situation, you could not open the package until you paid for it. Thus, packaging and careful choice of language is everything!

Reasonableness and adequate notice will always be questions of fact, but you should be able to ascertain how far you can go on the basis of common sense, since most of the commercial law of the United States and Great Britain has its origin in common sense and standard business practices (called "customs and practices" in the case law).

How Packaging Software Influences
Enforcement of Licenses

I have on my desk in front of me four examples of what appear to be the current software packaging from DEC®, IBM®, Lifetree Software, and Ashton-Tate. Except for Ashton-Tate, each of these companies packages its software in slipcases of approximately the same size (about eight by nine inches), with an outside case, and an inside book or tray holding the user manual and the software on a five-and-a-quarter inch diskette. Ashton-Tate uses a larger notebook, with no slipcase. All are tightly shrink-wrapped, and all but DEC's package have some sort of licensing or warranty notice visible on the outside. Each company deals differently with the diskette, the warranty, and the license. The key to enforceability of the warranty and the license may turn on how they are dealt with. Each of the following examples of software packaging is a lesson in itself.

Example Packaging.   DEC's license and warranty do not show on the outside, but the company provides computer stores with a large warranty notice for public display. IBM has its whole license and warranty form showing through the shrink-wrap, and Ashton-Tate and Lifetree (see Figure 11–1) have a large sticker stating that the software license and warranty is inside and should be read carefully. (See Chapter 12 for further comments on the warranty issues.)

IMPORTANT
Read Before Opening

This sealed package contains your Volkswriter® Deluxe software on diskette.

The following is also shipped separately from this sealed software package:

- Your End User License Agreement and Warranty
- Warranty Service Form

CAREFULLY READ THE END USER LICENSE AGREEMENT before opening this package. If you cannot or do not agree with the terms of the End User License Agreement, you may return the package *unopened* for a full refund. Note: This software is only licensed, not sold, for use in accordance with the terms of the License Agreement. Returns cannot be accepted after seven (7) days or if the diskette package seal is opened or broken.

By opening this package, you will have indicated your consent and agreement to the provisions of the End User License Agreement.

LIFETREE
SOFTWARE INC

Volkswriter is a registered trademark of Lifetree Software Inc.
Volkswriter Deluxe is a trademark of Lifetree Software Inc.

Figure 11–1

Inside the front of the user manual in each case is a neatly printed license and warranty form. Aston-Tate's is letter-sized, concise, and in easily readable print, which states clearly that if you open the sealed software envelope you have agreed to the terms of the license, and that you can return it if you don't wish to agree. It also includes an unsealed demonstration diskette, to be used before opening the sealed pack. Lifetree's packaging is about the same, except that it has a very noticeable booklet containing the license and the warranty printed in large type. The diskettes are packed in a separate shrink-wrapped container with a bright red warning notice about the license restrictions. The diskette label of both Ashton-Tate and Lifetree has a warning about the license provisions.

IBM's packaging is similar except that its software diskette is not in any way sealed; only the outside slipcase is sealed. There is a second copy of the software license in the box, ahead of the user manual. DEC has a manual with license and then a small paper box holding the diskettes, with the strongest transparent tape seal I have even seen. On the tape seal is a message in four or five languages to the effect that the software is licensed according to the license agreement packed with the box, and that you should not break the seal on the diskette box unless you agree to be bound by it.

THE IDEAL LICENSING PACKAGE

Based on the legal principles already discussed, and assuming you have a well drafted warranty and a carefully considered license agreement, the way to handle the actual packaging is along these lines:

- Always place a full copy of your warranty form on the outside of the slipcase, under the shrink-wrap, so that it can be read without opening the shrink wrap or removing the goods from the store. Or give an obvious, external notice that the warranty is in the box. As Chapter 12 points out, failure to do this or to follow the example of DEC by providing a warranty notice in the store, may destroy any effort to limit your liability. The warranty should also be repeated inside the manual or the box, just in case it is lost from the outside.

- See that some extremely visible form of notice is on the outside of the box, under the shrink-wrap, to the effect that the software is licensed. It is even better to place the whole license on the exterior of the package, if this can be in large enough type for the normal reader. This is not always feasible. If not, I would include a notice in twelve-point type and a contrasting color that says,

> PLEASE NOTE: This software product is distributed only under a comprehensive software license agreement and is never sold outright. The full license and additional warranty information is packed inside to insure that it is not lost. DO NOT OPEN THE ACCOMPANYING SEALED DISKETTE ENVELOPE UNTIL YOU HAVE READ THE ENTIRE LICENSE and the warranty. If you are unsure of the meaning of the terms of the license or the warranty, you may call the Customer Service number in the front of the user manual for further information. Thank you for selecting our software product.

- Seal the actual software diskette(s) in one envelope or small box in such a manner that it is reasonably difficult to break the seal. Place that envelope inside the slip case, at the back of the tray or manual, so that the user will see the license and warranty material before he or she comes to the sealed diskette package. If you include, as Ashton-Tate does, a demonstration diskette which the user can try before opening the sealed disk, *do not seal* the demo disk, and clearly mark it as a demo disk to be used to test the software for acceptability. Ashton-Tate's approach to this is excellent.

- In sealing the diskette package, consider the printed transparent tape with the warning notice on it in several languages, which DEC uses. The notice on the tape should say: "WARNING: Do not break this seal until you have carefully read the License Agreement. If you break this seal, you will be bound by the terms and conditions of the License." The DEC disk package is the clearest and best notice I have ever seen.

- Have your full license agreement drafted or reviewed by competent legal counsel and then have it typeset in ten-point type, with warranty or other provisions you wish highlighted in larger type or a different color. Include a warning notice at the beginning, like that in the Lifetree form, which states that use of the software or opening the sealed package is deemed agreement with the license terms. Ensure that the license agreement is the first thing a user sees when opening up the manual or notebook. Check carefully, during your quality control, that it is packaged in every manual.

- If you use a warranty card or a registration card, be certain that it is packed immediately after the license agreement so that it can be completed while the user in thinking about it. If you have adopted the positive type of warranty approach suggested in Chapter 12, it will serve as another good customer-relations tactic.

- To be certain that your license and warranty are read and that the user is aware of them, make reference to them on the first page or two of the text of your manual. You can also include a note there which says, *"Please remember that this software is licensed and not sold. Read the license agreement carefully."*

- See that a short notice about the license agreement, along with appropriate copyright notices, are placed on the actual diskette on a label in the upper corner, where you place the trademarks and program name. It can read, "This software is licensed and not sold. Use, copying, and distribution is governed by your license agreement. Copyright infringement is a serious civil and criminal matter."

- Place a short notice in the actual software, along the lines of the label notice spelled out in the previous item. This, together with a copyright notice, should display for a second or more whenever the software is initially read into the computer system. You may also wish to consider an initialization procedure whereby the software will not work until the first user types in his name and address, which there-after displays with the above message. All software should also have a unique serial number embedded in it, which may or may not display on the screen at sign-on.

• Above all, do NOT destroy all your good work with license agree-ments by including a friendly note in the manual or accompanying literature that says, "Thank you for *purchasing* this software. As the new *owner*, you will, etc." While this will not conclusively establish a first sale, it certainly will not help the situation. Be careful to review your contracts, advertising, and promotional literature, and remove all references to "sale," and substitute for that word the term "license."

SUMMARY

My goal in this chapter has been to provide a comprehensive explanation of what is necessary in an end-user software license, and how to present it to the public in a manner that will strengthen your company's legal position vis à vis pirates and other infringers.

The use of a properly drafted software license is mandatory in order to protect your software. Development of such licenses is not a job for in-experienced personnel, nor should a license be "lifted" from that of other companies. The control of software use and distribution can only be dealt with in such a license, and the draftsman of it needs to understand some very complex and changing laws.

Software rental and other current issues are still unresolved as of this writing, but the likely outcome is predictable on the basis of past case law in the movie industry. The enforceability of unsigned licenses is less predictable, but is still likely if a license is fair, if notice is given, and if the court is presented with the alternatives, and the customs and practices in the software industry.

12

Software Warranties and Limiting Liability

CATHY
By Cathy Guisewite

IS THIS THE WARRANTY REGISTRATION CARD YOU'RE SUPPOSED TO SEND IN FOR YOUR PHONE-ANSWERING MACHINE, CATHY?

YES, MOM. HERE. IT GOES IN THIS DRAWER.

YOU STUFF YOUR WARRANTY REGISTRATION CARDS IN A DRAWER??

WHAT DO YOU DO WITH YOURS?

I LET THEM SIT ON THE COUNTER UNTIL I SPILL SOMETHING ON THEM, AND THEN I THROW THEM OUT.

EVERY GENERATION HAS HER OWN SYSTEM.

Cathy, Copyright 1982 Universal Press Syndicate. Reprinted with permission.
All rights reserved.

Do you identify with this cartoon? Most of us do, because we, like Cathy, tend to ignore warranty cards that come with things we buy. We toss them in a drawer, leave them in the box, or worse yet, throw them out—until something goes wrong with the product, and then we scramble to locate them so we can complain to the manufacturer or the retailer from whom we bought the product. Consumers can afford this luxury because federal and state laws protect them—at the expense of you and your business!!

You, as a producer or distributor of software, need to be concerned about the effect of warranties, both express and implied, and the potential financial responsibility you may have under the federal and state consumer protection laws passed for the benefit of people like Cathy. These

*I am indebted to Robert T. Daunt, Esq., my professional associate in the law firm of Schroeder, Davis & Orliss Inc., Monterey, California, for the background research and an initial draft of this chapter.

laws are intended to shift the burden of losses caused by defective products from the purchaser to the producer. The computer hardware manufacturers are already learning the consequences of these laws the hard way. It is probable the software industry is next.

Products that do not work, that destroy data, or that have the potential for injuring people, can result in lawsuits and heavy damage awards. Stop and think about the possible effect of a $250,000 judgment against your business for defective software that you marketed. The chances are that such a judgment would put a sizeable dent in your ability to continue to do business. This chapter is about how you can limit your business's exposure to damages for defective software, and what can happen if you do not pay attention to this critical aspect of your software licensing documents. As such, it is a follow-on from Chapter 11.

NEW AND UNCHARTED WATERS FOR THE SOFTWARE INDUSTRY

Unresolved Issues

The extent and exact nature of liability of an American software author or publisher for defective software is simply unknown at this time. Just as the software industry raised many new and unresolved questions in copyright, trade secret, and patent law, it has the potential for a lot of interesting and expensive warranty and product liability litigation—at the expense of some of America's software houses. You don't need to be one of them.

What follows is an outline of the major legal principles applicable to this subject, together with some practical suggestions for avoiding problems, and some theories about which way the law will go during the next ten years. This chapter is only a summary, since a detailed discussion would fill a whole book. You should know that some lawyers in this field may, and do, disagree with me. I prefer the conservative approach of looking for possible problems and ways to avoid them, rather than waiting until they arise.

New Technology, Old Law

The law in this area is largely based on painfully detailed statutes, interpreted by courts that have increasingly found against the manufacturer and seller, regardless of what the parties to the transaction intended or had agreed in writing. It is fairly easy to identify the three legal theories forming the probable basis for imposing liability. It is very difficult to predict how these laws will be applied to a new technology. There simply have not been enough cases decided in the courts for anyone to draw an accurate picture of how the existing warranty laws will be applied to software licensing.

Goods versus Services

One major question that has as yet to be answered is whether computer software, as an intangible, is "goods" or merchandise in the the sense of more typical consumer items, like toasters or cars. Most warranty and consumer laws refer to the items sold as "goods," and goods are usually defined in terms of movable objects, capable of being physically possessed. Nothing is said about property which is but a magnetic image. If software is not to be classed as "goods," is it to be classed as a service? Services are not covered by most warranty laws.

The fact that software is usually licensed, and not sold, also raises some new legal issues. It has also been argued that software, when used in a business, is not a consumer product to which these laws apply. Computer software just does not fit neatly into the convenient categories with which lawyers and judges are comfortable.

Predicting the Future

I believe software will be classified as goods and merchandise, whether licensed or sold outright, and that consumer warranty laws will be applied to most software transactions—at least those in the microcomputer software industry. If I am correct, you will want to have read and applied the information in this chapter carefully. In my view the cost of compliance is extremely low compared to the financial risks of non-compliance. The choice is yours.

THE LEGAL BASIS FOR LIABILITY FOR DEFECTIVE PRODUCTS

The buyer of defective merchandise or goods has, today, three different legal theories by which he or she may be able to recover damages because of financial losses or personal injuries. There is a lot of history behind these theories, and some of them are still in the active process of development in this country. Nonetheless, any one or all of them could, potentially, apply to defective computer software. These theories are set out below.

Warranty. The most important concept of recovery, as you would suspect from the title of this chapter, is based upon contract law and is known as "breach of warranty." For example, if your new TV or VCR breaks down during the Olympics, you can take it back to the store and have it fixed without cost if it is still under warranty. Or if the diskettes you buy are defective, your local computer store will usually replace them.

The law of warranties originated in English Common Law—the decisions of the early English and later American courts. Today most of this law is found in the Uniform Commercial Code (UCC), a body of business laws enacted in all the fifty states, except Louisiana which follows French law. Additional consumer rights have been created in recent years by federal laws, which apply uniformly to every state. A few states have their own consumer protection laws, in addition to the UCC. We will explore all these laws in a moment.

Negligence.   Over the years another basis for recovery has grown up, called "negligence" or "tort liability." This body of law is based on the theory that if someone is injured by a product, either financially or physically, due to the carelessness of someone else, the injured party should have a basis for recovery even if he or she did not have any contract with the seller, and thus no basis for recovery under warranty law. While this law originated from court decisions, it is now based in part on actual state and federal statutes.

For example, if the wheel of a Buick going by your house comes off and damages the house and injures you or your family, you can sue the manufacturer and the repairer of the automobile. You can also sue your credit card company whose accounting software has a bug that erroneously causes your account to show as delinquent all the time, which fact causes you to have a bad credit rating elsewhere. There are some suggestions later in this chapter on avoiding claims of negligent programming.

Strict Liability.   Finally, as technology has led to the manufacture of more and more complex devices, foods, cosmetics, chemicals, and the like, the legal system has had to create a further remedy for those situations where there was no way the injured party could practically or economically prove negligence. Since the 1900's the courts have permitted recovery for injury and damages caused by defective goods where the manufacturer had reason to know that the items it made and sold were inherently dangerous to human beings and their property. In such cases, the manufacturer can avoid liability only if it can show that it did everything humanly possible to minimize these dangers and then advised the purchaser of the remaining dangers.

In holding the manufacturer of a power tool strictly liable for defects in its product design that caused a personal injury, the court in Greenman v. Yuba Power Products, a nationally famous California case, ruled that the manufacturer could not limit its liability by contract and did not have to be proven negligent to be liable. The court awarded damages on the theory that "The purpose of such liability is to insure that the costs of injuries resulting from defective products are borne by the manufacturers that put such products on the market rather than by the injured persons who are powerless to protect themselves." This remedy is based solely on court decisions. It probably applies only to computer programs used in industrial processes, although other possible cases are covered later in this chapter.

DEFECTIVE SOFTWARE—
A UNIQUE INDUSTRY PROBLEM

All Software Has Errors

You, as a professional programmer or software industry executive, can readily see that the software author and publisher has a unique problem if any one of these three legal theories is applied to defective computer software. There is no possible way for a product as complex as today's software to be free of defects or bugs during the first year or two of its use.

The programs licensed for most microcomputers have all sorts of possible errors which could create financial damage to a user, if the user, for example, lost all the data carefully input to a spreadsheet. Even software that has been on the market for ten years shows up errors from time to time, and most successful products undergo many revisions to fix bugs, as well as to add new features—which themselves may cause new errors. What then can be done to limit liability for these probable defects?

Business-to-Business Transactions

In the early days of the computer industry, programs were either prepared by the user or acquired from another business that wrote software to the specifications of the purchaser. Eventually, packaged software, like database programs, began to be developed and sold. Other software came directly from the manufacturer of the hardware. All of these transactions were between fairly large businesses, experienced in developing and using software, and the contracts for the acquisition of the software were negotiated or at least reviewed by legal counsel. The companies involved understood the risks and contracted accordingly. Historically, it has been possible under American law to limit liability by contract, especially where the contract was between businesses.

"As Is" Deals

The industry's solution was to sell or license the software on an "As Is" basis. This is the lawyer's way of saying "What you see, is what you get." If the software doesn't work later, it is the buyer's responsibility to fix it, or to have taken this condition into consideration at the time it contracted for the software. The "As Is" disclaimer presumes that the buyer is capable of evaluating the software before buying or licensing it, and that the buyer has some bargaining power with the seller.

A typical "As Is" disclaimer reads like this one from a $250 communications software package for the IBM-PC:

USER ACCEPTS THE PROGRAM AND MANUAL "AS IS" AND WITHOUT ANY WARRANTIES AS TO MERCHANTABILITY OR FITNESS FOR A PARTICULAR PURPOSE.

This practice carried over as minicomputers became popular, and carried over further into the beginnings of the microcomputer software industry in the late 1970's. Today's legal problem for the industry is that the parties who are contracting for and purchasing software are no longer only big businesses with million-dollar computers, but little people acquiring software for their own use. The laws that protected software houses in earlier days, by use of the "as is" disclaimer, may not apply to the current software business. The law has even changed as to the ability of businesses to limit their liability in transactions with other big businesses, as we will see in the FMC case described below.

The Problem in a Nutshell

The software industry's dilemma today is how to effectively limit its liability for damages that arise out of the sale or license of microcomputer software in the consumer and small business market. The risks of marketing software are greater today than ever before, for several reasons. "As Is" transactions may no longer be enforceable in the courts in today's software market. Recent cases involving computer hardware and operating systems reinforce this concern.

First, the price of the software is likely to be under $500 in almost every case, so that the risk is disproportionate from the days when the software license cost $100,000 for a database package. The possible damages could go into the hundreds of thousands of dollars. Second, the purchaser may well be considered a consumer under the federal and state laws, with strong statutory legal rights against you as the seller, which include penalties, prohibitions against waivers of some types of liability, and even provisions for attorney fees to the consumer that sues you. The rest of this chapter tells you what your liability could be, and how to reduce or eliminate that exposure.

WHAT IS A WARRANTY
AND HOW DOES IT WORK?

A warranty is a legally enforceable promise by the seller that certain facts or representations concerning the product are true. If a buyer relies on the warranty and suffers a loss because the warranty proves to be untrue, the buyer can recover damages from the seller. Warranties arise out of contracts and, in some cases, out of the conduct of the parties or the customs and practices of an industry, or from all of these factors.

Express Warranties

These promises may be "express," in which case they are actually set forth in the contract or the specifications for the product. If they are express, they cannot be disclaimed or waived by other provisions in the contract.

For example, in a 1983 federal case, Consolidated Data Terminals v. Applied Digital Data Systems, Inc., the appeals court ruled that when the manufacturer of the ADDS terminals put out specifications for its terminal saying it would operate at 19,200 baud, which it could not in fact do, it was liable to a business purchaser for damages, even though the sales contract attempted to disclaim all warranties. Even advertisements may be considered express warranties of performance, as though the statements in the advertisements were part of the contract.

Implied Warranties

There are a series of other warranties "implied" by the Uniform Commercial Code (UCC) in every sale, the most important of which are as follows:

- The implied warranty that the sale will pass good title to the buyer, and that it will not infringe the rights of any third party (UCC 2-312).

- The implied warranty of fitness of purpose, which means that if the seller markets a word-processing program for the IBM-PC, then a buyer can assume it will function as such, with reasonable functionality (UCC 2-315).

- The implied warranty of merchantability, which is legal shorthand for a promise to the buyer which can be implied from the fact the product is marketed, that it is reasonably fit for the ordinary purpose for which similar goods are used (UCC 2-314). In other words, the goods must meet the minimum standards of the marketplace and the customs of the industry.

The Effect of a Warranty

Because warranties are binding promises, the result of failure of a software package to measure up to those promises can be a customer claim for damages or for the return of the product. Sections 2-711 through 2-725 of the UCC give the buyer a whole array of remedies for breach of an express or implied warranty. The buyer may 1) refuse to accept the goods; 2) return them if accepted; 3) attempt to find acceptable goods at the expense of the seller; or 4) keep the goods and sue for actual, direct damages incurred because of the breach of the warranty. The buyer may also recover his or her "incidental damages" and, in some cases, "consequential damages."

Incidental damages are things like transportation expenses incurred in returning the goods, or storage costs. The real zinger is the possibility of the seller being liable for consequential damages. Suppose that you have marketed a medical billing package to a physician's office. It does not work because it loses patient records to the point that the office cannot bill the patients for six months while the system is straightened out. You could be liable for the interest the doctor has to pay on $200,000 that he borrows to meet his payroll in the meantime, plus the value of patients lost because of their annoyance at getting messed-up statements for services. Or suppose your new word-processing package loses the final twelve chapters of an author's new book, which he had to have finished to meet a contractual deadline? The liability picture is not pretty in either case.

A Real-Life Example from the Computer Industry

"How can all this be? You must be kidding. Nobody can sue a little software house or program author and get all that," you say. You better believe it, because while there have been, as yet, only a few suits against the publisher or distributor of a software package, there are a number of recent successful legal actions against major computer manufacturers for marketing defective combinations of hardware and software.

The Glovatorium Case.   For example, in 1982 the U.S. Ninth Circuit Court of Appeals upheld a jury award totalling $2,359,419 against NCR Corporation for misrepresentation of the capabilities of its Sprint/8200 system, which was to have provided certain accounting functions to the Glovatorium, a San Francisco Bay Area business. The problems alleged consisted of a combination of defective software, undelivered software, and hardware which could not meet its advertised specifications.

The award consisted of compensatory damages of $286,419 for various breaches of warranty resulting in lost profits and actual expenses, plus punitive damages of $2,073,000 for fraudulent misrepresentations. There are several other cases involving NCR, IBM, and Burroughs, which have had mixed results. Burroughs, in particular, has litigated and lost nearly half of the twelve or more B-80, B-700, and B-800 system cases, which went to trial. Many cases are still pending in the courts.

You need some way to eliminate or limit the damages for which you might be responsible if your program proves defective. How can you do this? There are several things you can do: Be careful not to make unintentional express warranties, and carefully and properly disclaim the implied warranties, if you can. However, these tasks are easier said than done.

Avoid Express Warranties

You can avoid the trap of unintended express warranties by establishing some simple procedures, and by being aware of the legal implications of making statements of fact or representations which are untrue or partially untrue. Statements which are partially false are perhaps the hardest things to avoid. Consider the following approach in reviewing your product literature and advertising:

- Carefully review all specification sheets, manuals, and advertising for statements which assign qualities or characteristics to your product.

Examples are "runs in 128K," "fully compatible with the IBM-PC operating system," or "handles data in any format."

- Unless assertions are true in all cases, be certain they are qualified, by saying, for example, "compatible with most IBM-compatible personal computers tested by us." Then list those on which you have actually tested the program.

- Be especially careful to review advertisements which were prepared before release of the final product, since the product's specs may have been changed between your original conversations with the advertising agency and final release. Manufacturers and authors often plan products which they find they cannot produce with all the planned characteristics in the amount of time left to get to market. If your product changes materially, then change the specification sheets, the manual, and the ads.

- Finally, be extremely careful about sales literature and sales letters which are written in the field. Sales persons are paid to sell, and they tend to describe products in glowing terms which may or may not be accurate. Bear in mind that your company is responsible for all such sales material, no matter where it came from, as long as it is used in the stream of commerce and you had any reason to know of it. This may even include sales brochures prepared by your dealers, which is why many companies will not permit dealers to prepare such brochures but rather take pains to provide all needed literature themselves. You can also control the use of your trademarks better in this way.

The Practical Side of Disclaiming Warranties

While you need to understand how and under what circumstances it is possible to disclaim or exclude express and implied warranties, you should also consider the commercial realities of the market. Some representations must be made about any software if it is to be advertised and marketed. Some of these representations about characteristics of the software will be considered express written warranties made by you as the publisher of the software. Some of them may prove untrue under circumstances beyond your control. What then?

If you cannot disclaim express warranties by a general waiver, as the ADDS terminal case holds, why do companies try to market software on an "as is" basis? The answer is a combination of fear of the unknown liabilities of marketing products that have never been mass-marketed before, and the feeling that consumers may be intimidated from suing by such language.

The most effective way to avoid customer complaints and litigation over defective products is to establish a reputation for standing behind products and living up to promises to customers. This means you not only use your best efforts to test software before it is released, and to notify customers promptly when errors do turn up, but also that you provide opportunities for feedback from customers. You should include forms with all software marketed, which indicate that you want to know about defects that show up and that you will make an effort to fix them. A form used by Digital Research for this purpose is set out as Figure 12–1.

If you elect this approach, you do not have to attempt to disclaim all warranties, but you must carefully condition what is said in your license and warranty forms so that it raises only realistic expectations. The example warranty form from Lifetree Software set out, starting on page 237, tries to do just this.

Perfection Is not Required in a Product

The consumer laws do not expect absolute perfection in every consumer product, only that the product not injure people or property and that it be truthfully represented to the user. The most effective way of dealing with possible defects is to tell the end user that defects show up in all software, and what you will do about this. The UCC and the consumer warranty laws discussed later in this chapter will usually accommodate this business position. For example, why not say in your manuals, specification sheets, and documentation, something like this:

> IMPORTANT NOTICE: This software has been developed, tested, and used on computer hardware equivalent to that described in the hardware specifications for use of the software. While we have used our best efforts to make it error-free, all software by its very complexity has the possibility of undiscovered errors. If you discover what you believe to be an error, or a situation in which the software does not perform according to the documented specifications, please notify us on the form at the back of the user manual. We will then use our best efforts to provide you with a correction, or an explanation of steps which can be taken to avoid the problem where it cannot be fixed.
>
> If, during the warranty period, the software proves to be unusable for the advertised purpose for which the product is licensed, because of significant errors which we cannot correct or help you work around, we and the dealer from whom you obtained this software will refund your license fee paid, upon evidence of payment and our inability to correct the problem. Since all software and data used on computers is inherently subject to loss because of hardware and software failures, we urge that you maintain complete back-up copies of the software and data, prepared on a regular basis. We cannot help you if you don't.
>
> We cannot be responsible for failures due to causes beyond our control, like subsequent hardware modifications or other software used with this product. Likewise, since we cannot con-

⫼ DIGITAL RESEARCH **SOFTWARE PERFORMANCE REPORT**

P.O. BOX 579
PACIFIC GROVE, CA 93950

Product Name and Version
Date
User Name
Company Name
Address

Report Type	Rate Problem Impact
☐ Problem/Possible Error	☐ 3 Shuts Down System
☐ Suggested Enhancement	☐ 2 Impairs System Performance
☐ Document Suggestion	☐ 1 Causes Inconvenience
☐ Other	☐ 0 Needs Suggested Enhancement

Phone   Ext.

Operating System Version and Serial Number (If different from Product Name shown above)	Product Serial Number	Language
	Microcomputer Manufacturer	Software Supplier Name and Address

Hard Disk(s)   Floppy Disk(s)   CPU Type (Z-80, 8080, 8086, etc.)

Size _____   Size _____

Capacity _____ Capacity _____   Memory Size   Memory Configuration   Peripherals

Density: Single_____ Double_____ Sides: Single_____ Double_____

Problem Description: (Please describe the problem and how it can be reproduced, your diagnosis and your cure, if known. Be concise and attach a listing, if available.)

User Name

FOR DIGITAL RESEARCH USE-DO NOT WRITE BELOW THIS LINE   ⬩1981 Digital Research

Date Received	Date Answered
Date Assigned	Log Number

Figure 12-1

trol the use to which you put this software, or operator error, we will not be responsible for any direct or indirect damages which you may incur, including incidental and consequential damages. These provisions allow us to market this software at a much lower price than would be the case if we had to accept liability for any damages which might occur due to errors and problems which can arise in the use of any software.

The Able American Software Company

THE HIGH RISKS OF LIMITING OR EXCLUDING WARRANTIES

Disclaiming Express Warranties

The wisdom of taking the practical approach rather than trying to exclude warranties becomes clear if you examine closely the provisions of the UCC concerning what you must do to disclaim warranties. You can legally disclaim all express warranties, as long as you don't make any. But UCC § 2-316 provides that where a disclaimer of express warranties conflicts with express warranties made, the disclaimers are ineffective if the existence of both creates an unreasonable agreement. The practical effect of this is to prohibit the disclaimer of express warranties if any express warranty is made. Remember that advertisements are often deemed to be express warranties or representations by the seller.

Disclaiming Implied Warranties

This same section of the UCC permits a disclaimer of implied warranties, but only if the written disclaimer is conspicuous and, in the case of disclaiming merchantability, those words must be used. In theory, all implied warranties can be disclaimed by an "As Is" statement similar to that used by IBM in its warranty which accompanies PC-DOS 2.0:

LIMITED WARRANTY

THE PROGRAM IS PROVIDED "AS IS" WITHOUT WARRANTY OF ANY KIND, EITHER EXPRESSED OR IMPLIED, INCLUDING BUT NOT LIMITED TO THE IMPLIED WARRANTIES OF MERCHANTABILITY AND FITNESS FOR A PARTICULAR PURPOSE. THE ENTIRE RISK AS TO THE QUALITY AND PERFORMANCE OF THE PROGRAM IS WITH YOU. SHOULD THE PROGRAM PROVE DEFECTIVE, YOU (AND NOT IBM OR AN AUTHORIZED PERSONAL COMPUTER DEALER) ASSUME THE ENTIRE COST OF ALL NECESSARY SERVICING, REPAIR OR CORRECTION. . . . .

IBM does not warrant that the functions contained in the program will meet your requirements or that the operation of the program will be uninterrupted or error free.

. . . .

IN NO EVENT WILL IBM BE LIABLE TO YOU FOR ANY DAMAGES, INCLUDING ANY LOST PROFITS, LOST SAVINGS OR OTHER INCIDENTAL OR CONSEQUENTIAL DAMAGES ARISING OUT OF THE USE OR INABILITY TO USE SUCH PROGRAM EVEN IF IBM OR AN AUTHORIZED IBM PERSONAL COMPUTER DEALER HAS BEEN ADVISED OF THE POSSIBILITY OF SUCH DAMAGES, OR FOR ANY CLAIM BY ANY OTHER PARTY.

Does this strike you as a reasonable warranty? *Do not use this form,* because it may well be unenforceable as an unreasonable and unconscionable disclaimer under the UCC and the consumer warranty laws.

Problems With The IBM Form

There are three serious defects in the IBM form, which many other software companies are currently copying. First, an "as is" disclaimer presumes an opportunity on the part of the buyer to inspect the goods, and that the buyer has some reasonable basis for making the decision to accept this limitation. This is clearly not the case in the consumer market, since the software is in a sealed box and most consumers do not know enough about the IBM hardware and operating system to intelligently waive their rights. The consumer has only two practical choices—accept the standard form or not buy the product. The terms are not negotiable. For this reason, alone, this disclaimer is probably unenforceable.

Second, the attempt of IBM to deny the purchaser any remedy for damages caused by defective software is in direct violation of UCC § 2-719, which permits alternative provisions for remedies, such as limiting the remedies to the purchase price or to the replacement of the product. The IBM form provides *no* remedy whatsoever, but says it is up to the buyer to fix the product.

Most important, since the UCC further provides that consequential damages may not be excluded if to do so would be unconscionable, this form probably does not effectively waive such damages, since the buyer has no remedy at all. This type of waiver has consistently been held unconscionable by the courts. This waiver is the most dangerous provision of all, since UCC § 2-719 provides that where proposed remedies or limitations fail, the buyer may rely on the general provisions of the UCC for his or her remedies. These are the very provisions the waiver tries to eliminate.

The Ultimate Danger—No Limits At All

Businesses that attempt to disclaim express and implied warranties, and to limit indirect and consequential damages, need to understand that if this effort is found to be "unconscionable" by the court, the buyer will have unlimited access to all of the remedies specified in the UCC. In short, if you push too hard, instead of limiting your financial exposure from defective software, you will open your company up to unlimited liability. This fact is obviously not understood by those software companies that continue to copy the IBM form. The IBM form has the potential for the disasterous litigation mentioned at the outset of this chapter.

A Classic Example.   A sizeable portion of the landmark opinion in a 1983 California case is quoted below, because it is one of the clearest statements of the law where a contract was held to be unconscionable.

In the case of A & M Produce Co. v. FMC Corporation, FMC recommended and sold a piece of complex tomato-processing equipment to A & M for $32,000, under a printed form agreement containing all the standard disclaimers of express and implied warranties, and a disclaimer of consequential damages in nearly the same words used by IBM in its disclaimer. Turning down a chance to settle the case for refund of the purchase price of the equipment, FMC took the case to trial and relied on its printed form disclaimers to defeat A & M's admittedly valid claim that the machinery did not work, and ruined A & M's tomato harvest. FMC lost, appealed, and the appeals court upheld the judgment against FMC of $225,000 for breach of various implied and express warranties, consequential damages, and $45,000 in attorney's fees.

The language of the appellate court opinion says it all, although I have omitted some elements of its decision so as to keep the quotation reasonably short:

> [U]nconscionability has generally been recognized to include an absence of meaningful choice on the part of one of the parties, together with contract terms which are unreasonably favorable to the other party. . . . "Surprise" involves the extent to which the supposedly agreed-upon terms of the bargain are hidden in a prolix printed form drafted by the party seeking to enforce the disputed terms. . . . [C]ommercial practicalities dictate that unbargained-for terms only be denied enforcement where they are also substantively unreasonable. . . . [T]he greater the unfair surprise or inequality of bargaining power, the less unreasonable the risk reallocation which will be tolerated. . . .
>
> [T]he facts of this case support the trial court's conclusion that such disclaimer was commercially unreasonable. The warranty allegedly breached by FMC went to the basic performance char-

acteristics of the product.... *Since a product's performance forms the fundamental basis for a sales contract, it is patently unreasonable to assume that a buyer would purchase a standardized mass-produced product from an industry seller without any enforceable performance standards. ...*

Especially where an inexperienced buyer is concerned, the seller's performance representations are absolutely necessary to allow the buyer to make an intelligent choice among the competitive options available. *A seller's attempt, through the use of a disclaimer, to prevent the buyer from reasonably relying on such representations calls into question the commercial reasonableness of the agreement and may well be substantively unconscionable.* ....

If the seller's warranty was breached, consequential damages were not merely "reasonably foreseeable"; they were explicitly obvious.... [R]isk shifting is socially expensive and should not be undertaken in the absence of a good reason.... FMC was the only party reasonably able to prevent this loss by not selling A & M a machine inadequate to meet its expressed needs.... If there is a type of risk allocation that should be subjected to special scrutiny, it is probably the shifting to one party of a risk that only the other party can avoid....

[T]hese contract clauses were oppressive, contrary to oral representations made to induce the purchase, and unreasonably favorable to the party with a superior bargaining position. No experienced farmer would spend $32,000 for equipment which could not process his tomatoes before they rot and no fair and honest merchant would sell such equipment with representations negated in its own sales contract. [Emphasis Added]

A Lesson for the Software Industry.   The lesson of the FMC case is clear: any software warranty that attempts to disclaim all liability, in the manner of the IBM form, simply will not work if contested in the right case, because it is unconscionable and unreasonable. It is also extremely dangerous to try to use such sweeping language, because to do so opens up the possibility that you will not be able to limit your liability at all.

It is even more dangerous for a software company to hide behind such sweeping limitations, since all software, like computer hardware, always comes with some technical documentation which lays out specifications for the product. If the product is defective, it does not meet those specifications, and there has been a breach of an express warranty, similar to the situation in the ADDS terminal case. If a court finds the attempted limitations or disclaimers unreasonable, as in the FMC case, you are vulnerable before the court and open to damages so disproportionate to the price of your product that it could be catastrophic to you.

FEDERAL AND STATE
CONSUMER WARRANTY LAWS

It isn't enough that you have to be concerned with the warranty provisions of the Uniform Commercial Code, but you also have to be aware of some even more stringent (and unreasonable) federal and state consumer warranty laws. The most important of these is the federal Magnuson-Moss Warranty Act, which applies to every sale of consumer products priced over $15.00. California, where forty percent of the computer industry is located, has an even more burdensome law, the Song-Beverly Consumer Warranty Act. Some other states have consumer laws, but few are as all-encompassing as that of California.

What They Require

Unlike the substantive provisions of the UCC, the federal and state consumer warranty laws aim primarily at requiring clear and simple language in warranties, and the inclusion of certain fixed terminology declaring what rights are available. In sum, the Magnuson-Moss Warranty Act (MMWA) mandates that warranty terms be available to consumers before the purchase, and prohibits disclaimers of some implied warranties. It provides for access to state and federal courts to enforce the rights granted and allows recovery of attorney's fees and costs, in addition to damages actually incurred. The California law sets up somewhat similar requirements, and in some situations prohibits the disclaimer of implied warranties in the case of consumer goods. The focus of this discussion will be on the MMWA because of its nationwide application.

BASIC REQUIREMENTS OF MAGNUSON-MOSS

The MMWA is administered by the Federal Trade Commission, which puts out a number of publications listed in the bibliography. It also has issued a full set of regulations under the law. You should get copies of them for your own study, since fully detailing the requirements of the MMWA would take hundreds of pages. All that can be done here is to touch on the highlights of this 1975 law.

The first issue to examine is whether the MMWA applies to software sales and licensing. It covers consumer goods, which are "any tangible personal property which is distributed in commerce which is normally used for personal, family, or household purposes." Pure business transactions involving software are not included, but what about software acquired for personal use in business? The law is silent on this issue. Based on past history it seems safe to assume that some day this law will be held to apply to most software transactions.

While the specific language requirements of the MMWA are frustrating and very unforgiving, the unfavorable financial penalties to a distributor or seller of goods are so potentially costly that it seems foolish not to comply, where this is possible. Section 2310 of Title 15 of the United States Code sets out the full range of consumer remedies for violation of this law by a seller. This includes the right to sue the seller in state or federal court, to recover not only damages but attorney fees and costs, and a number of other remedies. Given the fact that most software for micros sells in the under $500 range, the exposure to such broad liability for non-compliance does not make good business sense. Let's see what is required.

Full Warranties versus Limited Warranties

Unless you give the consumer the minimum rights specified in Section 2303 of the law, you must call your warranty a "Limited Warranty." This is why the IBM warranty quoted above used that heading. To have a "Full Warranty," which may be limited in time, you must, under § 2304, provide the following minimum rights:

- You must agree to remedy any defect without charge, within a reasonable period of time.

- You must place no limitation on implied warranties.

- You may not exclude or limit consequential damages unless you use clear and conspicuous language to that effect on the face of the warranty.

- You must agree to give the consumer either a complete refund or a full replacement if you cannot fix the defect within a reasonable period of time.

Limiting Implied Warranties

You may not disclaim implied warranties *if any written warranty is made to the consumer*. However, the implied warranties may be limited in time, if the duration "is conscionable and is set forth in clear and unmistakable language" prominently displayed on the face of the warranty. The IBM warranty quoted (but not in full) above may not comply with this requirement.

If you violate any material requirement of the MMWA, the consumer has access to all the court remedies and is not bound by your attempted disclaimer at all. This is similar to the UCC provisions which disallow all efforts at limiting warranties where the provisions are unconscionable, but is stronger than the UCC.

FTC Required Rules On Written Warranties

If you provide your customer with *any* written warranty, the FTC rules require that you disclose the following information in clear language in a single document:

- Who the warranty protects.
- Any parts or items not included.
- What the warrantor will do, including what replacements or repairs will be paid for and which will not be.
- When the warranty commences.
- Procedures necessary to obtain service, including addresses and phone numbers of warranty service centers.
- Any procedures for informal dispute resolution.
- Any time limits on implied warranties, with appropriate language indicating that some states do not permit such limitations.
- Any time limits on recovery of incidental or consequential damages, with appropriate language indicating that some states do not permit such limitations.
- A final clause to the effect that "This warranty gives you specific legal rights, and you may have other rights which vary from state to state."

The biggest problem that the software industry seems to have with these requirements is that most businesses seem completely unaware of the law. Many software houses apparently just copy, blindly, the language of any convenient warranty form they see. Obviously, this practice can get your business into trouble under this law.

Pre-Sale Availability of Written Warranty Terms

The most often ignored requirement, § 702.3 of the FTC rules, requires that the seller make available to the consumer *prior to the purchase* the text of any written warranty. There are several alternative ways to do this, such as posting the warranty near the product, having copies of warranties in binders, or printing the full text of the warranty on or attached to the product itself. You may notice signs in department stores calling attention to the fact that copies of all warranties are available at some convenient place in the store, which is an effort to comply with this rule.

To aid the seller, the manufacturer must provide the seller with these materials. You, as the software house actually providing the warranty, can meet the law in several alternative ways: 1) by providing a copy of the written warranty with every warranted consumer product; 2) by providing the warranty on a tag, sign, or other attachment to the product; 3) by printing the warranty on display cartons, and including a copy inside the box; or 4) by providing a sign or poster with the warranty on it, for display in the store, and in the box with the merchandise.

How to Comply. I have suggested to my clients that a complete, formal warranty document be included in the package the software comes in, preferably in the front of the user manual or loose in the box. In addition, you should ship to each dealer, with each shipment, a packet of warranty forms, including a sign to be posted by the shelf about the warranties. Most hardware manufacturers actually do this now.

Ideally, the full text of the warranty could be printed on your shrink-wrapped slip-case containing the software, but this is not aesthetically pleasing. You could combine automatic shipments of copies of the full text warranty to dealers and distributors, with a complete written warranty in each package, and with language on the outside of the box in conspicuous type:

> NOTICE TO BUYER: This product comes with a written limited warranty, the full text of which is packed inside this case. Ask your dealer for a copy of the warranty, or obtain his permission to open this case to see the warranty, if you wish to read it before licensing this software.

The Lotus™ 1-2-3 package has a notice, which also relates to the licensed nature of the software. While this notice does not fully comply with the law, it might work as well:

Conditions of Purchase

This product is subject to limitations on warranty and permitted uses customary in the *sale* of microcomputer software for personal use. The details of such limitations are set forth in the Lotus Customer Assurance Plan which is available from Lotus or from your dealer. Opening the diskette package indicates your acceptance of these limitations. [Italics added.]

Whatever you do, be very sure that you do not pack the warranty inside the box in such a way that the customer has to open the licensed software pack, described in Chapter 11, in order to see the warranty. This could destroy both the warranty limitations and the licensing restrictions. Make it easy for the customer to see and find the warranty; the chances are it will be ignored anyway, as the Cathy cartoon suggests.

Catalog Sales and Warranties

The FTC rules apply to disclosure of warranties before purchase even when you are distributing only by mail. If you market your software this way, you must, under Rule 702.3(c), clearly and conspicuously disclose in your catalog and your mail order advertisements that copies of warranties for your products can be obtained free on request from your place of business. Alternatively, you may print the full text of the warranty in the catalog or in a conspicuous place near the article. This is burdensome, but a standard practice of placing language like this in all ads and catalogs would be considered compliance with the law:

WARRANTIES. Copies of written warranties for all products advertised may be obtained free of charge, prior to licensing such products, by writing or calling the address or phone number for orders.

Requiring Warranty Cards

As a method of controlling and registering software licensees, many software publishers require as a precondition to support services that a warranty or registration card be returned to the publisher. This may work from the standpoint of software protection, but it may violate the MMWA or state consumer protection laws.

Section 700.7 of the FTC Rules provides that where you are providing a Full Warranty for a product, it is unreasonable to require such registration as a condition to service or warranty assistance. You may not, therefore, provide this as a condition. However, very few software warranties are Full Warranties within the meaning of the MMWA.

In the case of Limited Warranties, you may require, as a precondition to warranty service, the return of such a card. FTC Rule 701.4 requires that you disclose this requirement in the warranty form itself. If you do not require the card, you should disclose that it is not necessary to return it or you may be deemed guilty of an unfair trade practice under the FTC rules.

The following language should comply with this requirement:

WARRANTY SERVICE CARD. You must return the Warranty Registration Card, fully completed with the requested information, in order to qualify for warranty assistance. This is the only way we have of knowing that you are a legitimate licensee of this software. We will provide you with a substitute card if it has been lost or destroyed.

AN EXAMPLE OF STATE CONSUMER PROTECTION LAWS

Many small businesses are unaware of the existence of the numerous consumer protection laws in the various states. These laws can create serious problems for you if you fail to comply with them. The best way to learn about them is to check with your attorney or your state Department of Consumer Affairs. While it is impossible for you to package and warrant your software products for every state, realize that technically you must comply with the rules of each state into which your product goes.

The California Song-Beverly Consumer Warranty Act

Because so much software is produced and sold in California, the Song-Beverly Consumer Warranty Act, found in California's Civil Code §§1790–

1795.7, is briefly highlighted here as an example of state laws. Like the MMWA, this law covers only consumer goods, which probably includes most microcomputer software.

Unlike some states, California does not absolutely prohibit the disclaimer of implied warranties, but it requries that the implied warranties of merchantability and fitness of purpose have a duration equal to any express warranties made. Unless the goods are properly sold or licensed on an "as is" basis, these two implied warranties must last for at least sixty days in the case of consumer goods. This requirement means that it is unwise to market any software in California with less than a sixty-day warranty.

In addition, the laws of Alabama, Kansas, Maine, Maryland, Vermont, and West Virginia prohibit or severely limit the right to make warranty disclaimers for consumer products. You should carefully check the laws of the states in which you have your primary markets.

It is possible, under Civil Code §§ 1792.3 through 1792.5, to sell goods on an "as is" basis to consumers, but there must be the same clear notice to the buyer as required in the Magnuson-Moss Warranty Act. The buyer must clearly understand that "the entire risk as to the quality and performance of the goods is with the buyer," and that the buyer assumes all costs of repair and replacement if the goods prove defective. The IBM PC-DOS warranty form set out above is worded perfectly to meet this requirement under California law. Similar language must be set out in any mail-order offering or catalog sales on an "as is" basis, "as to each item so offered."

The Risk of Non-Compliance with Song-Beverly

Treble Damages. The risk of ignoring laws like Song-Beverly is that if the manufacturer is determined to have wilfully violated any of the provisions of the Act, or to have refused to comply with express or implied warranty obligations involved in a sale, the manufacturer may be liable for three times the amount of actual damages incurred, plus attorney fees and costs of the litigation. This could amount to the value of your company, if an irate consumer sues you.

Why not make an effort to comply with the Act, rather than risk an adverse court decision because of an illegal disclaimer of express or implied warranties? The business decision is simply whether the risk of suit *and treble damages* is worse than the costs of standing behind the software product for a sixty-day minimum period of time. The example warranty form toward the end of this chapter shows how you can comply at little actual cost.

Remedies for Retailers. California's statute also gives a right to suit under the Consumer Act to the retailer. The retailer must have been damaged by the manufacturer or distributor who wilfully failed to comply

with the Act, or who refused to meet express or implied warranty obligations undertaken at the time of sale. This makes the retailer your potential
enemy, rather than an ally. The retailer has the same treble damage and
attorney fees rights as the consumer. The retailer does not ordinarily have
this type of right under the UCC nor the federal laws.

Other State Traps for Sellers

In an effort to insure that California consumers have adequate warranty
service, there are provisions in this law requiring that every manufacturer
of a warranted consumer good, distributed in the state, maintain service
facilities within the State of California. These facilities must be
"reasonably close" to where the goods are sold. To comply with the law,
the manufacturer can contract with the stores that sell the goods or with
others who can perform authorized repairs. This law can be a real thorn in
the side of out-of-state businesses, since they cannot afford to do this
unless they are very large and nationwide.

Since there are provisions authorizing the manufacturer to "suggest
other methods of service and repair" in § 1794.5 of the Code, you should
give careful thought to being sure that mail-order repair facilities are
reasonably available, if you are out-of state, and that you consider use of
dealers for warranty claims. Due to the small cost of mailing diskettes to
and from the customer, it might be a much better solution to provide an
express warranty and remedy for defective software allowing the
customer to call the software house on a "hot-line," perhaps even toll-free.
You could provide that error corrections which cannot be handled in the
field will be shipped free of charge to the consumer from your facilities.
This should comply with the law.

A COMPLETE SOFTWARE WARRANTY FORM
INTENDED TO COMPLY WITH WARRANTY LAWS

Together we have reviewed most of the significant aspects of warranties
relating to software under federal and state law. We have looked at parts
of existing warranty forms actually in use in today's market. No sample,
model, or suggested form can take into consideration all of the factors
that might impact a particular product in the software business. No such
form will ever be perfect, even for a specific product. However, it will be
helpful for you to review a complete warranty form which was drafted with
the intent of complying, as much as possible, with the UCC, federal, and
state laws.

The following form, actually in use in slightly modified form by a
client of mine, is set forth in its entirety to give you an idea what one
should look like. You must keep in mind that a number of business decisions were made in developing it, and that it does not deal with some
issues that might be necessary in your own company's case. You should,

therefore, not use it without careful review by your own legal counsel, experienced not only in warranty law but also with the unique legal issues of the software industry. It is reprinted with permission of the copyright owner, Lifetree Software, Inc.

SAMPLE WARRANTY FORM

LIMITED WARRANTY
LIFETREE SOFTWARE, INC.
SOFTWARE PRODUCTS

What Is Covered:

LIFETREE SOFTWARE, INC. (LSI) warrants that the magnetic diskette(s) which the enclosed computer SOFTWARE is recorded on and the DOCUMENTATION provided with it are free from defects in materials and workmanship under normal use. LSI warrants that the computer SOFTWARE itself will perform substantially in accordance with the specifications set forth in the DOCUMENTATION provided with the SOFTWARE.

For How Long:

The above warranties are made for sixty (60) days from the date of original retail delivery to you or your company as the user.

What We Will Do:

LSI will replace any magnetic diskette or DOCUMENTATION which proves defective in materials or workmanship without charge.
LSI will either replace or repair any SOFTWARE that does not perform substantially in accordance with the specifications set forth in the DOCUMENTATION with a corrected copy of the SOFTWARE or corrective code. In the case of an error in the DOCUMENTATION, LSI will correct errors in the DOCUMENTATION without charge by providing addenda or substitute pages.
If LSI is unable to replace defective DOCUMENTATION or a defective diskette or if LSI is unable to provide corrected SOFTWARE or corrected DOCUMENTATION within a reasonable time, LSI will either replace the SOFTWARE with a functionally similar program or refund the fees paid for the SOFTWARE.

What We Will Not Do:

LSI does not warrant that the functions contained in the SOFTWARE will meet your requirements or that the operation of the SOFTWARE will be uninterrupted or error free. The warranty does not cover any diskette or DOCUMENTATION which has been subjected to damage or abuse. The SOFTWARE warranty does not cover any SOFTWARE which has been altered or changed in any way by any one other than LSI. LSI is not responsible for problems caused by computer hardware, computer operating systems or the use of LSI's SOFTWARE in conjunction with non-LSI software.

ANY IMPLIED WARRANTIES COVERING THE DISKETTE, THE DOCUMENTATION OR THE SOFTWARE PROGRAM INCLUDING ANY WARRANTIES OF MERCHANTABILITY OR FITNESS FOR A PARTICULAR PURPOSE ARE LIMITED IN DURATION TO SIXTY (60) DAYS FROM THE DATE OF ORIGINAL RETAIL DELIVERY. An implied warranty of merchantability means that the product will work normally and an implied warranty of fitness means that a product is suitable for the use for which it is advertised. Some states do not allow limitations on how long an implied warranty lasts, so the above limitation may not apply to you.

LSI SHALL NOT IN ANY CASE BE LIABLE FOR SPECIAL, INCIDENTAL, CONSEQUENTIAL, INDIRECT OR OTHER SIMILAR DAMAGES ARISING FROM BREACH OF WARRANTY, BREACH OF CONTRACT, NEGLIGENCE, OR ANY OTHER LEGAL THEORY EVEN IF LSI OR OUR AGENT HAS BEEN ADVISED OF THE POSSIBILITY OF SUCH DAMAGES. This means we are not responsible for any costs incurred as a result of lost profits or revenue, loss of use of the SOFTWARE, loss of data, costs of re-creating lost data, the cost of any substitute program, claims by any party other than you, or for other similar costs. Some states do no allow the exclusion or limitation of incidental or consequential damages, so the above limitation or exclusion may not apply to you.

What You Must Do:

You must return the defective item postpaid with the warranty service form provided, within sixty (60) days of your original retail delivery, and we must receive it within seventy-five (75) days of delivery. You must either insure the defective item being returned or assume the risk of loss or damage in transit. Address all warranty claims to: Warranty Service Department, Lifetree Software, Inc., 411 Pacific Street, Suite 315, Monterey, Califor-

nia 93940. Any claim under the above warranty must include a
dated proof of purchase such as a copy of your sales receipt or invoice.

Other Conditions:

This warranty allocates risks of product failure between
YOU and LSI. LSI's software pricing reflects this allocation of
risk and the limitations of liability contained in this warranty.
The warranty set forth above is in lieu of all other express warranties, whether oral or written. The agents, employees, distributors, and dealers of LSI are not authorized to make modifications to this warranty, or additional warranties binding on
LSI. Accordingly, additional statements such as dealer advertising or presentations, whether oral or written, do not constitute
warranties by LSI and should not be relied upon.

State Law Rights:

This warranty gives you specific legal rights, and you may
also have other rights which vary from state to state.

PROFESSIONAL LIABILITY
FOR DEFECTIVE PROGRAMMING

You will remember that one of the legal grounds for liability discussed at
the outset of this chapter was negligence or tort liability. Now that we have
covered the bases on warranty liability, we should look at this issue again
briefly because it could arise in several contexts.

Contract Liability

If you enter into a contract with a customer for custom programming,
based on specifications and detailed functionality, you may have legal liability to your customer arising from that contract. That type of exposure
can, to some degree, be limited by contract provisions expressly stating
the exact extent of your liability or non-liability. Give careful thought to
just what exposure you are willing to take, since these limits are generally
enforceable as a matter of contract law. This is a service contract and is
not subject to the UCC warranty rules nor most consumer protection laws.

Third Parties

However, suppose that the program you write is to be used to run the accounting aspects of a federal credit union, and you make some serious er-

rors that lose people's accounts or credit and debit things to the wrong accounts. You have no contract with the members of the credit union, but they may have the basis for a lawsuit against you for negligent performance of your duties as a programmer. This may be so even if your contract with the credit union limits or entirely disclaims any liability to the organization.

There have been very few cases in this field to date, but there is no reason why a programmer could not be put in the same situation by the courts as a lawyer or doctor who commits malpractice by making an error that injures someone financially or physically. Some insurance carriers, like St. Paul Fire & Marine Insurance Co., have recognized this possibility and will write insurance coverage for you to protect against claims for your professional errors and omissions. You should consider carrying such insurance if you do custom programming, since this insurance can cover both your contractual liability to the customer and your negligence liability to third parties.

Protecting Yourself from Programming Errors

There are other steps you can take to protect yourself and your company. As long as you do custom programming there is no way you can totally limit your liability for errors, since there are some implied obligations imposed on you which most courts will not let you disclaim by contract, and there are situations where you will make an error. Here are some suggestions to minimize those risks:

- Carefully plan the programming project with your customer, and insist on clear and unambiguous specifications, together with a set of real-life test data and expected results. The specifications should include the details of the exact hardware configuration on which the software is expected to run. If there are later changes in the specifications, be sure that they are feasible before you agree to them.

- Insist on a reasonable time schedule so that you can test and correct problems before you install the system, and so that you will not perpetually be under the gun to complete it. Stick to that schedule, or obtain extensions of time.

- Once you commence the work, keep detailed notes on problems encountered and the solutions used, so you can show that you tested things as you went along and that the system worked when you completed it. Keep the test data and results.

- When you have completed the software and installed it, perform an acceptance test with your customer, and have the customer sign-off with an acknowledgement that it works and that you are released from further liability. Provide for such a test and acceptance in your initial contract.

- Be certain that the operators are properly trained, and insist in your contract that you have specific input into such a training program beyond preparing and delivering a copy of a users manual to management. You will get valuable feedback as to potential problems during training, which will often signal possible design or coding errors in the program.

- Be responsive to early problems with the program, and bend over backwards to fix things that appear to be errors. Very few user organizations sue either programmers or computer manufacturers who are still actively working to fix problems. Most lawsuits come after the software house refuses to do anything further.

- Finally, *before you start such a project,* talk to your insurance broker about obtaining "Errors and Omissions" insurance which will cover you for legal expense and damages incurred if you do make serious mistakes in developing the program. Such insurance is not cheap, but if you do any significant amount of programming work the insurance costs are cheaper than being pushed into bankruptcy court by a judgment in a lawsuit you lose. You may be able to build these added costs into your programming fees.

Most of these steps amount to nothing more than common sense. Unlike producers of mass-distributed software, you have a direct relationship with the acquiring party, so you should be better able to design and control the use of the program, and to see that your duties specified in the contract are reasonable. You can negotiate your obligations, and so long as you do not undertake projects you are not qualified to do, you should be in a strong position to avoid unnecessary liability upon completion of your work.

STRICT LIABILITY FOR SOFTWARE ERRORS

The third legal basis for liability stemming from software development activities is known as "strict liability" for defects. It is highly unlikely that the average software business has any significant exposure to this type of liability, since it requires that the product be one that has inherently dangerous characteristics, such as industrial machinery, toxic chemicals, drugs, and other similar items. Nonetheless, it should be considered as a possible risk.

CAD/CAE/CAM Software

There are some cases where risk exposure under strict liability theories is not apparent on the surface. Several of my clients are engaged in developing CAD/CAE/CAM software. This type of graphics software is used in developing, designing and manufacturing equipment, buildings, refineries and many industrial processes. The software is used by the designer or engineer to design and permit manufacture of complex parts, machinery, and processes. Its very complexity permits the user to create things and processes that are beyond the capability of a human being unaided by the computer. As such, the designs may be so complex that a human designer/developer could not see potential errors until the product fails in actual use.

You can readily imagine how the designer of a bridge, airplane part, or industrial system could come to rely on the software to the point that he or she no longer questions the computer-aided designs produced. Suppose, for example, that the airplane part goes into production and is incorporated into the final aircraft, and then the part fails—causing the airplane to crash. In the search for someone to pay damages to the families and victims killed or injured in the crash, it is highly likely that the attorneys representing the plaintiffs would eventually trace the failure of the part to the failure of the software to produce a correct design. Even if the software were only one part of the equation causing the failure, it would involve a costly legal defense of product liability, professional malpractice, and other issues.

The Only Solution

Aside from the same suggestions made with respect to preventing negligence claims—care in developing and testing the software—the only effective method of dealing with this potential financial exposure under strict liability theories is to carry software errors and omissions insurance which specifically includes product liability coverage. There is no way you can contractually limit liability because the claimants will not have been a party to your software development or licensing agreements, and as a matter of public policy the courts will not let you limit your liability *if the product could foreseeably be dangerous to humans.*

Software is not inherently dangerous, but there are some types of software which, if defective, could do harm to people or property. In this case carry insurance, or don't develop and market software of this type at all. There are very high risks in creating and marketing such software, and you should not undertake such work lightly.

SUMMARY

The ultimate results of warranty and product liability litigation, and its effect on software houses and software authors, will depend largely on the reasonableness of the warranties used in this industry as it matures. If the industry tries to hide behind complex disclaimers that leave consumers and users with no remedies, it is not difficult to predict that the law will develop unfavorably from the viewpoint of the software industry.

On the other hand, if reasonable alternatives are provided, such as short but fair replacement and repair policies for defective software, then it is likely that attempts to limit uncontrollable consequential damages will succeed. The court system is not unaware that prices of products depend to some degree on the sharing of risks. If the risks are fairly spread, and the consumer is clearly told this, it is possible that attempts to limit consequential and indirect damages will be sustained.

In the final analysis, the outcome will depend on reasonable business policies, skillfully drafted legal documents, and well-presented and logical legal cases—all of which assume that the industry will mature to the point that mass-produced software will have a level of quality better than that which presently exists. There are encouraging signs of a trend toward higher quality, and the growth of small but established software houses into larger businesses should help. You can do your part by careful consideration of the ideas set out in this chapter.

13

Dealing with the Government: Licenses and Contracts for Software Acquisition

To be free is to live under a Government by law.

Lord Mansfield in King v. Shipley, 1784.

BIG BROTHER
AND THE SOFTWARE INDUSTRY

Contracting for the delivery of goods or services to the federal government is like dancing with a nine-hundred pound gorilla: you can dance any way you want, as long as that's the way the gorilla wants to dance.

Software sales or licensing agreements with the Department of Defense (DOD) and the National Aeronautics and Space Administration (NASA) can be particularly difficult and frustrating, because of the complex maze of rules and regulations that apply to contracts with those agencies. Fortunately, under the Federal Acquisition Regulations (FARs) licensing software to other government agencies is less complex. This chapter explains these procurement rules and their application to your software business.

Government Contracting Is Unique

If you contemplate licensing your software to the federal government, or if you are presently doing so, you need to understand that government procurement requests and agreements are not like the ordinary run-of-the-mill, commercial documents you are accustomed to signing without detailed review. When dealing with the federal government, you should not assume that your typical, carefully drafted, commercial software license will adequately protect you and your software business. Since the government creates the law, it is not bound by the same contracting rules that apply to other businesses.

Loss of Proprietary Rights.   Standard and special provisions in some government procurement regulations may inadvertently destroy your copyright, trade secret, or patent protection. If you are aware of the extent of your rights as a contractor with the government, there are special legends or provisions you can request to be inserted into government contracts. These provisions will protect your property rights, but still give the government what it needs. You must, however, understand the application of these rules in order to protect your software and documentation.

UNDERSTANDING THE FEDERAL PROCUREMENT REGULATIONS

After years and years of contracting for goods and services, the federal government has developed a body of laws and regulations which govern purchases from private contractors. Many of these rules are automatically incorporated into any contract you enter into with the U.S. Government, unless you provide to the contrary, in writing. For this reason, you should never agree to what you may be told is "the standard government contract" for software licenses. There is no such thing, since the language required to be used will depend on the circumstances under which the particular software was developed.

The Reasoning Behind Procurement Rules

The government buys billions of dollars of goods and services each year. It does not want to pay over and over again for things it needs. Where it has paid for the development of software and documentation under a specific contract, it must, by law, have an unlimited right to use that software in various government agencies around the globe, and not be restricted in its use to a specific computer or a particular building. This is different from most businesses and gives the government far more extensive rights.

On the other hand, the government recognizes that where a contractor has developed software at the contractor's own expense, the government cannot expect the same extensive rights for itself. Private businesses will not provide innovative, cost-effective computers and software to the government if the owners cannot protect their proprietary interest in such technology. This creates problems for agencies like the

DOD, which funds huge research and development contracts that include software, some of which is developed under the specific contract and some of which is "off-the-shelf" commercial software. The most difficult problem of all is dealing with software that is based on a commercial product, but is then adapted to specific government applications under a government contract.

THE FEDERAL ACQUISITION REGULATIONS

Federal procurement is divided between contracts with the military and NASA under the Armed Services Procurement Act (starting at Section 10 USC § 2301), and contracts with the General Services Administration (GSA) and the rest of civilian government under the Federal Property and Administrative Services Act (Section 40 USC §470 and 41 USC § 251). A significant amount of civilian agency procurements is handled by or through the GSA. Regulations adopted by the agency in question must be carefully followed by the contracting officer who is charged with administering them for each federal agency.

Uniformity and the New FAR's

To promote uniformity among the differing rules of many agencies, the government adopted on April 1, 1984, a comprehensive set of regulations known as the Federal Acquisition Regulations (FAR's). In theory, this set of regulations is to replace existing individual agency regulations, but in practice major agencies like the DOD have already issued their own supplemental regulations, which are pretty much the same as the rules they had before April 1984, but with different numbering systems. References should not be made in government contracts to the earlier Defense Acquisition Regulations (DAR) and Federal Procurement Regulations (FPR), since they are no longer in use.

Part 27 of the FAR's prescribes the policies, procedures, and contract clauses relating to patents, copyrights, and like matters. There is very little in the FAR's on the subject of computer software, so that virtually all the important rules affecting the software industry are to be found in the DOD Supplement to the FAR's and in the NASA Supplement. Since the latter rules are similar to those of the DOD, the discussion here is primarily based on the DOD regulations. There are, or will be, some rules concerning software issued by agencies such as the General Services Administration, the Department of Energy, and others.

Commercial Loose-Leaf Services.   The text of these rules is readily available to government contracting officers, but unless you have a copy of one of the commercial loose-leaf services like the nine volume CCH Government Contracts Reporter or some of the books listed in the bibliography, you will have a tough time finding the full text of these rules.

To assist you in understanding them, extracts of some of the pertinent sections are quoted in this chapter, but you should not rely on these as the current versions. Instead, ask the government contracting officer to send you a copy of the current regulations, or look them up yourself in the CCH Reporter.

Specific Rules Applicable. The basis for the DOD and NASA regulations on software and technical data is to be found in Subpart 27.4 of the FAR's, entitled "Rights In Data and Copyrights," but it is only one long paragraph, which contemplates separate regulations by various agencies. The applicable DOD supplemental regulations begin at Subpart 27.4 with section 27.400, which defines the scope of the rules for "Technical Data, Other Data, Computer Software, and Copyrights." The specifics of acquiring computer software start with section 27.404-1 of the DOD Supplement, which is discussed in detail below.

The actual language required in all DOD agreements and in solicitations for bids for software is found in section 52.227-7013 of the DOD Supplement. This section defines the applicable contract terms concerning software, documentation, and technical data, and exactly what rights the government seeks to obtain in a contract for computer software. It divides these rights into three classes, "Unlimited Rights," "Limited Rights," and "Restricted Rights." We will explore the distinctions between these classes below.

THE PROCUREMENT PROCESS AND GOVERNMENT RIGHTS IN YOUR SOFTWARE

The Government's Right to Infringe

When the government grants you a copyright or patent, it reserves certain rights. For example, it reserves the right to make use of any U.S. copyright or patent with or without your consent. In other words, unlike individuals and private businesses, it can infringe your copyright or patent at will.

Under Section 28 USC § 1498, your only remedy in this situation is to file suit in the U.S. Claims Court for the reasonable value of the rights used by the government, or by contractors acting on its instructions. You cannot enjoin the government from infringements. There is, however, a recent case, Megapulse, Inc. v. Lewis, which indicates that you can obtain an injunction if the government threatens to or does refuse to abide by the restrictive provisions under which you provided technical data or software. Such unauthorized disclosure could otherwise destroy a business relying upon continued confidentiality of the information.

DOD Supplemental regulation 27.404-1(d) even provides that no contract clause may be included which has the effect of prohibiting the government from infringing a patent or a copyright. However, contracting officers can agree to some restrictions on government use of your program and the documentation which accompanies it, as long as these restrictions are consistent with the rules and the three classes of government rights mentioned above, namely unlimited, limited, and restricted rights.

Government Acquisition
of Technical Data and Software

Distinguishing beween Technical Data and Software. The DOD's regulation 27.401 defines any recorded information of a technical or scientific nature as "technical data," including software documentation but excluding computer software itself. Computer software documentation includes "computer listings and printouts, in human-readable form, which (a) document the design or details of computer software, (b) explain the capabilities of the software, or (c) provide operating instructions for using the software to obtain desired results from a computer." In short, some of your most proprietary information is considered "technical data." "Computer software" is limited to "computer programs and computer data bases." This distinction is vital, because government rules relating to technical data or documentation are often different from these relating to software.

Acknowledging Copyright Law Rights. Section 27.402 of the DOD Supplement makes clear that, since most computer software and technical data are protected under the U.S. copyright laws, use or publication of them does not place them in the public domain. This section recognizes the fundamental rights of the copyright owner, but tries to establish a hierarchy of government rights by license, depending on who paid for the development of the software or technical data.

Work Prepared at Government Expense. The government, with one exception, permits the contractor who develops software at government expense to own the copyrighted work, so long as the government is granted a nonexclusive, paid-up worldwide license. The government must also be given the right to sublicense the use of such software and technical data to its contractors. In certain types of so-called "Special Work" (for example, highly classified projects involving national security), the development contract must provide that copyright, ownership, and control of the work be retained by the government, and that the contractor who prepares the work cannot assert any rights to or claim of copyright to such work.

Software Prepared at Private Expense. Even a computer program, developed at private expense by a contractor who then licenses it to the government, must be licensed on the basis that the government has a similar right to use and sublicense the software, subject, however, to restrictions on that use agreed upon at the time of preparation of the contract. The minimum rights the government contracting officer can accept are "Restricted Rights," as defined in DOD regulation 27.401. Most commercially developed software qualifies for this treatment.

The Basic Rights Clause. To implement the government's policy relating to use of software, DOD regulation 27.404-2(b)(2) provides that "The clause at 52.227-7013, Rights in Technical Data and Computer Software, shall be included in every contract under which computer software may be originated, developed, or delivered." This required clause, in turn, creates the three classes of technical data and software—Unlimited, Limited, and Restricted Rights. Restricted Rights usually only apply to software. Limited Rights usually apply only to technical data. Unlimited Rights could apply to either, although you obviously want to avoid this category if possible.

The government is also required to include in any contract solicitation involving software another contract clause, 52.227-7019, which requests that any contractor identify in his proposal to the government:

to the extent feasible any such computer software which was developed at private expense and upon the use of which he desires to negotiate restrictions, and to state the nature of the proposed restrictions. *If no such computer software is identified, it will be assumed that all deliverable computer software will be subject to unlimited rights.* [Emphasis added]

RESTRICTING THE GOVERNMENT'S USE OF SOFTWARE AND DOCUMENTATION

Commercial Software

The most restriction you can place on the government's rights in your software and documentation is through the "Restricted Rights" clause, defined in DOD regulation 27-401 and detailed in section 52.227-7013(b)(3). Restricted Rights primarily apply to software, but in the case of commercial software they will also apply to the documentation, if so identified. Where documentation does not qualify for Restricted Rights, as in the case of unpublished documentation, Limited Rights will often apply, thus treating unpublished documentation the same as technical data.

Commercial computer software is defined in the DOD Supplement as:

computer software which is used regularly for other than Government purposes and is sold, licensed, or leased in significant quantities to the general public at established market or catalog prices.

Section 27.404-1(f) says you have the right to ask for the Restricted Rights provisions for *both* software and related documentation:

> Commercial computer software and related documentation developed at private expense may be leased, or a license to use may be purchased, by the Government subject to the restrictions in subdivision (b)(3)(i) of the clause at 52.277-7013, Rights In Technical Data and Computer Software.

Privately Developed Software

Even if your software is not commercially marketed, it may still be entitled to Restricted Rights treatment if you, and not the government, paid for its development. In this case, the notice on the software will be slightly different, as the next section indicates. However, in this situation, your documentation will be subject to Limited Rights provisions, since technical data that is privately developed but not commercially distributed does not usually qualify for Restricted Rights treatment.

What Restrictions Can You Contract For?

The new regulations in DOD subdivision 27.404-2(b)(3) answer this question, which the old rules did not:

> Contracts under which computer software developed at private expense is procured or leased shall explicitly set forth the rights necessary to meet Government needs and restrictions applicable to the Government as to use, duplication and disclosure of the software. Thus, for example, such software may be needed, or the owner of such software will only sell or lease it, for specified or limited purposes such as for internal agency use, or use in a specific activity, installation or service location. In any event, the contract must clearly define any restrictions on the right of the Government to use such computer software, but such restrictions will be acceptable only if they will permit the Government to fulfill the need for which such software is being procured. The recital of restrictions may be complete within itself *or it may reference the contractor's license or other agreement setting forth restrictions.* If referencing is employed, a copy of the license or agreement must be attached to the contract. The minimum rights are provided in the Rights in Technical Data and Computer Software clause at 52.227-7013, and need not be included in the recital. [Emphasis added]

The new regulations are the first that recognize the reality of software licensing in the marketplace. They should make things easier for contracting officers to work with software companies.

Restricted Rights Legends

If you, as the contractor want to rely on restricted rights protection, then the following form of Restricted Rights legend must be placed on labels of diskettes or disks containing commercial computer software and related documentation, not in the public domain and developed at private expense.

RESTRICTED RIGHTS LEGEND

Use, duplication, or disclosure by the Government is subject to restrictions as set forth in subdivision (b)(3)(ii) of the Rights in Technical Data and Computer Software clause at 52.227-7013.

_____

(Name of Contractor and Address)

Where software requires a Restricted Rights legend because it is privately developed but not commercial software, the legend must be in this form:

RESTRICTED RIGHTS LEGEND

Use, duplication or disclosure is subject to restrictions stated in Contract No. _____ with _____ [**Name of Contractor**] _____.

Under DOD regulation 27.404-2(c)(3), the related computer software _documentation_ must, in both situations, include a prominent statement in human-readable form of the restrictions applicable to the software. Claims for restricted rights on _software_ "are of no effect unless the computer software is marked by the Contractor" with the restricted rights legend. The regulation further states, "Failure of the Contractor to apply a restricted rights legend to such computer software shall relieve the Government of liability with respect to such unmarked software."

Restricted Rights: What the Government Actually Obtains

When acquired by the government, commercial computer software and related documentation, accompanied by a Restricted Rights legend, is subject to the following restrictions (which can also apply to noncommercial, but privately developed software, if requested):

(A) Title to and ownership of the software and documentation shall remain with the Contractor.

(B) Use of the software and documentation shall be limited to the facility for which it is acquired.

(C) The Government shall not provide or otherwise make available the software or documentation, or any portion thereof, in any form, to any third party without the prior written approval of the Contractor. Third parties do not include prime contractors, subcontractors and agents of the Government who have the Government's permission to use the licensed software and documentation at the facility, and who have agreed to use the licensed software and documentation only in accordance with these restrictions. This provision does not limit the right of the Government to use software, documentation, or information therein, which the Government may already have or obtains without restrictions.

(D) The Government shall have the right to use the computer software and documentation with the computer for which it is acquired at any other facility to which that computer may be transferred; to use the computer software and documentation with a backup computer when the primary computer is inoperative; to copy computer programs for safe-keeping (archives) or backup purposes; and to modify the software and documentation or combine it with other software, *provided,* that the unmodified portions shall remain subject to these restrictions.

(E) If the Contractor, within sixty (60) days after written request, fails to substantiate by clear and convincing evidence that computer software and documentation marked with the above Restricted Rights Legend are commercial items and were developed at private expense, or if the Contractor fails to refute evidence which is asserted by the Government as a basis that the software is in the public domain, the Government may cancel or ignore any restrictive markings on such computer software and documentation and may use them with unlimited rights. Such written requests shall be addressed to the Contractor as identified in the Restricted Rights Legend.

This is the basis for the legend form referring to 52.227-7013(b)(3)(ii), from which this exact language comes.

THE LIMITED RIGHTS LEGEND

Protecting Technical Data and Documentation

The next less restrictive rights you can grant the government are Limited Rights. Your contract must specifically state that the government is entitled only to Limited Rights as defined in Section 52.277-7013(b)(2) for this restriction to apply. This classification is not what you really want from the contracting officer for your documentation, but unless your software is a standard commercial product it may be all you can get. Limited Rights apply only to technical data which have not been published (released to the public) or which have been released only under restrictions like trade secret agreements. This classification most often applies to detailed software documentation of large semi-custom software and hardware projects.

The Form for a Limited Rights Legend

A Limited Rights legend must be placed in the software documentation in a form which shows the number of the prime contract under which the material is to be delivered, the name of the contractor and subcontractor by whom the data was generated, and an explanation of the method used to identify data to which the limited rights apply. Such a legend should read as follows:

LIMITED RIGHTS LEGEND

Contract No. _____
Contractor: _____
Explanation of Limited Rights Data Identification Method Used:
_____
_____
_____

The blank lines above should be completed with an explanation as to how your software and documentation are marked to identify them as subject to this limitation. You should usually state in these lines, "Identified by a Note on the beginning of each module of software and on the title page of the documentation and manuals." Obviously, if you use some other method, you would so indicate.

The Effect of a Limited Rights Legend

You should follow the Limited Rights legend with this full explanation of its effect:

Those portions of this technical data indicated as Limited Rights data shall not, without the written permission of the above Contractor, be either (a) used, released or disclosed in whole or in part outside the Government, (b) used in whole or in part by the Government for manufacture or, in the case of computer software documentation, for preparing the same or similar software, or (c) used by a party other than the Government, except for (1) emergency repair or overhaul work only, by or for the Government, where the item or process concerned is not otherwise reasonably available to enable timely performance of the work, provided that the release or disclosure hereof outside the Government shall be made subject to a prohibition against further use, release or disclosure, or (2) release to a foreign government, as the interest of the United States may require, only for information or evaluation within such government under the conditions of (1) above. This legend, together with the indications of the portions of this data which are subject to such limitations shall be included on any reproductions hereof which includes any part of the portions subject to such limitations.

UNLIMITED RIGHTS: THE GOVERNMENT GETS IT ALL

DOD Supplemental regulation 27.404-1, as well as the comparable NASA regulations, provide that all technical data and computer software purchased or licensed by the federal government without restrictions is available to the Government with unlimited rights. Unlimited rights are defined by DOD regulation 27.401 to mean "rights to use, duplicate, or disclose technical data or computer software in whole or in part, in any manner and for any purpose whatsoever, and to have or permit others to do so."

If your software was developed at government expense, if it is in the public domain, or if it is furnished without restriction by you as the contractor, it will be considered as subject only to these Unlimited Rights provisions. You will then have lost all control over it. Worst of all, DOD regulation 27.404-1 specifically provides that "no payment will be made for rights of use of such software in performance of Government contracts or for the later delivery of such computer software." There are some provisions for payment by the government to the contractor for software conversion to a particular format or for reproduction, but not for anything else.

UNRESOLVED PROBLEMS REMAIN EVEN WITH RESTRICTED RIGHTS

It appears from the government's copyright licensing regulations at Section 52.227-7013(c) that even the restricted rights clauses could be interpreted as authorizing the government to make copies of software and documentation for one particular facility, and to permit other contractors or subcontractors working at that facility to use them without additional payments to the original contractor. The subcontractors do have to agree to respect the Restricted Rights of the original contractor. However, the language of this section is not at all clear. If the software is not intended to be commercial software but merely privately developed software, then there are no specific restrictions in the regulations on government copying of restricted rights software or limited rights documentation, except those restrictions you obtain by negotiation.

Other Contract Provisions

The government does not, in the restricted rights clause, recognize the other restrictions usually placed in software package licenses, such as limitations on liability and warranties, termination provisions for violations, and other standard commercial licensing practices. However, new language in the regulations at Section 27.404-1 spells out the right of the contractor to "negotiate" restrictions on the use and duplication of the software and documentation, so long as the government obtains at least the Restricted Rights provisions.

The problem of negotiating with the government on commercial software is that the software sale or license price is often so small that it is not economically feasible to spend much time on the contract negotiations. Furthermore, most software marketing and contracting personnel are unaware of all these complex rules, or of the major changes that have occurred in them with the adoption of the FAR's and the new DOD Part 27 Supplement in 1984.

CUSTOM MODIFICATIONS TO COMMERCIAL OR PRIVATELY DEVELOPED SOFTWARE

One of the toughest problems in contracting with the government arises when you license off-the-shelf commercial or privately developed software, but are required by the contract to make special modifications in it in order to adapt it to a particular government project. Such software is technically a derivative or adaptation under the copyright laws, and you should be the owner of it. The government, however, will often argue that it paid for the modifications and should, therefore, be entitled to Unlimited Rights in all the software. The DOD regulations at Section 27.404-2(b)(4) provide that only that portion of the software which is still "recognizable" will be considered developed at private expense. The recognizable part is the only portion that qualifies for Restricted Rights treatment.

How extensive do these changes have to be before a program is legally no longer "commercially available software," developed at private expense? If you can separate the development work for the government into modules which are not part of the commercial program, you may be able to take Restricted Rights in your commercial software, and give the government Unlimited Rights only in the portion developed for its purposes. This is a good solution in most cases.

However, in some cases this solution may not be worth the trouble, and you could decide not to take the project rather than give up some of your proprietary rights. Be sure, however, that whatever you agree to with the government does not adversely affect the copyright and trade secrets you claim in your basic commercial package. Try to protect your original source code from unlimited use and disclosure, even if you permit unlimited copying and use of the object code. Because this object code is a unique version it may not have much value to others, and you may be able to afford to concede Unlimited Rights to the object code only.

WAIVER OF COPYRIGHTS
TO SOFTWARE AND DOCUMENTATION

You may be faced with a request (if not a demand) on the part of the government contracting officer to delete the copyright notice on all copies marked with the Restricted Rights or Limited Rights legends. You should refuse to do so, since this is both dangerous to the validity of your copyright in the commercial market, and not required by DOD regulation 52.227-7013.

Such a request (or demand) flies in the face of DOD regulation 27.403-3(c)(2), which says that while you cannot place restrictive markings on technical data or software, unless negotiated prior to delivery of it to the government, "Copyright notices as specified in Title 17, United States Code, Sections 401 and 402 are not considered 'restrictive markings.'"

Never agree to strike out the copyright notices, because if you do, you may be placing your software in the public domain, even though the government has restrictions placed on its use. Furthermore, Section 401 of the Copyright Act requires this notice on all copies, if you consider the software to have been published. (See Chapter 5 for the exceptions, and the effect of failure to use the copyright notice.)

If, as part of your government contract, you do agree to permit reproduction of your software and technical data, you should insist that all copies bear the supplemental legend authorized in DOD regulation 52.227-7013(c)(4): "This material may be reproduced by or for the U.S. Government pursuant to the copyright license under the clause at 52.227-7013 (date)." This will protect your copyright in the material, as long as it also has your copyright notice on it.

OTHER GOVERNMENT CONTRACT
PROVISIONS

Government contracts can, and do, contain many other provisions. For your part, you will need to consider carefully which other provisions of your standard software and documentation license you wish to have included in the government contract.

Limiting Liability and Warranties

In most cases, except where a contract is based on advertised specifications and contract provisions, the government will negotiate a reasonable limitation on liability or warranty clause. FAR 46.703 specifies that "The use of warranties is not mandatory." There are numerous forms of warranty and other contract clauses which may be proposed as part of your government contract. However, you will have to ask for what you want, or you will only get what the government gives you.

Deferred Ordering and Deferred Delivery Provisions

You should be wary of any attempt by the government contracting officer to include contract clause 52.227-7026 relating to Deferred Ordering of Technical Data or Computer Software. This clause gives the government the right to order any software or technical data originally delivered under a contract *or a subcontract,* for a period of two years after the date the contractor accepts the last delivery from the subcontractor under the contract.

There are also provisions in contract clause 52.227-7027 allowing deferred delivery on orders. In either instance, such provisions would permit a government contract to drag on for years after you may think you have fully complied with a subcontract. You should avoid these clauses if you can. They are not practical in most cases involving commercial software and they are subject to changes and other modifications.

THE GSA PURCHASING SCHEDULE

The General Services Administration (GSA) is charged with providing services and goods to most government agencies other than the DOD and NASA. The GSA has a procedure by which contractors desiring to do business with the government can list their goods (including software) on the GSA Schedule, on which they agree in advance to prices and terms. Agencies can then purchase the goods from this list, with much less formal contracting methods. Under this procedure, substantial amounts of software and computer-related items are sold or licensed to the government. Commercial microcomputer software is a perfect candidate for such a procedure, since, if you take the time to get on the GSA Schedule, then many of the steps described in this chapter will be eliminated.

The rules and forms for participation change from time to time, but you can obtain detailed information from your nearesst GSA office. These offices are located across the country in most metropolitan areas.

SUMMARY

If you license software and documentation under the GSA Schedule or to goverment agencies other than the DOD or NASA, then dealing with the government has some differences from dealing with private parties, but it is not usually that difficult. Above all, be sure you understand what you are asked by the government contracting officer to sign.

If software is licensed under DOD or NASA regulations, licensing privately developed software can be frustrating because of the need to protect your company by using the Restricted Rights provisions of the regulations. In any transaction with the DOD or NASA, the rules of these government agencies can make software licensing complex and expensive to do. Again, be very careful what you agree upon in such contracts.

Should you be developing and licensing truly custom software for the government, the rules are such that you need a government contracts specialist to help you. In such case, the material in this chapter can only alert you to the possible problems.

14

Dealing with the Government: Export Controls On Computers and Computer Software

LEARNING ANOTHER SET OF GOVERNMENT RULES

A series of government laws restrict the right to export your software, so that the management of every software business must be aware of the U.S. export control laws and their impact on the computer and software industry. Just as Chapter 13 showed a need to understand government regulations in the field of government software procurement, this chapter will acquaint you with the U.S. Export Administration and its arcane rules and regulations. It also discusses how unintentional noncompliance with government export laws could result in huge fines and even denial of the right to export your software and other products.

Little Businesses With International Character. The incredibly fast pace of the computer industry and its growing international character have meant that numerous small software houses are actually engaged in significant international transactions, primarily with European businesses. This foreign activity subjects American companies, and possibly their foreign subsidiaries, to some of the more esoteric and incomprehensible government regulations ever written. Worst of all, most such businesses and their legal advisors are not even aware of the existence or scope of these laws and the severe penalties for violation of them.

THE EXPORT ADMINISTRATION ACT AND REGULATIONS

Export Restrictions and the Commodity Control List

Unless you are an avid reader of international business publications, you are probably happily unaware that virtually everything produced by American businesses (other than agricultural and food products) is on a government list of ten categories or items that may not be exported to any place other than Canada without some form of government approval. High on this list of restricted items are computers and computer software.

This list, called the Commodity Control List (CCL), is part of a regulatory scheme enacted under the Export Administration Act of 1979 (EAA) by Congress. While the 1979 law was originally scheduled to expire on May 31, 1984, it was extended and somewhat modified by Congress in the summer of 1984. The military and some government officials still want to strengthen the law, while the electronics industry and others feel that parts of it are unrealistic and should be eliminated or substantially modified. Either way, the law can cause you grief.

The Purpose of Export Regulations

The present law is supplemented by a four-inch-thick book of export regulations issued by the Office of Export Administration, International Trade Administration, Department of Commerce, Washington, D.C. The full text of these regulations can also be found in Title 15 of the Code of Federal Regulations, which is anything but light reading. You should verify the current status of the EAA any time you deal with it, since the law has changed considerably over the past six years, and the regulations interpreting it have been revised extensively. *(See pages 272–273 for 1985 changes.)*

If you were to read through the EAA and the regulations, you would learn that in order to protect the military security of this country, to implement foreign policy, and to protect the country from depletion of scarce resources, Congress created a system for licensing the export of commodities. Part 370.3 of the Regulations expressly prohibits the export from the United States of any controlled commodity, unless the exporter has a license from the appropriate government agency authorizing it.

The Export of Computers and Software Is Controlled

Computers, and the software that comes with them, are one of the more important commodities covered by the law. Computers are listed as "Export Commodity Number 1565A" on the Commodity Control List. Commodity Control Number 1572A, covering recording devices and magnetic media for use in them, is another related, but important, item on the list.

Significantly, the law also restricts export of technical data related to these commodities, and the plants or facilities that could manufacture or process them. Therefore, substantially all software is a controlled commodity, subject to the full scope of the licensing requirements.

Software Is Controlled As Technical Data.   To the extent that software is not inherently incorporated into a computer as a functional part of its operation, computer software is considered "Technical Data" under this law. The term technical data is used differently here than in the government procurement rules described in Chapter 13, since here both the documentation and the actual software are classified as technical data. The potential impact of these restrictions on commercial business and personal software exports can be far more serious than might be expected, and it introduces further paperwork into your business. The following material explains the procedures and rules for licensing software exports.

Countries Are Grouped for Control Purposes

Depending on the seriousness of any perceived military or political threat and the foreign-policy implications of the restrictions, all countries except Canada are listed in seven Country Groups, lettered Q, S, T, V, W, Y, and Z. The regulations then impose restrictions on the various groups with varying degrees of severity. (There are almost no restrictions on exports to Canada, if they are intended for use there.) The current list of Country Groups is set out on the next page for your convenience, since the list, which changes from time to time, is not easy to come by.

THE TYPES OF EXPORT LICENSES— GENERAL AND VALIDATED

Every export shipment, by mail or by any other means of transportation, of a controlled commodity to a member of the Country Groups is subject to the requirement of an export license. There are two types of export licenses:

- **General Licenses.** These are automatically granted by the regulations, without specific application to the Export Administration, if the controlled commodity or technical data fall within specific classes of items and meet detailed rules set forth in the regulations. For example, one class of General License, called type GLV, exempts nearly all shipments under $1,000 in value to most countries. No actual license papers are issued under the General License classification. Most business and personal software for shipment to Western Europe and Japan will qualify for one or more General Licenses.

Export Licensing General Policy and Related Information   Supplement No. 1 to Part 370—page 1

COUNTRY GROUPS

For export control purposes, foreign countries are separated into seven country groups designated by the symbols "Q", "S", "T", "V", "W", "Y", and "Z". Listed below are the countries included in each country group. Canada is not included in any country group and will be referred to by name throughout the Export Administration Regulations.

Country Group Q
Romania

Country Group S
Libya

Country Group T

North America

Northern Area:
  Greenland
  Miquelon and St. Pierre Islands

Southern Area:
  Mexico (including Cozumel and Revilla
    Gigedo Islands)

Central America
  Belize
  Costa Rica
  El Salvador
  Guatemala
  Honduras (including Bahia and Swan
    Islands)
  Nicaragua
  Panama

Bermuda and Caribbean Area:
  Bahamas
  Barbados
  Bermuda
  Dominican Republic
  French West Indies
  Haiti (including Gonave and Tortuga
    Islands)
  Jamaica
  Leeward and Windward Islands
  Netherlands Antilles
  Trinidad and Tobago

South America

Northern Area:
  Colombia
  French Guiana (including Inini)
  Guyana
  Surinam
  Venezuela

Western Area:
  Bolivia
  Chile
  Ecuador (including the Galapagos
    Islands)
  Peru

Eastern Area:
  Argentina
  Brazil
  Falkland Islands (Islas Malvinas)
  Paraguay
  Uruguay

Country Group V

All countries not included in any other country group (except Canada).

Country Group W
Hungary
Poland

Country Group Y
Albania
Bulgaria
Czechoslovakia
Estonia
German Democratic Republic (including
  East Berlin)
Laos
Latvia
Lithuania
Mongolian People's Republic
Union of Soviet Socialist Republics

Country Group Z
Cuba
Kampuchea
North Korea
Vietnam

Export Administration Regulations   EAB 228   January 9, 1984

Figure 14–1

- **Validated Licenses.** These licenses must be applied for by the exporter, by submitting an application to the Office of Export Administration (OEA) in Washington, D.C. After three to five weeks of processing, the license is either issued or denied. Almost all computers and computer-related equipment, except some older, limited-capacity systems, must have Validated Licenses. Virtually all software destined for Iron Curtain countries, and any software used for military or nuclear-energy purposes, requires a Validated License.

Software May Qualify for Either License

Software shipments could fall within either license classification, depending on the proposed use and the country of destination. The General License is essentially an exception to the requirement for the more burdensome Validated License. Software that is shipped with a computer, such as an operating system, is usually licensed with the computer; while packaged software, shipped separate from the computer, is normally classed as Technical Data and most often qualifies for one of the General Licenses. *(See pages 272–273 for 1985 changes.)*

There are some eighteen subclasses of General Licenses established in Part 371 of the regulations, of which only three or four are of particular interest to the software industry. After a brief explanation of the Validated License procedures, the applicable General Licenses will be discussed in detail.

How to Tell Which Countries
Require Validated Licenses

For the present, the OEA considers that the export of virtually all computer software requires either a General or Validated License (except to Canada for use there). Validated Licenses are needed for software exports to all Communist and "terrorist" countries. As a result of recent changes, special rules apply to software exports to the Peoples' Republic of China. Because of these restrictions, special attention must be paid to any requests from customers in, or exports to, any country in a Country Group lettered Q, S, W, Y, and Z. For all practical purposes export licenses will not be granted to Groups S (Libya) and Z (Cuba, Vietnam, Cambodia, and North Korea) for any commodity. Most high-technology items will be subject to very careful review before a Validated License is granted for export to any of the Country Groups other than T and V, which represent countries of the Free World.

The only sure way to know which countries are covered and what items are covered is to review these complex, changing regulations periodically. To do this, you may call or visit the branch offices of the Export Administration in major U.S. cities, or the main office at Box 273, Washington, D.C. 20044. The phone number of the main office is

202-377-4811, while the phone number of the 47 branch offices will usually be listed under the United States Government, Department of Commerce, International Trade Administration, in the local telephone directory.

Apply for a Validated License.   Three to four weeks is about the normal processing time for Validated Licenses to Free World countries, while export approval to restricted Communist countries will take five or more weeks. Longer delays have been experienced by many exporters. If the software has military implications, it is unlikely to receive a license for export to other than "friendly" countries like the NATO bloc.

Since software exported to the Free World is not normally subject to use of Validated Licenses, and because the detailed provisions of applying for and using the Validated License are the better part of the whole set of the Export Control Regulations, detailed information on obtaining a Validated License is not covered here. If you need more information on applying for a Validated License, consult in particular Parts 372 and 375 of the Export Control Regulations. You should also call and talk to the Export Specialists in the Department of Commerce field offices.

Software for Military Use or Nuclear Facilities

There are even more restrictive export control laws administered by the Defense and State Departments governing software that could be part of a military weapons system or a nuclear facility. While these rules are not discussed here, if your software is part of such a system, plant, or method, you should seek information from the appropriate agency before you ever consider exporting such items or even discussing them with foreign nationals. Under Section 387.1 of the Regulations, the penalties for intentional violation of export controls on national security items are up to $1 million for companies, and $250,000 and 10 years imprisonment in the case of individuals.

RESTRICTIONS ON EXPORT OF TECHNICAL DATA

While export of computers and recording devices has long been regulated, the export of "technical data" related to these systems has only fairly recently been regulated. To stop the flow of technological information, Part 379.1 of the regulations defines technical data as information of any kind that can be used, or adapted for use, in the design, production, manufacture, utilization, or reconstruction of articles or materials. Technical data may be tangible, like maintenance manuals, or intangible like technical services or computer programs. Software is technical data unless it is shipped with and part of a computer, in which case the license is for the computer and not the software.

General License Classifications
for Technical Data

The OEA has set up several classifications of technical data, depending upon the general availability of such data. These classifications recognize that there is little that can be done to stop export of information which is readily available in the press or public libraries. As a result, the following General Licenses apply to qualifying software.

GTDA Licenses—for Generally Available Information. A General License designated "GTDA" is available for export of data or information which is generally available either free or for nominal cost, without restriction (i.e. unlicensed); other generally available scientific and educational data not specifically related to design, production, or utilization in industrial processes; and certain patent applications. Almost all computer program user manuals and documentation, which do not require a license, may be exported to any country, by complying with the rules for use of the GTDA License, which rules will be described below. Game software probably falls into this class as well.

GTDR Licenses—for Most Computer Software Under License. A General License designated "GTDR" authorizes export of all other technical data that does not qualify under the GTDA General License. Since almost all computer programs are licensed in some form, they are not considered to be "generally available," and hence not able to receive a GTDA License. Nearly every licensed computer program, whether in source or object-code form, will by definition therefore come under the GTDR License. Under a new rule, Part 379.4(g), all software exported under the GTDR License must have a Letter of Assurance, or Written Assurance, as described below.

Restricted Countries and Items. No GTDR technical data, including computer programs, may be exported to Country Groups S and Z, and there are detailed restrictions on export of technical data under the GTDR License to Country Groups, Q, W and Y, as well as to Afghanistan and the Peoples' Republic of China. Most such technical data will require a Validated License. Likewise, any software for use in a nuclear facility, or for electronic surveillance (such as radar systems), requires a Validated License, regardless of the Country Group.

Possible Exemptions—Games and Family Computer Software. The Export Administration has considered creating exemptions from the export licensing requirements for games and personal computer software, but no regulations have been issued to date. In fact, contrary to this planned liberalization, recent news articles have indicated that "lap" computers like the TRS-100 and the Convergent Technologies' "Workslate" computer may require export licenses, even for travelers. Major changes were made in the export rules for software and small personal computers, effective January 1, 1985. See pages 272–273 for details.

Use G-DEST General Licenses
for Small Computers and Game Software

A G-DEST General License is sometimes available for software such as that used in cartridge games and small family-type computers, but not office and personal computers. Unfortunately, the current hardware limitations disqualify any system with more than 32K of internal memory available to the user. This exempts many game systems, but restricts the current versions of most 8 and 16-bit personal computers. Therefore, if your software is for games and home systems, you may wish to use the G-DEST General License. You do not then need a Validated License for exports to Free World customers, but you must still comply with the requirement for the Shipper's Export Declaration (described below) if the value exceeds $500. This license is not available for exports to Country Groups S and Z.

Procedure Involved.   To use the G-DEST license, you must first submit a written request to the OEA, with the details of what you expect to export and why you think it qualifies. If, in the opinion of the OEA, it does qualify, the OEA will grant written approval of the exemption from a Validated license for all qualifying shipments. This exemption, if applicable, usually can be easily obtained.

Use GLV General Licenses
for Small Shipments

Another type of General License, designated "GLV" for General License—Valuation, is available for small shipments of computers, recording devices, and media intended for export to the Free World, usually to the Country Groups T and V. Although use of the GTDR General License would appear more appropriate for software, the GLV License is sometimes used for shipping magnetic media and handheld computers. This license is automatic for any shipment that has a net value, less shipping costs, of $1,000 per *single* entry on the Commodity Control List. GLV may not be used for exports to the Peoples' Republic of China.

Limitations on Use of the GLV License.   Using the GLV License, you may make no more than one shipment of $1,000 net value per week by mail to a particular consignee, and you may not split up orders to get around the dollar limit. This General License is obviously the one to use for simple shipments to a single export customer in the Free World, since it is free of all the questions that plague the other General Licenses. Unfortunately, it does not cover the typical OEM shipment of reproduction disks, nor of large quantities of software intended for resale or sublicensing in foreign countries. You must use the Shipper's Export Declaration form (described below) for this type of license.

Exporting Magnetic Media With Technical Data

No one has yet been able to resolve satisfactorily the issue of whether a separate export license is needed for the magnetic media on which the technical data, in the form of software, is exported. Magnetic media is a separate class on the Commodity Control List (# 1572A) from the computer and the software (# 1565A). However, since the magnetic media value is so small most people ignore it and rely simply on the technical data export license requirements of the GTDR License.

USE OF THE SHIPPER'S EXPORT DECLARATION (SED)

There is a pile of paperwork associated with the export of software and computers. In order to collect data on exports of various commodities, the Bureau of Census regulations (Part 30) require exporters, or in some cases the transportation companies, to complete a Shipper's Export Declaration form for each shipment. This requirement applies to nearly all exports of computers and computer parts, but in some cases does not apply to technical data (software). The rules are not crystal clear, and the conflicting statements in the Export Regulations make it worse.

Census regulation § 30.54 states that the SED form is not required, regardless of value or licensing requirements, if the shipment is technical data sent by mail. This would appear to exempt all software mailed for export. These same rules state that no SED is required for mail shipments: 1) if either the sender or receiver is not a business concern; 2) if the shipment is valued at $500 or under; or 3) if the goods are not sent as a commercial transaction. Notwithstanding these exceptions, if a Validated License is required then the SED is needed.

In § 386.1(c) the Export Regulations also provide that no SED is required for exports by means other than mail to Country Groups T or V (generally, the Free World), if the shipment is valued at les than $500. It is also exempt if the transportation company or the broker is reporting the same information under certain bulk provisions on a monthly basis. Thus, software and other technical data, shipped by air, sea, or other than mail, is exempt from use of the SED if valued at less than $500 in each shipment. It is required for shipments over that amount, or if a Validated License is involved. You cannot, however, split shipments to get around this set of rules.

When required, the SED form is to be delivered with your shipment to the Post Office if by mail, or to the carrier or Customs Office if by common carrier, like airlines and shipping companies. Details about filing out the

FORM NO. 7525-V (7-22-80)

U.S. DEPARTMENT OF COMMERCE – BUREAU OF THE CENSUS – ITA, BUREAU OF EAST-WEST TRADE

SHIPPER'S EXPORT DECLARATION

OF SHIPMENTS FROM THE UNITED STATES

Export Shipments Are Subject To Inspection By U.S. Customs Service and/or The Office of Export Control

READ CAREFULLY THE INSTRUCTIONS ON BACK TO AVOID DELAY AT SHIPPING POINT

Declarations Should be Typewritten or Prepared in Ink

Form Approved O.M.B. No. 41-R0397

CONFIDENTIAL – For use solely for official purposes authorized by the Secretary of Commerce. Use for unauthorized purposes is not permitted (Title 15 C.F.R. section 30.91, Title 13 U.S.C. section 301, as amended, P.L. 96-275).

Authentication (When required)

DO NOT USE THIS AREA	DISTRICT	PORT	COUNTRY (For Customs use only)	

File No. (For Customs use only)

1. FROM (U.S. port of export)

2. METHOD OF TRANSPORTATION (Check one)
   ☐ VESSEL (Incl. ferry) ☐ AIR ☐ OTHER (Specify) _____

2a. EXPORTING CARRIER (If vessel, give name of ship, flag and pier number. If air, give name of airline.)

3. EXPORTER (Principal or seller – licensee)   ADDRESS (Number, street, place, State)

4. AGENT OF EXPORTER (Forwarding agent)   ADDRESS (Number, street, place, State)

5. ULTIMATE CONSIGNEE   ADDRESS (Place, country)

6. INTERMEDIATE CONSIGNEE   ADDRESS (Place, country)

7. FOREIGN PORT OF UNLOADING (For vessel and air shipments only)

8. PLACE AND COUNTRY OF ULTIMATE DESTINATION (Not place of transshipment)

MARKS AND NOS. (9)	NUMBERS AND KIND OF PACKAGES. DESCRIPTION OF COMMODITIES. EXPORT LICENSE NUMBER OR GENERAL LICENSE SYMBOL. (Describe commodities in sufficient detail to permit verification of the Schedule B commodity numbers assigned. Do not use general terms) (10)	SHIPPING (Gross) WEIGHT IN POUNDS (REQUIRED FOR VESSEL AND AIR SHIPMENTS ONLY) (11)	DF (TYPE OF MOVE) (12)	SCHEDULE B COMMODITY NO. (Include Commodity Control List italicized digit, when required) (13)	NET QUANTITY SCHEDULE B UNITS (State unit) (14)	VALUE AT U.S. PORT OF EXPORT (Selling price or cost if not sold, including inland freight, insurance and other charges to U.S. port of export) (Nearest whole dollar, omit cents figures) (15)

VALIDATED LICENSE NO. _____   OR GENERAL LICENSE SYMBOL _____

16. BILL OF LADING OR AIR WAYBILL NUMBER

17. DATE OF EXPORTATION (Not required for shipments by vessel)

18. THE UNDERSIGNED HEREBY AUTHORIZES _____ TO ACT AS FORWARDING AGENT FOR EXPORT CONTROL AND CUSTOMS PURPOSES.

(Name and address – Number, street, place, State)

EXPORTER _____ BY _____   (DULY AUTHORIZED OFFICER OR EMPLOYEE) _____

▶ 19. I CERTIFY THAT ALL STATEMENTS MADE AND ALL INFORMATION CONTAINED IN THIS EXPORT DECLARATION ARE TRUE AND CORRECT. I AM AWARE OF THE PENALTIES PROVIDED FOR FALSE REPRESENTATION. (See paragraphs 1 (c) and (e) on reverse side.)

SIGNATURE _____   FOR _____
(Duly authorized officer or employee of exporter or named forwarding agent)   (Name of corporation or firm, and capacity of signer, e.g., secretary, export manager, etc.)

ADDRESS _____

▶ Declaration should be made by duly authorized officer or employee of exporter or of forwarding agent named by exporter.

a If shipping weight is not available for each Schedule B item listed in column (13) included in one or more packages, insert the approximate gross weight for each Schedule B item. The total of these estimated weights should equal the actual weight of the entire package or packages.

b Designate foreign merchandise (reexports) with an "F" and exports of domestic merchandise produced in the United States or changed in condition in the United States with a "D." (See instructions on reverse side.)

DO NOT USE THIS AREA

Figure 14-2

SED, the number of copies, and the disposition of the form are set forth in Regulation 386.3, which you should read.

The regulations say the blank SED forms are available for purchase from U.S. Customs Offices, the District Offices of the Department of Commerce, and the Government Printing Office. However, the Export Control offices of the Department of Commerce have recently refused to provide them, insisting that you purchase them from commercial stationers, or from the GPO—which sells them for $6.50 per hundred and takes several months to deliver them. Since the form may change from time to time, check with your shipping company or the Department of Commerce offices as to the current version.

You will need to refer to the regulations and information accompanying the form to complete it, but generally it calls for information on the parties involved, addresses, values, and Commodity Control Entry Numbers. If you are relying on a General License such as the GLV or G-DEST licenses, you must so indicate on the form. If you need to prepare and file the SED, you should place Destination Control Statements on the freight waybills or airbills and other shipping documents. These statements, contained in Part 386.6, remind the consignee that under American law the commodities involved have restrictions on their further export.

Use Destination Control Statements

In nearly every case it would appear to be good operating practice to include the standard Destination Control Statement on all commercial invoices and shipping documents of software, diskettes, and computer documentation, in the following form:

FORM OF DESTINATION CONTROL STATEMENT
UNDER PART 386.6

This technical data is licensed by the United States for ultimate destination to *** [here fill in the country it is going to] *** and for distribution or relicensing in any destination except the Soviet Bloc, Poland, Hungary, Romania, Laos, Libya, North Korea, Vietnam, Kampuchea (Cambodia), or Cuba, unless otherwise authorized by the United States. Diversion contrary to U.S. law prohibited.

Where you have done this, you have established your good faith effort to obtain compliance by the foreign importer. Consequently, unless you have reason to know or suspect that violations are intended, it is highly unlikely that you would ever be considered in violation of the export control rules. You should also obtain the Written Assurances language in each license agreement or contract with the proposed recipients.

Documenting Exports when
Using the General Licenses

As noted, the regulations impose on the shipper (and the common carrier where one is involved) paperwork requirements like marking packaging, marking invoices and waybills, and the use of the Shipper's Export Declaration. Since the rules distinguish between exports by mail and those sent by other means, you need to review this list of requirements.

If your shipment qualifies for the use of either the GTDA or GTDR License, because it is technical data and is going by mail, you:

- DO have to mark packages mailed with the license letters, either GTDA or GTDR, but nothing else. The rules may exempt even this marking, but it is so simple to do that it seems worth the minute it takes.

- Do NOT have to complete a Shipper's Export Declaration, since technical data is exempt from this requirement—unless it is on five-and-a-quarter inch diskette, in which case you may need an SED just because of the diskette.

If the shipment consists of technical data, is licensed under GTDA or GTDR, is shipped other than by mail, and is valued at less than $500, you:

- DO have to make a statement on the waybill or bill of lading of your reason for omitting the SED. Usually, the letters GTDA or GTDR will be sufficient, together with a statement that it is valued at under $500.

- Do NOT have to complete the SED.

Finally, if you are using the G-DEST or GLV General Licenses (or GTDA, or GTDR, and the shipment is over $500 and other than by mail), you:

- Must complete a Shipper's Export Declaration.

- Must mark the address side of the package, if mailed, with the legend "G-DEST—Export License Not Required" or "GLV-Export License Not Required," if these are the licenses relied upon.

- Must place the same license legend on the shipping documents in all cases, if sent other than by mail.

- Must place the same license legend on the Shipper's Export Declaration Form.

Validated Licenses. If you are exporting either commodities or technical data under a Validated License, then the outside of all packages, the Shipper's Export Declaration, and the shipping documents must all list the Validated License number and its expiration date.

OBTAIN WRITTEN ASSURANCES OF COMPLIANCE

Assurances in Licenses or Contracts

To protect yourself from potential problems caused by later export or reexport of your software by your customer, you should obtain, in every software-license agreement with a commercial establishment, a written assurance against violation of the U.S. Export Control law. The language can be similar to that formally required in some cases by Part 379.4(f) of the regulations. You may also obtain such assurance in a letter or other written form, but since you will undoubtedly have a formal written license, especially in the case of OEM-type transactions, it is best to include these provisions even in domestic OEM licenses.

Suggested Language

To comply with current law, I would suggest language along the following lines:

FORM FOR WRITTEN ASSURANCE AS TO EXPORT CONTROLS

Licensee acknowledges that the software and other technical data licensed hereunder is subject to export controls imposed on Licensor and Licensee by the provisions of the United States Export Administration Act of 1979, as amended, and that export of the subject matter hereunder may presently be accomplished under a General Export License, designation GTDR. Most related user Documentation may be exported under a General License, designation GTDA. Licensee certifies to Licensor that neither the technical data (in the form of software or manuals) nor the direct product thereof is intended to be shipped, either directly or indirectly, to Country Group Q, S, W, Y or Z, nor Afghanistan or the Peoples' Republic of China, without further compliance with the Validated License requirements of the Office of Export Administration, United States Department of Commerce. This technical data is for use only at authorized destinations, and Licensee will not knowingly permit exportation or transshipment in violation of the above law and regulations thereunder.

To protect yourself from heavy fines for violation of the Export Control Laws, it is also highly desirable to add the following indemnity:

Licensee agrees to indemnify and hold Licensor harmless from any and all costs, damages, fines, or other expense incurred by

Licensor by reason of Licensee's violation of these representations of Licensee.

REEXPORTING AND FOREIGN SUBSIDIARIES OF AMERICAN COMPANIES

If your company has a controlled foreign subsidiary operating in any part
of the world, remember that the Export Control laws have extraterritorial
application. This means that the U.S. Government expects your company
to prevent its foreign subsidiaries from violating the Export Control laws,
even if the subsidiaries are operating in a foreign country and are subject
to different foreign laws. This can leave you and your subsidiary in a real
box, as many companies found out when President Reagan tried to stop
the Russian gas pipeline in 1982.

Furthermore, the provisions of Section 374.1 of the regulations pur-
port to prevent reexport of any commodities or technical data from the
original country of destination. In other words, if you ship software to a
customer in France, that French customer is supposed to be bound by
American law, which would prohibit him from shipping the software to
Russia. Therefore, always include Destination Statements in your invoices and shipping documents,, and obtain from all your commercial
licensees Written Assurances of continued compliance with the Export
Control Laws.

PENALTIES FOR EXPORT REGULATION VIOLATIONS

Knowingly violating the law by exporting the more standard items on the
Commodity Control List without a license can result in heavy penalties.
These can be fines of no more than five times the value of the exports involved or $50,000, whichever is greater, or imprisonment of not more
than five years, or both. Civil penalties of up to $10,000 per violation may
also be imposed, in addition to or in lieu of other liability. A civil penalty
may apply even if the act took place in ignorance of the law.

Furthermore, anyone who violates the law may have his, her, or its
right to export commodities or technical information suspended, re-
voked, or denied entirely, after appropriate civil hearings before the Export Control Administration.

1985 CHANGES IN EXPORT CONTROL REGULATIONS

Consistent with the prediction in the Preface about last minute events, the
OEA published twenty-four pages of sweeping changes in the rules for exporting software, computers and telecommunication software and equipment that take effect on January 1, 1985. As it is impossible to change the
chapter text at this point, the new rules are summarized below.

Software is now explicitly a Controlled Commodity, under new class 1566A, which however excepts from the need for a Validated License most personal and business applications software. The exceptions are for (1) accounting, payroll, personnel records, receivables, inventory control and general ledger software; (2) data entry and text manipulation such as text editing and word processing, sort/merge, and presumably spreadsheets; and (3) data retrieval and report generation for the functions listed above. *The excepted categories and other software not on the 1566A list are still subject to Part 379 and the need for a GTDR General License.*

High level language development systems, cross-hosted compilers and assemblers, disassemblers and decompilers (except simple debuggers and tracers), and diagnostic or maintenance systems may require a Validated License if they are used to create or maintain equipment or systems which are themselves on the Controlled Commodity List or for use on computers made in controlled areas. Operating systems for high speed mainframes and applications software with cryptologic uses are also controlled, along with most artificial intelligence and expert systems software.

The new rules except from export control most civilian market 8-bit CPU digital computers with processing rates below 2 megabits/sec, and most common computer peripherals like impact printers, CRT's, floppy disk drives, simple plotters, OCR character recognition equipment, keyboards and keypunch equipment. Ruggedized portables and compact computers that could be used by the military are severely restricted.

Because of the extraordinary complexity of the 1985 changes, it is imperative that anyone exporting computer hardware and software consult them or the OEA before changing existing export practices. Most of what was said in this chapter still applies, only some of the detail has changed.

SUMMARY

U.S. Export Administration laws and regulations apply to virtually everything that a software company ships outside the country, although most such businesses are unaware of these complex rules. Violation of these laws is a serious civil and criminal offense, yet the actual language of the regulations are hard to come by.

There are two types of export licenses available. The Validated License for exports to Communist countries, and countries characterized by a rule of terror, is time-consuming to obtain since you must send in an application for it to the Washington office of OEA. On the other hand, use of the General License for exports to most other countries is a simple matter of complying with rules requiring package marking, invoice marking, and obtaining written assurances from customers that they will comply with this law.

15

International Aspects of Software Protection

It may be that computer software can, in a few countries, be adequately protected without any change in existing laws. But, due to the newness of computer technology and the consequent scarcity of judicial decisions, and to disagreement among legal experts, there is a considerable state of uncertainty in this field.

Model Provisions on the Protection of Computer Software, WIPO, Geneva, 1978, p. 4.

This quotation from a 1978 report by the World Intellectual Property Organization (WIPO) still reflects the situation in 1985. If anything, the explosive growth of the microcomputer industry and the worldwide sale of millions of personal computers has made international protection of software an even more critical subject. If the legal system of the United States (the country that invented the microcomputer) cannot adequately deal with these technological changes, there is scant hope that a hundred radically different legal systems can do so on the international level within the foreseeable future. The subject is still under study by WIPO.

This chapter describes where we are today, and what can be done to protect your software in the international marketplace.

INTERNATIONAL ISSUES AFFECT ALL SOFTWARE COMPANIES

During the past few years, virtually every kind of software developed in America has found its way overseas. Computers manufactured in Japan, England, Italy, and elsewhere all run with American operating systems,

274

American computer languages, and American applications software. English, as the commercial language of the world, has become the basis for the world's computer languages. Japan and China, for example, have such large character sets in their national languages that virtually all their software is either in English or in a subset of a language that allows reproduction of the software from English.

The international nature of software and American leadership in this field has led to wholesale importation and translation of American software into European languages, as well as those of the Far East. American software businesses, even those that do not intentionally export their products, are now faced with the question of how to protect software from illegal copying and use overseas. Microcomputer software is so portable that it can be mailed or carried from country to country in days or even hours. This characteristic increases the risk of unauthorized duplication or more subtle forms of misuse. What protection, then, does exist for American software once it leaves our shores?

The laws of most countries, including the U.S., seek to protect the property rights of an owner from theft or misuse. Such laws normally make distinctions, described in Chapter 3, between tangible property like automobiles and intangible property like copyrights and patents. Each legal system will, however, deal with such issues slightly differently and each may use different terminology. The more industrially developed a country, the more highly structured the laws usually are, and copyright and patent laws are among the most highly structured of all laws.

RELIANCE ON COPYRIGHT LAWS

The primary legal protection for software exists in the form of copyright laws of each nation and under international copyright treaties. Nearly every country grants copyright protection to the author of written materials. The issue is often whether software is treated as a "writing" or "literary work" to be protected by copyright law. For example, an Australian trial court recently held that software is not a "literary work" within the meaning of that country's copyright law. Although reversed on appeal, that decision is now the basis for an Australian legislative study intended to favor software copyright protection.

In addition, patent and trade secret laws have some application to software in foreign industrial nations. However, these laws often only protect nationals of the local country, in absence of treaties or local registration or filing. Foreign legal systems place different social values on the various classes of intellectual property, resulting in legal and public policy decisions contrary to the U.S. For example, software is, by statute, not patentable in France or Germany (although one recent French case has held to the contrary if software is part of an industrial process). On the other hand, copyright law, being substantially similar in every country and with fewer local variances, tends to be more universal in scope and coverage.

As the world becomes more and more an "information society," connected by computers and instantaneous satellite communication, every country has a vested interest in protecting the intellectual efforts of its citizens from theft or misuse, not only by its own nationals but also by persons or businesses in other countries. This national concern is the basis for most international treaties, which extend some of the principles of local law to citizens of other countries by mutual agreement. Some of the oldest of these treaties are in the area of copyright law, the strongest present form of software protection for authors and publishers.

RELIANCE ON THE UNIVERSAL COPYRIGHT CONVENTION

The best-known and most important of the international copyright treaties is the Universal Copyright Convention (UCC). American software authors have almost automatic copyright protection in the international arena under the UCC, which became effective in 1955 and was later modified in 1971. The U.S. was an original signatory in 1955 and signed the amended Convention in 1974.

As its name indicates, the UCC is intended to provide nearly universal copyright coverage to authors and artists by establishing certain uniform rights in each country for the benefit of nationals of the other countries that subscribe to the UCC. The UCC exists as much to protect foreign authors and artists in the U.S. as it does U.S. citizens and their software in foreign markets. It is important to understand that the UCC gives foreign nationals rights which a local citizen might not have. For example, the complex notice, registration, and publication rules in the U.S. Copyright Act do not exist in Europe, Japan, or most other industrial countries. The UCC gives foreign authors the same protection a national has in the U.S. through use of the ©, even when the work was not registered in the U.S.

The Berne Convention

The UCC was created in large part to accommodate the problems caused by our unique U.S. copyright laws. Because of the formalities of these laws, the U.S. has never joined the Berne Convention, an earlier international treaty signed in Berne, Switzerland, in 1886, and revised a number of times since then. This treaty protects the works of authors of most industrial and commercial countries without any formality required other than publication within a country that is part of the Berne Copyright Union.

The only time you need to resort to protection under the Berne Convention is when you are dealing with a country that is not a signatory to the UCC; there are not many countries that fall into this group. It is possible to obtain protection under the Berne Convention by simultaneous publication in the U.S. and any Berne country (like Canada), since its provisions protect nonmember nationals in such cases. However, this may be impractical in the case of software, which is rarely marketed in foreign countries until it is well established at home. The Berne Convention defines "simultaneous publication" as "general commercial availability," in any Berne country, of a book or work within thirty days of initial release in the author's own country.

How the UCC Works to Protect Foreign Authors

For the reasons cited above, the key clauses of the UCC found in *Article II* are extremely important:

1. Published works of nationals of any Contracting State and works first published in that State shall enjoy in each other Contracting State the same protection as that other State accords to the works of its nationals first published in its own territory.

2. Unpublished works of nationals of each Contracting State shall enjoy in each other Contracting State the same protection as that other State accords to unpublished works of its own nationals.

These provisions mean, for example, that if English law grants copyright protection to computer software written in English by an English citizen, then an American author who wrote a computer program in the U.S. is entitled to copyright protection for that software in England even though the program was not written or originally published in England. In the opinion of various English legal writers (cited in the bibliography), computer programs *are* covered by copyright law in the U.K. There have been a few lower-court cases and one recent appeals court case in England confirming this position.

Since the U.K. is a member of the UCC, an American citizen who first publishes software in the U.S. has automatic copyright protection in England. The U.K. is one of the many countries that does not require registration or deposit of materials to obtain copyright protection, so an American citizen or company does not have to do anything to gain protection other than comply with the minimal formalities of the UCC. These are described below.

UCC Formalities—General

There are countries that have various formalities such as registration, deposit, notice, payment of fees, or a requirement that the publication must first occur in *that* country. To deal with this situation (in which case the U.S. is the most formal), Article III of the UCC says that all local formalities of the second country shall be deemed complied with, if the following conditions are met:

1. The work is first published outside the second country.
2. The author is not a national of the second country.
3. From the time of first publication by authority of the author, the work bears the international copyright symbol "©," the name of the copyright owner, and the year of first publication, placed in a manner giving reasonable notice.

On the other hand, a "Contracting State" (to use the term found in Article II of the UCC) may impose more formal requirements on its own citizens (nationals) for works published anywhere in the world, and for works of any national which are first published in that country. This means the U.S. can set additional requirements for its own nationals publishing elsewhere, and for nationals of any country who first publish in the U.S. An American author, for example, must register his copyright in the U.S. before he can bring a copyright infringement suit, but an English author bringing suit in the U.S. would not need to have registered the work in the U.K., since his country does not require registration as a precondition to filing an infringement action. However, Professor Nimmer, the American copyright expert, suggests that failure of the English author to register in the U.S. may cause the loss of the right to attorney fees and statutory damages. This seems at variance with the explicit language of the UCC.

UCC Formalities—The Copyright Notice

The value of the rights to be gained by complying with UCC Article III are such that virtually any software you write or publish should use the appropriate notice if you want to be certain of international protection. This international notice is almost identical to the U.S. copyright notice (see Chapter 5), and at an absolute minimum it should read, "© 1984, Shauna Scientist."

Actually, you will normally see the following international notice, which also complies with the notice form required by Section 401 of the U.S. Copyright Act and the Buenos Aires Convention (discussed below): "Copyright © 1984, Shauna Scientist. All Rights Reserved."

It is, of course, best to use the latter, longer version since it will definitely satisfy both the UCC, U.S. law, and even the Buenos Aires Convention, which covers most South American countries; the shorter form will not necessarily do so.

The Term of Protection under the UCC

The UCC term of protection and renewal rights are not normally of any international consequence for software, since software often has a relatively short useful life. The UCC minimum protection term is for twenty-five years from publication, or for the life of the author plus twenty-five years where the author is the publisher. The Berne Convention, on the other hand, provides for life plus fifty years, which is the same as that established in our 1976 U.S. Copyright Act.

South America and the Buenos Aires Treaty

The Buenos Aires Convention, ratified by the U.S. in 1911, governs the copyright relationships of the U.S. and most of the South and Central American countries. At present, all but four of its signatories are also members of the UCC. The one variation under the Buenos Aires treaty is that the copyright notice must state that the owner claims a "reservation of the property right." The usual form added to the U.S. and UCC format is the language, "All Rights Reserved." Since nearly all countries subscribing to the Buenos Aires Convention are also UCC members this may be excessive caution, but it is so easily accomplished it should always be done.

Special Problems with Alternatives to the © Symbol

One major concern of lawyers who work with software protection is that many computer printers and computer terminals use only a standard ASCII character set, with which there is no way to create what is called the "circle C" (©) on a screen or in computer printed materials. Most people use "(C)" or even "[C]" as an alternative. A rational person would assume that this alternate form is acceptable, but there is no present authority in any case, treaty, or law that supports this variation. In fact, the U.S. Copyright Office published a circular in 1982 which casts doubt on the use of anything except the © symbol under U.S. law. However, U.S. law, unlike the UCC, does permit the alternatives of the word "Copyright" or the abbreviation "Copr." In 1984, the District Court in Videotronics, Inc. v. Bend Electronics did, however, conclude that a C in a hexagon on the screen was sufficient under U.S. law. This may help the issue.

Until both domestic law and international treaties like the UCC are changed or the issue is clarified, it is unwise to use anything but the © symbol on printed materials like labels or books. There is not much that can be done with computer-terminal screen messages or computer listings on ASCII printers, since neither device supports the © symbol. As of publication of this book, legislation is pending in the U.S. to allow the alternate forms (C) or [C] domestically, but this does not answer the question under the UCC.

Since the UCC has many other provisions which can adversely affect copyright claims, it is vital to have a competent intellectual-property attorney review any proposed international software transaction. Even if the proper international copyright notice form has been used, a suit for infringement will require use of local legal counsel. Furthermore, there are many other issues of contract and tax law that should also be considered carefully before signing any international agreement for software distribution. A brief discussion of some of these issues follows.

COMPULSORY LICENSES
AND FOREIGN LANGUAGE TRANSLATIONS

American companies are beginning to realize that their software is more marketable in foreign countries if the screen messages and the manuals are in the local language. The U.S. Copyright Act and the UCC both give the author the exclusive right to make, publish, and authorize the making and publication of translations protected by the Copyright Act or the UCC. Many companies do, in fact, arrange for such translations. Such work should be done under a contract which clearly provides that ownership of the translation belongs to the software company and not to the translator.

You should think carefully about how your company handles this situation, because it has copyright, trademark, and other legal implications that you may not have considered. For example, under current law in France, all documentation for software and hardware brought into that country must be in French, or importation rights may be denied. And in a case involving some Visicalc® program documentation, a German court has held that the former German distributor was guilty of copyright infringement when it translated these materials into German without permission.

What if you don't feel the market to be large enough to justify doing the translation of your software and documentation? You may be surprised to learn that at the behest of the "developing countries," the UCC has a provision giving any national of another country the right to make a translation into the local language if that has not been done within seven years (or three years in the case of "developing countries") of first publication. These provisions, found in UCC Article V, provide for royalties and a procedure for obtaining permission from the author or the local government. These rules could be very dangerous to a software publisher or author unaware of them. There is no known software case where this has occurred, but the Japanese government is considering a similar law.

POSSIBLE EFFECTS OF THE EUROPEAN
"MORAL RIGHTS" THEORY

Due to the differences between American and European copyright law, a final issue of interest involves the principle of the author's "moral right." While this right, found in many European countries and exemplified in the following Article 6 *bis* of the Brussels 1948 revision of the Berne Convention, primarily applies to books and works of art, there is no reason that it could not be applied to computer programs:

> Independently of the author's copyright, and even after the transfer of the said copyright, the author shall have the right, during his lifetime, to claim authorship of the work and object to any distortion, mutilation or other alteration thereof, or any other action in relation to the said work, which would be prejudicial to his honor or reputation.

The Berne Convention, and most other countries that subscribe to the principle of the author's "moral right," even extend this right to the heirs or successors to the copyright after the author's death. At least one 1976 American case seems to recognize the same principle.

Since this "moral right" could be applied to a computer program, a software publisher might someday be faced with objections from the program author to changes made in later versions of the original work, or perhaps in the documentation or manual which accompanies the program. This raises the question of who is deemed to be the author of a translation of a program or manual into a foreign language. Under the laws of most countries, works written by employees belong to the employer as author, while an independent contractor is deemed to be the author even if he or she has assigned all rights to the party paying for the work.

Because of these principles it is wise to have a provision in the translator's contract expressly stating that the translator acknowledges that he or she is *not* the author of the work, and to identify the actual author of the work being translated as either the original individual author or the original employer. It is also important to identify the author(s) because the various treaties make many of the rights granted depend on the citizenship or domicile of the author(s).

A SURVEY OF INTERNATIONAL SOFTWARE COPYRIGHT PROTECTION

International software copyright protection would appear to exist in most countries, but it is a complex area of the law. The software author can, at the very least, obtain basic protection by complying with the expanded UCC notice form "Copyright © 1984, XYZ. All Rights Reserved." Contracts for international use or creation of software should be examined very carefully in light of the various problems mentioned above. Thought should also be given to the effect of various government regulations relating to exportation of technology, and to tax laws discussed elsewhere in this book.

As of publication of this book, there are cases in the countries listed below which have dealt with copyright protection of computer software, with the result indicated. There could be other cases, but they have not been publicized in the U.S. Remember that this law is so dynamic that new cases could obsolete this information over the next few years.

Australia. Copyright protection for computer programs was denied in an Apple Computer case involving Apple's ROM code and decided in December 1983. In May 1984 this case was overruled by an appeals court in a lengthy opinion. As a result of the trial court opinion, legislation was passed in 1984 making clear that software is covered by copyright.

Canada. Canadian copyright laws are presently similar to those in Australia, England, and the U.S. A precedent-setting case, IBM Corp. v. Ordinateurs Spirales Inc., et al, involving claimed infringement of the IBM Personal Computer "Basic Input-Output System" (BIOS), seems to place Canada squarely in the same camp as the U.S. with regard to software protection. In June 1984 the Canadian trial court granted an injunction against the defendant's further sale of a Taiwanese-made PC-compatible computer containing a ROM that duplicated the IBM-copyrighted BIOS ROM. In the course of concluding that the Canadian Copyright Act protects computer programs in object code in a ROM, the court cited and discussed with approval cases from the U.K., South Africa, Australia, and the U.S. It adopted the same general position that the U.S. courts did in the Apple-Franklin and Apple-Formula cases.

However, the Canadian Copyright Office refuses to accept videogames for copyright. The Canadian Government has also just concluded a study recommending a major revision of the copyright laws. It specifically suggests protection for machine-readable computer software.

France. Over the past three years there have been a series of lower court cases holding that computer software is protected under French copyright law. This includes ROM code and operating systems, as well as videogames and source code. A 1982 case also held that even if the copyrightability question had not been determined under French law, a U.S. registered videogame must be granted protection in France under the UCC. This latter opinion takes French law farther than most other countries would go.

Germany. The District Court of Appeals in Karlsruhe ruled in 1983 that computer programs are subject to copyright, but that the algorithms used in them are not; what is to be protected is the form of the program and the "flow" of the data. Since then several other German courts have reached the same conclusion. On the other hand, the Frankfurt Appeals Court ruled in several 1983 decisions that videogames are not protected by copyright since they are not inventive nor complex enough to justify such protection. Simple software that does not qualify under the copyright law may, however, be protected under the unfair competition law.

Earlier, in 1982, a trial court in Munich granted injunctions in favor of Visicorp against its former distributor for copying computer programs and documentation. A German Federal Labor Court also ruled in 1983 that computer programs are protected by the copyright law. It held that an employee who prepares programs does not own them and may not use them, even if the employment contract does not expressly assign them to the employer.

Hong Kong.   Apple Computer has won several preliminary injunction actions in Hong Kong against software and hardware copiers. Piracy, however, is reported to be rampant, and other cases are pending.

Japan.   It was assumed by most Japanese copyright experts that computer programs would be protected under Japanese law. In December 1982, the first of several cases was decided confirming this position. It involved a videogame programmed in assembly language and stored in ROM. A 1984 decision granted protection to video game images, in addition to the program. Since then, Japan's Ministry of International Trade & Industry (MITI) has been actively pushing legislation in the Diet (the legislature), which would expressly recognize software copyrights, but would limit the copyright term to fifteen years.

However, this legislation has been opposed in Japan by U.S. companies and the U.S. Government, since it also contains provisions allowing MITI to force a company to license others if MITI feels that that is in the national interest, or if the proposed licensee has substantially altered another company's software package and wants to resell it.

Mexico.   In October 1984 the Mexican copyright office began accepting software for registration for a 30 year term of protection under its laws.

Singapore.   Apple has successfully prosecuted several copyright infringement cases involving its software in ROM and on diskette, as well as unfair competition and trademark cases.

South Africa.   Apple and several other companies have received rulings in this country protecting computer software in various forms.

Taiwan.   After some initial skirmishes which it lost, Apple has finally won civil and criminal court victories in this country in favor of copyright protection for its ROM code and operating system.

United Kingdom.   In the U.K. there have been a number of lower and one or two appellate court cases which have established protection for computer programs under the U.K. copyright law. One of the appellate level cases involved videogames with code in EPROMS. As early as 1980, Microsoft and Tandy obtained injunctions permitting seizure of pirated copies of BASIC and other software. It is now fairly well established in England that software in all forms is copyrightable.

INTERNATIONAL PATENT PROTECTION FOR SOFTWARE

There is presently little in the way of international patent protection for software since, as discussed in Chapter 9, patent law is not practical for run-of-the-mill software. It may work, however, for software used in process control situations, as mentioned in the French case noted.

Local Law Governs

Patents, trademarks, and protection for industrial designs are normally only available in the country in which an owner has formally registered the claim. Thus, the scope of protection available for software must be determined in each case by local legal counsel and the national government. There is no such thing as a universal patent or trademark right, as there is under the copyright conventions.

The Paris Convention

However, the various nations do cooperate on some procedural matters. An international convention known as the International Convention for the Protection of Industrial Property, originally concluded in Paris in 1883, and amended many times, now covers international patent protection procedures between some eighty-eight countries. This treaty, called the "Paris Convention" for short, is administered from Geneva, Switzerland, by the World Intellectual Property Organization (WIPO). It operates on the principle that each participating state must treat nationals of other member states as it treats its own nationals. It also provides a system whereby the filing of a patent or other application in one country gives rise to a twelve-month priority in all other countries, which is very important in patent applications where rights depend on who files first.

As far as Europe is concerned, Article 52(2)(c) of the European Patent Convention contains an express provision that computer programs and algorithms cannot be regarded as patentable inventions. Essentially this same provision is also part of the U.K., French, and German patent laws. However, it may be possible in one or more of these countries, as in the U.S., to obtain a patent on a process or machine incorporating a computer program in the steps which make the process or machine accomplish its objective. However, it does not appear that European courts and patent offices view this idea with much favor.

As for the U.K., Professor Bryan Niblett's book, *Legal Protection of Computer Programs,* contains an extensive analysis of patent protection for software in the U.K., but leaves open many questions. Niblett also cites a number of European treaties and international arrangements in this area that will have an effect on future cases. His book should be consulted if you have questions regarding the state of software patent law in the U.K.

The Issues of Novelty and Disclosure

As with domestic software patent protection, the same international threshold problem is whether or not the necessary novelty can be established to meet the invention requirements of patent law. Most programs do not do anything really new; they just do things quicker and better and on a computer. Novelty may be hard to establish since there is no depository of prior art, and it is difficult to make patent searches in this subject, in most countries. Finally, the adequacy of disclosure in software patent applications is a real problem, since no author would want to reveal the source code of an entire program. However, the principle of full disclosure is the basic tenet of patent laws in every country, so that a conflict would arise if an exception were to be made in the case of software. Because of all these difficulties, patent protection may not be a practical alternative for computer programs except in the industrial process control field.

In spite of a growing number of patent law treaties and conventions in Europe and elsewhere, the subject of international patent protection may continue to founder for some years until some satisfactory solution is arrived at for the difficulties outlined above. The WIPO study quoted at the outset of this chapter essentially writes off patent protection and concentrates (as this book has) on copyright protection, with some reliance on licenses, contracts, and trade secrecy laws.

INTERNATIONAL PROTECTION OF TRADE SECRETS AND "KNOW-HOW"

An earlier chapter covered the domestic U.S. law of trade secrets and the licensing of technology as it relates to computer programs and documentation. On the international level, most other nations have reasonably well-developed (and similar) laws covering the protection of what is often called "industrial property" or "know-how". The subject of trade secrecy, called "The Law of Confidence" in England, is also recognized in most countries in some form or other, but often under different names. This body of law should be useful to U.S. companies engaged in the software business in these countries.

Most foreign laws rely on the same principles we have adopted in the U.S., which stem from the rule that it is illegal to steal ideas, processes, and intellectual property that other people or companies spent time and energy developing. This general rule will not change, so that under it some protection should be available in every industrial country. The question of protection will usually turn on the value of the know-how, what steps were taken to develop and protect it, and whether someone is making unfair use of it.

There is some evidence, for example, in a 1981 French case that software may also be protected as a trade secret. The French court concluded that an employee was guilty of a felony for transmitting a program of his former employer to a third party. The French penal code makes the divulgence of trade secrets a crime punishable by a stiff fine and prison sentence, which is more serious if the information is passed to or by foreigners than for local recipients.

INTERNATIONAL LICENSES AND CONTRACTS

The value of software contracts and licensing agreements has been referred to elsewhere in this book, especially in Chapters 11 and 12. In spite of differences in language, legal systems, and legal principles, most well-written agreements between commercial enterprises are upheld when litigated in foreign countries—unless they run afoul of some national public policy. In light of this, it is foolish for software authors and companies to draft and sign international agreements without consultation with legal counsel familiar with the applicable international laws. It is important to realize that domestic and international agreements are just *not* the same.

Choice of Law Clauses

At the very least, careful consideration should be given to the "choice of law" clauses normally included in contracts, since a provision that "This Agreement shall be governed by California law," for example, will normally be given effect by a foreign court. Because it is known to you and your attorney, it is in your best interest to settle disputes under principles of U.S. law. A choice of law clause will provide that benefit when included in the agreement.

Jurisdictional Clauses

The other types of clauses to be included are less obvious. A jurisdictional paragraph, by which the parties agree that all disputes will be settled in the Superior Court of Santa Clara County, California, or the U.S. District Court for the Southern District of New York, may or may not be enforced, but this surely provides a better basis for commencing a lawsuit than no provision at all. You really do not want to be litigating over a software contract in a French court, in French, if you have an alternative. The time, cost, and uncertainty of dealing with another legal system can be very unpleasant and frustrating.

The full extent of problems that can turn up in international contracts involving the computer industry is covered in an excellent recent book by Hilary Pearson, entitled *Computer Contracts: An International Guide to Agreements and Protection.*

Other International Issues to Think About

While related to software protection only in the sense of protecting royalties from the license, international contracts must deal with such things as the currency in which payments are to be made, currency controls, the place of payment, and the effect of international tax laws which may require withholding of sizeable sums of royalties in lieu of income taxes. Failure to consider these issues may leave the author or publisher of software with only part of the desired return for the license. There are many unanticipated traps in international transactions, which can be unpleasant and expensive surprises.

ARBITRATION AS AN ALTERNATIVE TO FOREIGN LITIGATION

As an alternative to litigation in a foreign or domestic court, it is possible to include arbitration clauses in software licenses and other international computer contracts. Awards made by arbitrators acting under such clauses can now be enforced in most foreign countries, because of an international treaty known as the United Nations Convention on the Recognition of Foreign Arbitral Awards. This treaty covers most countries with which U.S. businesses ordinarily have dealings.

There are many benefits to use of arbitration at the international level, not the least of which is that the parties can agree in advance on many issues that would otherwise cause serious inequities if decided by local law. Arbitration allows you greater certainty about how disputes will be resolved. You should carefully consider use of arbitration in any international transaction.

At a minimum, arbitration clauses in international contracts should deal with the following items:

- A description of the issues which are open to arbitration, or which must be arbitrated.

- Identification by the parties of the international organization they desire to be used for administration of the arbitration proceeding. There are numerous international Chambers of Commerce, any of which can be of help. They include The Japan-American Chamber of Commerce, The International Chamber of Commerce in Paris, the

American Arbitration Association, and The London Court of Arbitration.

- The issue of whether there are to be multiple arbitrators or a single arbitrator.
- The official language of the arbitration proceeding.
- The national law that shall govern the arbitration.
- The desired location of the hearing.
- How the costs of the proceeding should be divided or assessed.
- A specific statement that the agreement to arbitrate and the arbitration award is intended to be enforced under the UN Convention mentioned above.

SUMMARY

The laws of foreign countries vary considerably, not only from country to country, but also from those laws we are used to dealing with in the U.S. Unfamiliar foreign business practices, reflecting these different laws, make international software licensing and contracting a potentially hazardous endeavor for your business. You can become involved in international transactions almost without realizing it. This is an area where you and your business need competent legal and accounting help from the outset.

The extent to which software can be protected under foreign laws is not completely clear in many countries, although there is a strong tide surging toward the same types of legal theories and court decisions that we have seen in the U.S. International copyright protection is particularly valuable because of an extensive network of copyright treaties. Other types of legal protection for intellectual property are less universal.

There will be many opportunities for American software companies in the international market, but such opportunities must be approached with care, planning, and the knowledge that there are very real differences between the international and domestic scene.

16

Sales Taxes and Local Taxes on Software

Taxes are what we pay for civilized society . . .

Justice Oliver Wendell Holmes (1927).

THE IMPORTANCE OF UNDERSTANDING SALES TAXES AND LOCAL TAXES

You may wonder what a chapter on sales taxes and local taxes on software has to do with protecting and marketing software. Well, your financial interest as an author, publisher, or other producer of software depends on the return you earn. Failure to take into consideration the taxes exacted by state and local authorities can materially reduce your revenues. It can also drag your company into audits and litigation with the government, or, worse yet, with some of your customers. If you plan carefully, you may be able to avoid or minimize these taxes. This chapter is intended to help you anticipate these issues, as well as to avoid penalties and interest charges.

This chapter can only acquaint you with some of the principles of sales, use, and property tax law as they relate to software development. This is, therefore, another area of your software business where competent legal and accounting advice is important.

DEFINITIONS OF SALES, USE, AND PROPERTY TAX

State and local taxes are generally categorized into *sales, use,* and *property* taxes. Significant portions of state and local government revenues come from these taxes, so you can expect them to impact your software business more and more.

Sales Tax

Sales tax is usually defined as a tax levied on the sale of goods (and sometimes services), which is normally calculated as a percentage of the purchase price. The seller is required to collect and remit the sales tax to the government agency involved. It may apply to leases, rentals, and royalties, as well as traditional sales of goods. A more detailed discussion of sales tax as it applies to software is set forth below.

Use Tax

Use Tax is the flip side of sales tax, intended to catch transactions which do not qualify as a sale in the state where the buyer resides. It is a tax on the use, consumption, or storage of goods acquired from a retailer without being subjected to the sales tax. For example, it is typically the tax you are supposed to pay your state of residence on a car which you buy in another state with the intention of using in your state. If the car is brought into your state of residence within a short time after purchase, use tax may be assessed by your state. It is computed the same way as sales taxes.

Property Tax

Property tax is levied by state and local governments on the right to own personal and real property. Software is considered personal property, so we are not concerned here with real property taxes. Traditionally, personal property taxes were assessed only against tangible (physically visible) property. But as states have become more concerned about revenue sources, they have applied this tax more and more to *intangible* personal property as well, like software.

In the examples which follow, California is often used as the reference point. This is done because California is not only the largest single source of software development, but also the largest single market. Its government agencies also happen to hold some of the more extreme positions on these issues, which are often adopted later by other states. Forewarned is forearmed.

PRINCIPLES OF SALES TAX AND USE TAX LAW

Imposition of sales taxes started in the U.S. in the 1930's, and presently all but five American states impose sales taxes on some types of transactions. In most states, the sales tax is imposed upon the retailer for the privilege of selling tangible personal property at retail. It is normally passed on, or collected from the consumer, based upon the gross selling price of the goods purchased. While there are some exceptions to the general application of the sales tax law, most states have increasingly applied it to more and more classes of goods. A few states (Illinois, for example) even have a service occupations tax, which taxes that portion of the cost of services involving the parts used, if any. The sale of the assets of a business (including software) may even be taxable, if the seller holds a sales tax permit, even though the sale is for the purpose of going out of business.

To catch transactions that might otherwise escape the reach of the sales tax laws, sales tax laws are paired with use tax laws. Technically speaking, use tax is a tax on the use, consumption, or storage of goods acquired from a retailer without being subjected to a sales tax. Out-of-state sellers, who maintain branch offices in the state where the buyer resides, must collect the use tax on sales into such state. For example, because the National Geographic Society maintains two small advertising offices in California, it is required to collect use taxes on mail-order sales into California, even though its main office filling the order is in Washington, D.C. Because of this pairing of these two taxes, nearly everything said about sales taxes will usually apply to use taxes.

Factors Causing Taxability

Three factors determine whether a transaction is likely to be subject to sales or use tax. These are sound, but not infallible guidelines:

1. Is the transaction one at retail, that is, one made between the seller and the final consumer or user of the goods? Intermediate transactions, such as wholesaler to retailer, are not taxable unless the retailer is going to use the goods rather than sell them.

2. Does the transaction involve tangible or intangible personal property? Normally, the sales or use tax applies only to sales of tangible property. Most of the litigation over the taxability of software has turned on this issue. Where software has been held to be tangible personal property, it is almost universally taxed when transferred or sold.

3. Where were the goods delivered? If otherwise taxable, goods delivered in the same state as the seller will always be taxable. If delivered out-of-state to a non-resident buyer, the sale will usually (but not always) be nontaxable. Even if the sales tax does not apply, use tax may be applicable where the out-of-state seller has some connection with the state in which the goods are delivered. Sometimes, determining whether title passed in the seller's state or the buyer's state will make a difference.

Out-of-State Sales Exemption

Generally speaking, sales are deemed to have occurred where the retailer is located. However, because of constitutional prohibitions, where the buyer is an out-of-state resident the state of the seller cannot collect sales tax from the non-resident if the goods are delivered elsewhere than the seller's state of operation.

For this reason, even though there is a California sales tax on floppy disks purchased in California, a shipment sent by a California retailer in interstate commerce from California to New York is not taxable by California, or New York, unless some special rule applies.

The rules for determining whether a use tax or a sales tax applies to out-of-state sales are complex and beyond the scope of this discussion. If you have no office, representative, or warehousing in the other state, the sale is probably nontaxable. If you operate in several states, be extremely careful to check out this question.

Exceptions to Sales Tax

The major exception to sales and use tax is a sale to someone who purchases goods for resale. This is typically a sale by a distributor to a dealer, or a manufacturer to a distributor. The performance of services is also not a sale of goods at retail and is therefore not subject to sales tax.

Most states consider you a retailer if you make more than two or three retail sales in a twelve-month period. If you fail to collect sales tax from the consumer, you must pay it yourself. Lots of things you wouldn't think of as being retail sales are considered as such. For example, leases or rentals of almost every kind of personal property are treated as continuing sales by the lessor or owner and sales tax applies. For this reason, if your state taxes the sale of software, then sales tax may apply to the licensing, leasing, or rental of such software.

If your business is obligated to collect sales or use taxes, it is required by most states to obtain a Sales and Use Tax Permit, so the authorities can tell that you are collecting the tax and can cause you to file regular monthly or quarterly sales tax returns. Although you do not take out the permit, or do not collect the tax you are supposed to collect, the state will hold you liable anyway.

Even if you didn't realize that you were supposed to collect sales tax on your software, this does not excuse you from paying the tax, which may not be collected from you until several years later—long after your customer, from whom you should have collected the tax, has left your area. Severe penalties and interest are imposed on delinquent returns and overdue sales taxes. A number of California software houses have recently learned this the hard way, years after the original software transactions.

UNIQUE PROBLEMS OF THE SOFTWARE INDUSTRY

Tangible versus Intangible Property

Nobody worried about the taxability of software in the early mainframe days, since sales tax was applied to hardware while the software was "free." Once IBM unbundled software and created the software industry, the question of software taxability began to arise. Since software is intangible, intellectual property, it is difficult to see how it could be classified as tangible, personal property for sales tax purposes. Furthermore, development of software, at least in the case of custom programming, is a service and not a sale. Unfortunately, this logic conflicts with the growing revenue needs of some state and local governments.

Revenue-hungry states like California see revenues from a growing industry which they would otherwise miss. These states claim that, since software is delivered on a tangible object like a floppy disk or computer tape, the whole transaction is one involving the taxable sale of tangible, personal property. As a result of litigation, other states like Illinois and Texas have seen the light, and no longer attempt to impose a sales tax on licensing of software. Almost uniformly where the issue has been litigated, the courts have held that software is intangible property and not subject to sales tax. But then the state legislatures sometimes step in, as in Illinois in 1984, and propose to make it taxable anyway.

Custom versus Off-the-Shelf Software

Some states take an intermediate view and acknowledge that software that is custom written for a particular customer is, in reality, a service which should not be taxable. They ignore the minor value of the tangible personal property involved, when the software is delivered on tape or diskette. To avoid the tax on the software, some states require that the service element and the tangible property element be separately stated on the invoice. If not, then the whole transaction is taxed. In many states the only form of software that is taxable is standard off-the-shelf packaged software. This is taxed on the theory that it is simply another form of merchandise, part of which happens to be recorded, as are phonograph records and videotapes.

As a result of litigation and finally legislation in California, the sale or licensing of custom software at retail is expressly exempted from sales tax. A custom program, according to Revenue & Taxation Code § 6010.9, is one prepared to the special order of the customer. But the issue is not dead, since there are nearly always bills pending in the California legislature to repeal or materially modify this exception.

On the other hand, California has always taken the position that "canned programs," those intended for general or repeated use, are subject to sales tax. In the case of modifications to canned programs, any portion of the price for such services which is separately stated is considered exempt, but otherwise the entire price is taxable, regardless of whether the cost of the changes is more than the cost of the original program.

Sources of Current Information

The issues mentioned above are being litigated and argued in the courts and legislatures of the various states almost monthly, so that it is difficult to tell what the situation is in each state at any given moment. As an aid that should remain reliable for a year or two, you should consult the table of software taxation which is set out on pages 295–96 of this chapter as Table 16-1. The source of the information varies, but a particular case or regulation that is the basis for the information is indicated as such.

Other sources of current information are trade associations like ADAPSO, 1300 North Seventeenth Street, Arlington, Virginia 22209, which has participated in some of the state sales tax litigation, or the Computer Law and Tax Report, published by Robert P. Bigelow. Bob and his law partner also publish an annual compendium of tax laws relating to computers, called the "State Computer Tax Report," containing information collected by them from the various state agencies. If you are going to be involved with your own sales outlets on a multistate basis, you should subscribe to their reports.

SOME EXAMPLES OF CURRENT SALES TAX DISPUTES

Resale Certificates

Sales of software to wholesalers, distributors, and dealers are exempt from sales and use taxes. However, the burden of proof is on your company to show that the sale was exempt under the law. If you cannot do so, you have to remit the tax anyway. California is notorious for auditing a business and seeking adjustments because of the inability of that business to prove the level of the sale. Do not fall into this trap.

The way to avoid these problems is to insist that the wholesaler, dealer, or other person purchasing or licensing software from you for resale or sublicensing, provide you with what is often called a "Resale Certificate." This is simply a signed statement, which you should obtain from the purchaser, stating that the purchase is for the purpose of resale and not for use or consumption. You are entitled, if you act in good faith, to rely on such a certificate; see that you have a copy of it in the invoice file of all your nonretail customers.

TABLE 16–1
Sales & Use Tax Status of Computer Software (1) (4)

State	Canned Program	Custom Program	Authority
ALABAMA	T	E	Rule C28–001
ARIZONA	E	E	Rule 15–5–1853(C); Rule 15–5–1513(C)
ARKANSAS	T	T	GR–25 (1982)
CALIFORNIA	T	E	Regulation 1502; R & T Code 6010.9
COLORADO	E(2)	E(2)	Regulation B
CONNECTICUT	T	T	Sec 12–407(2)
DISTRICT OF COLUMBIA	E	E	*District of Columbia v. Universal Computer Associates, Inc.* 465 F.2d 615 (D.C. Cir. 1972)
FLORIDA	E	E	Rule 12A–1.32(4).
GEORGIA	T	T	Informal opinion. (1983)
HAWAII	T	T	Informal opinion (1982)
IDAHO	T	T	Regulation 12–2
ILLINOIS	E	E	86 Ill. Adm. Code Section 130.1935.
INDIANA	E	E	Revenue Information Bulletin #8
IOWA	T	T(3)	Rule 18.34
KANSAS	T	T	K.S.A.. 79–3603(S)
KENTUCKY	T	T	Informal opinion (1983)
LOUISIANA	E	E	Article 47:301(16)
MAINE	T	E	Informal opinion (1984)
MARYLAND	T	E	*Equitable Trust Co. v. Comptroller of the Treasury,* Maryland Court of Appeals, 8/11/83
MASSACHUSETTS	T	T(3)	Regulation 64H.06.
MICHIGAN	T	E	*Hastings Mutual Insurance Co. v. State of Michigan, Dept of Treasury,* Michigan Court of Claims, No. 82–453, 1/23/84
MINNESOTA	E	E	Section 297A.01; Reg. 610
MISSISSIPPI	E	E	Informal opinion (1984)
MISSOURI	T	E	*James, Director or Revenue v. Tres Computer Systems, Inc. et al.,* Missouri Supreme Court No 63662
NEBRASKA	E	E	Rev. Stat. 77–2702(C)
NEVADA	T	T	Informal opinion (1984)
NEW JERSEY	E(3)	E(3)	N.J. Adm. Code Sec 18:24–25.1
NEW MEXICO	T	T	G.R. Regulation 3(K):2; Regulation 3(F):64
NEW YORK	E	E	Technical Services Bulletin No. 1978–(1) (S)
NORTH CAROLINA	T	E	N.C. Gen. Stat. § 105–164.3(20)
NORTH DAKOTA	E	E	Technical Memorandum
OHIO	T	T	Ohio Rev. Code § 5739.01
OKLAHOMA	T	E	Section 1354(H), Title 68

(Continued)

TABLE 16-1 (cont.)

State	Canned Program	Custom Program	Authority
PENNSYLVANIA	T	E	Regulation 31.32
RHODE ISLAND	T	T	Formal Rule
SOUTH CAROLINA	T	T	Regulation 117-174.262; *Citizens and Southern Systems Inc. v. Commissioner,* South Carolina Supreme Court, 1/10/84
SOUTH DAKOTA	T	T	Regulation 64:06:02:79 and 64:06:02:80
TENNESSEE	T	T	Section 67-3002(b)
TEXAS	T	E	H.B. 122
UTAH	T	E	Informal opinion (1984)
VERMONT	T	E	*Chittenden Trust Co. v. King,* Vermont Supreme Court, 465 A2d 1100 (1983)
VIRGINIA	T	?	Advisory opinion (1983)
WASHINGTON	T	E	ETB 515.04.155
WEST VIRGINIA	T	T	Informal opinion (1984)
WISCONSIN	T	T	Proposed Rule 11.71
WYOMING	T	T	Sec 39-6-404(a)(xiii)

NOTES

(1) This status chart represents a state's position as of October 1984 and is subject to change. Keep in mind that the data on the chart has been generalized for ease of reporting. It is recommended that you review the applicable cites to make sure that they are relevant to your particular fact situation. There are exceptions in many cases.

(2) To be considered exempt, preparation or selection of the program for the customer's use requires an analysis of the customer's requirements by the vendor, or the program requires adaptation, by the vendor, to be used in a specific output device.

(3) Custom programs are taxable if sold, leased, or licensed in machine readable form, but are exempt if sold, leased, or licensed in human-readable form.

(4) Computer games and similar software in cartridge form sold over-the-counter are taxed in most states.

This table was originally developed by Ronald Palenski, Esq., Tax Counsel of ADAPSO, Arlington, Va., was modified by the author, and is used with permission.

Service Transactions

Very few jurisdictions tax transactions that are clearly services, as opposed to delivery of actual goods. In California, for example, providing processing of customer data like payrolls and inventory reports is considered a service and is exempt from tax. Likewise, sale of time on a timesharing system, even using standard software, is exempt as a service. In most states consulting, designing, and implementing computer systems and software, as well as other forms of technical assistance, are nontaxable services. In each case the determining factor is whether the objective of the transaction is the processing of information, or some physical object like a deck of punched cards. The former is a service, the latter a sale of goods. Be sure your invoices are phrased in terms of services rendered, and not the sale of goods.

California Regulations.   Although it has not yet been revised to reflect the details of the new law exempting custom programs, California-based software authors and software houses should refer to Regulation 1502 of the State Board of Equalization for a detailed analysis of the rules of that agency, which is responsible for collection of sales and use taxes in California. Be aware, however, that this Regulation is based on the Board's own (sometimes idiosyncratic) interpretation of the Sales Tax Law. The Regulation provides examples of things which it considers taxable, and those which it does not.

How Do You Protect Your Company from Uncertainty?

If you are not certain whether your transaction is going to be taxable, and where the sales or use tax is relatively small, should you then try to collect the sales or use tax anyway? This is easier said than done, since many businesses object to paying taxes for what appears to be a service or a nontangible goods transaction. There is also the problem that improperly collecting sales tax, when it is not really due, may be treated by the state authorities as a fraud on your customers. You are caught in a bind.

A more viable alternative is to include the following form in virtually every sales or license transaction involving software. This language should go into the initial contract with the customer, or if there is no written contract, at least on the invoice. This is especially important if your business is subject to California law, since Civil Code § 1656.1 sets up a series of rules for determining whether you may collect the sales tax from your customer. It says that your ability to be reimbursed by the customer "depends solely upon the terms of the agreement of sale." In other words, if you don't provide for reimbursement, and have not met the other conditions of the law, you cannot collect reimbursement later on even if you have to pay it.

Suggested Form for Collection of Sales, Use, and Property Tax.

Sales, Use and Property Tax.   Customer (Licensee) shall be solely responsible for payment or reimbursement to Seller (Licensor) of all sales, use, or similar taxes imposed upon this transaction by any level of government, whether due at the time of sale or asserted later as a result of audit of the financial records of either Customer or Seller. Customer shall also pay all personal property taxes levied by government agencies based upon Customer's use or possession of the software acquired or licensed in this transaction.

A Sales Tax Trap for the Unwary

The California Board of Equalization has taken a position on software licensing agreements that all authors, software publishers, and licensors must take into consideration. California is now trying to impose a sales tax on OEM contracts involving software delivered to the OEM (hardware manufacturer) in California or to companies subject to the use tax. This position is based upon a case involving the Simplicity Pattern Company in 1980, which taxed the sale of intangible property in exchange for stock in a new company. A number of California companies have recently been audited on this issue. It could be a major and expensive problem for you.

The significance of this position is perhaps not obvious until explained. Many software houses contract directly with hardware manufacturers who wish to distribute specific computer programs on their machines, either because they intend to bundle the software into the price of the hardware or because they expect to offer a particular machine-dependent version of software with their machine.

In such a case, the OEM might pay the software house $100,000 for the unlimited right to distribute a particular word-processing program on the OEM's machine. This software is usually delivered to the OEM by the software publisher on a set of one or two master diskettes, which are then used by the manufacturer as masters for reproducing all necessary copies. Printed listings or documentation often accompany the diskettes. The value of the tangible personal property delivered to the OEM is perhaps fifty dollars (out of a $100,000 transaction), yet the California Board of Equalization takes the position that the entire amount of money received by the software author or publisher is taxable under the sales tax law, because it is deemed the sale (or licensing) of tangible personal property.

This transaction often is a wholesale transaction, because the OEM intends to resell or sublicense the software to the end user. Sometimes, the license to the OEM will limit the number of copies that can be made to 100,000 which again suggests a wholesale rather than a retail transaction. Therefore, the Board of Equalization's position seems untenable on its face. But that agency has consistently held views not substantiated by the existing state laws, and because no one contested them they in effect became law.

Several Possible Remedies. There are several ways around this situation, two of which have been approved by the Board of Equalization in private rulings:

1. Provide in the software license that the software will be delivered electronically over the phone or a datalink, and that no physical media (including manuals) are to be delivered to the licensee.

2. Provide in the software license that the licensee will bring its own media to the licensor's place of business, where the software will be placed electronically on the media belonging to the licensee.

Note that if the licensee or agreement provides for either alternative, it will still be taxable if you do not actually deliver it as specified, *or* if you deliver printed manuals in addition to the software. Everything must be done in electronic form, with no physical media changing hands.

Sales tax should also be avoidable by separately stating in the license agreement the retail price for the media used and for the documentation delivered, based on a fair market price, and then stating that the license fee does not include media or documentation. This technique has worked for some years in the construction business, where the materials are taxable and the services are not.

Out-of-State Contractors.   Because of the large amounts of potential sales tax involved, out-of-state software houses dealing with California companies should be sure a use tax does not apply to deliveries to California customers. Likewise, try not to take delivery from a California software firm *in California* if there is any alternative, or unless you are sure it is exempt from sales tax. Do use the sales tax language set out in the form above, in case your transaction is later audited and you are charged the tax.

PROPERTY TAXES ON SOFTWARE

Nearly all the discussion in this chapter has focused on sales and use taxes. But you should be aware that some jurisdictions levy a personal property tax on the right to own, possess, or use computer software. This tax is based on the fair market value of the items taxed, as of an annual assessment date. Software is property, just like your computers, but because it is intangible it is harder to see why it should be taxed.

In theory, you could be taxed on your "inventory" of computer programs held for distribution, as well as the applications software used in your business; you would then have to pay tax on any prepackaged software you held for shipment to customers. In practice, however, the states that levy property tax on software normally treat software as another form of equipment used in the business, such as cars and business machines. For example, the laws of the State of California permit property taxes only on "basic operational programs" under Revenue & Taxation Code Section 995, which means the tax applies only to the operating system software, and not to applications programs.

In the past, property taxation of software has only been a significant burden to banks, large businesses, and computer service bureaus, all of which have large investments in software. On the other hand, such taxation is not likely to affect you if you merely own or use some microcomputer software as a user. However, as tax collectors increasingly realize

that owning and possessing the "master" of a popular applications program like Lotus 1-2-3™ is of immense economic value, that situation
could change. If these master copies were to be taxed as business personal
property, software authors and publishers could have serious tax problems. Fortunately, very few taxing authorities have, as yet, considered this
issue.

Once again, the one area where you can usually protect your business
lies in the language of your agreements with licensees. If your state or
local government assesses property taxes on software, then any license
agreement should make clear that while your company retains title to
licensed software, the property taxes assessed on its use and possession
are to be paid by the licensee.

SUMMARY

Software businesses need to be more aware of the potentially adverse impact sales and use taxes can have on software transactions that might not
be thought taxable. Such taxes are increasingly being applied to the licensing and sale of software, as more and more state governments realize
the revenues involved.

With proper planning it is possible to shift the burden of such taxes to
the buyer/licensee, but this can only be done if the documents used contain the proper provisions to protect the software company from audits
and later adjustments. There are also a number of simple procedural steps
you can take to establish that some transactions are nontaxable. Be sure
you fully understand the application of your own state sales tax laws to
your business.

Because the software industry is new, government agencies have not
yet thought through the application of existing laws, so that you may find
it necessary to contest some of their positions. Most state taxing agencies
look to leadership from the California authorities, so you should watch
especially carefully for developments under California laws.

17

Income Tax Aspects of Software

Anyone may so arrange his affairs that his taxes shall be
as low as possible; he is not bound to choose that
pattern which will best pay the Treasury; there is not
even a patriotic duty to increase one's taxes.

Judge Learned Hand in Helvering v. Gregory,
69 F2d 809, 810 (1934).

THE BACKGROUND TO INCOME TAX LAW

Nobody likes to pay income taxes, especially those that can be avoided by advance planning. Software is treated differently under the federal income tax laws than most other business assets. So are the authors of software. For this reason, anyone involved in writing, publishing, or acquiring software needs to know something about the federal tax treatment of software. This chapter will provide you with a framework in which to plan, and could save you time and money.

A single chapter like this can only touch on the major income tax themes affecting software. Federal income tax law applies to all individuals, partnerships, corporations, and other business organizations operating in or from the U.S. State income tax laws tend to follow the general principles of Federal law, but vary drastically from state to state; so this chapter has no separate coverage of state law. When you complete the chapter, you will find additional resources in the Bibliography.

As with many other matters covered in this book, you can gain a good, general understanding from this material, but you should also use it to discuss your future business plans with your tax attorney or accountant. Determining the correct outcome of some of the complex legal and factual issues relating to federal tax law and the software industry is difficult. The cost of being wrong can be very high.

THE RANGE OF INCOME TAX ISSUES

The federal income tax law applies to software transactions in a number of contexts, and raises some interesting questions:

- First, how can you deduct or recover the cost of purchasing or developing software as a business operating expense? The answer varies, as we shall see in a moment, depending on a number of factors you may be able to control.

- Once you own the software, how do you determine the tax effects of selling, leasing, or licensing your software to others? The income received in such a case is often taxed at the higher ordinary income tax rates, rather than at the more desirable capital gains rates. Even if you cannot change the applicable rate, you may with a little planning be able to push the income and the tax into another year.

- Since growing businesses are often incorporated as they mature, what will be the effect of incorporation on your income taxes? There are some possible surprises here.

- Finally, what will be the effect of an outright sale of your software business or of the stock of your corporation? This presents some intriguing issues which neither you or your attorney may have considered, but which you should think about.

DEVELOPING OR PURCHASING SOFTWARE

Typically, you will decide that your business needs some software to accomplish a particular business application, such as an inventory-control system or an accounts-payable program. The software is then either developed in-house or purchased from an outside vendor. If acquired outside, it will either be licensed "off-the-shelf" or custom-developed for you as the end user. What income tax treatment is accorded to this type of transaction? Does it make any difference that you develop it for license or sale to others?

After a number of years of inconsistent positions, the IRS, in Revenue Ruling 60-20, established a set of tax guidelines which the developer or purchaser (or licensee) of the software can rely upon. Essentially, the ruling differentiates between software purchased from third parties, software leased or licensed with continuing payments, and software actually developed by the taxpayer. Some recent pronouncements of the IRS, discussed below, originally cast doubt on the viability of this old ruling, but in April, 1983, the IRS reconfirmed its position.

Software Development Costs

If you develop software yourself, whether for use in your business or for sale to others, the IRS gives you two alternatives for recovering the software development costs. Since these costs are considered research and development expenses under Internal Revenue Code (IRC) § 174, they are a business expense deductible in either of two ways:

- The entire cost of such development may be deducted, currently each year, as provided in Section 174(a); or

- Alternatively, the IRS allows the costs to be set up as an asset on the books (capitalized) and then deducted (amortized) over a five-year period, or such lesser period as you can show to be reasonable.

Once you elect one or the other method, you may not, according to Revenue Ruling 71-248, change the method of accounting for these costs without IRS approval. Remember also that you can only make a choice if all of the costs attributable to such development are consistently treated, both *during* the year and *from* year to year.

Accounting Treatment. From an accounting standpoint, the different effect of the two possible choices could be critical. Expensing the software costs annually, as developed, reduces reportable income during the development period, while capitalizing the costs creates an asset on the balance sheet of the business, which can then be written down over the period of time during which the software is sold or licensed. The U.S. Securities & Exchange Commission has proposed that publicly-held companies not be allowed to capitalize internally-developed software. This has created a stir in the industry since some companies do show software development costs as assets on their balance sheets, while others do not. The Financial Accounting Standards Board (FASB) issued, in late 1984, a detailed proposal. Each software developer should carefully consider the effect of these rules, since they can change reported earnings substantially, which can in turn affect the value of the business.

Amortizing Purchased Software

There is no election to be made in the case of software purchased outright. The cost of such software *must* be capitalized and amortized over five years, or such lesser period as the taxpayer can justify. The IRS guidelines for determining the number of years to be used (called ACRS) do not apply to software, so the actual useful life of the software is the determining factor. In spite of this rule, most purchases of software costing under $1,000 are written off in the year of purchase as current operating expenses.

To a software publisher who purchases a major computer program for the purpose of marketing it, this rule means that the cost of such software must be treated as the acquisition of an intangible asset and recovered by annual amortization deductions over a period of years. With the rapid changes in microcomputer software marketing, some software packages may have a useful life of less than five years.

Furthermore, once the purchased software package is set up as an asset, under the IRS rulings, all additional developments and enhancements have to be capitalized and then amortized over a further period of years. This would seem to present some consistency problems to a company which both develops and purchases software, since the rulings require consistency in treatment of software costs. There is no definitive answer to this difference in treatment.

Currently the IRS appears to recognize but one exception to the requirement of amortizing software purchased. In a 1981 letter ruling, the IRS concluded that where custom software is ordered and paid for on a progress payment basis, and where all the risk of successful completion of the project lies with the purchaser, the costs incurred may be deducted on a current basis. There are earlier rulings that seem to conflict with this, especially where the risk of completion is not with the buyer. Thus, if you desire current deductibility of custom software, it may be possible to structure the contract in such way as to do so.

Deducting Periodic Lease or License Payments

Where software is leased or licensed with a continuing, periodic payment due, the IRS rulings permit the cost of such lease of license payments to be deducted on an annual basis as rental payments under Section 162 of the Internal Revenue Code. If you are merely using the software as part of your business, this makes good accounting sense. But in the case of a software publisher, the fact that such continuing expense is deductible does not settle how the initial downpayment or usual "front-end" money to an author is to be treated.

Most software authors try to obtain an initial payment from the publisher for the right to publish and sublicense their software. After the initial payment, the publisher is usually obligated to pay further royalties on a per-copy-sold or licensed basis. It seems logical to treat the initial payment as just one of a series of continuing payments, and to deduct it in the year of payment. Again, in case of audit by the IRS, consistency in treatment of such amounts paid is of vital importance.

Combinations of Hardware and Software

On the other hand, the IRS requires that where software is purchased with hardware, and the software price is not separately stated, the hardware and software costs must be written off (depreciated) together over the useful life of the computer itself. In the case of expensive hardware with a useful life longer than the software, this could be disadvantageous to you as the purchaser since it would result in having to write off the software over a period longer than five years. But if the software is purchased bundled with a personal computer like the Corona or Columbia Data, the software and the computer itself could easily be depreciated within five years due to the rapid technological obsolescence of such small systems.

Computer hardware placed in service after 1980 must be depreciated using the IRS Accelerated Cost Recovery System (ACRS). This method applies accelerated methods of cost recovery over a fixed number of years and is applicable to most types of depreciable tangible property. According to ACRS classifications, computer hardware must be depreciated over not less than a five-year period. However, computer software, as such, does not fall within ACRS because it is an intangible asset. In the past several years the ACRS guidelines have been considered too liberal by Congress, so the write-off period for some equipment may eventually be lengthened. Check the current tax law to be sure, since proposals for 1985 would materially change or eliminate ACRS.

Tax Credits for Software
Acquisition and Development

In addition to depreciation (or amortization, which is essentially the same thing), businesses are entitled to take direct credits against the income tax otherwise payable, based upon the cost of purchasing equipment or for expenditures in the nature of research and development. These are called "Investment Tax Credits" and "Research and Development Credits." They are intended to encourage businesses to spend money on capital equipment and on research and development.

As this is being written, one of the hottest software issues is whether the cost of development of computer software is entitled to the 25% research and development tax credit permitted by Section 44F contained in the 1981 Economic Recovery Tax Act. From income taxes otherwise due, this law permits a deduction of 25% of the increase in actual expenditures (over a base period) for the development of computer software.

Until recently it was assumed by tax advisors that all software development fell within the provisions of this very favorable law. However, the IRS has suggested in proposed regulations under IRC § 174 that a taxpayer would only be entitled to the credit for software development if there were some doubt as to its success. The proposed change is aimed at preventing use of the credit for upgrading existing software or the development of routine applications software. This IRS position has created an uproar in Congress, which believes the tax credit should be more widely applicable, and the final outcome is not yet clear. Because of the substantial tax benefit of this credit, the software developer should carefully consider it in every situation. Changes may occur in 1985.

Research and Development Partnerships.   The eligibility of software as the object of research and development partnerships is beyond the scope of this chapter. However, you should be aware that there are many unresolved questions in this area, which are affected by the preceding discussion and many other thorny and undetermined issues. Be very careful to seek highly specialized and experienced tax counsel before entering into a research and development partnership.

Regular Investment Tax Credit.   Earlier rulings, such as Revenue Ruling 71-177, have made clear that the regular 10% investment tax credit is available for the cost of software that is purchased with a new computer, where the cost of the software is not separately stated. However, software purchased separately does not qualify for any regular investment tax credit because this is available only for tangible personal property with a useful life of three years or more ("qualified Section 38 property"). The IRS, in Regulation § 1.48-1(f), has taken the position that software is intangible property and therefore not qualified.

INCOME TAX ON THE SALE OR LICENSING OF SOFTWARE

Royalty income from licenses permitting the use of software has always been considered ordinary income in the same sense as rental income, whether it was earned by the author or some third party. The same rule applies if a copy of the software is "sold." However, following the tax rules in other similar fields, such as patent tax law, you would think that income from the outright sale of all rights to a computer program would result in the more favorable capital gains treatment. Wrong.

Generally No Capital Gains Treatment for Software

Generally speaking, all income received by the developer or author of copyrighted material, such as software, is always treated as ordinary income, whether based on an outright sale of all rights or on the income from a license. Since software is almost universally copyrighted and copyright protection in the U.S. is automatic unless the author intentionally avoids it, this creates a tax inequity for software authors, who would prefer to obtain capital gains treatment on the sale of all rights to the software. Long-term capital gains are taxed at a maximum 20% rate, and ordinary income at a maximum 50% rate.

Ordinarily, the owner of a valuable asset such as real property or most types of personal property is entitled to treat such assets as capital assets, with the result that sales proceeds from such property are capital gains. In fact, Section 1235 of the Internal Revenue Code specifically accords the owner of a patent long-term capital-gains treatment, without regard to the one-year holding period otherwise required, if the owner transfers all substantial rights in the patent or an undivided interest in all such rights. Thus an inventor who sells his patent, even though he bases the price on royalties to be paid him, obtains capital gains treatment for his inventive efforts.

No such luck for the author of software, or any other copyrightable work, because Section 1221(3)(A) and (C) of the Internal Revenue Code states that copyrights cannot be capital assets. Copyrighted software is not entitled to capital gains treatment when sold by "a taxpayer whose personal efforts created such property," nor by a taxpayer who has previously acquired the copyright by gift, nor in most tax-free transactions like an incorporation. Likewise, Section 1231(b)(1)(C) says such copyrights are not considered property used in the trade or business of the taxpayer, which may deny other benefits to the author.

These provisions are the legacy of what is known as the "Eisenhower Amendment," adopted by Congress in 1950 after General Eisenhower worked out a tax-based transaction involving the sale of his book "Crusade In Europe". This transaction resulted in his receiving several million dollars in capital gains, instead of ordinary income. Congress decided from then on that since the income from writing was similar to the type of income that other workers earn, authors should not be entitled to capital gains treatment.

Exceptions to the Rule.   However, if a seller is someone who purchased the rights from the software author for value, then that seller may be entitled to capital gains if he or she is not engaged in the trade or business of selling or licensing software. Conversely, if a seller is engaged in the software business, then the amounts received are treated as ordinary income. The difference is because the first seller is considered to have a capital asset in the form of a computer program, while the second seller is deemed to have the program in inventory as an asset held for sale in the course of business.

In spite of these confusing rules, it is clear that the income of a business entity which has its employees create copyrighted programs is entitled to capital gains treatment on the sale of such works *where all rights to the program are sold,* unless the business is engaged in the trade or business of buying and selling programs, in which case this is treated as ordinary income. In this latter instance, such a business will also incur ordinary income if nonexclusive licenses are granted or copies of the software are sold. Most software houses, even those whose employees are also partners or shareholders, will be treated as a seller who is not the author or the author's donee. There are some unusual exceptions, several of which are discussed below, such as the Section 341 problem.

Timing Considerations.   You should always consider the timing of receipt of taxable income, since you may be able to defer or otherwise reduce income taxes. Even if the royalties or selling price are to be treated as ordinary income, it may be in your best interest to provide in a license that the licensee may commence use immediately but pay the license fee in January of the following year. Or, if you expect the current year's income to be materially lower than next year, take the income in the present year when your tax rates should be lower. Your accountant should help you plan this strategy.

THE EFFECT OF INCORPORATING A SOFTWARE BUSINESS

As a software business grows, it will probably wish to incorporate in order to limit liability and to more easily raise working capital from shareholders. This can ordinarily be accomplished in a tax-free transaction under Section 351 of the Internal Revenue Code. Such transfers are not subject to tax if the owners of the original business receive solely stock or securities in the corporation, and if, immediately after the exchange of stock for the assets, they are in control of the corporation.

While there is no conclusive authority, it is generally believed that the contribution for stock of all rights in existing computer software is considered transfer of property, which will qualify as a tax-free incorporation. One 1980 letter ruling permitted software to be treated as property in such a transaction, and many software companies have been so incorporated in the past few years. There are, however, some other problems here to be considered.

Personal Holding Companies

One issue often overlooked by lawyers, accountants, and their business clients, is that there is a good chance that a software house, which is incorporated by the authors of its software, will be considered a "personal holding company" under IRC Section 543. Most of the income of such a software corporation would be royalties from the sale or licensing of the software. The undistributed income of a personal holding company is taxed at a special penalty rate, imposed on top of the regular corporate income tax. This is a highly technical tax trap, which should be avoided at all costs.

A personal holding company is a corporation in which 50% or more of the stock is owned by five or fewer persons during the last six months of the taxable year, and as to which corporation at least 60% of adjusted gross income is personal holding company income. Copyright royalties can be personal holding company income. This is an extremely complex and detailed issue beyond the scope of this book.

There is serious question whether Congress intended software companies to come under this punitive tax, but there is virtually no guidance available on how to avoid it. Some day Congress may change or clarify the law. Until it does, bear this possibility in mind when incorporating a software business, since the consequences could be a disastrous additional tax, litigation, or both.

Collapsible Corporations

Once the corporation is set up and the owners decide to sell the stock held by them to a third party, there are still other traps lying in wait for them. One such trap is called the "collapsible corporation," created by the provisions of IRC § 341. If the corporation meets the definition, and otherwise falls under § 341, the shareholders owning 5% or more of the stock will receive ordinary income treatment on the proceeds of the sale of their stock, instead of the capital gains they expected. A similar result may follow from liquidating the corporation.

A collapsible corporation is one formed principally to construct or produce certain types of assets (called "Section 341 Assets") such as movies or other intellectual property, which have the potential for producing large amounts of ordinary income from rents or royalties. If the corporation is liquidated or the stockholders sell within three years after acquiring the § 341 assets, the company is presumed to have been formed to avoid tax, and capital gains treatment is denied. In a 1974 case, Computer Sciences Corp., the IRS took the position that computer programs are Section 341 assets but lost; there is reason to believe the IRS may try again. There are exceptions and a number of complex rules that might avoid this tax disaster, but they are beyond the scope of this book.

Holding Period for Capital Gains

Even if the provisions of Section 341 do not apply to the sale of your stock in a software corporation, you might still have an unpleasant surprise when you sell your stock. Under the capital gains provisions, IRC § 1222(3), you must ordinarily have held the asset sold for more than six months, if acquired after June 22, 1984. Normally, the period you owned the computer program transferred to the corporation on incorporation would be added to the time you held the stock, for purposes of determining if you have met the six-month holding period. This is not the case where the author of software exchanges it for stock under § 351. Since computer software is neither a capital asset nor Section 1231 property, if you as the author exchange it for stock, then the holding period of the stock starts over again on the day you receive it. You must, therefore, hold the stock for more than one year if acquired by June 22, 1984 or six months if after that date in order to obtain capital gains treatment, no matter how long you owned the computer software before the incorporation.

SUMMARY

Federal and state income taxes can play nasty tricks on your pocketbook and your software company's balance sheet, if you do not plan carefully and have sound legal and accounting advice *before* you engage in any major transaction. Some of these laws appear to be biased against the owner of copyrights and other intangible property like software. Tax laws are very complex, sometimes downright punitive, and always changing. Due to the drastic changes proposed in 1985 for federal tax laws, you should be very careful to check on the current state of the law as it may differ from these comments made in 1984.

Any transaction involving the sale, license, or development of software should be looked at from an income tax viewpoint before you sign any documents. You may be able to create a large deduction or tax credit if you handle a purchase or sale correctly. Deferral of income is sometimes possible, where desirable.

Should you be considering incorporation, reorganization, or other changes in your business structure, it is vital that you plan in advance. Many such changes can be handled with little or no resulting income tax, but once the steps are taken it may be impossible to correct the adverse effects of taxable transactions.

Assume that every major transaction involving software has important income tax consequences, and you will never be sorry.

18

Copyright Infringement Remedies

THE SCOPE OF COVERAGE

No discussion of software protection would be complete without an analysis of the remedies available to a copyright owner under the U.S. Copyright Revision Act of 1976. Unfortunately, the moment your software is generally available, someone will probably copy it illegally. Therefore, once you as the author or publisher have completed the necessary steps for copyright registration, it will be natural for you to want to know how to counteract such infringement or illegal activity.

The subject can be very complex and would require a lengthy discussion of all the nuances if it were to be presented in detail. I have, therefore, chosen to provide you here with a summary of the key legal issues and the various remedies available to prevent and compensate for copyright infringements. The index at the back of the book will also lead you back to parts of other chapters where you can find additional answers to your questions about infringements.

For lawyers and judges interested in a much more detailed legal treatment of the subject, there are several other sources. In the bibliography for this chapter, I have listed a number of recent legal publications gathered from seminars and elsewhere, including an extensive, continually updated legal memorandum of my own, which is available from my office as listed in the bibliography.

THE LEGAL RIGHTS
OF THE COPYRIGHT OWNER

Once you have complied with the detailed requirements of the 1976 Copyright Act, there should be some material benefits to reward your efforts. There are, and these can be very effective in the case of a commercial copyright infringement. However, with individual infringers, these remedies are often too costly and impractical to utilize them.

The Basic Rights

First, it is important to remember what constitutes an infringement of the copyright on your program. Section 106 of the Copyright Act gives you, as the owner of a copyright, the exclusive right:

- To make copies of the copyrighted work.
- To make derivatives or follow-on types of works, including translations and new versions.
- To distribute copies of the work, by the sale or other transfer of ownership, or by lease, rental, or loan.
- To perform the work publicly in the case of a play, for example.
- To display the work publicly in the case of a painting, for example.

The Software Exception
in the Copyright Act

The major exception to these exclusive rights is Section 117, which gives the "owner of a copy of a computer program" the right to make or authorize the making of another copy or adaptation of that computer program if this copy is essential to the use of the program or if it is for archival purposes. The original and all copies must be transferred to the new owner of the original copy of the program when that is sold or otherwise transferred to someone else. However, the adaptations cannot be transferred without the copyright owner's permission.

An Example of Infringement

If I license a copy of a computer program from its publisher, all I can do with it is use it myself. I cannot reproduce it nor distribute copies of it to the public, not even to my friends, without infringing the copyright of the owner. Nor can I use more than small portions of the source or object code to create my own programs for public distribution, since the use of portions of the original work together with my additions would constitute a prohibited derivative. Use of the "library" of a compiler is an exception.

Likewise, I cannot translate the program and documentation into another computer language (or a foreign language) for redistribution without infringing the copyright of the owner. It appears from Section 117 that I could translate or "adapt" the program for my own use without infringing the copyright, but I could not transfer title or the right to use the modified version.

How Much Can You Copy?
The IBM BIOS Issue

Everyone in the computer industry is painfully aware that is is nearly impossible today to market a personal computer that is not "IBM compatible." To manufacture an IBM-compatible computer requires that the manufacturer duplicate the functionality of the IBM BIOS, which is in Read-Only-Memory (ROM) and copyrighted. Since IBM has sued four manufacturers in the U.S. and one in Canada for duplicating too much of this code, and subsequently settled with permanent injunctions, it is not presently clear just how far you can go in creating a "compatible" machine.

To better understand this, you may want to review Chapter 8, which discusses in some detail the idea/expression dichotomy. The important point to remember is that you are not an infringer if you only copy the idea expressed in a copyrighted work. The problem, however, is that in creating a compatible computer it is necessary to use the same locations in memory for some functions and to perform certain functions exactly the same way that IBM does. Otherwise, the programs written for the IBM PC will not run on your own computer.

Compatibility between the IBM PC and your own computer may require that some of the assembly language code used in the latter be, line for line, almost identical to the code used by IBM in its published BIOS. If this cannot be avoided through lack of an alternative, then the identical lines are not deemed an instance of infringement but merely functional. However, if there *are* alternative ways to derive compatibility, then copying the code does become an infringement. This is a tough legal problem, which cannot be resolved except on a case-by-case basis.

Renting Software—Licenses
versus Outright Sales

Even under Section 117, there are some subtle differences between the rights of an "owner" of a copy of a program and those of a "licensee" of a program. When you carefully read the software license form which comes from most major software companies, you will see that you have not purchased ownership of the copy of the software, but only acquired a license to use that copy under the specific terms of the license. That license probably restricts you to use of the program on one computer at a time. It may restrict the number of copies you may make and may impose other conditions. It probably also restricts your right to transfer the software to others. This is the only way the copyright owner can place restrictions on the "owner" of a copy of the software.

The First Sale Doctrine

These restrictions and the licensing concept, discussed in Chapter 11 on License Agreements, are necessary because of what, under the copyright law, is called the "first sale" doctrine. Section 109(a) of the Copyright Act provides that once a copy of a copyrighted work is sold and title to it passes to the purchaser, that purchaser may thereafter dispose of it as he or she wishes. Therefore, if you wish to control subsequent use of your computer program, you must not sell copies of it but instead must lease or license the use of it.

While reselling a copy of software that you have purchased is not an infringement, selling a copy that was licensed to you with prohibitions against resale is an infringement. Yet, in both cases it is clearly an infringement to *duplicate* either a purchased or a licensed copy and to distribute those copies. Whether an infringement has truly occurred will depend on whether the software was purchased, leased, or licensed, and on the terms of any license restrictions.

WHO IS AN INFRINGER?

An infringer is someone who, without authority from the copyright owner and without a license, exercises one or more of the rights reserved to the owner by Section 106, as modified by Section 109 in the case of sales or Section 117 in the case of computer programs. However, if the person exercising these rights does have a license, then that person is not an infringer so long as he or she is abiding by the restrictions of that license.

If your company has set up its licensing forms and distribution network properly, you will have preserved these rights. Should someone attempt to commercially exploit your program product, you can stop that person with a copyright infringement action in the U.S. District Court. If you can prove your case, you can recover damages at least equal to the *profit* earned by the infringer, if not *all* the revenues received by the infringer in the process of infringing your rights.

PROVING AN INFRINGEMENT CASE— THE THREE ELEMENTS

If you have complied with the formalities of the Copyright Act outlined in Chapters 5 through 8, you are entitled to file an infringement suit against the infringer. You should win that suit, and successfully remedy the infringement, if you and your attorney can prove just three elements at the time of trial. Sections 501 through 510 of the Copyright Act provide all your remedies and most of the rules to be followed during the case.

- *First,* you must establish your ownership of the copyright and the fact that you have registered a copy of your software with the Copyright Office. This is accomplished by providing the court with a certified copy of your registration certificate. Under the provisions of Section 411, registration is a prerequisite to bringing an infringement action. You are presumed to be the owner of the copyright by virtue of the registration certificate having been issued to you.

- *Second,* you need to show that copying of your work has actually occurred. In some cases this is easy, such as where there has been a direct or verbatim copy. It is for this reason that you should place serial numbers, initials, and other identifying features in all of your software, since few pirates will take the time to look for such methods of identification or to remove them. These safeguards make proof of copying elementary. (See Chapter 8 for some examples of the value of this technique in the case of videogames.)

  If the copying has been less direct and obvious, perhaps by means of paraphrasing your program, then the task of proving your case gets tougher. In this situation, you must prove that the defendant had access to your copyrighted material and that what he or she produced is similar in appearance or pattern to your work. The clear impression of someone looking at your original work and the infringing work must either be that they are the same, or that they are likely to have come from the same source. This may require expert and highly technical testimony as to the similarities between the two works.

- *Third,* if you have satisfied the requirements of the first two elements of your case, you must then show damages to your business by reason of the copying. In copyright cases, damages are awarded on the basis of your lost profits or, where the infringer cannot show what his costs were, *all* the revenues earned by the infringer from selling or licensing your software. All you have to do is show how much the infringer took in, and then it is up to the infringer to show what his costs were.

THE SPECIFIC REMEDIES AVAILABLE

Briefly, your specific remedies are these:

- An immediate preliminary and, later, a permanent injunction that will put a stop to the continuing infringement.
- Damages for the profits you lost and the money the infringer made.
- Recovery of your attorney fees and costs of the lawsuit.

Seeking an Injunction

The first thing you want to do when you have proof that someone has been illegally copying and selling (or licensing) your program to others is to quickly put a stop to these actions by obtaining a court order in the form of an injunction. There is a good chance that the infringer will go to jail or be heavily fined if he ignores the injunction. The effect of an injunction can be devastating to the infringer, and it often puts a stop to the whole case at this point.

If you have a strong case of obvious copying, your attorney may be able to obtain a temporary restraining order or even a preliminary injunction against the defendant, shortly after the case is filed. An injunction normally lasts until the case is over. Although there are good tactical and legal reasons for not seeking a preliminary injunction in some cases, preliminary injunctions are very effective in a fast-moving market like software, because by the time the case comes to trial the market will have moved on.

If you don't choose to seek a preliminary injunction, the defendant can continue licensing your software until the trial is over. But if he or she does so, and you win the case, you will then be entitled to money damages for the wrongful actions, as well as a permanent injunction.

Money Damages

Where you prevail in the litigation, you are entitled to recover the money you lost because of the infringement, plus any additional profits made by the infringer. You have a choice between these so-called "actual damages," or a special kind of damages which the court awards you as punishment to the infringer for the unlawful activities; these are called "statutory damages." Statutory damages can be very large, sometimes in the hundreds of thousands of dollars. In a case where five programs were copied and sold commercially, MicroPro International and Digital Research obtained a judgment for $250,000, plus attorney fees and interest.

As statutory damages, the court may award you any sum between $250 and $10,000 for all infringements of any one program, "as the court considers just." If you can show that an infringement was committed willfully, then the award can be for an amount up to $50,000. Conversely, if the court believes the infringement occurred innocently, damages for all infringements of the one work can be as low as $100. Like most laws, there are some exceptions to these rules.

Limits on Recovery

An important limitation is that you cannot recover statutory damages or attorney fees if an infringement of your work occurred before it was registered with the Copyright Office, unless you registered it within three months of publication. This rule exists to encourage people to file promptly for registration. If you were late is registering, you must prove the actual damages incurred by your business in order to recover any money. The amount of the actual damages will depend not so much on what the judge or jury does or thinks, as on the quality and quantity of evidence presented by you and your attorney.

Attorney Fees

Finally, if you registered your work before the infringement occurred, and if you win your case, then you are entitled to recovery of "reasonable" attorney fees and the court costs of your lawsuit. These fees can be considerable, since litigation is expensive. The amount you receive may be less than your actual costs, however, since the sum recoverable is determined by the judge. Very rarely does a *defendant* in a copyright case recover any attorney fees, even when he wins. The few awards of legal fees to defendants involved cases where it was obvious that the plaintiff brought a lawsuit in bad faith, knowing that he or she had a poor or nonexistent case.

WHAT IS THE COST OF BRINGING AN INFRINGEMENT ACTION?

As a businessperson, you will need to know what the likely cost of all this litigation can be. There are two answers to this: nothing (except a lot of your time) if you win and the court awards you all your actual attorney fees and costs; or a lot of money in the form of your own legal fees (and your time) if you lose.

Typical Legal Costs

The average, fairly simple infringement lawsuit including a one or two-day trial will probably result in legal fees of $20,000 to $40,000. These fees would cover not only the trial itself, but also conferences between you, your employees, and experts, and other investigation time, plus the preliminary proceedings and court appearances that usually precede trials.

This probably seems like a lot of money for a couple of days of trial proceedings, but the actual time spent by your attorney could be hundreds of hours, as he or she investigates, prepares pleadings, does legal research, and makes court appearances. Your attorney will also spend a great deal of time with you and your programmers, trying to understand exactly what has been copied or otherwise misused. Software copyright infringement cases are often much more difficult to try than those involving books or other media.

Court Costs and Other Expenses

The out-of-pocket costs in such litigation can also be considerable, since such cases often require the services of computer and legal experts to interpret the evidence for the judge. If the witnesses or parties are from different parts of the country, the travel and lodging costs can mount up quickly, too. You always need to think about the value of your own time, and that of other company personnel, since you cannot be out selling software or managing your company when you are in court or educating your attorney about the technical aspects of software and its misuse.

Out-Of-Court Settlements

If you successfully obtain a preliminary injunction before the trial, then the case will often be settled without an actual trial, because the defendant infringer is now unable to continue to distribute the infringing software. In such case, the parties may agree upon a negotiated license from the plaintiff to the defendant. Under an agreed license, as the plaintiff you would be paid royalties for past sales by the defendant, and for continuing use of your software by the defendant.

Alternatively, the defendant might offer to pay a lump sum to you as the plaintiff, in order to get you to drop the lawsuit and reduce the risk of having to pay you damages and attorney fees if you win. This happened in 1984 in the Apple-Franklin case, after Franklin had lost in the Court of Appeals and before the Supreme Court could hear the case. Franklin decided to pay Apple $2.5 million and agreed to rewrite the Apple-compatible operating system it had used on the Franklin microcomputer. Most of this money was probably eaten up by the legal fees which Apple paid to take the case to the point of settlement. But Apple won in what proved to be litigation that set a precedent for future software copyright cases.

Losing the Case

The down side is that if you lose your case, you will have to pay your own legal fees and probably the court costs of the defendant, as well. It is rare for the plaintiff to have to pay the legal fees of the defendant, unless the plaintiff's case was totally unreasonable from the start. You should remember, however, that you will have to advance sufficient legal fees to pay your attorney until the case is over, even if you expect to win, unless you previously arranged to have the case handled on a contingent fee basis. Be sure you carefully investigate apparent infringements, because in more than one case what looked like an infringement was not. A case like that could be very embarrassing, not to mention expensive.

DEFENSES AGAINST COPYRIGHT INFRINGEMENT CASES

Obviously, a defendant will try to put up strong defenses against your assertion of copyright infringement. These defenses can range from the claim that you do not legally own the software copyright in question to a complex series of antitrust arguments. The imagination of defense counsel is almost unlimited.

One of the hazards of bringing a lawsuit is that the defendant can strike back by claiming that you or your company did something illegal or in violation of a contract. Such assertions, called "cross-complaints," can add to the complexity of the lawsuit and confuse some of the issues. It is becoming almost automatic for defendants in computer litigation to claim than plaintiffs have violated some antitrust law, or breached some agreement that may have had little to do with the actual infringement case. You need to anticipate these defensive reactions.

HOW LONG DO ALL THESE PROCEDURES TAKE?

At the outset even your trial attorney can probably only guess how long your infringement action might take. Once the lawsuit has been filed, preliminary testimony called "depositions" are taken, and only after your attorney has more information with which to evaluate the evidence can he or she give you a better idea as to the time involved.

While the majority of copyright infringement cases could be tried in several days, it often takes up to six months to get merely to the stage of the court actually issuing a preliminary injunction. This is because your attorney will methodically have had to gather the facts by interviewing you and others involved, prepare the papers to be filed with the court (called "pleadings"), and then take the testimony of at least some of the defendants—all this before he or she can even intelligently present the arguments for the preliminary injunction to the court. The court then often takes several weeks to act on the request for a preliminary injunction. Once the injunction is granted, it can take from several months in smaller communities to three or even five years in metropolitan areas to bring your case to trial. The trial courts of Los Angeles, New York or Chicago, for example, are incredibly clogged.

Frankly, most clients get very frustrated during this long process, since they see dollars being spent with little in the way of results until many months after the case commenced. One way to minimize this frustration is to insist that your attorney keep in regular communication with you during the whole process.

Always remember that you are the client and that it is your money being spent. You are entitled to know what is going on and to make decisions about whether to continue with the case or to settle it. At the same time, if you have selected a competent and experienced lawyer, he or she will be able to help you evaluate the alternatives. Many very fine lawyers settle more cases than they take to trial. Some lawyers in fact rarely try cases if a trial can be avoided, since they are acutely aware of the high cost of litigation.

REMEDIES FOR INFRINGEMENT
OF OTHER RIGHTS

While this chapter has not mentioned the possible remedies for violation of your trade secret rights, contracts, or patent infringements, these legal rights are also protected in similar ways. However, the laws relating to protection of trade secrets vary from state to state and are not as specific as copyrights. Patent and trademark infringement actions are fairly similar to copyright actions, but are governed by other statutes which were mentioned or listed in Chapters 9 and 10.

You should know, however, that allegations of infringements of patents, trade marks, contracts, licenses, and unfair competition are sometimes combined in the one lawsuit, where this is appropriate. Trade secret cases are harder to win, and contract cases are fairly routine but do not have the same preliminary remedies. Patent infringement cases tend to be very complex and expensive. In most situations, your software infringement case will be best served by relying on copyright law, supplemented by claims under the other applicable laws.

SUMMARY

If you think you have a possible copyright infringement on your hands involving one of your software products, the information in this chapter should enable you to collect the necessary facts so you can talk with your lawyer and decide what course of action to take. (You might also want to turn to Chapter 20, at this point, on selecting a lawyer for an infringement action.) Bear in mind that swift action is often the most effective deterrent to other infringers or persons contemplating copying.

If you want further helpful information on the legal aspects of prosecuting a copyright infringement case, the bibliography contains references to other books on this and related subjects. Books and articles will keep you alert to the changing aspects of this industry, the laws that apply to it, and the various remedies available. A subject as complex and dynamic as software protection is never going to stand still.

19

The Future Course of Software Protection

As computers become the printing presses of the twenty-first century, ink marks on paper will continue to be read, and broadcasts to be watched, but other new major media will evolve from what are now but the toys of computer hackers. Videodisks, integrated memories, and data bases will serve the functions that books and libraries now serve, while information retrieval systems will serve for what magazines and newspapers do now. Networks of satellites, optical fibers, and radio waves will serve the functions of the present-day postal system.

Ithiel de Sola Pool. *Technologies of Freedom,*
Belknap Press of Harvard University:
Cambridge, MA, 1983, p. 226.

SOURCES OF FUTURE CONFLICT

This prophetic quotation from a newly published book about the possible effects of the "Information Age" seems apt here for its vivid pictures of the course of future technology. It is reminiscent of George Orwell's earlier attempt to predict future life in *1984.* Today's continually exploding technology will strongly influence the software and computer industry for years to come.

Any technology growing this rapidly creates social changes, which in turn carry with them a need for the American legal system to grow. The key question is whether the law can expand and keep pace with the technology. One thing is abundantly clear—the economic value of software in a computer-based information age will not diminish, but increase. This will lead to more litigation and more need to define the extent of the shelter which the law can provide for software authors and publishers. It may also lead to major modification of copyright law, or to the creation of an entirely new body of "Information and Industrial Copyright" law to deal with electronic communication and information. Or it may prove that our legal system can adapt to technology better than it has during the first thirty years of the computer.

AREAS OF LEGAL CONCERN

While no one can accurately predict the specific areas of high technology that will create future legal problems, the present picture of major technologies indicates these four groups will constitute the next frontiers:

- **Computerized Input Technologies,** such as Optical Character Recognition (OCR) readers for ordinary printed text or even handwriting, voice-recognition systems, and data and program generators.

- **Data and Program Storage Devices** connected with, or used in, computers, such as bubble memories, laser disks, holograms, and, in the more distant future, molecular memories and molecular computational devices.

- **Computerized Output Devices,** such as video and printer output from computer/laser disk combination devices, computer-generated human speech systems, and, in the more distant future, direct electrochemical transfer of information to the human body from computer systems.

- **Communications Networks And Systems,** such as multiuser, multisite computer systems (based on what is currently a Local Area Network or LAN), which utilize small personal computers and sophisticated communications hardware to tie dozens of small computers together, regardless of their physical location.

The Roots of the Problem

Each of these four emerging technologies is bound to create new issues under copyright law and the other forms of intellectual property protection. Each is so new that the existing laws have no predetermined slot into which to fit them, and no analogue to which to compare them.

To find this fit for the four new technologies and the other scientific developments that are sure to follow, the whole orientation of the copyright laws will have to be changed to accommodate the essential intervention of the computer into human activities. There will have to be a recognition that human beings can generate and retrieve electronic information (through the use of the computer) that is never seen in traditional forms of human expression. To do this, the courts will have to deal with the twin questions of whether human authorship is involved and whether the human-authored instructions to a machine *become* the machine. Let's briefly review the historical basis of the problem.

Human Authorship and Readership. The copyright system was originally intended to protect "the writings of authors." The assumption was that a human being would do the writing *and* that a human being would do the reading. No one contemplated that machines could read and write, almost without human intervention.

Who Created the Information? The law protects the expression (writing) regardless of whether the information used by the computer is intended for human use or for machine use. If the copyright system is to protect electronic information, the courts will have to conclude that if human thought started the chain, all intermediate forms of the expression of information are protected, unless the expression is so machine-oriented that it is not a form of communication. So long as the information is intended for direct use by a human being, or for *indirect* human use through a machine communicating with a human, it is expression that should be protected by the copyright law. A human, not a machine, will lose legal rights unless all forms of electronic information are protected.

Software v. Machines. The stumbling block seems to be the point where human authored software has changed form so much that it is no longer software, but a machine. This was at the heart of the arguments in the Apple Computer cases, and is a legitimate and current legal issue in other cases involving microcode, now on appeal. By stating a specific series of instructions in a program, which are held copyrightable, the author of microcode could prevent anyone else from causing a machine (a computer, in this case) to take a particular action. If there is only one way of writing the microcode, that author would, in effect, be obtaining a patent on the machine process without the normal patent examination procedures. The issue is not an easy task for the courts, since there is a point where the software is so specific in its instructions to the machine that the program and the machine merge. In reality, there are very few situations where this could occur. This should be the legal question on which protection turns, and not whether the software is intended for machine use versus human use.

Electronic Communication. As Professor Pool has so accurately pointed out in the above quotation, society is no longer dealing with the written or printed word, but with electronic information and images created and communicated from point to point by computers. It will no longer be clear who the author is, whether electronic images are human authorship, or even *if* there is an author, within the definition of the copyright laws. The newer forms of electronic media which will hold or transmit computer programs, such as laser disks, read-only memories, and optical fibers will make it even less clear.

The guiding principle must be to protect the intellectual efforts of human beings from misappropriation, and not to focus on whether the form in which the data is communicated or stored is human readable or directly human usable. Virtually all the High Tech devices mentioned above are but "data carriers"—a form of electronic paper which can be read directly only by computers, but not by people. The mechanical intervention of a machine should not, and does not, make electronic information any less human authorship.

In a future computer age it may be that humans will eventually give up all use of handwritten and printed materials, and rely entirely on electronic information and communication, because of the computer's superior ability to move, sort and retrieve the information in this fashion. Only time will tell, but the law will have to adjust.

FUTURE SCENARIOS AND THE LAW

Each of the four areas of new technology listed above represent possible future legal disputes. In each is an element where the computer intervenes so strongly that it is not clear either who the author is, or whether the computer has taken over so completely that the program and the computer merge as one.

Examples that Defy the Legal System

The following hypothetical examples are particularly intriguing, because it is doubtful that anyone could accurately predict how they would be dealt with by the American legal system.

Example 1: Input Technology. Suppose, for a moment, that voice-recognition devices were perfect enough that a programmer, using only his voice, could dictate and test a computer program to control a robot used for household chores. There would be no record of his voice, as such, since the computer would interpret his instructions directly into object code. All the information would exist in electronic form, and its sole purpose would be to control a machine. The program is not designed to communicate anything to a human, although the robot would be used by humans and could be instructed by them.

Is this a literary work, a "writing" protected under the copyright laws? Is it a patentable machine, when even the inventor of it cannot tell you how it was done, since the computer did it by interpreting the inventor's instructions? And yet, given the trouble that the inventor went to, shouldn't the work be protected from someone copying the object code and selling it in competition with the inventor/author?

Example 2: Program Storage Devices. Imagine, somewhere in the future, that someone invents a computer that can develop reproducible three-dimensional holograms stored on laser disks. This would be based on input from an artist who places the image in front of the machine, and controls the colors and dimensions of the image by moving his hands *near* control panels that modify the actual image recorded by the computer. The image is now reproducible at will, by merely "playing it" as one would a phonograph record.

Is the laser disk an audiovisual work, a computer program, or a pictorial, graphic, or sculptural work, under the copyright laws? There is no writing, the artist never touched the work, and yet it is the artist's "programming" of the computer that allows it to be reproduced. How, if at all, will the laser disk be protected? There are no cases holding that laser images, which do not exist until reconstructed on a monitor or screen, are copyrightable. Perhaps, in this example, no program would even exist, since the laser disk simply has the data necessary to construct the holographic image. Who is the author/artist of this image, the computer or the human being?

Example 3: Output Devices. Assume that ten years from today it is possible to make a direct transfer of information from various state-of-the-art memory devices to the human brain, by use of a small electrical device that fastens to your wrist. This device creates nerve impulses, which your body receives through the skin, and direct images of the information are reproduced in your brain. Because of the immense amount of storage possible on laser disks, all the worlds' literature and written information (including computer programs) is stored in the system, for instant retrieval over satellite links connected to the computer storage.

How do we pay the authors of electronic information on this system for use of the system? Is the author in fact entitled to any royalty, since there is no output that can be "seen" or perhaps even measured? Assume, for the moment, that the images created in Example 2 were available on this system. Are they protected in this example? Realizing that no such image ever exists, except in the receiver's mind, is there a fixation of the author/artist's work sufficient to satisfy the copyright laws? It would seem on the face of it that there are "copies" of things on this system, but there is no way anyone can perceive them without the direct nerve transfer device. How do you make a copyright law deposit in order to register the work?

Example 4: Communications Networks. Unlike the previous hypothetical cases, this example is already at hand. Today, it is possible to have one copy of a computer program physically recorded on a hard disk drive on a computer located in New York, which can be used by anyone connected to the telephone system anywhere in the world. The user, say, in Monterey, California, can either submit data to the computer in New

York over the phone and receive the results at home on a screen; or the user can ask the New York computer to "down-load" the actual copy of the program to the user's disk drive, where it can thereafter be used time and again wthout being reloaded. Once the program is on a hard disk, there is no technological means presently known to prevent a licensee of a microcomputer program from down-loading.

How do software houses license programs in this situation? They have no control over software once it leaves a store, and most of these communications networks leave no record of how and when programs are used or remotely accessed. Virtually anyone in the world who has access to a computer, disk drive, and communications capabilities can take advantage of this technology, if permitted access to the network.

This is not a question of piracy but of practical business facts. Once the software house has licensed the one base user, in this example, literally thousands of people can download and use the software without payment of further license fees or royalties. The only known remedy is to take legal action against the owner of the base system that has the copy of the program, but you must prove he or she has it and that others have accessed the program without your permission. For many software houses this may mean the difference between financial success and disaster.

Orwell Was Right.   George Orwell was right, in his novel *1984,* about the instant access of information to governments, but he overlooked the fact that the citizenry might also have access to the same communications network, which changes the problem of software protection drastically. The software industry awaits some solution to this potential disaster, brought about by its own industry.

HARDWARE AND SOFTWARE PROTECTION SCHEMES

Let's examine, briefly, what technological means may be available in software or hardware to physically protect the software from being copied illegally. Most such attempts have been technologically unsuccessful for a variety of reasons, and most consumers appear to resist them, aggressively. Such devices must either be in or connected to the hardware, or be an integral element of the software.

Hardware Protective Devices

For years mainframe manufacturers have serialized the software and placed a corresponding serialized hardware device in the computer system, which must be present and operating for the software to work. Unfortunately, when dealing with small microcomputers and mass distributed software the element of control of the hardware and software environment is missing, so the software must either be recorded in such manner that it cannot be copied or accessed (except for legitimate use) or it must be tied to a serial number or code that is input by the user or by other software.

Software Locks

Currently, there are a number of "software locks" available which preclude copying by the average user, but most such systems can be subverted if the user has the time and the equipment to discover the scheme being used. Many systems involve deliberate recording aberations, such as a nonstandard disk track, physically damaged media which confuse copying programs, or even hidden tracks and programs which the computer looks for before it will run the software. Other systems are coded and require the user to obtain a code number to use the software, or require use of two disks at the same time, one with a serial number and the other with the program or data.

The Need to Back Up Programs

Most of these schemes fail because they preclude making backup copies and they often preclude transferring the software to hard disk systems. Where the protection scheme works too well, the users revolt and license competitive software which is not protected. Furthermore, these systems are the target of computer hackers, who spend days or weeks trying to break them, and then broadcast or publish the solution to defeating them if they are successful. Most protection schemes are like locks, they work well with honest people but can be overcome by any professional willing to take the time.

Future Devices

There are a number of devices either on the market or in development which will probably defeat all schemes that rely on recording tricks, since it is theoretically possible to devise a machine that copies the flux reversals on the magnetic media, regardless of tracks, errors and the like. Perhaps the use of read-only laser disks will help somewhat. All existing schemes have significant drawbacks to universal use in place of legal remedies. Until an infallible technical solution is devised, the software industry will have to rely on legal remedies, and suffer from the imperfections of an imperfect legal system devised for imperfect humans.

Recent Cases

In recent years commercial, coin-operated disk copying machines (like a Xerox® machine) have been invented, which will copy anything placed in it. Mail order catalogs currently list cassette-tape copiers and game-cartridge copiers. In late 1983, in Atari v. JS&A Group, Inc. Atari was successful in obtaining an preliminary injunction against a game cartridge copier. However, the 1984 Supreme Court decision in Sony Corp. of America v. Universal City Studios, Inc. has considerably weakened the theory of "contributory copyright infringement" which might otherwise have served as a legal basis to stop the sale and use of these disk-copiers.

In the Sony case the Supreme Court held that a manufacturer of a device used for copying videotapes could not be held liable for contributing to copyright infringement unless the device was "unsuited for any commercial noninfringing use." This means that software publishers and authors may be unable to prevent the use of disk-copying devices, placed in libraries or computer stores, which can be used for copying commercially distributed disks. Unfortunately, there is no way for a software publisher to prove that such a device is intended only for infringing purposes. This issue is bound to be litigated in the next few years, along with the others posed in the hypothetical examples. The outcome, however, is not predictable.

SUMMARY

The only certainty about the effects of changing technology on the law of software protection is that there will be more changes in the law, more problems, more conflicts, and more compromises between the various players in the game. The changes in technology, which will not satisfy everyone, will lead to changes in the law, which will not satisfy everyone. They will be changes, however, that you should carefully watch, since they will strongly influence the economics of your business in future years.

20

Selecting a Lawyer for Your Software Business

We lawyers are always curious, always inquisitive, always
picking up odds and ends for our patchwork minds,
since there is no knowing when they fit into some
corner.

Charles Dickens, *Little Dorritt.*

CHAOS, CONFLICT AND COMPLEXITY

Let's face it, lawyers are not popular; most people go to them with the
same anticipation usually reserved for dentists. However, this need not be
the case. An experienced and competent lawyer can be of significant help
to a software business.

If your software business is like most high-technology enterprises, it
is growing rapidly and almost out of control. Often, the original
entrepreneurial management lacks business experience and has a genuine aversion to the complexity of the thousands of laws, rules, and
regulations created almost daily by government. Lawyers, on the other
hand, are trained to cope with chaos, conflict, and complexity. Many of
them seem to thrive on it. Some of them even find computers and technology challenging. These are the lawyers you want for your business.

DIFFERENT KINDS OF LAWYERS
FOR DIFFERENT PROBLEMS

Even though I am biased, since I have been a practicing lawyer for twenty-
six years, I agree that legal services are expensive, and that clearing

business decisions with legal counsel is a time-consuming process. But the alternatives—unhappy customers, protracted business disputes, government investigations, or litigation—are even more expensive and time consuming. Given the complexities of our society, there really is no reasonable alternative. There are, however, ways of using legal services that make the most of what you pay for and that allow you to exercise some control over the costs.

Lawyers as Specialists

It is not intuitively obvious that there are many different kinds of lawyers, and vastly different kinds of law firms. As the law has become more complex, lawyers have become specialists, rather than the generalists they were in Abraham Lincoln's day. This provides clients with more knowledgeable, but also more expensive lawyers. Because of their specialized knowledge, however, they can demand and receive higher legal fees than the average lawyer.

Law specialties may be substantive, like computer software law, or procedural, like trial law or lobbying activities. The disadvantage of specialist lawyers to business clients is that such lawyers tend to know less about the detailed operations of your business than a general business lawyer might. They are often unaware of the day-to-day problems you have to face. If you are worrying about your whole business, a tax specialist may only be concerned with minimizing your taxes, even if that is not the best business decision for you.

Full Service Law Firms

To avoid some of these problems, some "full service" law firms have grown up in the larger metropolitan areas. These firms, which start out small, add one specialist after another, as their clients' needs dictate, until they aggregate hundreds of lawyers in one firm. Such law firms become awesome (but very expensive) resources for specialized legal information. The high cost of such firms stems from the need to support highly paid specialists, administrators, clerical help, and prime office space.

To utilize such a firm for day-to-day legal advice rapidly becomes prohibitively expensive, since the client no longer has any control over who does the work, or even what is done. The secret is to use these big firms only when needed, and to know when they are required.

General Counsel

The type of lawyer that a typical small business has is often called its "General Counsel," which term recognizes that his or her role is one of providing day-to-day counsel on general matters as they arise. This lawyer is sometimes called "House Counsel" when employed directly by a company. Such lawyers, in-house or outside, work directly with management and call in specialists where necessary. If you don't have such a lawyer, the task of using lawyers properly must be worked out by you.

WHEN TO USE A LAWYER

It is hard to decide when to use your "General Counsel" to review or draft a contract. Numerous factors enter into such a decision. My feeling is that lawyers are least expensive when brought in at the beginning of a negotiation to give you advice on how you might best structure the contract transaction. Many times they can point out legal and practical flaws in a business contract well in advance of its implementation. At that stage, the cost of changing the contract will be minimal. Business lawyers can also point out what problems to look for in working out a deal. For example, what are the possible tax or antitrust implications, what alternative forms of business relationships are possible, or what copyright and intellectual-property considerations apply? You can then negotiate the business terms yourself, consulting by phone with your business lawyer if new developments come up. Then, when it comes to documenting the transaction, the lawyer is already apprised of your objectives and his drafting time is minimized.

Know What You Want from Your Lawyer

Legal time is most expensive when the transaction is not thought through in advance by the businessman, so that legal drafting has to be done over again and again. Costs accumulate when the business lawyer is only brought into the negotiations at the last moment and has to spend time understanding the situation before drafting documents. There are times when a transaction is so routine that a business lawyer becomes unnecessary, especially if a standard form has already been worked out with that lawyer for routine business arrangements. However, the cost of developing (or revising) any standard form should be considered a long-term investment, like the foundation of a building which is never seen once completed. This is where a specialist in software licensing and computer law can work well with your existing general business lawyer.

The effective use of legal time and talent is an important determinant of its ultimate cost. The way a lawyer is used by a business also depends on what talents and time are available within the company. When small companies start up, a good business lawyer may be used as though he or she were one of the company's full-time officers, since no one else may be available. As the company grows, a business lawyer's time should be used, instead, for consultations in advance of major projects, in a preventative law capacity, to review forms and procedures (like pricing or distribution agreements, when they are established or changed), and for drafting complex agreements which require considerable experience and legal training. Your own management personnel can otherwise handle many of the day-to-day negotiations, if they have the backing of your business lawyer and can go over knotty questions with him or her on the phone.

Selecting Specialists

Your business lawyer should be used to help determine when to call in the expensive specialists, like international tax lawyers, securities lawyers, and the like. A lawyer probably has many past contacts with such experts and can sometimes see the legal need for them before your company does. It is your lawyer's duty to know who a good specialist is in tax shelters, for example. Just as you would have your internist help you select a brain surgeon, you should use your business lawyer to select other lawyers.

Employing House Counsel

From time to time, other specialized counsel can be obtained as necessary for special problems. As the company grows you may wish to hire inside or "house" counsel, but do not be deluded into thinking that such assistance is inexpensive. It is not. Law firms run overhead (aside from lawyer salaries) of forty-five to fifty percent of income, and your company's associated costs of support of house counsel will be nearly as high. Your true costs of inside legal counsel will include many hidden items, like rent, books, seminars, secretaries, office furniture, phone systems, and fringe benefit expenses, which your lawyer or law firms now pay out of the legal fees they receive.

Planning Advice

Your lawyer's greatest value should be as a legal consultant and planner on all general matters, including software licensing and protection, acquisition negotiations for software and software companies, drafting, and bringing in specialists where necessary. If your lawyer does not have the necessary background in some of these areas, he or she has a professional obligation to obtain that experience elsewhere for you, rather than to learn it at your expense. In the long run, it is least expensive if most of your lawyer's time is used in direct consultation with you, and other company officers, in advance of major transactions. This is what is meant by preventative law.

Develop a Legal Services Plan

Establishment of an organized plan to provide legal services to any company over the years requires careful thought and judgment. Proper use of the lawyers you have, and those you "acquire" in various ways, will make a difference in cost and in the benefits you obtain from the dollars spent over the years.

LAWYERS WITH "PATCHWORK" AND "BATHTUB" MINDS

The earlier quotation from Charles Dickens describes the type of legal, "patchwork" mind you need in a good general business lawyer. Such people are extremely rare, but invaluable if you work in a fast-moving high-technology environment like the software business. They have the ability to learn quickly and solve problems creatively, they find change exciting, they are solution-oriented rather than problem-oriented, and their patchwork minds enable them to understand complex problems.

Good business lawyers need creativity, intelligence, integrity, interest, judgment, experience, and sound training. Because of the variety of legal issues facing a business, they also need what Judge Learned Hand once called "a bathtub mind." They have to be able to fill their heads with the facts immediately necessary, then pull the plug, scour away all recollection of the last problem, and then refill quickly for the next situation. It is just this quality that attracts good lawyers to business law work, and other talented attorneys to trial practice. Such lawyers are not easily found.

Finding Lawyers—All Are Not Created Equal

Speakers And Writers.   There is no one place to find such unusually talented people, but there are situations which tend to attract them. One of them is at seminars and conventions, where they may speak. Another source is from magazines and books, where they may exhibit what they have thought and written. All lawyers were not created equal. Some are good, some bad, and most average, but these types of situations will enable you to evaluate their true worth.

Ask Other Lawyers.   A second source for finding good lawyers is through other laywers you may know or meet during travel or in business negotiations. Good lawyers know instinctively how to spot other competent professionals, and they will usually share this information with anyone who seems genuinely interested. It is fruitful to keep in touch with such people, to write to them or seek them out at conventions, trade shows and similar gatherings.

Ask Others in Your Business.   Third, if you cannot find a good lawyer using the first two approaches, contact other business people in your field and ask them for their experiences with particular lawyers. You should be a bit wary if your business contacts recommend their own lawyers, since they are unlikely to tell you that the lawyer *they* selected is a dud. Ask them instead to tell you about lawyers they have dealt with on the other side of the table in negotiations or trials.

Select Experienced Lawyers.   Generally speaking, it's best to select the more senior and busier lawyer. Although they may be more expensive on an hourly basis, because they are busy they will often make better use of their and your time. It is the old saw that the busy person is always the one who can find time to do the necessary things.

COMPUTER LAW SPECIALISTS

When looking for a lawyer with experience and interest in the specific field of computer law and software, the problem is a great deal more difficult. There are, as yet, only a few hundred lawyers in this field who actually have the background and experience you need for your unique legal and business problems. As the field grows in interest and breadth there will be more lawyers specializing in software and computer law.

Questions to Ask a Computer Lawyer

Most computer lawyers are either patent lawyers or business lawyers with an interest in technology and an active curiosity. You should always ask a prospective computer lawyer how long he or she has had a computer. Lawyers unwilling or unable to at least use a computer for applications like word-processing, scheduling, legal research, or the like, would seem to be poor candidates to advise a high-technology business.

A second question to ask prospective computer lawyers is what trade and legal publications they regularly read. If they are too busy to do so, they are too busy to advise you. A third question to ask is whether they attend any trade shows or conventions in the computer fields they represent. If they don't, then it will be hard for them to advise a business in this field, because they will have no idea of the problems that can be expected or the coming changes in technology.

Computer Law Association

There is a professional organization of lawyers expressly interested in computer law, called the Computer Law Association, which now has nearly 1,000 members, many of whom are working inside companies in the industry or as outside legal counsel. While the CLA will not recommend lawyers to you, it will provide you with the names of any members in your general area of the country. The address of the CLA is 6106 Lorcom Court, Springfield, Virginia 22152.

Don't Forget to Talk to Your Existing
Business Lawyer

In your business you may have a business lawyer who has worked with you for a period of time. Just because you go into new fields, do not abandon the knowledge of your existing business lawyer. Sit down and discuss with him or her your strong feeling that you need more specialized knowledge in the software protection and licensing field, and ask for help in finding someone. Most computer lawyers are quite happy to work with your existing counsel, if there is a clear delineation of responsibility and authority, which only you, as the client, can create.

SUMMARY

This chapter has recommended striking a middle path: do not use lawyers unnecessarily for routine transactions, but do use them for more complex situations. It is patently absurd to assume that all of the legal matters of any small, medium, or large business need to be handled exclusively by lawyers; for one thing the cost would be immense. On the one hand, laypersons can do many of the things discussed in this book, at a cost much less than if you have to hire lawyers. On the other hand, using laypersons to draft complex software licensing agreements may represent suicidal risks for a business. Just apply common sense to your decisions, and ask your lawyer how to keep legal costs down.

Bring in a computer law specialist if your lawyer does not have the necessary knowledge or experience. You should not have to pay to educate your existing lawyer who has an obligation to get and give you the best legal help available.

I commenced and completed this book in the hope that it would provide the accurate information about this subject which is necessary for lawyers and their software clients to discuss software issues. I also hope the book will help programmers and software industry management to ask more intelligent legal questions and to recognize legal issues they might have otherwise missed.

The fundamental element of business is risk-taking and risk-spotting while in search of profit. It is up to you and your lawyer to balance the risks—but in the final analysis it is your money and your business, not your lawyer's. You have to make the decision each time. If this book helps you to do that, it has achieved its objective.

Glossary
of Computer Terms

Application Programs Computer programs written to perform a particular function or solve a set of problems, like word-processing or payrolls. WORDSTAR® and VISICALC® are examples.

ASCII American Standard Code for Information Interchange. The standard binary code used by manufacturers to represent letters, numbers, and punctuation in computers and in communications.

Assembly Language A programming language closely following machine language, except it uses mnemonics (ADD or JMP, for example) instead of numbers for instructions. Sometimes called an "Assembler."

BASIC Beginner's All-purpose Symbolic Instruction Code. The simplest of the so-called high-level languages. Available on nearly every computer system.

Binary Number A base two number system in which the only digits used are 1 and 0. They are usually represented in the computer by ON and OFF conditions of the electronic logic.

Bit A Binary Digit. Either a 1 or a 0. The lowest level of representation of numbers in a computer.

Bug An error in a computer program. Debugging is the process of finding such errors in a previously written program.

Byte A group of eight bits which the computer treats as a unit when representing numbers, letters, or punctuation. One byte of memory is needed to hold each character.

C A high-level computer language becoming very popular because of its transportability from one computer system to the next. Bell Labs developed this language for systems programming purposes.

CAD/CAM Computer-aided design/computer-aided manufacturing. Computer hardware and software used in a system to design and manufacture items through use of the computer.

Chip An integrated circuit logic component used in a computer. Usually manufactured from a small piece of silicon, hence the term "chip."

COBOL Common Business Oriented Language. A high-level language developed under government auspices in the late 1950's, used extensively for accounting-type programs.

Compatibility The ability of a computer to run programs written for another manufacturer's computer. An IBM PC compatible program would be one that will run on any computer with a hardware architecture similar to that of the IBM PC.

Compiler A computer program that is used to translate a high-level computer source language program into machine language or object code.

CPU The Central Processing Unit of a computer. The part that does the actual computing of numbers or comparing of values.

CRT A Cathode Ray Tube. The screen portion of any computer terminal on which the computer can display alphanumeric data.

Data Information used by the computer, which may be numbers, codes, letters, or punctuation marks. The computer processes data using instructions from a computer program or "software."

Disk Any of several forms of iron-oxide-coated circular magnetic disks used for external storage by the computer system. Sometimes called (depending on the form) a diskette, a floppy disk, a magnetic disk, a hard disk, or a Winchester disk. Data is recorded magnetically on the disk as it spins in the disk drive. Data on the disk can be erased and re-recorded in split seconds.

Firmware Software or computer instructions that are permanently stored on a computer memory chip in such a manner that they are not lost if the power is turned off. A form of ROM.

FORTRAN Formula Translation Language. An older high-level language primarily used in scientific and mathematical environments.

Graphics Computer devices and computer software intended to reproduce graphical representation of data, such as bar charts, pie charts, and line drawings or text intended for slides. A rapidly developing part of the computer industry.

High-Level Language   A computer language which more closely approximates normal human language than does machine language or assembly language. COBOL, FORTRAN, PASCAL, and BASIC are all considered high-level languages.

IC   An Integrated Circuit chip of any type.

Interface   The point at which two computers or devices communicate with each other. Thus the ability to transfer data from one to the other.

Internal Memory   That portion of the computer memory which is used for temporary storage of data during processing. Controlled by the program and the CPU. Loses stored data when the power is off.

Interpreter   A form of computer program which translates a high-level language program directly into executable machine language on a line-by-line basis, as the program is typed into the computer. BASIC is the most common interpreted language.

K   Abbreviation for 1,024 bytes. A term usually associated with internal or external memory capacity, measured in bytes of memory. Often rounded off to the nearest 1,000, as 64K for the actual number 65,536 (1,024 × 64).

Low-Level Language   The term usually applied to machine language or assembly language. Any language which is close to the form of instructions directly understood by the computer.

Machine Language   The lowest level of instructions for a computer program, normally expressed in binary, octal, or hexadecimal numbers. A program in machine language is usable by the computer without further translation or interpretation.

Mainframe   The largest type of computer commonly in use, the type used by banks and the government. In terms of cost, usually over $250,000 and up to millions of dollars.

Microcode   Code stored in permanent memory, used to control a machine or computer.

Microcomputer   The smallest type of computer, usually called a personal computer (PC), although this classification includes any small computer used in business, which usually costs under $20,000.

Minicomputer   The middle-size computer often used in factories and laboratories for process control, communication, and scientific computations. A DEC PDP-11 is the most common "mini."

Modem   A communications device, technically called a MODulator-DEModulator, which converts analog signals to digital signals and back again, in order to carry them over normal analog phone lines.

Object Code   A computer program in machine language, after compilation or interpretation by the computer. Only a highly skilled programmer could read this form of a program, although the computer uses it directly.

OEM Original Equipment Manufacturer. One who makes or assembles (or buys and labels as his own) equipment for sale to others.

Operating System A computer program designed to control the various elements or units of a computer. It acts like a traffic policeman in that it directs the flow of data from one unit to the other, assigning priorities as necessary.

Output The data or information which the computer has processed and sends directly to the user or to an external storage device for later use.

Parallel A form of computer communication in which all eight bits of a byte of information are simultaneously sent or received. Opposite of serial communication.

PASCAL A modern high-level language used extensively on microcomputers, and in teaching programming.

Peripherals Any device intended to be attached to a CPU and controlled by it. Disk drives, printers, and CRT terminals are typical examples.

Programs Computer software or instruction sets for the computer.

RAM Random Access Memory. Internal storage memory to which the CPU sends and from which it receives data. So named because the data may be stored and retrieved from random locations within it. Loses the data when the power is turned off.

ROM Read Only Memory. Sometimes called "Firmware." Internal memory which is pre-programmed so that it cannot be changed and does not lose data when power is lost. Often found in games and devices like calculators, as well as in some general purpose computers.

Serial A form of communication in which data is sent and received one bit at a time, as opposed to parallel communication.

Software A computer program in any form or language, and regardless of the media on which it is stored.

Source Code The form of a computer program in which it was originally written by the human programmer, usually in a high-level language like PASCAL or FORTRAN. Such programs are normally readable by anyone, although full comprehension will depend on programming training. Source code must be compiled or translated into machine language (object code) for a computer to use it directly.

Terminal Any piece of computer hardware with a keyboard or other input device intended for communication with the CPU. The CPU may also output to it, as on a screen attached to the keyboard.

Appendix:
Selected Bibliography

Chapter 1: A Magnetic Image in Time—An Introduction

BIBLIOGRAPHY

Books and Articles

Fitzgerald, Edward, trans. Undated. *The Rubiyat of Omar Khayyam.* 4th ver. New York: Barse & Hopkins.

Chapter 2: What is this Thing Called "Software"?

BIBLIOGRAPHY

Books and Articles

Barden, William. 1977. *How to Program Microcomputers.* Indianapolis: Howard W. Sams.

Computer Software Issue, *Scientific American* 251 (Sept. 1984): 1–232. (The entire issue is devoted to articles on computer software.)

Creekmore, Wayne. 1983. *Through the MicroMaze.* Culver City: Ashton-Tate.

International Microcomputer Dictionary. 1981. Berkeley: Sybex.

Pool, Ithiel de Sola. 1983. *Technologies of Freedom.* Cambridge: Belknap Press of Harvard University. Chapter 8, "Electronic Publishing," pp. 189, 214.

Weller, Schatzel, & Nice. 1976. *Practical Microcomputer Programming.* Chicago: Northern Technology Books.

Cases

Apple Computer, Inc. v. *Franklin Computer Corp.* 545 FSupp. 812, 215 USPQ 935 (D. E.D. Pa. 1982), rev'd. and rem'd. 714 F2d 1240, 219 USPQ 113 (3d Cir. 1983).

Chapter 3: Who Owns Ideas and Other Intellectual Property?

BIBLIOGRAPHY

Books and Articles

Epstein, Michael A. 1984. *Modern Intellectual Property.* New York: Law & Business.

Kintner, E., & Lahr, J. 1982. *An Intellectual Property Law Primer.* New York: Clark Boardman.

National Commission on New Technological Uses of Copyrighted Works (CONTU), *Final Report of the National Commission on New Technological Uses of Copyrighted Works.* 1979. Washington: Library of Congress.

Cases

Cheney Bros. v. *Doris Silk Corp.*, 35 F2d 279, 280 (2d Cir. 1929), opinion by Judge Learned Hand.

Statutes and Related Materials

15 U.S.C. §§ 1051–1127 (Trademark law provisions, generally.)

17 U.S.C. §§ 101–912 (Copyright law provisions, generally.)

35 U.S.C. §§ 1–376 (Patent law provisions, generally.)

Chapter 4: How to Protect Software as a Trade Secret

BIBLIOGRAPHY

Books and Articles

Brosnahan, Carol S., ed. 1971. (Supplemented, May 1981.) *Attorney's Guide to Trade Secrets.* Berkeley: California Continuing Education of the Bar.

Browne, Allan, ed. 1981. (Supplemented, April 1983.) *The Law of Competitive Business Practices.* Berkeley: California Continuing Education of the Bar.

Jager, Melvin F. 1983. *1983 Trade Secrets Law Handbook.* New York: Clark Boardman.

Milgrim, Roger M. 1984. *Trade Secrets.* New York: Matthew Bender. (3 vols., supplemented annually.)

Pooley, James. 1982. *Trade Secrets.* Berkeley: Osborne-McGraw Hill.

Protecting Trade Secrets. 1981. New York: Practising Law Institute.

Cases

M. Bryce & Associates v. *Gladstone,* 319 NW2d 902, CCH Copyright L.Rep. ¶ 25,418 (Ct.App. 1982). (1976 copyright law did not preempt state trade secret laws.)

Colony Corp. of America v. *Crown Glass Corp.,* 102 Ill.App. (1st Dist., 3d Div. 1981). (Not a trade secret if product on market readily discloses the information.)

Compco Corp. v. *Day-Brite Lighting, Inc.,* 376 U.S. 234, 140 USPQ 528 (1964). (Preceded Kewanee. Decided with Sears case.)

Data General Corp. v. *Digital Computer Controls Corp.,* 297 A2d 28 (Del. Ch. Ct. 1972), aff'd. 297 A.2d 437 (D. Del. 1972); later opinion, 357 A2d 105, 188

USPQ 276 (Del. Ch. Ct. 1975). (Six thousand copies of manual distributed and still a trade secret.)

Diodes, Inc. v. *Franzen,* 260 CA2d 244 (Cal. 1968), (Special rights of employee to use knowledge to support himself.)

E. I. DuPont de Nemours & Co. v. *Christopher,* 431 F2d 1012, (5th Cir. 1970). (Injunction granted to prevent use of trade secret obtained by aerial photos.)

IBM Corp. v. *Hitachi Corp.,* —— FSupp. ——, (D. N.D. Ca. 1983). (Civil version of criminal case over theft of trade secrets of IBM by Hitachi representatives.)

Jostens, Inc. v. *National Computer Systems, Inc.,* 318 NW2d 691, (Minn. Sup. Ct., 1982). (Failure to treat material as trade secret or to identify it as such, fatal to request for relief.)

Kewanee Oil Co. v. *Bicron Corp.,* 416 U.S. 470, 181 USPQ 673 (1974). (Trade secrets protected by state law, even when patentable.)

Rigging International Maintenance Co. v. *Gwin,* 180 Cal.Rptr. 451 (Cal. 1982). (No trade secret where employer makes no effort to treat material as such.)

Sarkes Tarzian, Inc. v. *Audio Devices, Inc.,* 166 FSupp. 250 (D. S.D. Cal., 1958), aff'd. 283 F2d 695 (9th Cir. 1960). (Unfair to preclude employee from use of skills gained in job.)

Sears, Roebuck & Co. v. *Stiffel Co.,* 376 U.S. 225, 140 USPQ 524 (1964). (Earlier than Kewanee, indicated patent law might preempt all state trade secret law.)

Sheridan v. *Mallinckrodt, Inc.,* 26 PTCJ 294. (D. N.D. N.Y. 1983). (Clear competitive advantage of trade secret shown.)

Technicon Medical Info Systems v. *Green Bay Packaging, Inc.,* 480 FSupp. 124 (D. E.D. Wis. 1979). (1909 copyright law did not preempt state trade secret law.)

Telex Corp. v. *IBM,* 367 FSupp. 258, 179 USPQ 777 (D. N.D. Okla. 1973), aff'd in part and rev'd. in part, 510 F2d 894, (5th Cir. 1975). (Hiring away key employees to obtain trade secrets.)

Videotronics, Inc. v. *Bend Electronics,* CCH Copyright L.Rep. ¶ 25,579, (D. D.C. Nev. 1983). (State law preempted by fact computer program was subject to copyright law. Case may be wrong.)

Warrington Associates v. *Real-Time Engineering Systems, Inc.,* 522 FSupp. 367 (D. E.D. Ill. 1981). (Breach of trust by former employee enjoined.)

Wexler v. *Greenberg,* 160 A2d 430 (Penn. 1960). (Right of employee to support himself from occupation versus right to protect information developed by employer.)

Statutes and Related Materials

California Bus. & Prof. Code §§ 16600–16601 (Anti-trust law of California.)

California Lab. Code § 2860 (Inventor's protection law.)

California Penal Code § 499c (Trade secret criminal statute.)

Restatement of Torts, ¶ 757, Comment b., Philadelphia: American Law Institute, 1939.

Chapter 5: The Basics of Copyright Law

BIBLIOGRAPHY

Books and Articles

Boorstyn, Neil. 1981. (Supplemented yearly.) *Copyright Law.* Rochester, NY: The Lawyers Cooperative Publishing Co.

Copyright Law Reporter. 1984. Chicago: CCH. (2 vols. looseleaf, supplemented monthly.)

Johnston, Donald F. 1982. *Copyright Handbook.* 2nd ed. New York: R. R. Bowker.

Kintner, E., & Lahr, J. 1982. *An Intellectual Property Law Primer.* New York: Clark Boardman.

Latman, Alan. 1979. *The Copyright Law.* 5th ed. Washington: BNA.

Melville, L. W. 1979 (Revised 1983.) *Forms and Agreements on Intellectual Property and International Licensing.* 3rd ed. New York and London: Clark Boardman/ Sweet & Maxwell.

National Commission on New Technological Uses of Copyrighted Works (CONTU), *Final Report of the National Commission on New Technological Uses of Copyrighted Works.* 1979. Washington: Library of Congress.

Nimmer, Melville B. 1984. *Nimmer on Copyright.* New York: Mathew Bender. (4 vols., supplemented yearly.)

Cases

Aldon Accessories Ltd. v. *Spiegel, Inc.,* 738 F2d 548, 28 PTCJ 295 (2d Cir. 1984). (Contrary to "work for hire" definition in §101 of the 1976 Act, court holds that this term includes a person working under the direction and supervision of the "hiring author," even if that person is a contractor and not an employee in the sense of having a regular job with hiring author.)

Apple Computer, Inc. v. *Franklin Computer Corp.,* 545 FSupp. 812, (D. E.D. Penn. 1982), rev'd. and rem'd. 714 F2d 1240, (3d Cir. 1983). (Since settled by stipulation in which Franklin agreed to pay Apple $2.5 million and to develop and use its own operating system.)

Baker v. *Seldon,* 101 U.S. 99 (1879). (Bookkeeping system not copyrightable.)

Data Cash Systems, Inc. v. *JS&A Group, Inc.,* 480 FSupp. 1063 (D. N.D. Ill., 1979), aff'd. 628 F2d 1038 (7th Cir. 1980). (Trial court decision aff'd, on grounds not discussed by trial court, that ROM lacked any copyright notice, which was fatal under 1909 law.)

Jerome N. Freedman v. *Select Information Systems, Inc.,* 1983 Copyright Law Dec. (CCH) ¶ 25,520, (D. N.D. Cal. 1983). (Preliminary injunction granted to prevent distribution of copyrighted work licensed under oral arrangement.)

GCA Corporation v. *Raymond Chance,* No. 82–1063–MHP, 1982 Copyright Law Dec. (CCH) ¶ 25,464 (D. N.D. Cal., Slip Opinion 1983). (Object code protected in ROM.)

Hubco Data Products Corp. v. *Management Assistance Inc.,* 1983 Copyright Law Dec. ¶ 25,529, 219 U.S.P.Q. 450, (D. Ida. 1983). Appeal discussed by stipulation, 1984. (Preliminary injunction granted to prevent unauthorized derivative work which acted to speed-up operating system.)

Mazer v. *Stein,* 347 U.S. 201 (1954). (Purpose of intellectual property laws is to encourage creativity.)

Sony Corp. of America, et al. v. *Universal City Studios, Inc., et al.,* —— U.S. ——, 104 S.Ct. 774, 80 L.ed.2d 148 (1984), reversing *sub. nom., Universal City Studios, Inc.* v. *Sony Corp. of America,* 659 F2d 963 (9th Cir. 1981); which in turn had reversed the trial court opinion under the same name, 480 FSupp 429 (D. C.D. Cal. 1979). (The Betamax VCR case.)

Videotronics, Inc. v. *Bend Electronics Co.,* 564 FSupp. 1471 (D. Nev. 1983). ("C" in hexagon on videoscreen meets notice requirements.)

Statutes and Related Materials

California Ins. Code §3351.5.
17 C.F.R. 201.20. (Rules of Copyright Office on Notice Placement.)
U.S. Constitution, Art, I, Sec. 8, Cl. 3, and 8.
17 U.S.C. §§101–912. (The U.S. Copyright Law.)

Chapter 6: Why Register Your Software Copyrights?

BIBLIOGRAPHY

Books and Articles

See books relating to copyrights listed in Chapter 5.

Cases

National Conference of Bar Examiners v. *Multistate Legal Studies, Inc.*, 692 F2d 478,
    216 USPQ 279 (7th Cir. 1982), cert. denied, 1983.

Statutes and Related Materials

17 U.S.C. §§407–412. (Provisions of law concerning deposits and registration.)
37 CFR Part 202.19 (Final rules concerning deposits for Library of Congress.)
37 CFR Part 202.20. (Final rules concerning deposits for copyright registration.)
37 CFR Part 202.21. (Final rules concerning deposit of identifying material instead
    of copies.)
37 CFR Part 202.23. (Interim rules concerning full term retention of copyright
    deposits, effective July 19, 1983.)

Chapter 7: The Rules for Copyrighting Video Games

BIBLIOGRAPHY

Books and Articles

See books concerning copyrights listed in Chapter 5.

Cases

Atari, Inc. v. *Amusement World, Inc.*, 547 FSupp 222 (D. Md. 1981). (Injunction
    denied, despite many similarities, since the idea cannot be protected).
Atari, Inc. v. *JS&A Group, Inc.*, —— FSupp. ——, No. 83 C 8333, 27 PTCJ 171, (D.
    N.D. Ill. Slip Opinion 1983) (PROM BLASTER sale enjoined on basis it has no
    substantial non-infringing use, other than to copy game cartridges). On ap-
    peal, 1984.
Atari, Inc. v. *North American Phillips Consumer Electronics Corp.*, 217 USPQ 1265,
    (D. N.D. Ill. 1981); rev'd., 672 F2d 607, (7th Cir. 1982). (Injunction granted on
    appeal; because of similarities in characters and overall feeling of copying.)
Innovative Concepts In Entertainment, Inc. v. *Entertainment Enterprises, Inc., et al.*,
    No. 83 C 4732, (D. E.D. N.Y., Slip Opinion, December 13, 1983). (Defective
    notice may be cured on game chips by prompt action under 17 USC §405(a).)

Midway Mfg. v. *Artic International,* 704 F2d 1009, (7th Cir. 1983) (Speed-up kit infringes basic copyright as prohibited derivative.) Lower court opinion, 211 USPQ 1152, (D. N.D. Ill. 1981.)

Midway Mfg. Co. v. *Bandai-America, Inc.,* 546 FSupp 125, 216 USPQ 812 (D. N.J. 1982). (Idea-versus-expression dichotomy and scope of protection.)

Midway Mfg. Co. v. *Dale Dirkschneider,* 543 FSupp. 466, 214 USPQ 417 (D. Neb. 1981), subsequent case, 571 FSupp. 282 (D. Neb. 1983). (Expression covers sights and sounds of audiovisual work.)

Midway Mfg. v. *Roger Strohon,* 546 FSupp. 741, 219 USPQ 42 (D. N.D. 1983). (Object code of games in ROM protected, rejecting utilitarian object argument.)

Stern Electronics, Inc. v. *Harold Kaufman,* 523 FSupp. 635, (D. E.D. N.Y. 1981), aff'd. 669 F2d 852 (2d Cir. 1982). (Video game sufficiently fixed to be copyrightable as audiovisual work.)

Videotronics, Inc. v. *Bend Electronics,* 586 FSupp. 478, No. CV-R-83-310-ECR (D. Nev. Slip Opinion April 26, 1984). (Copyright notice appearing randomly on screen of videogame is insufficient compliance with notice requirements.)

Williams Electronics, Inc. v. *Artic International,* 685 F2d 870 (3d Cir. 1982). (Copyright upheld for object code of game in ROM.)

Statutes and Related Materials

17 U.S.C. §101. (Definition of audiovisual works.)
17 U.S.C. §102(a). (Works protected by copyright.)

Chapter 8: Unresolved Problems with Copyrights and Software

BIBLIOGRAPHY

Books and Articles

Brooks, Daniel T., and Keplinger, Michael S., eds. 1982. *Software Protection.* New York: Law & Business.

Davis, G. Gervaise. 1984. IBM PC Software and Hardware Compatibility. *The Computer Lawyer.* July. 1: 11–17.

Goldberg, Morton David, ed. 1983. *Software Protection and Marketing.* (2 vols.) New York: Practising Law Institute.

Laurie, Ronald S., and Everett, Stephen M. 1984. Protection of Trade Secrets in Object Form Software: The Case for Reverse Engineering. *The Computer Lawyer.* July. 1: 1.

Reznick, Allan E. 1980. Synercom Technology, Inc. v. University Computing Co.: Copyright Protection for Computer Formats and the Idea/Expression Dichotomy. *Rutgers Computers, Technology and the Law.* 8: 65.

Cases

Alfred Bell & Co. Ltd. v. *Catalda Fine Arts, Inc.,* 191 F2d 99 (2d Cir. 1951).

Apple Computer Corp. v. *Formula International, Inc.,* 562 FSupp. 775 (D. C.D. Cal. 1983); 725 F2d 521, (9th Cir. 1984), upholding preliminary injunction granted in trial court.

Apple Computer Corp. v. *Franklin Computer, Inc., supra.,* Chap. 5.

Atari v. *North American Philips Consumer Electronics Corp., supra,* Chapter 7.

Baker v. *Selden, supra,* Chapter 5.

Hubco Data Products Corp. v. *Management Assistance Inc., supra,* Chap. 5. (Preliminary injunction granted to prevent unauthorized derivative work which acted to speed-up operating system.)

International Business Machines Corporation v. *NCR Comten, Inc. et al,* Civil No. 83-0563-RMT (D. C.D. Cal. Slip Opinion 1983).

Landsberg v. *Scrabble Crossword Game Players,* 736 F2d 485, CCH Copyright L.Rptr. ¶ 25,637 (9th Cir. 1984), vacating and remanding Dist. Ct. opinion. (Idea-versus-expression dichotomy and similarity of factual works.)

Micropro International Corporation v. *United Computer Corporation et al,* Civil No. C 83-3019 WWS (D. N.D. Cal. Slip Opinion 1983).

Micro-Sparc, Inc. v. *Amtype Corp.,* 592 F Supp 33 (D. Mass.). Section 117 does not allow others to copy software for use by owner of copy.)

Morrisey v. *Proctor & Gamble Co.,* 379 F2d 675 (1st Cir. 1967).

Peter Pan Fabrics, Inc. v. *Martin Weiner Corp.,* 274 F2d 487, 489, (2d Cir. 1960).

Rand McNally & Co. v. *Fleet Management Systems, Inc.,* CCH Copyright L.Rptr. ¶ 25,624, 27 PTCJ 285 (D. N.D. Ill. 1983). Summary judgment motion by plaintiff denied, subject to showing at trial. (Mere compilation of mileage between towns is copyrightable, when it took independent effort. Utility of work never questioned.)

Sony Corporation of America, et al. v. *Universal City Studios, Inc. et al., supra,* Chap. 5. (The Betamax VCR case.)

Synercom Technology, Inc. v. *University Computing Co.,* 462 FSupp. 1003 (D. N.D. Tex. 1978).

Tandy Corp. v. *Personal Micro Computers, Inc.,* 524 FSupp. 171 (D. N.D. Cal. 1981).

Technicon Data Systems Corp. v. *Curtis 1000 Inc.,* 29 USPTCJ 82 (Del. ch. 1984). (Reverse engineering of hardware and software enjoined as improper means.)

Toksvig v. *Bruce Publishing Co.,* 181 F2d 664 (2d Cir. 1950).

Videotronics, Inc. v. *Bend Electronics Co.,* 564 FSupp. 1471, (D. Nev. 1983). (An earlier argument in the same litigation referred to in Chapter 7.)

White-Smith Music Co. v. *Apollo Co.,* 209 U.S. 1 (1908).

Statutes and Related Materials

17 U.S.C. §101-912. (The 1976 copyright law.)

Chapter 9: Patent Protection for Computer Software

BIBLIOGRAPHY

Books and Articles

Fox, Harold G. 1947. *Monopolies and Patents—A Study of the History and Future of the Patent Monopoly.* Toronto: University of Toronto Press.

Kintner, E., & Lahr, J. 1982. *An Intellectual Property Law Primer.* New York: Clark Boardman.

New York County Lawyers' Association. 1982. *Handbook on Patents, Trademarks and Copyrights.* New York: Clark Boardman.

Cases

In re Abele, 214 USPQ 682 (CCPA 1982).

Dann v. *Johnston,* 425 U.S. 219 (1976).

Diamond v. *Chakrabarty,* 447 U.S. 303 (1980). (A man-made organism is patentable under 35 USC §101 even though new and unanticipated by Congress at time Patent law adopted.)

Diamond v. *Diehr,* 450 U.S. 175 (1981).

Gottschalk v. *Benson,* 409 U.S. 63 (1972).

Mackay Co. v. *Radio Corp.,* 306 U.S. 86, 94 (1939). (Novel and useful invention incorporating scientific principle or mathematical formula may be patentable.)

In re Meyer, 215 USPQ 193 (CCPA 1982).

O'Reilly v. *Morse,* 56 U.S. (15 How.) 62 (1953). (Patent claim overly broad in part.)

Paine, Webber, Jackson & Curtis, Inc. v. *Merrill, Lynch, Pierce, Fenner & Smith, Inc.,* 564 FSupp. 1358, 218 USPQ 212, (D. Del., 1983). (Cash management business system is patentable, since not purely a mathematical formula. Patent involved is No. 4,346,442.)

In re Pardo, 214 USPQ 673 (CCPA 1982).

Parker v. *Flook,* 437 U.S. 584 (1978).

In re Prater, 415 F2d 1378 (1968); modified on rehearing 415 F2d 1393 (CCPA 1969).

Rubber-Tip Pencil Co. v. *Howard,* 87 U.S. 498, 20 Wall 498 (1874). (Ideas as such are not patentable.)

In re Taner, 214 USPQ 678 (CCPA 1982).

Statutes and Related Materials

U.S. Const. Art. I, Section 8, Cl. 8. (Authorization to Congress to grant authors and inventors certain exclusive rights in the form of copyrights and patents.)

35 USC §§1–376. (Contains the patent laws of the United States and is the authority for the PTO regulations.)

Chapter 10: Trademarks as a Form of Software Protection

BIBLIOGRAPHY

Books and Articles

Gilson, Jerome. 1982. *Trademark Protection and Practice.* New York: Matthew Bender. (2 vols., supplemented annually.)

Infringement of Trademarks. New York: Practising Law Institute, 1981.

Kintner, E. and Lahr, J. 1982. *An Intellectual Property Law Primer.* New York: Clark Boardman.

McCarthy, J. Thomas. 1984. *Trademarks and Unfair Competition,* 2d ed. San Francisco: Lawyers Co-operative Publishing.

N.Y. County Law Lawyers Association. *Handbook on Patents, Trademarks & Copyright.* New York: Clark Boardman, 1982.

Seidel, Arthur H. 1984. *What the General Practitioner Should Know About Trademarks and Copyrights.* 5th ed. Philadelphia: ALI-ABA.

U.S. Trademark Association. 1981. *Trademark Management.* New York: Clark Boardman. (An excellent paperback, full of highly practical advice on the use and adoption of trademarks, specifically designed for use by business people.)

Cases

Computerland Corp. v. *Microland Computer Corp.*, 28 PTCJ 158 (D. N.D. Cal., 1984) (the term "Computerland" is not protectible since it is descriptive and generic.)

Invicta Plastics (USA) Ltd. v. *Mego Corp.*, 523 FSupp. 619 (D. S.D. NY, 1981) (Truthful references to another's trademark on competitor's packages are permissible, but only if the unauthorized reference does not create confusion as to the source.)

Merriam-Webster, Inc. v. *Cornucopia Software, Inc.*, No. C-84-1120-MHP (D. N.D. Cal., Slip Opinion 1984). (Suit to prevent use of name and trade dress of Webster's dictionary—settled by admission of Cornucopia that its "Electric Webster" infringed trademark, with agreement to cease use of present name and packaging.)

Technical Publishing Co. v. *Lebhar-Friedman, Inc.*, 729 F2d 1136 (7th Cir. 1984). (The name "Software News" held generic and not trademarkable nor protectable.)

Vuitton et Fils, S.A. v. *Crown Handbags, Inc.*, 492 FSupp. 1071 (D. S.D. NY, 1978), aff'd. 622 F2d 577 (2d Cir. 1980). (Expansion of coverage of §43(b).)

Statutes and Related Materials

15 USC §§1051–1127. (Federal trademark statute—Lanham Act.)

Chapter 11: Why Software is Licensed and Not Sold

BIBLIOGRAPHY

Books and Articles

Brooks, Daniel T. 1984. "Shrink-Wrapped License Agreements: Do They Prevent the Existence of a 'First Sale'?" *The Computer Lawyer.* April. 1: 17–22.

Brunsvold, Brian G., ed. 1983. *1983 Licensing Law Handbook.* New York: Clark Boardman.

Goldscheider, Robert, and Arnold, Tom, eds. 1983. *The Law and Business of Licensing.* New York: Clark Boardman. (3 vols, supplemented.)

Hoffman, Paul S. 1984. *The Software Legal Book,* 2nd ed. Croton-on-Hudson: Shafer Books. (Contains forms and discussion.)

Nimmer, Melville B. *Nimmer on Copyright.* 1984. New York: Matthew Bender. (4 vols., supplemented yearly.)

Raysman, R. and Brown, P. 1984. Computer Law: Drafting and Negotiating Forms and Agreements. New York: Law Journal Seminars —Press. (Text and numerous forms.)

Scott, Michael D. 1984. *Computer Law.* Somerset, N.J.: Wiley Law Publications. (Contains forms for licenses.)

Cases

Albers v. *County of Los Angeles,* 62 C2d 250 (Cal. 1965). (A party may not take the benefits of a bargain without assuming the burdens of it, citing Civil Code §§1589 and 3521.)

American International Pictures, Inc. v. *Foreman,* 576 F2d 661, 198 USPQ 580 (5th Cir. 1978). (First sale extinguishes copyright owner's right to control distribution.)

Bobbs-Merrill Company v. *Straus,* 210 U.S. 339 (1908). (Genesis of first sale cases.)

Durgin v. *Kaplan,* 68 C2d 81, 65 Cal. Rptr. 158, 164, 436 P2d 70, (Cal. Sup. Ct., 1968). (Acceptance of benefits in silence, when they could be rejected, creates an obligation to accept the burdens of the agreement.)

Emmylou Harris v. *Emus Records Corporation, et al,* No. 81-5753; No. 82-5613 (9th Cir. Slip Opinion 1984). (Licensee has no interest in or right to assign the license or the copyright.)

Gilliam v. *American Broadcasting Companies, Inc.,* 538 F2d 14 (2d Cir. 1976). (Scope of license exceeded; author's right to control use.)

Harrison v. *Maynard, Merrill & Co.,* 61 F 689 (2d Cir. 1894). (Buyer of waste paper including copyrighted works cannot be controlled once first sale occurs.)

Independent News Co. v. *Williams,* 293 F2d 510 (3d Cir. 1961). (Buyer of waste paper including copyrighted works cannot be controlled once first sale occurs.)

Lawlor v. *National Screen Service Corp.,* 349 U.S. 322 (1955). (Copyright owner has a limited monopoly on his material.)

Lipp v. *National Screen Service Corp.,* 368 U.S. 835 (3d Cir. 1961).

Platt & Munk Co. v. *Republic Graphics, Inc.,* 315 F2d 847 (2d Cir. 1963). (Possessor of copies after first sale cannot copy the works.)

Pollitz v. *Wabash R.R. Co.,* 207 N.Y. 113, 129, 100 NE 721, (1912). (Conduct of a party, after notice of a transaction, supports the reasonable conclusion that he has accepted it.)

George Simon, Inc. v. *Spatz,* 492 FSupp. 836 (W.D. Wis., 1980). (Right to license is one incident of ownership of copyright.)

Smithers v. *Metro-Goldwyn-Mayer Studios,* 189 Cal.Rptr. 20 (1983). (On appeal to California Supreme Court and may not be cited in litigation, since opinion withdrawn by Supreme Court.) (Obligation of good faith and fair dealing in all contracts, not just insurance.)

United Merchants Realty & Improvement Co. v. *Roth,* 193 N.Y. 570, 581, 86 NE 544 (1908). (Overt act of another may result in a contract.)

United States v. *Wise,* 550 F2d 1180 (9th Cir. 1977). (Exhibition license of movie upheld and conditions defined.)

Uproar Co. v. *National Broadcasting Co.,* 8 FSupp. 358 (D. Mass., 1934); modified 81 F2d 373 (1st Cir. 1936). (Implied agreement in every contract and license to act in good faith.)

Statutes and Related Materials

17 USC §106. (Rights of copyright owner.)

17 USC §109. (Basis of first sale doctrine.)

17 USC §117. (Software users rights.)

17 USC §202. (Ownership of copy gives no rights to copyright itself.)

17 USC §§204 and 205. (Assignments of copyright.)

California Civil Code §§1589 and 3521. (Acceptance of benefits makes contract.)

Restatement of Contracts Second, §69. Philadelphia: American Law Institute 1981. (Contract may arise by conduct.)
Uniform Commercial Code §2–204(1). (Mode of acceptance of offer.)

Chapter 12: Warranties and Limiting Liability

BIBLIOGRAPHY

Books and Articles

"Computer Programs as Goods under the UCC," *Michigan L.R.* 77 (April 1979).

Gemignani, Michael C. "Product Liability and Software." *Rutgers Computer & Technology L.J.* 1981. 8 (No. 2): 173.

Holmes, Robert A. 1982. "Application of Article Two of the Uniform Commercial Code to Computer System Acquisitions." *Rutgers Computer & Technology L.J.* 1982. 9 (No. 1): 1.

Nycum, Susan. 1979. "Liability for Malfunction of a Computer Program." *Rutgers Computer & Technology L.J.* 7 (No. 1): 1.

Warranties and the Practitioner. 1981. New York: Practising Law Institute.

Warranties in the Sale of Business Equipment and Consumer Products. 1982. New York: Practising Law Institute.

Warranties: Making Business Sense Out of Warranty Law. (No date.) Washington: FTC.

Writing Readable Warranties. 1983. Washington: FTC.

Cases

A & M Produce, Inc. v. *FMC Corp.*, 135 CA3d 473 (Cal. 1982).

Consolidated Data Terminals v. *Applied Digital Data Systems, Inc.*, 708 F2d 385 (9th Cir. 1983).

Glovatorium, Inc. v. *NCR Corp.*, 684 F2d 658 (9th Cir. 1982).

Greenman v. *Yuba Power Products*, 59 CA2d 57 (Cal. 1963).

Statutes

15 USC §2301 et seq. (Magnuson-Moss Warranty-Federal Trade Commission Improvement Act.)

California Civil Code §§1790–1795. (Song-Beverly Consumer Warranty Act.)

FTC Warranty Rules 40 FR 60188, Dec. 31, 1975.

Uniform Commercial Code, Division 2—Sales. (Enacted in various states with slightly different number breakdown and with some additions and omissions.)

Chapter 13: Dealing with the Government—Licenses & Contracts for Software Acquisition

BIBLIOGRAPHY

Books

Federal Contracts Report. (No date.) Washington: Bureau of National Affairs. (2 vols. annually, regularly supplemented loose-leaf reporter.)

Government Contracts Reporter. (No date.) Chicago: CCH. (9 vols., loose-leaf reporter, supplemented regularly *during* the year.)

Cases

Megapulse, Inc. v. *Lewis,* 672 F2d 959, (D.C. Cir. 1982). (While the government may not ordinarily be enjoined for patent or copyright infringement, it may be where it proposes to or does release technical data subject to Restricted Rights limitations in government contracts.)

Statutes and Related Materials

48 CFR Chapter 1—*Federal Acquisition Regulation System,* Parts 1 through 69, 1984. Published in 48 Federal Register No. 182, September 19, 1983. U.S. Government Printing Office, Washington, D.C.

DOD FAR Supplement. April 1984 edition, as supplemented by Defense Acquisition Circulars, commencing with DAC 84–1. Published by the Department of Defense, but available only from the U.S. Government Printing Office, Washington, D.C.

GSA FAR Supplement. April 1984 edition. Published by GSA, but available only from U.S. Government Printing Office, Washington, D.C. and Commerce Clearing House.

NASA FAR Supplement. April 1984 edition. Published by NASA, but available only from the U.S. Government Printing Office, Washington, D.C. and Commerce Clearing House.

Chapter 14: Dealing with the Government—Export Controls on Computers and Computer Software

BIBLIOGRAPHY

Books and Articles

"Export Controls: The Battle Lines Are Drawn." *Electronic Business.* August 1983. pp. 42–44. (Discusses conflicts between the AEA and electronics industry on one hand and the government on the other.)

Tittman, Harold H. "Extra-territorial Application to U.S. Export Control Laws on Foreign Subsidiaries of U.S. Corporations: An American Lawyer's View from Europe." *The International Lawyer.* 1982. Fall. 16: 730.

U.S. Export Weekly. Washington: Bureau of National Affairs. (No date.) (A weekly loose-leaf service concerning all aspects of exporting rules, regulations and laws, including export controls.)

Statutes and Related Materials

Export Administration Act of 1979, as amended by the Export Administration Act of 1981, and extended by interim legislation to 1985. Public Law 96–72, September 29, 1979 and PL 97–145, December 29, 1981.

15 CFR, Chapter III, Subchapter C, Parts 368 to 399, inclusive, containing the Export Administration Regulations. (Also available in loose-leaf form from Superintendent of Documents, Government Printing Office, Washington, D.C. 20402, for current annual subscription rate of $95.00, or from District Offices of the OEA.)

Chapter 15: International Aspects of Software Protection

BIBLIOGRAPHY

Books and Articles

Brett, Hugh, and Perry, Lawrence, eds. 1981. *Legal Protection of Computer Software.* Oxford: ESC Publishing Limited. (An excellent summary of the law as of 1981. Brett is a solicitor in Oxford and editor of the European Intellectual Property Review, a periodical much used in the EEC. Perry died in 1980.)

Niblett, Bryan. 1980. *Legal Protection of Computer Programs.* London: Oyez Publishing Limited. (Good but now dated coverage of the subject by a recognized U.K. barrister and computer scientist.)

Pearson, Hilary E. 1984. *Computer Contracts: An International Guide to Agreements and Software Protection.* New York: Chapman and Hall. (Good current advice on international computer contracts and issues by a lawyer trained in both U.K. and U.S. law.)

Protecting Intellectual Property in Asia-Pacific. 1984. London: Oyez Longman.

Tapper, Colin. *Computer Law.* (2d ed.) 1982. London and New York: Longman Group Limited. (A more general work on the subject, including software protection, by a respected U.K. professor at Oxford.)

The White Paper. 1984. Ottawa, Canada: Canadian Dept. of Consumer and Corporate Affairs & Dept. of Communications. (A study of proposed revisions to the Canadian Copyright Act, granting protection to machine-readable computer programs.)

Cases

Apple Computer Inc. v. *Computer Edge Pty. Ltd. and Michael Suss,* Federal Court of Australia, May 24, 1984. Unreported as yet.

Gilliam v. *American Broadcasting Companies, Inc., supra,* cited in Chap. 11. (U.S. recognition of moral rights of author.)

IBM Corp. v. *Ordinateurs Spirales, Inc., et al.,* Federal Court of Canada, Case T–904–84, June 27, 1984. Unreported as yet.

Northern Office Micro Computers (Pty.) Ltd. and Others v. *Rosenstein,* [1982] FSR 124 (Sup.Ct. S. Africa).

Sega Enterprises Limited v. *Richard and Another,* [1983] FSR 73 (UK High Ct. Ch. Div.).

Taito Co. v. *I.N.G. Enterprises Co.,* 25 PTCJ 139. (Japanese recognition of copyright for software.)

Thrustcode Limited and Another v. *W. W. Computing Limited,* [1983] FSR 502 (UK High Ct. Ch. Div.).

Videotronics, Inc. v. *Bend Electronics,* 586 FSupp. 478, 28 PTCJ 125 (D. Nev. 1984). ("C" in a hexagon on video terminal screen meets U.S. notice requirements.)

Statutes and Related Materials

Berne Convention.
Buenos Aires Convention.

Rome Convention.

Universal Copyright Convention.

Note: These conventions have been amended from time to time. Both the original treaty and later amendments of each are reprinted in the *CCH Copyright L.Rptr.* commencing at ¶ 11,250.

Chapter 16: Sales and Local Taxes on Software

BIBLIOGRAPHY

Books and Articles

Bigelow, Robert, & Saltzberg, J. 1983. *State Computer Tax Report.* Woburn, MA: Bigelow & Saltzberg.

Cases

Chittenden Trust Co. v. *King,* 465 A2d 1100 (Vt., 1983). (Canned software delivered on tape is subject to use tax.)

Controller v. *Equitable Trust Co.,* 464 A2d 248 (Md., 1983). (License Agreement for use of software is a "sale" which is subject to sales tax.)

District of Columbia v. *Universal Computer Associates, Inc.,* 465 F2d 615 (DC Cir., 1972). (Software held to be intangible and therefore not taxable).

First National Bank of Fort Worth v. *Bullock,* 504 SW 2d 548 (Tex. Civ.App., 1979). (Purchase of software not subject to sales tax).

Simplicity Pattern Company, Inc. v. *State Board of Equalization,* 27 Cal 3d 900, 167 Cal.Rptr. 366 (Cal. 1980). (Sales tax imposed on sale of intangible property).

National Geographic Society v. *California Board of Equalization,* 430 U.S. 551 (1977). (Seller required to collect use tax where it had minimal contacts with state).

Statutes and Related Materials

Calif. Civil Code §1656.1.

Calif. Rev. and Tax Code §995.

Calif. St. Bd. of Equalization Reg. 1502.

Chapter 17: Income Tax Aspects of Software

BIBLIOGRAPHY

Books and Articles

Estate Planning for Authors and Artists. 1982. Washington: BNA. (Supplemented as required during the year.) Part of the BNA Estate Tax Estate and Gift Tax Service.

Kintner, E., & Lahr, J. 1982. *An Intellectual Property Law Primer.* New York: Clark Boardman.

Master Tax Guide. 1984. Chicago: CCH.

Patent Law Assoc. of Chicago. *Tax Guide for Patents, Trademarks & Copyrights.* (5th ed.) 1984. New York: Clark Boardman.

Cases

Computer Sciences Corporation v. *IRS,* 63 TC 327 (1974).
Helvering v. *Gregory,* 69 F2d 809 (1934).

Statutes and Related Materials

26 USC §§1–9602. (Internal Revenue Code of 1954, as amended.)

Rulings

Rev. Rul. 55–706, 55–2 CB 300, superseded on other grounds by Rev. Rul. 61–141, 62–2 CB 182.
Rev. Rul. 71–177, 71–1 CB 5.
Rev. Rul. 71–248, 71–1 CB 54.
Rev. Proc. 69–21, 69–2 CB 303.
Rev. Proc. 74–36, 74–2 CB 491 (Procedure to obtain advance Ruling on the tax-free transfer of know-how to a corporation in exchange for stock.)
Ltr. Ruling 8034096 (5/29/80).
Ltr. Ruling 8136024 (5/27/81). (Allows current deduction of custom software.)
IR News Rel. IR–83–74, April 19, 1983. (Rev. Proc. will not be superseded by proposed regulations under Code Sec. 174.)

Chapter 18: Remedies for Copyright Infringement

BIBLIOGRAPHY

Books and Articles

Computer Law Institute. 1983 and 1984. New York: Practising Law Institute. (A broad survey of computer industry related subjects. Different papers each year.)

Computer Litigation 1984. 1984. New York: Practising Law Institute. (A handbook on litigation involving computers and proprietary rights by attorneys practising in the field.)

Computer Litigation 1983. 1984. New York: Practising Law Institute. (Previous year's seminar, which contains completely different papers, including one by this author on "Remedies For Copyright Infringement.")

Davis, G. Gervaise. 1984. *Remedies For Copyright Infringement.* (Current Memorandum). Monterey, CA: Schroeder & Davis Inc. (Available from the author, Box 3080, Monterey, California 93942 for $25.00, postpaid including tax.)

Samuels, Jeffrey M., ed. 1984. *Patent, Trademark and Copyright Laws.* Washington: Bureau of National Affairs. (A useful compendium of all relevant laws on the subject, including those in other titles of the United States Code.)

Software Protection and Marketing. 1983. New York: Practising Law Institute. (Broad coverage of the subject by knowledgeable attorneys. 2 vols.)

Note: Because of the rapid changes in this field, any book that is over two years old is likely to be very dated and perhaps dangerously wrong. Use caution in relying on older materials.

Cases

Aldon Accessories Ltd. v. *Spiegel, Inc.,* 738 F2d 548, 28 PTCJ 295, (2d Cir. 1984). (Contrary to "work for hire" definition in §101 of the 1976 Act, court holds that this term includes a person working under the direction and supervision of the "hiring author," even if that person is a contractor and not an employee in the sense of having a regular job with hiring author.)

Apple Computer, Inc. v. *Franklin Computer Corp.,* 545 FSupp. 812, (D.E.D. Penn. 1982), rev'd and rem'd., 714 F2d 1240, (3d Cir. 1983). (Since settled by stipulation in which Franklin agreed to pay Apple $2.5 million and to develop and use its own operating system.)

Apple Computer Corp. v. *Formula International, Inc.,* 562 FSupp. 775 (D. C.D. Cal., 1983); 725 F2d 521, (9th Cir., 1984), upholding preliminary injunction granted in trial court.

Atari, Inc. v. *Amusement World, Inc.,* 547 FSupp. 222 (D. Md., 1981). (Injunction denied, even where many similarities, since the idea cannot be protected.)

Atari, Inc. v. *JS&A Group, Inc.,* —— FSupp. ——, No. 83 C 8333, 27 PTCJ 171 (D. N.D. Ill. Slip Opinion, 1983). (PROM BLASTER sale enjoined on basis it has no substantial non-infringing use, other than to copy came cartridges.) On appeal, 1984.

Atari, Inc. v. *North American Phillips Consumer Electronics Corp.,* No. 81 C 6434, 217 USPQ 1265 (D. N.D. Ill. Slip Opinion, 1981); rev'd, 672 F2d 607, (7th Cir. 1982). (Injunction granted, on appeal, because of similarities in characters and overall feeling of copying.)

Baker v. *Seldon,* 101 U.S. 99 (1879). (Bookkeeping system not copyrightable.)

Alfred Bell & Co. Ltd. v. *Catalda Fine Arts, Inc.,* 191 F2d 99 (2d Cir. 1951).

Data Cash Systems, Inc. v. *JS&A Group, Inc.,* 480 FSupp. 1063, (D. N.D. Ill., 1979); aff'd. 628 F2d 1038 (7th Cir. 1980). (Trial court decision aff'd. on grounds not discussed by trial court that ROM lacked any copyright notice, which was fatal under 1909 law.)

Jerome N. Freedman v. *Select Information Systems, Inc.,* 1983 Copyright Law Dec. (CCH) ¶ 25,520 (D. N.D. Cal., 1983). Preliminary injunction granted to prevent distribution of copyrighted work licensed under oral arrangement.)

GCA Corporation v. *Raymond Chance,* No. 82–1063–MHP, 1982 Copyright Law Dec. (CCH) ¶ 25,464 (D. N.D. Cal. Slip Opinion 1983). (Object code protected in ROM.)

Hubco Data Products Corp. v. *Management Assistance Inc.,* CCH Copyright L.Rptr. ¶ 25,529, 219 USPQ 450 (D. Ida., 1983), appealed to 9th Cir. 1983, but case sealed by stipulation and settled. (Preliminary injunction granted to prevent unauthorized derivative work which acted to speed-up operating system.)

Innovative Concepts In Entertainment, Inc. v. *Entertainment Enterprises, Inc., et al.* No. 83 C 4732 (D. E.D. NY. Slip Opinion, December 13, 1983). (Defective notice may be cured on game chips by prompt action under 17 U.S.C. § 405(a).)

International Business Machines Corporation v. *NCR Comten, Inc. et al,* Civil No. 83–0563–RMT (D. C.D. Cal., Slip Opinion 1983).

Landsberg v. *Scrabble Crossword Game Players*, 736 F2d 485, CCH Copyright L.Rptr. ¶ 25,637 (9th Cir. 1984), vacating and remanding Dist. Ct. opinion. (Idea/expression dichotomy and similarity of factual works.)

Mazer v. *Stein*, 347 U.S. 201 (1954). (Purpose of intellectual property laws is to encourage creativity.)

Micropro International Corporation v. *United Computer Corporation et al*, Civil No. C 83–3019 WWS (D. N.D. Cal., Slip Opinion 1983.)

Midway Mfg. v. *Artic International*, 704 F2d 1009, (7th Cir. 1983) (Speed-up kit infringes basic copyright as prohibited derivative). Lower court opinion, 211 USPQ 1152, (D. N.D. Ill. 1981).

Midway Mfg. Co. v. *Bandai-America, Inc.*, 546 FSupp 125, 216 USPQ 812 (D. N.J., 1982). (Idea versus expression dichotomy and scope of protection.)

Midway Mfg. Co. v. *Dale Dirkschneider*, 543 FSupp. 466, 214 USPQ 417 (D. Neb, 1981); later opinion, 571 FSupp. 282 (D. Neb, 1983). (Expression covers sights and sounds of audiovisual work.)

Midway Mfg. v. *Roger Strohon*, 546 FSupp. 741, 219 USPQ 42 (D. N.D., 1983). (Object code of games in ROM protected, rejecting utilitarian object code argument.)

Morrisey v. *Proctor & Gamble Co.*, 379 F2d 675 (1st Cir. 1967).

National Conference of Bar Examiners v. *Multistate Legal Studies, Inc.*, 692 F2d 478, 216 USPQ 279 (7th Cir. 1982), cert. denied, 1983.

Peter Pan Fabrics, Inc. v. *Martin Weiner Corp.*, 274 F2d 487, 489, (2d Cir. 1960).

Rand McNally & Co. v. *Fleet Management Systems, Inc.*, CCH Copyright LRptr. ¶ 25,624, 27 PTCJ 285 (D. N.D. Ill., 1983). Summary judgment motion by plaintiff denied, subject to showing at trial. (Mere compilation of mileage between towns is copyrightable, when it took independent effort. Utility of work never questioned.)

Sony Corp. of America, et al. v. *Universal City Studios, Inc., et al.*, —— U.S. ——, 104 S.Ct. 774; 80 L.Ed.2d 148 (1984), reversing sub. nom., *Universal City Studios, Inc.* v. *Sony Corp. of America*, 659 F2d 963 (9th Cir. 1981); which in turn had reversed the trial court opinion under the same name, 480 FSupp 429 (D. C.D. Cal. 1979). (The Betamax VCR case.)

Stern Electronics, Inc. v. *Harold Kaufman*, 523 FSupp. 635 (D. E.D. N.Y., 1981), aff'd. 669 F2d 852 (2d Cir. 1982). (Video game sufficiently fixed to be copyrightable as audiovisual work.)

Synercom Technology, Inc. v. *University Computing Co.*, 462 FSupp 1003 (D. N.D. Tex. 1978).

Tandy Corp. v. *Personal Micro Computers, Inc.*, 524 FSupp 171 (D. N.D. Cal. 1981).

Toksvig v. *Bruce Publishing Co.*, 181 F2d 664 (2d Cir. 1950).

Videotronics, Inc. v. *Bend Electronics Co.*, 564 FSupp 1471 (D. Nev. 1983). ("C" in hexagon on videoscreen meets notice requirements.)

White-Smith Music Co. v. *Apollo Co.*, 209 U.S. 1 (1908).

Williams Electronics, Inc. v. *Artic International*, 685 F2d 870 (3d Cir. 1982). (Copyright upheld for object code of game in ROM.)

Statutes and Related Materials

17 USC §§501–510. (For basic provisions governing suit for infringement; but see also §§411–412 concerning prerequisites to suit.)

28 USC §1338, §1391, §1400, and §1498. (The basic jurisdictional statutes concerning legal actions against infringers.)

Chapter 19: The Future Course of Software Protection

BIBLIOGRAPHY

Books and Articles

Pool, Ithiel de Sola. 1983. *Technologies of Freedom.* Cambridge, Belknap Press of Harvard University. Chapter 8, "Electronic Publishing," pp. 189, 214.

Cases

Atari, Inc. v. *JS&A Group, Inc., supra,* Chap. 7.
Sony Corporation of America, et al. v. *Universal City Studios, Inc. et al., supra,* Chap. 5.

Statutes and Related Materials

17 USC §117 (Rights of owner of a copy of computer program.)

Index

Index

References are to page numbers except where specified otherwise (tables and figures are listed by page number). *See also* references are to either a heading of this Index or to a chapter of the book. The Glossary and Bibliography are not indexed beyond one page reference to the beginning of each. Pages in boldface are for primary entries.